The
OPERA LOVER'S
Guide to
EUROPE

EUROPE

KEY TO CITIES

1. Graz
2. Innsbruck
3. Linz
4. Salzburg
5. Antwerp
6. Charleroi
7. Ghent
8. Liège
9. Mons
10. Verviers
11. Bordeaux
12. Colmar
13. Lyon
14. Marseille
15. Mulhouse
16. Nice
17. Strasbourg
18. Toulouse
19. Aachen
20. Cologne
21. Dortmund
22. Dresden
23. Duisburg
24. Düsseldorf
25. Essen
26. Frankfurt
27. Hamburg
28. Hanover
29. Karlsruhe
30. Krefeld
31. Mannheim
32. Mönchengladbach
33. Münster
34. Munich
35. Nuremberg
36. Stuttgart
37. Wiesbaden
38. Wuppertal
39. Florence
40. Milan
41. Naples
42. Venice
43. Barcelona
44. Bâle
45. Geneva

The
OPERA LOVER'S
Guide to
EUROPE

John Philip Couch

First Limelight Edition January 1991

Copyright © 1991 by John Philip Couch

All rights reserved under international and Pan-American Copyright Conventions.
Published in the United States by Proscenium Publishers Inc., New York, and
simultaneously in Canada by Fitzhenry & Whiteside, Limited, Toronto.

Library of Congress Cataloging-in-Publication Data

Couch, John Philip.
  The opera lover's guide to Europe/John Philip Couch. —1st
Limelight ed.
     p.   cm.
  ISBN 0-87910-145-8
  1. Opera—Europe.   2. Europe—Description and travel—1971-
3. Theaters—Europe.   I. Title.
ML1720.C68   1990
792.5′094—dc20   90-40433
                                                         CIP
                                                         MN

For Fanny Ruprecht Potts

CONTENTS

FRANCE

GERMANY

GREAT BRITAIN

HOLLAND

HUNGARY

ITALY

SPAIN

SWITZERLAND

ACKNOWLEDGEMENTS

I am much indebted to the advice and encouragement of many people in putting together this book. For their editorial help I want especially to thank Ms. Maribeth Anderson Payne, Mr. David Perry, and Ms. Kitty Benedict, each of whom in turn offered invaluable suggestions about better defining the focus of this guide. Mr. Perry and Ms. Benedict read the manuscript in its later stages. Any lapses in the clarity of the writing are of my doing, not theirs.

In every opera house in Europe, whenever I wanted or needed more information about the theater, people everywhere were patient and coopera-tive, going out of their way and taking precious time to answer my endless questions. I wish I could thank each of these persons individually, but the list would be extremely long. Also I would have to omit the names of many of those whose names I never learned. All of the foreign-government tourist offices, both in this country and in Europe, were likewise of great help in providing maps and information about hotels and other matters pertaining to travel. Without the assistance of these agencies my darting about from city to city would have been very difficult.

Finally, there are the loyal and patient friends who read portions of the manuscript and commented on the contents and style. I would not have been able to finish the book without their constant reassurance and encourage-ment. My heartiest thanks to Mr. George Ashley, Ms. Anne Baecker, Ms. Jean Buchert, Ms. Virginia Heady, Mr. Charles Jardis, Mr. William Kulp, Mr. Robert Newell, Mr. William Tucker, Ms. Shirley Whitaker, and the late William Branch Whitehurst.

The computer facilities of the University of North Carolina at Greens-boro were used in the final preparation of the manuscript.

PREFACE

This guide is for the adventurous but budget-minded opera lover who wants to discover the exciting riches of opera-going in Europe, away from the big tourist centers such as London, Milan, Munich, Paris, and Vienna. Although I include these cities and describe how you can find tickets even when the opera is "sold out," my basic argument remains: you can see wonderful opera and avoid the hassle over tickets when you go elsewhere. Often too in a "big" house in Europe the performance may closely parallel what is available on a good night (or maybe a bad one) in New York, San Francisco, Chicago, or Dallas. Why cross the Atlantic to hear and see singers, conductors, directors, and designers quite readily available in the USA? For much more stimulating opera and unusual repertory I strongly recommend visiting the smaller cities on the Continent, those places where the tour groups never stop and where you're unlikely to encounter any Americans, tourists or others. Ticket prices are much, much cheaper, and even at the last minute, good seats are almost always available. Also, hotel costs and other amenities are far more reasonably priced than in the big cities. Finally, in your free time during the day there is the pleasure and adventure of discovering new sights, off the beaten path, and at night, the joy of hearing and seeing opera performed by polished ensemble groups.

It is so easy, comfortable, convenient, and inexpensive to get around Europe by train it would never occur to me to travel by any other means. With a Eurailpass, a recent copy of Thomas Cook's *European Timetable,* and lots of stamina it is conceivable that you could see fifteen different operas in fifteen different cities in the same number of days. Certainly in Germany, the "core" of this book, that could easily be done because there are so many good opera houses and the distances between them are so short. I don't propose such a hectic itinerary for the readers of this guide, but opera-viewing and travel at that pace are quite feasible. (On two occasions I've almost matched this dizzying schedule because different German theaters happened to be presenting an extremely varied and interesting range of works.) Also, another advantage of traveling by train is that in all but a few cases the station is within easy walking-distance of the local opera house. Hotels as well (in all categories) are usually clustered around the main station. Inside or very near it you will usually find tourist information for the local sights, convenient hours for changing money, food at almost any time of the day, and most important, main connections with all the local transit lines: trams, busses, and subways. For that reason I've designed directions for getting about each city with the assumption that the opera lover will come and go by train.

For this edition of the guide I have described some eighty opera and concert houses in ten European countries: Austria, Belgium, France, Germany (including East Berlin), Great Britain, Holland (the Netherlands,), Hungary, Italy, Spain, and Switzerland. Each city, chosen because the opera fare is quite good or because the tourist is likely to go there, is arranged alphabetically within each country. Only with Austria, France, and Great Britain do I violate this alphabetical arrangement, describing their capital cities first, because each plays such a dominant rôle in the country's musical life. Also most visitors to those countries are obliged to begin their travels in those cities. Yet I hope I can arouse the reader's curiosity to explore the richness that lies elsewhere, beyond the capitals. In the case of France the justification for visiting the provinces is particularly strong. In the section on Great Britain, for quite different reasons, I have limited the detailed information to London and have not given comparable data about the excellent regional companies that are thriving in other parts of the country. There are two causes for this: these companies are basically touring groups, and to describe each of the many cities and theaters in which they perform would comprise in itself another thick guide; second, without a language barrier the English-speaking visitor can easily obtain the needed information about tickets and such. My notes for opera outside London should prove to be quite adequate. For Italy I have given details about only five centers: Florence, Milan, Naples, Rome, and Venice. Unfortunately, travel in Italy these days has become a very chancey undertaking what with sudden work stoppages scrambling a traveler's schedule and causing great inconvenience. Disruptions inside the opera houses as well compound the problem by forcing last-minute changes in schedules. If you succeed in attending an opera in each of the cities I have described, I think you can count yourself very lucky and blessed by the gods. A complete guide to all of Italy's opera houses north and south, following the pattern I have used here in this guide, is perhaps another book project for someone else to attempt when and if that wonderful but maddening country ever calms down.

To obtain opera schedules for Europe there are now five good publications (American, English, French, German, and Swiss-German) providing excellent coverage. Each of these magazines has its own particular merits and strengths, depending on what kind of information you are seeking. In the first section of this guide, following the Preface, I describe these magazines and how to obtain them. Depending on the scope of your travels you may need only one or two of them. The problem is that in order to plan your itinerary in advance not all of the European publications are readily available in this country. Unfortunately as well, the foreign-government tourist agencies in this country and their various branches in Europe are of little help in giving precise opera schedules. The two exceptions are the Austrian National Tourist Office in New York which will send you a relatively accurate calendar for the Vienna Staatsoper and the Volksoper, and the German National Tourist Office which provides schedules only for West Berlin and Munich. All of the foreign tourist agencies are quite helpful with hotel and travel arrangements, but often you may not know where you'll be staying until you know the opera schedules.

My old travel habits, I fully realize, would not appeal to most people because I used to leave for Europe only with a Eurailpass, a timetable, and some notes garnered from *Opera News,* fully confident that once I left my "base" in either Paris, London, or Frankfurt, in whatever direction I traveled, I would find excellent opera. The first thing I would buy, before marking off a day to recover from jet-lag, was one of the European magazines giving opera calendars. Then with the schedules in front of me I would work out a tentative itinerary, not worrying about tickets or hotels until I got where I was going. Only once in six years have I not been able to get into every performance that I wanted: that was a Christmas-night gala in Munich with Kleiber conducting Gruberova and Domingo in *Traviata.* Little wonder! There I was a victim of not following my own formula for success: stay away from the big opera centers except when they are presenting some unusual work that scares off the tourists and many of the "locals"! I wouldn't be so bold or foolish as to make an unconditional "guarantee," but once you try the less well-known theaters— almost any of the German or Swiss ones, the theaters in the French provinces, Brussels, Liège, Antwerp, Amsterdam, and so forth—you'll be astonished at the quality of the productions and the ease with which you can find inexpensive tickets. (Quite surprisingly, on week-day nights many of the German theaters play to half-filled houses.) Nor do I propose that you imitate my gypsy-like wanderings and begin your trip with only a small idea of where you might be headed. In the introductory section, "What, Where, and When," you will discover directions about where you can find opera schedules. In the main part of this guide, the addresses and telephone numbers given with each opera house can prove indispensable when used in conjunction with the hours when Box Offices are open. (You, a friend who knows the language, or a hotel clerk in the country where you've been booked into your lodgings can make the call.)

The alphabetical arrangement of the guide should make it very easy to use. First, the countries are put in alphabetical order, and then under the heading for each country (with the exceptions noted above) the sequence of opera houses. For the benefit of the first-time visitor, a brief description is given of the country's opera-going habits and/or musical traditions and then, with each city, a few general observations about that city's cultural attributes. For each city I give the following:

A description of the opera house, its history, acoustical properties, comments about the atmosphere or ambiance of the theater, and a general appraisal of the seating.

The repertory characteristics and scheduling: does the company use the "repertory-system" (several different works performed on alternate days) or the "stagione-system" (also called the "block-system," when only one work is on the schedule and then repeated a fixed number of times with intervals of varying length between performances)? Are ballets and other musical events also offered and how many? In what ratio is the "heavy" repertory interspersed with "lighter" works, such as operettas and musical comedies (mainly pertinent to the smaller Austrian and German companies and some of the French "provincial" companies)?

Comments about the quality of the singers, chorus, and orchestra (to what extent are "star" or visiting singers brought in from the outside?)

Length of the season, when it begins and ends

Frequency of performances (e.g.: what days the theater is "dark" and is there a pattern to those times when no performances are scheduled?)

Box Office location (with telephone numbers) and hours

Ticket prices and the various types of seating (with translations of the foreign terms into their nearest equivalents in English)

Method of payment (by cash, a check in the local currency, or by credit card)

Ordering tickets by mail or telephone

Tourist Office location, hours, and services

The location of hotels with respect to the railroad station and the opera house

Changing money, where and at what hours

At the back of the guide there are three Appendices:

APPENDIX I contains a list of the most important summer opera festivals with their approximate dates, a description of their usual repertory, and how to obtain information about them. This list goes beyond the geographical scope of the main part of the guide and includes as well festival sites in Scandinavia and some of the Eastern-block countries.

APPENDIX II gives a list of useful addresses, such as the various foreign Tourist Offices (with their branches) throughout the USA and Canada, where to obtain rail passes, travel guides and maps, and finally, how to obtain a list of the addresses of American Express and Thomas Cook/Wagons-Lits agencies in Europe.

APPENDIX III is a brief summary of the USA dollar value of each of the European currencies mentioned in this guide. The rates of exchange are based on the value of the dollar as of October 1990. (Canadian readers will have to submit to one further calculation and convert their currency to USA dollars.) Because of the volatile nature of exchange rates, when the prices in foreign currency for tickets and other services are mentioned in the text, the cost in dollars is rarely given.

Finally, some personal comments. This guide came about because of the difficulty in trying to remember a multitude of small details. Even though I might have visited the same opera house three or four times it was impossible to recall when the Box Office was open so as to know about tickets. It was frustrating to make a telephone call and get no answer (because they were closed) and then to have to go over to the opera house and find out once more the hours. I began to take notes. Each theater in each city seems to have its own hours: this one closed for a long lunch hour, that one open only in the morning. And in a few cities there is no day-time Box Office in or near the theater itself: to buy tickets you go to a quite separate building (in the case of Bonn a mile away in a different part of town). Next was the problem of season opening and ending times, and when, in the course of a week, an opera house would always be open or closed. Then, as I began to visit more and more theaters, always trying to stay within a tight budget, I found that in many cases the least expensive seats at the top and back of the hall or even on the sides often were just as good as those much more costly seats, dead-center, one or two levels down. A look at a seating plan was not the same as getting inside the theater. In the same spirit my directions about hotels were guided by an effort to combine convenience with moderate prices. In some cases, when an opera house is not near the train station, "convenience" may be determined by the availability of public transit or by other amenities, such as finding restaurants open *after* a performance. Obviously in these matters each visitor has his or her own choices to make. Finally, in putting together my observations about cities, especially those many large and small industrial cities in Germany not usually on the tourist circuit, I have tried a delicate "balancing act": do the merits of the opera outweigh the dullness, ugliness, or banality of the city? And taken in a contrary sense, there are a few interesting cities, again in Germany, which do not have very good opera companies.

Travel companies (who will remain nameless!) for a hefty $7000 or $8000 will get you to Europe for two weeks, take you to three or four of the big opera houses for at most five or six operas (filling in the other evenings with ballets, recitals, and receptions), treat you to a few meals in fine restaurants, and see that you sleep on only five-star beds in five-star hotels. Most of your meals and many other amenities will be extra. Though this guide will not provide you with an invitation to tea at la Contessa so-and-so's, you should be able to see many more operas and visit many more cities at a fraction of the price charged by the tour groups—and probably enjoy yourself much more because you are not subject to the dictates of a tour director and can come and go as you please. And even if you should arrive in Europe without *any* itinerary planned in advance, the richness and diversity of what the European houses have to offer, and the sheer number of them so close together, offer an unbelievable opportunity for discovering so much that is new and exciting: simply buy a magazine with opera schedules, get on a train, travel a few miles, and you'll find yourself sitting in a handsome theater watching the curtain go up. All for very little money and very little effort.

The
OPERA LOVER'S
Guide to
EUROPE

WHAT, WHERE, AND WHEN

Before you leave the United States on your trip to Europe it is possible to have a fairly good idea of what operas are playing and where. But to learn the exact date for a particular performance is much more difficult. Unfortunately, even if you can visit, write, or telephone the tourist office of your soon-to-be host country, opera schedules are not generally among the items of information that are known and made available to the public or kept up to date.

Each year in mid-July, for example, the Swiss National Tourist Office puts together a detailed list of all of the concerts scheduled for the entire coming season. This impressive calendar will give you the program and conductor of a concert to be given in Lausanne on a date in March, eight months away, just as you can learn the name of a solo recitalist performing in St. Gallen or Winterthur in May. But with dates for operas, with the exception of Geneva, only the premières are listed, giving no hint at all of the many other operas that fill out the schedules in Basel and Zürich. The German National Tourist Offices in New York and Los Angeles will provide you with helpful information about Munich and Berlin, but they have nothing on any of the other major (or minor) theaters. There is a monthly German publication that gives in day-to-day detail every cultural event occurring in every city and town throughout Germany (I have often consulted this calendar in the Paris office of German Tourist), but in this country they do not receive the publication and do not plan to do so. The Austrian National Tourist Office will send on request copies of the tentative schedules of both the Vienna Staatsoper and the Volksoper, but as these lists are put together well before the season is underway, do not be surprised to find when you arrive in Vienna that dates and operas have been scrambled and some of the previously announced works changed. Likewise, late in the fall, the Italian Government Travel Office (ENIT) may be able to give you the programs for three or four of the more prominent houses in that country, but at best these schedules are very, very tentative. The French sometimes can give you a few dates for operas in Paris, and an in-house periodical does contain a schedule for the Opéra du Rhin (Strasbourg), but otherwise no attempt is made to provide information about the many other companies performing in "the provinces." And both the Belgians and the Dutch apologize that in this country (and in their European branches as well) they can furnish no opera schedules because they are not supplied with anything from their home offices. Unless there happens to be someone working in the office you visit or call who by chance is himself or herself an opera lover, do not waste time and money hoping to receive much information from the foreign government tourist bureaux. Let two brief examples suffice: though helpful in every other respect the German tourist office in Paris had no information about an act of sabotage that had devastated the Frankfurt opera two months earlier in the fall of 1987. In the late spring of 1988 the Belgian tourist office in Paris was unable to explain why the opera in Antwerp was not answering their telephones; only after traveling to Antwerp did I discover that the opera had been closed down for six weeks because of a very bitter strike. If you have friends in Europe whom you can call on to give you current information, by all means do so. Most of what you want to know, while still in this country, you will have to get on your own. But it isn't as difficult as I may make it seem.

Once you've landed on the Continent there are the very useful opera magazines that all publish schedules in advance for the coming month. It would be nice, if the mails offered faster service and printing lead times were longer, to have in hand one or two of these magazines before you plan your trip to Europe, but unfortunately, unless your departure date falls very late in the month and mail service is quite exceptionally fast, it is unlikely that the magazine you ordered will arrive before you leave. Don't despair! Plan your trip around two or three operas, the dates of which you are sure of, then discover once you are in Europe all the wonderful performances which you didn't know about beforehand. Distances being so short, you can quickly and easily scoot back and forth on the train between cities, building an itinerary around what you'd like to see. Remember that in the smaller or less-visited cities finding a good ticket, at almost any price, is not going to be a big problem.

How do you start to plan such a trip?

Opera News, published bi-weekly during the Met broadcast season and monthly from May through November, is readily available and can be used judiciously as your best domestic source of information about what is in the repertory of many of the European houses. (There is no complete calendar for Europe comparable to what is presented for theaters throughout North America.) The "Opera Watch" section of the magazine lists summary announcements of what the major companies are doing but usually gives specific dates only for the opening performances. The names of some singers may be mentioned but usually only in connection with a listing of the new productions. News releases of this sort tend to be scattered at random throughout the year, not in any single issue of the magazine or at any given time before the start of the season. You will have to play detective and keep careful notes over a period of several issues or months. Look as well at the advertisements for those deluxe, very expensive opera tour groups: often they will include the name of an opera you might try to see at a later performance, when the tourists have left town.

Another method of coming up with a specific date for a specific opera is to follow where and when certain featured singers will be appearing later in the season. Often I have been able to "spot" the date of a production of a work I very much wanted to see in Europe because a singer appearing at the Met was to be in the cast. Once again, the "Opera Watch" section of *Opera News* is invaluable because certain singers may later be making guest appearances in some of the smaller European houses. Also, when new singers are making their débuts with the Met or with other American companies, mention is often made of their forthcoming engagements elsewhere. Many young Americans, still unknown in this country, are under contract to sing in the ensembles of quite an impressive number of European opera companies, both large and small.

The magazine prints numerous reviews of operatic performances throughout Europe. These generally are of more substance than some of the reviews of productions by smaller American companies and can be very helpful in revealing the great diversity of operatic fare on the Continent, especially in the smaller theaters. But for planning your own trip they are not of much use. The lead time between the date of the performance and the appearance of the critique can vary from two months to as much as half a year or more.

Opera News is published by the Metropolitan Opera Guild, Inc., 1865 Broadway, New York, New York 10023. A year's subscription (17 issues annually) costs $30 ($39.50 for other countries). Membership in the Guild, which begins with a contribution of $40, also includes a subscription to the magazine.

Each of the monthly magazines I have listed below, all published in Europe, contains a calendar of opera performances scheduled for the month bearing the date of that issue. Only the French *Opéra International* goes one step further and provides a calendar giving the reader two months' worth of temptation. All of the magazines follow to some extent the pattern established by *Opera News* in writing about opera: general articles, interviews, reviews, and most important here, a listing by countries and cities of coming events. While *Opera News* restricts its calendar only to the United States and Canada, all of the European publications, in varying degrees of inclusiveness, reach out to Western Europe, the British Isles, the New World, and in some cases Eastern Europe, the Middle East, and Australia.

Opera, the British "companion" to *Opera News,* is the smallest in format and most modest in appearance of the six periodicals looked at here. It however has a prestigious reputation for the quality and depth of its critical reviews, which can make for some lively, instructive, and often very entertaining reading. For the traveler foraging for opera in both London and other cities and towns in the British Isles the "Home" calendar is indispensable. Most useful and comprehensive too are the schedules published for opera performances on the stages of London's concert halls. In their calendars the editors follow a system not seen in other magazines of giving a day-by-day run-down of what will be performed, from the first day of the month to the month's end. (Other magazines name the opera and then indicate next to it all of the dates on which it will be repeated.) In contrast to the thoroughness of the "Home" calendar, the listings for "Abroad" are somewhat erratic and less complete, at least with respect to the many smaller German houses (and a few French ones) that are *not* listed. For an inexperienced traveler, another problem might be the fact that all the cities mentioned on the Continent are given alphabetically in a single list and not grouped or identified by countries. More useful and better organized is the section giving advance announcements from various companies of their plans for their coming seasons; specific dates, when known, are often provided for each performance. Equally instructive is the "Festivals" section with repertory and performance dates. These schedules, appearing in successive issues of *Opera* and at irregular intervals, are published only when the various opera companies release such information to the press. *Opera* appears 12 times annually and subscriptions may be purchased for the USA at £35 (or US $53.00, by surface mail) and £48 (or $73.00, by air). Single copies in England are priced at £1.80. For subscriptions write: OPERA, D S B, 14/16 The Broadway, Wickford, Essex, SS11 7AA, Great Britain; the telephone number for subscription information is (0268) 766-330. (Copies of *Opera* can be found in the USA in some specialized music stories, such as G. Schirmer's in New York near Lincoln Center, and in larger public and university libraries. Kiosk in San Francisco usually has a recent issue. The Met gift shop at Lincoln Center has experienced long delays in the delivery of their copies and now no longer stocks it. It is difficult to get your hands on a current copy unless you subscribe and have the magazine sent by air. Though *Opera* can be easily found in London at most large newsstands, in the shops associated with Covent Garden and the ENO, and at both the Barbican and Royal Festival Hall, I have never succeeded in finding copies at either Gatwick or Heathrow. On the Continent the branches of Steinway Haus in Germany stock *Opera,* and in Brussels the magazine is on the shelves of that ever-reliable bookshop in the Théâtre de la Monnaie.)

In London a new and glitzy monthly, *Opera Now,* appeared in April of 1989 with its first issue. On slick paper, large in format, and lavish with photographs in color, it is indeed a handsome magazine to leave out on one's coffee table to impress one's yuppie friends (or the English equivalent thereof). Some of the reviews and articles in the first year's issues seem gushing and quite superficial, but perhaps one should take heart that the editors are reaching out to instruct and appeal to a new audience not very familiar with opera. One welcomes the idea of increasing the size of the opera-loving public, but there is good reason to wonder if the snob-approach will create a lasting audience . . . and in the end guarantee the success of the magazine. Yuppie tastes have proven to be extremely volatile. In any case, though the calendars for London are adequate (they fortunately no longer give one-sentence critiques of what is "in"), to date there is little in the way of schedules outside of England. Single copies of *Opera Now* cost £2, and an annual subscription in England of 12 issues is priced at £32. For the USA, sent by air, subscriptions cost £55. Write: *Opera Now* subscriptions, 5 River-park Estate, Billet Lane, Berkhamsted, Herts HP4 1HL. Telephone inquiries: (0442) 876-661. (In New York copies may be found at The Magazine Store, on Broadway across from Lincoln Center; in San Francisco the magazine is available at Kiosk.)

From France comes *Opéra International* which gives in more detail than elsewhere news of operatic activity in Paris and the French provinces. Yet *Opéra International* lives up to its title and like its Swiss-German counterpart, *Opernwelt,* ranges even as far as Australia in giving news of operatic events. (Starting with the January issue in 1989 the magazine slicked up its appearance, inside and out, and improved the quality of the paper on which it is printed. The format is large-sized, making the magazine somewhat heavy, but if you are concerned about the weight of your baggage, you can always clip out the pages with the schedules.) The critiques of performances are good reading and are grouped alphabetically by cities, first with a group of what might be considered "major" performances, followed by a series of what the editors choose (quite arbitrarily) as less important performances. These reviews generally appear quite promptly, within a month or even less following the date of the performance. Another special feature of the magazine is the fact that its calendar is lengthened to include two months of announcements, rather than being limited to just one. This could be very important and useful in shaping your travel plans before you leave the United States. There is also a very valuable section giving the next season's proposed repertory, dates, and casts for many theaters throughout Europe and North America. Normally there is no set time when theater managers release this information to the press. Two other things about *Opéra International* deserve special mention: the reviews are accompanied by a very generous number of photographs in color, giving you a good sense of the style of the production. Second, should you so wish, you can telephone most of the box offices of the theaters listed (including many to be found in the USA!), but I would not recommend your trying to call Strasbourg or Essen unless you are fluent in French or German. The telephone numbers I have been able to verify are however quite accurate. *Opéra International* appears 11 times a year, and single copies cost 30 francs. Subscriptions are available for one or two years (in the past the two-year rate offered a small discount, but now is double the one-year price, with only the advantage of avoiding the seemingly annual price increase). A supplement of an undetermined amount, over and above the surface rates given below, provides delivery by air; to know this cost for each country you must write or telephone the subscription department. One year: 290 francs (France only); 360 francs (abroad). Two years: 580 francs (France); 720 francs (abroad). Write: *Opéra International,* 122 Champs-Elysées, 75008 Paris, France. Telephone: (1) 42-25-31-62. (In New York this magazine can be found at the Magazine Store on Broadway between 62nd and 63rd Street, and in San Francisco at Kiosk in all three branches; normally these stores receive their copies towards the middle of the month inscribed on the cover. The Met Gift Shop in Lincoln Center does not carry it. In France, especially in Paris, you should have no trouble locating a current copy, as most larger street kiosks stock it, but in England I was told at the ENO bookstore that delivery delays preclude their trying to sell it. In German-speaking countries you will find *Opéra International* in all of the branches of Steinway Haus. And in Brussels, as to be expected, copies are available at the shop in La Monnaie.)

The magazine I most prefer is the German *Das Opernglas,* from Hamburg. One superficial reason for liking it is perhaps its resemblance to the familiar format and cover-design of *Opera News.* Also it is not bulky and not padded with excessively long evaluations of discs, as with the French publication discussed above. The feature opera reviews are held to a dozen or so, most of them of new productions in the "big" houses, including usually one or two from the United States. Shorter reviews appear in a separate section. A lot of succinct information is compressed into *Das Opernglas* because almost a third of its pages are done in a greatly reduced typeface. The *Spielpläne* or calendar is arranged alphabetically by city and not broken down into countries (see the comments about this kind of listing in the discussion of *Opera* above), but I find the schedules quite useful because the emphasis is put on the title of the opera, listed first, then on the dates when it is repeated. This format seems to me most convenient when you are mapping out an itinerary for yourself. Also, with the advantage of the small print, the reader has at one glance and in a very few pages the schedule of most of the operatic activity across Western Europe. Single copies of *Das Opernglas* cost 6,80 DM. A year's subscription for 11 issues, within Germany, is priced at 74,80 DM. Delivery by air to the USA costs 120,00 DM. Write: *Das Opernglas,* Lappenbergsallee 45, 2000 Hamburg 20, West Germany; telephone: (040) 850-3395. (*Das Opernglas* without any doubt is the most efficiently distributed of all the magazines listed here. It is available in the USA in New York: at the Met, Rizzoli, G. Schirmer, and in San Francisco: at Kiosk, and probably in other metropolitan centers with international news shops. You can find it as well at the ENO shop in London, and with the exception of France, where I have never been able to locate a copy, you will see it throughout the German-speaking countries. And copies of course are available at the shop in La Monnaie.)

Opernwelt, the Swiss-German magazine edited in Zürich, is rather formidable, and, excuse the term, teutonic in its outlook. Among the many correspondants on its staff is Andrew Porter, the extremely gifted and articulate music critic of *The New Yorker.* But on the whole, in spite of *Opernwelt*'s claim in a subtitle to be *"die internationale Opernzeitschrift"* ("the international journal of opera"), its focus is mainly on news from the German-speaking countries of Europe, with most of its emphasis on German opera and German musicians. In comparing the two magazines, *Das Opernglas* is perhaps less serious and scholarly, but it ranges more widely in both its feature articles and opera reviews. *Opernwelt* gives the reader two very different and quite separate schedules: first, a list of premières of coming new productions or revivals, most of them in German-speaking cities, with the names of the conductors and production staff; oddly, the casts of singers are not mentioned. Its second calendar, set up by countries (Germany, East Germany, Austria, Switzerland, and lastly "elsewhere abroad") lists alphabetically the cities under each heading and then with each city the coming performances; with the large companies the casts are given, but for most of the others only the title of the opera. However, *Opernwelt* is not cheap: a single issue, in German marks or Swiss francs, costs 14 DM/SFr. A year's subscription consists of 12 issues with an annual yearbook; the cost of a subscription for Germany and Switzerland is 141 DM/SFr., with the yearbook an additional 26 DM/SFr. Prices for delivery abroad and/or by air are not given. Write: Orell Füssli + Friedrich Verlag AG, Dietzingerstrasse 3, CH-8003 Zürich, Switzerland; telephone: (01) 466-7711. (Copies of *Opernwelt* are available in New York City at Rizzoli and G. Schirmer and in San Francisco at Kiosk; in London they are found at the ENO shop; in Brussels at La Monnaie; and *Opernwelt* is widely distributed throughout the German-speaking countries of Europe. I have never succeeded in finding a copy in a Paris music store.)

To sum up: A careful reading of *Opera News,* followed over several months, should give you some idea of what is happening on the stages of some of the opera houses in Europe. But in planning a trip, when you want more precise coverage and specific dates, you will need to consult one of the foreign magazines listed above. The music libraries of larger universities and conservatories may be able to help you. Or if you live in a city with a bookstore stocking foreign publications, try them; if they do not have the magazine, perhaps they can order it for you. (Ordering your own copy from abroad could be done but is both complicated, expensive, and slow, what with the need to send a check in foreign currency.) If you have had no success elsewhere, I suggest your calling any of the following shops and arranging for one or more of the magazines to be sent to you:

Kiosk, Magazine Imports, 1504 Haight Street, San Francisco, California 94117 (telephone: (415) 626-2436)

The Magazine Store, 1886 Broadway (across from Lincoln Center), New York, New York 10023 (telephone: (212) 397-3061)

Rizzoli, 31 West 57th Street, New York, New York 10019 (telephone: (212) 759-2424)

G. Schirmer, 40 West 62nd Street, New York, New York 10023 (telephone: (212) 541-6236)

Once you are in Europe you should encounter few problems in obtaining many of these magazines. Only the French still maintain difficult "nationalistic" barriers against the "outsiders"; Brentano's, that otherwise fine international bookstore on the Avenue de l'Opéra in Paris, will be happy to take your money for a subscription, but they have no single copies of any foreign opera magazine (except for an occasional issue of *Opera News*). In England the situation is much better, with the music shop operated by the English National Opera next door to the theater, your best source for any of the German-language publications. In Brussels there is the excellent opera shop just off the outer lobby of the Théâtre de la Monnaie where the range of magazine choices in all languages is quite complete. Likewise, in Germany in the various branches of Steinway Haus the magazine racks are kept up to date and quite full. (The Hamburg store is at the top end of the Colonnaden, just behind the Hamburg opera house; the Berlin store is on Hardenbergstrasse, about half-way between the Zoo Station and Ernst-Reuter-Platz; other branches of the Steinway business are probably found in other major German cities and in Vienna, but I have not yet visited them.) In the case of finding just the German-language magazines, most large railroad stations have at least one store with a wide selection of serious or specialized periodicals, and you can almost always find copies of *Das Opernglas* and *Opernwelt* prominently displayed on their racks.

IMPORTANT NOTES ABOUT TIMES, MONEY, AND TELEPHONE NUMBERS:

1. All times are given using the 24-hour system.
2. In indicating prices I have followed the European custom of using a

comma where in the USA we use a period. And with figures over a thousand, common in Italy where the Lira's value has been undermined by inflation, a period replaces the comma. For example, the German price of DM 15,50 would be transcribed by us in the USA as Deutsche marks 15.50, fifteen Deutsche marks and fifty pfennigs. As the period in Europe is interpreted as a comma, this means that Lit. (or L.) 4.300,00 for any European is: four thousand three hundred Italian Lire. Only the English hold on to the period and comma as we use them in the USA, but this may change when the new Common Market rules take effect in 1992.

3. You will notice that the number of digits in telephone numbers for many European countries varies from four to eight. A few years ago France adopted an eight-digit system which is now in use throughout the entire country. Theoretically these eight numbers allow you to call anywhere within France without using a prefix, but I have found that sometimes to call Paris from the provinces you will need to know a locally-used prefix. Elsewhere in Europe there is no such uniformity or consistency. Austria is currently in the process of converting to a new seven-digit system, but it is not unusual to find that "old" numbers of five digits are still in use on a different line within the same office.

The numbers given between parentheses are the area codes for each city. To call from one country to another you will have to add the prefix for that country.

AUSTRIA

VIENNA (German: Wien) All the old clichés about the Viennese are quite true: "they live and breathe music," and they have "music in their blood." In no other city in the world is so much of the public so reverent and well-informed about things musical. The audiences still tend to be very conservative and not very curious about what the Berios and Stockhausens of the avant-garde are doing, but they do know the old classics of the repertory backwards and forwards. The behind-the-scenes gossip from the opera houses and concert halls seems to be a more popular subject than the previous day's soccer scores. Certainly in the press, music politics commands more attention than the day-to-day affairs of running the government. One of the largest items in the Austrian national budget continues to be the annual subsidy handed over to Vienna's two opera houses. Yet this is a country in which Mozart was allowed to die a pauper (other countries have not always done much better by their own artistic geniuses), and when the Austrians fervently embraced the Nazis, they forced into exile many of their best and most famous musicians—or at least those who had the means to get out.

Some people would like to believe that the image of Vienna is best expressed through Strauss's waltzes (certainly the promoters of tourism want us to think this): joyous, full of life, and exuberant, but there are also many waltzes with a darker underside: bittersweet, nostalgic, and with strong hints of melancholy. Equally Viennese are the intensely tragic fatalism and world-weariness of Mahler, where the waltz is almost turned upside-down. Some critics claim that the city's spirit between the wars is best summed up in the lushly decadent romanticism of Alban Berg (never a favorite composer of his fellow countrymen), music that powerfully evokes the doom that enveloped all of Austria during and following the Second World War.

Though now stripped of its empire and without the endless line of Hapsburgs who once ruled it, Vienna still looks and feels like a capital city, hauntingly beautiful in certain sections and still rich in all the treasures heaped up by the more enlightened of its monarchs. Very much like Venice it is obsessed with its past, but the old and dying aristocratic order instilled in the people of Vienna a precious and enduring legacy: a graceful and winning charm. It has often been repeated that the old Hapsburg empire was put and held together not through military victories but through a long succession of adroitly-arranged marriages. Now with no empire to expand and command, Vienna has given itself the mission of conquering the rest of the world through its cultivation of music.

DIE WIENER STAATSOPER At the heart of Vienna's musical life is the Staatsoper (the State Opera), located perhaps symbolically at the intersection of the city's two most important streets: the Ring and the Kärtner Strasse. It was the first (1869) of the public buildings to be put up on the Ring and embodies all of the best and worst elements of the ponderous, "declining-Hapsburg-Empire" style. Left as a burned-out shell at the end of World War II, the building was redesigned and rebuilt within the old walls. The interior of the "new" house has a clean and simple elegance, pleasing to modern tastes but far removed from the eclectic clutter so cherished by Franz Joseph and his architect. (You can get a good idea of what the old house looked like from the murals and mosaics surrounding the grand staircase. This one part of the building partially survived the war-time bombardments and was restored to its original appearance when the opera reopened in 1955.)

The theater is an acoustical marvel: the unforced sound of the voices from any part of the stage blends beautifully with the rich, clear sound of the orchestra. The orchestra is the splendid and world-famous Vienna Philharmonic, known as the Staatsopernorchester when inside the theater accompanying opera or ballet, but called by its other name, the Wiener Philharmoniker, when outside, giving concerts in any other auditorium. Basically the theater has a semi-circular shape, elongated with the balconies almost parallel as they near the stage. The orchestra pit is unusually large and shallow, none of it covered by an overhang. (Richard Strauss was very fond of this theater, perhaps in part because his huge orchestral forces were always in full view of the audience!). Above the orchestra level (the *Parkett* and at the back, the *Parterre*) there are five rings of seats. The lowest three tiers of Boxes are made up first of the *Parkett Logen,* then of two levels of *Logen;* then comes the *Balkon,* and at the top, the fifth level, the *Galerie.* The last two tiers are open rows of seats, quite deep and steeply raked at the center, and not blocked by partitions.*

The Staatsoper has seating for 1709 people, but sight-lines are quite poor in the rear of a good half of the Boxes closest to the stage. (There are 13 Boxes on each side of the hall.) Further upstairs, in the *Balkon* and *Galerie*, the same problem exists as you approach the stage. Here the labels attached to the seating areas are quite forthright as one moves from the rear and center of the theater and closer to the stage: *Mitte* means "in the middle"; *Halbmitte* comes next and means "halfway from the middle"; then *Seite*, "on the side"; and finally *Ganzseite*, "really, truly on the side" (where you won't be able to see much at all of the stage).

Vienna's attitude towards music and musicians is perhaps best summed up by their policy towards Standees. "Officially" there is space for 567 Standees, but depending on whom you ask, the figure often goes as high as 700. Either way, no theater anywhere that I know of allows so many people to enjoy opera and to pay so little for the pleasure. The prices? 20 Austrian schillings for the downstairs *Stehplätze* (between 170 and 200 spaces are sold) and upstairs, for between 400 and 500 people, only 15 schillings, roughly $1.25 (by the April 1990 rate of exchange). What is more, the downstairs *Stehplätze* are in a very choice position: dead-center, just behind the *Parterre*, and steeply raked so that all have a clear view of the stage. Likewise, upstairs at the back and center of the *Balkon* and *Galerie*, where there could be another three rows of seats on each level, many selling for 25 times the price, Standees are given priority. Also, when other prices in the theater are doubled, such as on an evening when Domingo is in the cast, the *Stehplätze* prices remain unchanged: always 15 and 20 schillings.

Now for some impressive statistics. The season at the Staatsoper begins on 1 September and ends 30 June. In the course of the 1988–89 year some 54 different operas were presented, 10 of them in new or revised productions,

---

*Most of the German terms you will need for buying tickets in Vienna are given in the introductory section for Germany. At the Box Office for the state-run theaters on Goethegasse/Hanuschgasse you will find a few attendants who speak English, so it is unlikely that you will need to practice your German. At other theaters and concert halls your German may turn out to be better than their English.

Otherwise, my observations about opera in Germany apply as well to Austria, but there are two notable exceptions. Unlike Germany and Switzerland, theaters and concert halls in Vienna have one or two aisles splitting the seating in the orchestra section, which means in short that the Austrians follow the pattern of almost all other theaters on the Continent, in England, and the USA. (Unless you go to your seat early in a German theater, it is often a nuisance, for you and for others, to have to squeeze your way past some fifteen or twenty other people who are already in their places.) The second difference between Austria and Germany is of only minor importance but to be noted all the same: during intermissions the Austrians eat and drink far less than their German-speaking neighbors. There is food and drink available, but they indulge in far less of it. A quite trivial point, I admit!

plus nine different programs of ballet, of which two were new. Performances are given seven nights a week (plus a small number of Sunday matinées). One knows in advance that out of the entire season the Staatsoper will be closed on two nights: Christmas Eve and Good Friday. Also one can anticipate additional seven- to nine-day periods, spotted throughout the year, when the theater is closed because of rehearsals. On a few evenings performances are given to special audiences, and the general public is not admitted. The ratio of ballets to operas is relatively small, averaging around five per month. For the 1988–89 season some interesting figures show that the chances are unlikely that you will find many ballets on the schedule: in February only one was given; only two in two other months; and only one month (April) with as many as eight.

Curiously, the repertory is almost identical to that of New York's Metropolitan, but Vienna does in one season what the Met does in two or three, even without the ballets. A glance at the singers' and conductors' rosters also shows many of the same stars traveling regularly between Vienna and New York (and to many other theaters throughout the world), but Vienna has its own loyal stalwarts who rarely leave the city. These are the many singers whose names are thoroughly familiar through numerous recordings.

Using the 1988–89 repertory as an example, chronologically it runs from Gluck to Schönberg and von Einem, with Mozart's *Nozze di Figaro* the most frequently performed (15 times) and *Tosca* a close second (13). For this particular season the Italian composers and their works (from Rossini and Donizetti to Verdi and Puccini) far outnumber the Germans (Wagner and Richard Strauss)—leaving Mozart aside as a kind of mandatory "house specialty"—but these are generalizations that quickly change from one year to the next.

The Box Office for the four subsidized theaters in Vienna (the Staatsoper and the Volksoper, and for plays: the Burgtheater and the Akademietheater, which don't concern us here) are grouped together off a courtyard in a building bounded on one side by Goethegasse and, on the side nearest the opera house, by Hanuschgasse. (Goethegasse comes off the Ring where you see a statue of Goethe sitting in an armchair and is the last small street just before Operngasse, the street that runs along the left side of the Oper. Hanuschgasse comes off Operngasse at an angle to the left, at Albertina-Platz, where you find the Café Mozart and the side of the Hotel Sacher.) The signs pointing to the Box Office are on Hanuschgasse, but it is possible, if you are on Goethegasse, to get to the Box Office through the first wide carriage entrance on your right. The multiple windows for ticket sales are quite visible when you enter the courtyard. Inside and off to the right there is someone at an information window who speaks some English. The hours are as follows: Monday through Friday, from 0800 to 1800; Saturday, from 0900 to 1400; and Sunday and holidays, from 0900 to 1200.

Ticket prices at the Staatsoper are divided into six different categories, but neither the sixth and highest ("S") nor first and lowest ("I") is much used. "S" is reserved for special occasions, such as operas cast with Domingo or a comparably popular artist; "I" exists virtually in theory and is given for reference only. Describing this pricing scale is complicated by the fact that there is no "II" between "I" and "III"; it is skipped entirely, with "III" in second place, "IV" in third place, and so on. To give some idea of how the system works and beginning at the bottom after "I," the second category "III" is mostly reserved for ballets; "IV" is for Bartòk and Schönberg (the "difficult" works the public shuns) and at the other extreme, Smetana; most of the operas fall into the "V" and "VI" slots, the distinction between them being mainly a matter of how many star-singers are featured in the cast. I give prices below beginning with the most expensive seats and then use a cut-off point with the prices in the second row (and back) of the *Halbmitte* of the *Galerie;* the other seats with very poor sight-lines upstairs all remain below 200 schillings. In general all the prices in the two top rings and the seats with poor sight-lines in all of the *Logen* down below do not advance at all in price between categories "IV" and "S." The seats that are expensive to begin with (throughout the Orchestra and the first rows in all of the Boxes) are those that show a steady, step-by-step increase from one category to the next. From the most expensive category to the lowest and showing the price ranges between the *Parkett* and a "compromise" price in the top tier:

"S" (for *Sonderpreise*) used on special occasions: S 2500,- to S 280,-
"VI" operas with all-star casts: S 1800,- to S 280,-
"V" most operas: S 1600,- to S 280,-
"IV" for less popular operas (with exceptions): S 1400,- to S 280,-
"III" ballets, no operas: S 1200,- to S 240,-
"I" almost non-existent, for reference only: S 800,- to S 160,-
Standing Room tickets *(Stehplätze),* on sale one hour before curtain-time: S 20,- and S 15,-

Tickets go on sale seven days before a performance, i. e., on Monday for the following Monday, Tuesday for the following Tuesday, and so forth. (This is for when you go in person to the Box Office.) Telephone orders from outside Vienna are taken on the sixth day before the performance and may be charged to any of the major credit cards (American Express, Diners Club, Visa, MasterCard, and Eurocard); the telephone number is: (1) 513-1513. (The use of credit cards has only been in effect since December of 1988.) Information about the opera schedule may be obtained by calling: (1) 514-44, Ext. 2960 or 2959.*

---

*In Vienna many telephone numbers with five or six digits are now being replaced by numbers with seven digits. However in many places with two or more lines you may find an "old" number

Mail orders for tickets are honored if they arrive no later than fourteen days before a performance. (No date or time is given as to what limits are imposed on how early one may apply for tickets.) Credit cards are accepted for payment, but you have no way of knowing, until you arrive in Vienna, that your order has been filled or not. This address is: Osterreichischer Bundestheaterverband/Bestellbüro, 3 Hanuschgasse, 1010 Vienna.

Tickets will be held for you at the Box Office on Hanuschgasse or one hour before curtain-time may be picked up at the *Abendkassa* (*Kassa* I) at the opera house itself. From the Ring and facing the theater, *Kassa* I is to the far right in the long hall at the base of the grand staircase. *Kassa* II at the other (left) end of this hall is where last-minute *Stehplätze* (Standing Room tickets) are bought.

Standing Room is sold from an entrance on Operngasse, at the side of the theater. (This is the same door where you go when you sign up for the afternoon tours of the house.) When a very special performance is on the schedule, such as a gala or première, you are likely to see people with sleeping bags and thermos bottles lining up on Hanuschgasse; for a long vigil the line starts there and then shifts to across the street shortly before tickets go on sale. Sometimes Domingo and Pavarotti bring out the crowds two and three days in advance! On these occasions, beginning at 6 AM on the morning of the performance, the opera management has a sane and indulgent policy of handing out priority numbers to those who have been waiting all night: they can now go home and get some sleep! Those with numbers 1 through 200 will be admitted to the house three hours before curtain-time; those with numbers 201 and on up, two hours before curtain-time. Ordinarily, for most performances, around 1630 you will see a line forming along Operngasse. Those toward the front of the line will have priority for the spaces sold downstairs. *Kassa* II inside the opera house is mainly used at slack times for selling Standing Room and for the sale of discounted tickets to those who qualify (like students, opera employees, etc.).

How do you get tickets if you cannot or don't want to try working through the Staatsoper Box Office? There are many ticket agencies in the streets very close to the opera house, and they are quite experienced and reliable in finding tickets for foreigners. By law only a 22% surcharge is allowed over the price of each ticket. In some cases, should you arrive in Vienna and want to get into a sold-out performance, these people may often be able to help. Each agency in the list I give below has its own requirements for being paid, be it by check in Austrian schillings, credit card, or cash, and each of them has a different way of getting the tickets to you. With no

---

still in use side by side with a "new" number. As of June 1989 the area code for Vienna has been changed from (222) to (1), as given here.

exception do they like to mail them, as there is usually not enough time. Your order for tickets either by mail or by telephone should be made as early as possible: from six weeks to a month in advance and not later, unless you can persuade someone to make special arrangements for you.

First, to know what is to be performed if you have no other sources of information, the Austrian National Tourist Office in New York puts together in the summer tentative schedules for the coming seasons of both the Staatsoper and the Volksoper. They also compile a list of important concerts to be given throughout the year. All of these dates should be accepted as tentative because they are published well before the season has begun. (Also you will find the Staatsoper to be more flexible than most big American companies in rearranging its schedule on short notice.) Together with these lists the Tourist Office has the names and addresses of several ticket agencies in Vienna. Some of these, which are not on my list below, will find you opera tickets only in conjunction with your making hotel and other travel reservations with them. The address: Austrian National Tourist Office, 500 Fifth Avenue, New York, New York 10110. The telephone: (212) 944-6880. You will find them very friendly and helpful.

In the following list of Vienna ticket agencies I only mention those who are accustomed to dealing with orders from abroad. There are other agents located quite close to the opera house who did not wish their names listed because they are not equipped to handle large orders from overseas. These people might be of some help in an emergency (when you've arrived in Vienna and are still without tickets), but you will have to find them on your own.

1. Dr. Degener/Reisebüro (Attn: Johannes Knittl) is directly across the Ring facing the Staatsoper. You can see the signs for Dr. Degener from the front steps of the Oper, but these signs are for the Travel Agency section of the business. Herr Knittl's office is in the same building but on the second floor through an entrance that is closer to Kärtner Strasse. (About 30 yards/30 meters from the corner, look for the clothing store, "Factory Boutique," and just beyond it a hallway leading inside the building; to your right take the stairs up one flight and follow the corridor to your right; "Dr. Degener" will be door 107 on your left.) Herr Knittl and his staff are quite experienced in finding tickets for foreigners. They accept only checks in Austrian currency (readily available through any large American or Canadian bank). No credit cards. If you ask, they will try to find tickets at more moderate prices. Their hours, Monday through Friday, are from 0900 to 1700. In the summer, or more accurately, April through October, they have Saturday hours, from 0900 to 1200. They also have Salzburg Summer Festival tickets, but these are in a "package" that requires you to accept a recital (or something not most in demand) when you want tickets for a major event (such as an opera).

They do not mail tickets but prefer to deliver them to your hotel (if known in advance) or have you pick them up at their office. Should you arrive in Vienna on a weekend, arrangements can be made in advance for you to retrieve your tickets at the Travel Agency division of the business on the ground floor, several doors down. They keep longer Saturday hours.

The mailing address is: Dr. Degener/Reisebüro, Attn: Johannes Knittl, 3-5 Opernring, A-1010 Vienna. The telephone numbers are: (1) 587-15-56/ or 57/or 58 and Telex: 136 900. Everyone in the office speaks very good English. (Incidently, there is no longer a "Dr. Degener"!)

2. Erika Roessler at 33 Kärtner Strasse has a ticket-sales counter just inside the doors of a large store selling fabrics (three blocks down from the opera house, on your right going towards St. Stephan's, just before the corner of Johannesgasse). She and her staff deal quite regularly with orders from abroad. She will also send on request a monthly music/theater calendar, but this is of little use if sent across the Atlantic (or Pacific) because of the slowness of the mails (up to three weeks for delivery). Frau Roessler has two telephone numbers: (1) 513-1104 and 52-38-02. Checks must be in Austrian schillings. No credit cards. She will try to find you seats at moderate prices. Tickets (when paid for) may be picked up at her agency or at the Abendkassa (Kassa I) of the opera house. Mailing address: Erika Roessler, Theaterkarten-büro, 33 Kärtner Strasse, 1010 Vienna. The office hours are Monday through Friday, 1000 to 1200 and 1400 to 1700; Saturdays: 1000 to 1200. Her Telex numbers are: 013 60 44 and 013 18 36 (backh a).

3. Karin Kolerus at Reisebüro Intropa on Kärtner Strasse (in the Hotel Sacher building immediately behind the opera house) also accepts orders from abroad. She will try for tickets not in the most expensive categories and will put the charges on most credit cards when the tickets are picked up at her office. No orders for Salzburg Festival seats. The hours are Monday through Friday from 0900 to 1730. The mailing address is: Frau Karin Kolerus, Theaterkartenabteilung, Reisebüro Intropa, 38 Kärtner Strasse, A-1015 Vienna. The telephone is: (1) 515-14-225 and the Telex is: 112 521.

4. Katia Zirngast in the Reiseabteilung of American Express, 21-23 Kärtner Strasse, also takes orders for opera tickets. (American Express is in the fourth block after the opera house, on the right.) Tickets are to be picked up at her desk, and payment accepted only in cash or with the American Express card. She will try to find tickets in all price categories. The hours are Monday through Friday, 0900 to 1730; Saturday, from 0930 to 1200. The mailing address is: Fräulein Katia Zirngast, Reiseabteilung, American Express, 21-23 Kärtner Strasse, A-1015 Vienna. The telephone is: (1) 51540, Ext. 56 and the Telex is: 111 770.

5. There are two travel/ticket agencies almost side by side in the Opern-passage, the large underground tunnel lined with shops, linking the four corners of the intersection of Kärtner Strasse and the Ring. This is down an escalator or one flight of steps in front of the opera house. The first agency,

Austrobus, will accept credit cards if the charges are more than 500 schillings (quite a modest sum for reasonably good opera tickets!). They are open seven days a week from 0900 to 1900. The mailing address is: Austrobus, 15 Opernpassage, 1010 Vienna. The telephone number is: (1) 56-43-12.

6. The second agency in the Opernpassage is called Wienerstadthalle-Kiba/Information and also takes orders for tickets. They accept major credit cards. Their hours are Monday to Saturday, 0900 to 1800, and on Sunday, from 0900 to 1400. The mailing address is: 1-7 Opernpassage, 1010 Vienna. The telephone numbers are: (1) 586-2352 and (1) 586-2346.

If you are without luck and still have no ticket, and all the Standing Room is sold out, sometimes someone calling for reservations at the *Abendkassa* (No. I) will have one or two extras. Usually there are hordes of people milling about, some waiting in line at this window too, but it is worth a try. It may be naïve on my part, but I have never seen any evidence of scalpers plying their trade in Vienna, certainly not inside the theater and under the watchful eyes of guards.

DIE WIENER VOLKSOPER The Volksoper was built in the 1890's and originally called the Kaiser-Jubiläums-Stadttheater. After the First World War and the collapse of the old Hapsburg Empire the theater was given its present name and gradually assumed its present function as a *Volksoper* or "Peoples' Opera." This is where from 1 September through the end of June (paralleling the Staatsoper season) you can indulge your taste for Viennese operetta, a genre that continues to delight audiences the world over. In translation the Volksoper also performs in a polished and quite unpretentious style many other popular operas. Some of the composers represented are Bizet, Puccini, Offenbach, Rossini, Weber, Smetana, d'Albert, and Mozart (his Italian-language works in German translation). This is a true repertory company, performing seven nights a week, week after week, and like the Staatsoper, closing only on Christmas Eve and Good Friday and extremely rarely for rehearsals. There are no internationally-known casts brought in to sing a series of performances, who then fly off to other opera-centers.

The theater, holding 1473 with Standing Room for 102, has a pleasant and modest coziness about it, nothing elegant. There is a large orchestra-level section divided into the *Parkett* across the front and the entire center section and a *Parterre* on both sides towards the rear. Two large and wide balconies span the back of the theater, I *Rang* (First Balcony) and II *Rang* (Second Balcony). The only Boxes (32) to be found in the theater are quite small and flank the orchestra pit near the stage. The sight-lines throughout are excellent, with the exception of the Proscenium Boxes and a scattering of a few seats situated behind supporting columns. The acoustics are quite good, with an ideal blend between the stage and the orchestra. Standing Room is behind the *Parkett* (center) and to either side, behind the last rows of the *Parterre;* upstairs, Standees take their places at the back of the Second Balcony.

During a typical season a fairly even balance is maintained in the schedule between operettas and operas, although in the course of a single week there might be a run of more of the one than of the other. Fourteen operettas and fifteen operas were in the 1988–89 repertory, which also included two American musicals, *My Fair Lady* and *Kiss Me Kate.* One ballet figured as well in the schedule, but it was performed only one to three times each month.

The Box Office for the Volksoper shares the same address with the Staatsoper: Goethegasse and Hanuschgasse. Telephone orders can be made through that office: (1) 513-1513 or directly to the Volksoper itself; for the latter use a different number: (1) 514-44-3318 or (1) 514-44-3319. For this house too all major credit cards are accepted for telephone charges. The rules for ordering by mail are also the same as those for the Staatsoper.

Prices are much lower in this house, in keeping with the policy of providing affordable entertainment for *das Volk* (the audiences are however much more middle class than proletarian). Tickets are also somewhat easier to obtain because there are fewer seats sold by subscription and fewer tourists compelled to have their one visit to the opera. Though four pricing categories exist on paper, only two are really used: "III" and "IV," and of these two, "III" is hardly ever in effect. For the 1988–89 season one can safely say that prices were virtually the same night after night. The most expensive seats on the "IV" scale are in the first nine rows of the *Parkett* and the front row of the First Balcony (I *Rang*); these tickets in schillings cost S 500,-. After that, very good seats can be had for S 400,-, S 200,-, and S 150,-. Standing Room *(Stehplätze)* costs the same S 15,- upstairs and downstairs; tickets go on sale one hour before curtain-time at the Volksoper *Abendkassa.*

The Volksoper is at 78 Währinger Strasse where it intersects with the Währinger Gürtel in the northwest section of the city. From the Ring, at Schottentor, you will have to change to a # 40, 41, or 42 tram which goes out Währinger Strasse; get off at the stop, marked Volksoper, just before the Gürtel. From the West Bahnhof, southwest of the theater, take either a # 8 tram or the Underground, Line U6, to the Währinger Strasse/Volksoper stop.

THEATER AN DER WIEN This, the oldest of the city's surviving public theaters, is managed independently and not tied in with the Box Offices on Goethegasse and Hanuschgasse. Though now mostly serving as the stage for a long succession of Andrew Lloyd Webber musicals, it has an illustrious past. It opened in 1801 with Schikaneder as its first manager (he was the librettist and original Papageno of Mozart's *Magic Flute*). It is also rich in associations with Beethoven, who occupied rooms in part of the building and composed his Third Symphony, the Kreutzer Sonata, and part of *Fidelio* while living there. *Fidelio* was given its first performance in this theater but was not an immediate success. Later in the century several of Johann Strauss' most triumphant operettas, beginning with *Die Fledermaus* (1874), had their premières on this stage. For ten years after World War II the old theater hosted the Staatsoper company while their bomb-wrecked structure was being rebuilt. Extensively modified throughout its long history, the Theater an der Wien was itself closed for renovations in 1960 and then reopened in 1962 after a restoration that attempted to match more closely the appearance of the theater in Beethoven's time. The façade and main entrance fronting on Linke Wienzeile are late nineteenth century, entirely disguising the old theater to the rear, but inside and on the side and back streets you gain a better sense of just how old the building really is. In recent years Nikolaus Harnoncourt has been using the theater frequently for his presentations of eighteenth-century operas. The more intimate atmosphere of the hall is ideally suited to the style of his productions.

The theater holds between 1017 and 1125 people; those figures vary depending on how many seats are added or removed at orchestra-level to make room for the pit. There are five rings of shallow balconies, with only the seats closest to the stage having poor sight-lines. It is a bright and cheerful hall with excellent acoustics. There is no point in trying to give an accurate indication of the prices for seats because of the great variety of uses to which the theater is now put. For Harnoncourt's *Entführung* in May of 1989 tickets sold for between S 20,- (for Standing Room) and S 1200,-. Only 70 standees are admitted, and these tickets go on sale one hour before the performance begins (the entrance for Standees is inside the theater, to the left of the main Box Office).

The Theater an der Wien is easily reached from the long tunnel extending from the Opernring to Karlsplatz (overhead on street-level several tram lines converge, just in front of the Staatsoper, and underground there are stations for three connecting subway lines). Go out the exit marked for the Secession Building and Friedrichstrasse. The Secession Building is distinguishable by the large rounded gilded ornament on the roof. The theater is one block beyond, bordering on Linke Wienzeile in front and Millöckergasse on the side. The area in front of the theater is lined with market stalls.

There are two Box Offices, one inside at the front, at 6 Linke Wienzeile, and one at the back, 5 Lehárgasse. Both are open daily, including Saturdays, Sundays, and holidays, from 1000 to 1300 and from 1400 to 1800. The telephone numbers are (1) 58-830-0 and (1) 58-830-265. The mailing address is: Theaterkassen, Theater an der Wien, 6 Linke Wienzeile, 1060 Vienna.

Vienna's two famous and rival concert halls, the MUSIKVEREIN and the KONZERTHAUS, have both played an important rôle in the city's musical history. Every visitor to Vienna should try to attend some kind of event in both, but it is highly unlikely that you will encounter an opera. The fare in both halls is excellent, but it consists mostly of orchestral concerts, large works for orchestra and soloists, recitals, and chamber music. The Viennese, unlike audiences in London and New York, do not seem to warm to opera, unusual or not, done on the concert stage. In looking over the 1988–89 schedules for both halls I find only two such performances, an operatic rarity by J. C. Bach and Donizetti's *La Favorita*. The same situation exists in the listings for the 1989–90 programs: almost no opera in concert form. You will have to be like the Viennese who seem content with the choices they are offered on the stages of their opera houses. When they go to a concert hall they expect to hear orchestral music. There are however marked differences in the programming policies of these two concert halls: the Musikverein is staunchly conservative, only rarely straying from the treasured Austrian "classics"; in contrast, the Konzerthaus is much more adventurous (by Viennese standards), offering its subscribers a fair sampling of contemporary music along with the repertory staples.

The length of the concert season in Vienna closely parallels that of the opera houses, though the concerts start a bit later in September and end earlier in June. Unlike the theaters there are long breaks at Christmas and again around Easter.

THE MUSIKVEREIN with its distinctive coral-colored walls is within easy walking-distance of the Staatsoper. (From the intersection of Kärtner Strasse and the ring you can choose to go two blocks down the Ring and then turn right, or two blocks down Kärtner Strasse and turn left.) Anyone who grew up in the 1930's and 40's will have very sentimental feelings about the Musikverein. This goes back well into the 78 rpm era, a time before easy jet excursions, and when one traveled through one's ears. Some remarkable recordings were made in this hall, with the Vienna Philharmonic led by Felix Weingartner performing Beethoven, and Bruno Walter leading the orchestra in some "live" and unforgettable Mahler. (Most of these recordings survived as LPs and now are reappearing as CDs.) Much more recently, millions of people around the world have come to know the Musikverein through television, usually with the Vienna Philharmonic once again on stage. A famous chorus of professionally-trained amateurs also calls this their "home"; they are known by their very long title: der Singverein der Gesellschaft der Musikfreunde in Wien. Musicians enjoy performing in this hall, and acoustical experts rate it as one of the great concert halls of the Western World.

The Musikverein has scarcely changed since its inauguration in 1870. Its rich and florid interior, liberally highlighted in gold, defies classification as to its style, but no one would dare tone down the excessive ornamentation for fear of harming the full and mellow sound. (The building came through the last war without a scratch.) It is basically shaped like a long and narrow shoe box with a small balcony at the rear. The large section of seats at orchestra-level is flanked by Boxes *(Logen)* and by a second row of Boxes *(Balkon Logen)* above them, but these are not "Boxes" in the true sense because the partitions between them are at waist-level, not blocking off either the sound or the view (what qualifies them as "Boxes" is the fact that each one has a door at the back). For a solo recital, when seats on the stage and to each side of the organ loft are sold, the hall will hold as many as 1700, plus 300 in Standing Room. Standees occupy the space at the back, behind the orchestra-level *Parterre*. For an orchestra concert, with or without an accompanying chorus, the seating capacity is reduced by as much as 150 to 200.

By long-established tradition the Vienna Philharmonic used to give all of its subscription concerts in the Musikverein, but this custom is no longer followed. (This orchestra, it should be remembered, is the same group that in the pit at the Staatsoper is known as the Staatsopernorchester, made up of some 144 musicians—not all of them playing of course at the same time!) The city's second orchestra, the Vienna Symphony (the Wiener Symphoniker), claims 1900 as its founding date. Until it moved in 1913 into the newly-opened Konzerthaus (down the street from the Musikverein) the group had led a spotty existence supporting its serious concert programs by often hiring itself out as a salon orchestra. During the 1920's and 30's the Symphony, still based in the Konzerthaus, never enjoyed the prestige that clung to the much older and solidly entrenched Philharmonic, but shortly after the end of the war in 1945 it was thrust into prominence during the bitter competition between Furtwängler and Karajan for control of Vienna's music establishment. Caught up in the middle of the struggle the Vienna Symphony for the first time became a finely-honed ensemble, leaner in its sound and more of a virtuoso orchestra than the somewhat staid Philharmonic. Soon Vienna found itself with two rival orchestras to support, and the solution was a compromise worthy of the genius of the most talented Hapsburg emperors: each orchestra would no longer be permanently attached to either of the city's main concert halls, the Musikverein and the Konzerthaus, but with each season would alternate between them. Though the pattern is not always rigidly followed, during 1989–90 the Vienna Symphony is presenting most of its subscription concerts in the Musikverein and the Philharmonic its series in the Konzerthaus; in 1990–91 each orchestra will go back to the hall just vacated by its rival. This arrangement has apparently worked out well, but it must be somewhat confusing to each group's more faithful subscribers.

The Box Office for the Musikverein is on the right side of the building, around the corner from the main front entrance. They are open Monday through Friday from 0900 to 1800; on Saturday from 0900 to 1200; and closed on Sundays and holidays. (They are closed in August and until the season gets underway in September have shortened hours during the first few weeks of that month.) An *Abendkassa* is located inside the main lobby; it opens one hour before the start of a concert. Standing Room tickets with but few exceptions are priced at S 30,-. Beginning in September of 1989 tickets may be charged to Diners Club but to no other credit cards. (People appear to be unhappy with this exclusive arrangement which probably will be modified some time during a later season.) The Box Office telephone numbers are: (1) 65-85-90 and (1) 505-8190. The mailing address is: Gesellschaft der Musikfreunde, 6 Karlsplatz, 1010 Vienna. Tickets for many of the most popular events on the schedule are usually bought up by subscribers well before the season even opens. Subscribers pay an annual membership fee entitling them to buy several concerts grouped into a single cycle; membership privileges also include (with certain restrictions) single tickets from a wide range of other series. At the last minute however a few tickets can found for most events, either at the Box Office, at the door from patrons who have extras, or through ticket agents.

Tickets are also available at the Box Office for recitals and chamber music concerts presented in the Brahms-Saal. This is a small rectangular hall, seating approximately 550, flanking one side of the Grosser-Saal. The ideal dimensions and unobstructed sightlines provide a pleasant intimacy and warmth to the room. Like its larger neighbor, the Brahms-Saal too has served as a famous venue for distinguished recordings. During the late 1940's and throughout the 1950's, when labor costs in Vienna were still quite low, sound engineers from the major (and minor) record companies were leasing this hall from dawn to dusk, putting on tape recitals by many of the most celebrated vocalists and instrumentalists of the time.

THE KONZERTHAUS, a cluster of three halls, opened its doors in 1913, just on the eve of the First World War. Inside, the decorative style of the Grosser Saal, part Jugendstil, part restrained Austrian baroque, and mostly neo-classical around the stage, is still much more chaste than that of the Musikverein. It is an imposing auditorium, seating approximately 1840, but rather cold in its "feel"; the acoustics, though quite good, seldom receive the lavish praise heaped on the Musikverein. The seating arrangements are not very different, though with its wider, more squarish dimensions, the Konzerthaus has more seats on the sides, facing inward rather than towards the stage (the *Estraden-Sitze*). An upstairs balcony circles the entire hall with only the seats on the sides divided into Boxes *(Balkon-Logen);* at the back of the hall, above the Balcony area, is the steeply-raked *Galerie.* Unlike the Musikverein there is no seating on, above, or behind the stage.

The Konzerthaus also contains two other smaller halls. The larger of the two, the Mozart-Saal, appears from the seating plan almost as if it were the Grosser Saal in reduced form: squarish, with a balcony (not split up into Boxes) circling the auditorium. The seating capacity is just over 700. The smaller Schubert-Saal, seating 336, would be an exact replica of the Musikverein's Brahms-Saal were it not for the fact that all of it is on one level, with no balcony on the sides and at the back.

If you have found your way to the Musikverein, it is then easy to locate the Konzerthaus, less than a ten-minute walk away. (Again from the Opernpassage in front of the Staatsoper, follow the Kärtner Ring to where it turns at a sharp angle to become the Schubertring—this is where the Schwarzenberg-Platz intersects with the Ring; go one short block, turn to the right on Pestalozzi-gasse, and a short distance away, just in front of you, is the Konzerthaus. Or, when you leave the Box-Office side of the Musikverein, go along the side of the building towards the back; this is Lothringer Strasse, which then crosses the wide Schwarzenberg-Platz, and one block beyond is the Konzerthaus.) The Box Office is separate and off to the left from the main entrance to the concert halls. Someone is there, Monday through Friday, from 0900 to 1800; on Saturdays, from 0900 to 1300; it is closed on Sundays and holidays. All major credit cards are accepted for charges. The Box Office telephone number is: (1) 72-12-11, and the mailing address is: 20 Lothringer Strasse, 1037 Vienna. As with the Musikverein, the Konzerthaus is managed as a privately-run association with subscribers. Many of the events scheduled for the year are sold out long before the season opens, but tickets at the last minute are always available. As with the details given above in the description of the Musikverein, try first at the Box Office and then see a ticket agent. As a last resort, on the evening of the concert, stand conspicuously in front of the main doors and hope someone turns up with some extra tickets.

Tourist Information is available at three locations in the city: (1) The main office, on Kärtner Strasse, is in the building housing the Hotel Sacher just behind the opera house; (2) at the Westbahnhof; and (3) at the Südbahnhof.

1. The office at 38 Kärtner Strasse (they recently moved from the Opernpassage) is open daily, throughout the year, from 0900 until 1900. They make hotel reservations: you pay the first night's room charges plus a fee of S 35,-. You can buy here the special transit passes (see below under Transportation). The Tourist Office does not deal in theater or opera tickets.

2. The Westbahnhof office has the advantage of keeping much longer hours. They open at 0615 and close at 2300 and are open daily. Most tourists normally would be coming into this railroad station when traveling from France, Germany, Switzerland, or any part of northern Europe. The office is on the ground floor of the station, off to the far left if you are coming from

the train platforms upstairs. They provide the same services as the main office on Kärtner Strasse.

3. The small Südbahnhof office is used mostly by people coming from Italy or southern Austria. Though on the ground floor of the station, the office is a bit difficult to find because it is "stuck away" underneath one of the main ramps leading from the train platforms directly to the outside of the station. You may have to ask directions. The hours are daily from 0630 to 2200, and the same services are provided as with the other tourist offices. The fee however for making hotel reservations is slightly lower than elsewhere: S 30,-. There are also facilities for changing money.

Hotels in all categories are scattered throughout most of Vienna. The hotels in the immediate neighborhood of the Staatsoper are all luxury establishments, but further into the old city, that part of Vienna enclosed by the Ring, there is more variety, including a good number of pensions. One big disadvantage to staying "inside" the old city and too far from the Ring is the lack of public transportation. Bisecting this part of Vienna there is one subway line, with one station at Stephans-Platz, and no other way of moving about except on your own two feet—or by taxi. Since you will probably be buying one of the transit passes anyway, almost any part of the city, if near a tram or subway line, is convenient for getting back and forth to the opera house.

The Westbahnhof neighborhood is crowded with hotels, as is that part of the city north-northeast of the station behind the Rathaus (the City Hall). Everywhere in this area there is a dense network of tram and bus lines connecting with the frequent tram service going in both directions on the Ring. Though the transportation facilities are good for access to the Ring, there are very few hotels to be found in the vicinity of the Südbahnhof.

Public transit in Vienna is beautifully organized, allowing the visitor to get to almost any part of the city quickly and efficiently. The transit passes available at any Tourist Office come in two forms: the 72-hour pass, for one person, costs S 92,-, and the 8-day pass, costing S 200,-, is composed of eight sections and may be used by one person for eight days or by two people for four days, etc. Single tickets are sold in multiples of five and cost S 19,-; should you transfer from the subway to a tram you would have to use two of your five tickets during one trip—not an economical way to see the city.

Money can be changed at both of the railroad stations: in the Westbahnhof (not at the Tourist Office) at bank windows on the upper level, off to your left as you leave the train platforms; the hours are daily from 0700 to 2200. At the Südbahnhof money may be changed in the Tourist Office, daily, from 0630 to 2200. The main Tourist Office "downtown" on Kärtner Strasse will change money daily between 0900 and 1900. Other places (for reference only) keeping longer hours than banks are as follows: the City Air Terminal (in the Hotel Hilton Wien), 0800 to 1230 and 1400 to 1800, and at Schwechat Airport, 0630 to 2300.

Though Vienna obviously remains at the center of musical activity in Austria, four other much smaller cities in the "provinces" have repertory companies regularly producing some kind of lyric theater. In Graz, Innsbruck, Linz, and Salzburg do not expect to find the same smooth professional level that is usually the norm in Austria's capital, but in and among the long runs of operettas, musicals, and routinely-staged operatic staples you may find on occasion some interesting revivals of works rarely performed elsewhere. Or you may sometimes encounter new and exciting young singers who will soon be on their way to international stardom. (A good number of young Americans serve out their early years of "apprenticeship" in these smaller companies.) Unlike many of the generously-subsidized German theaters in small cities of comparable size, where artistic standards are extremely high, these Austrian houses are the "poor cousins" of their wealthy Viennese relations. When these companies strain their resources and try some of the "bigger" or more difficult operas there is almost always some element in the performance that is flawed: though the singing is excellent the orchestra or the conducting may be weak, or an otherwise commendable production is marred by poor staging and shabby sets, or, fortunately more rarely, the lead singers are far outclassed by those cast in the secondary rôles. It is nearly impossible to find critical reviews of new productions launched by these companies; a few of the major opera magazines, if they report at all on these cities, usually limit their coverage to the revivals of rarely-seen works. I don't want to discourage people from attending an opera (or an operetta) in Graz, Innsbruck, Linz, or Salzburg. But without being patronizing it is only fair to point out that these are small houses with limited budgets. If you enjoy operettas or musicals you can count on seeing these done to perfection. And if you are adventurous, independent-minded, and can tolerate a bit of roughness or unevenness in an operatic performance you will still experience many moments of great pleasure when you visit one of these theaters.

Some travel tips: By train Graz, Linz, and Salzburg are all less than three hours from the Austrian capital, and each city in itself is well worth a visit. Graz is especially attractive and quite off the regular "tourist-beat"; Salzburg at the height of the travel season is usually overrun with tourists, with its Mozart-industry operating at full tilt, but from September through late May the city recovers much of its charm; the old "core" of Linz is quite interesting, but it is small; Linz also serves as the jumping-off spot for the Abbey of St. Florian, so closely associated with Anton Bruckner. Innsbruck is about five hours distant by a spectacular train-ride from Vienna but is more quickly reached from Munich (slightly over two hours), on your way into or out of Austria; the Alpine setting of Innsbruck is magnificent.

To find out about the opera schedules in each of these cities the two German-language opera reviews, *Das Opernglas* and *Opernwelt,* both give complete titles and dates but usually list no casts (*Opera,* the English magazine, and the French *Opéra International* list the calendar for both the Staatsoper and the Volksoper but rarely anything else for Austria). The two German magazines are readily available in Vienna in large book stores and in shops specializing in music publications. To these two should be added the Austrian monthly, *Die Bühne,* similar in format to *Opera News* and *Das Opernglas,* but giving news and reviews of both plays and opera. There is some coverage of the concert scene and even a few reviews of both plays and operas outside of Austria's borders, but the information for the most part is directed to those interested in opera and theater activity in Vienna. *Die Bühne* also has complete listings for opera houses and theaters throughout Austria and might in some cases prove to be more up-to-date with the schedules than magazines published in Hamburg and Zürich. The address for subscription information is: Geyer GesmbH, 1-7 Arbeitergasse, A-1051 Vienna; the telephone number is: (1) 55-56-41, Ext. 46. Single copies of *Die Bühne* cost S 50,-; a year's subscription abroad, by surface mail, costs S 720,- (airmail must be arranged and is more).

GRAZ

GRAZ is a gem of a city and rarely visited by tourists, except in the summer, and then, mostly by vacationing Viennese. Tucked away in the Styrian hills in Austria's southeastern corner (and near the borders of both Hungary and Yugoslavia), Graz is a comfortable 2½-hour train ride from Vienna through some spectacular mountain scenery. (Some trains are direct from Vienna while others require a quick transfer in Bruck-an-der-Mur.) There is much to explore in this city which has carefully preserved or restored many of its most interesting Renaissance and baroque buildings. A pamphlet outlining a good walking-tour is available for 10 schillings in the Tourist Offices. Graz has as much (or more!) charm as Salzburg, and besides, it has none of the commerce sadly exploiting the memory of Mozart.

The opera house is in the old part of the city, well over a mile (c. 2.3 kilometers) from the Hauptbahnhof. Tram lines #1 and #7, leaving from the side of the station, stop just behind the theater. Lines #3 and #6 begin in the loop just in front of the station but go only as far as Jacomini-Platz, which is about 500 feet (180 meters) from the theater. A single tram ride costs S 15,-, and a Tageskarte for unlimited rides within 24 hours costs S 42,-; both can be bought from the driver.

Though inaugurated in 1899, the theater is a splendid imitation of Austrian baroque at its most delicate and most exuberant (in the style of the master architect of Austrian baroque, Fischer von Erlach, who happens to have been a native of Graz). But for its large size, seating close to 1400 with 120 *Stehplätze,* it has the appearance of a court theater constructed in the early 1700's, as if designed as an adjunct of a royal palace. In 1984 the entire building was renovated, with extensive work in revamping and modernizing the stage and wings. Inside and out the theater sparkles with freshness. The rich red plush covering the seats and the inner walls of the boxes accentuates the florid gold and ivory ornamentation of the balcony supports and of the ceiling; the foyer could easily have inspired the sumptuous sets seen in Act Two of the Met's current production of *Der Rosenkavalier.* A number of celebrated musicians have been associated with Graz: Karl Muck led the opening performances, and in turn Robert Stolz, Karl Böhm, and Clemens Krauss served in various administrative capacities. Richard Strauss was a frequent visitor, beginning with his conducting the first Austrian performance of *Salome.*

In a rather unusual arrangement there are Boxes only along the sides of the theater, beginning with three levels near the front, then only two levels further towards the rear. Instead of Boxes directly facing the stage at the back of the theater, a wide and deep *Balkon* with open rows of seats takes the place of what could have been a continuation of two rings of Boxes. These are the best seats in the house. Above this Balcony and the two levels of Boxes, circling the auditorium at the top, is the *Galerie,* again with open rows of seats. Most of these seats, those that are opposite the stage, are also quite good, both for unobstructed sight-lines and for the sound.

The season in Graz runs from the end of September to the end of June. The repertory is surprisingly large, with some 15 to 16 different operas given in the course of each of the last two seasons (1988–89 and 1989–90). The non-German works, sung usually in their original languages, match in number the German titles. For 1989–90, in collaboration with Salzburg, a complete *Ring* cycle is in the schedule. Graz has not been slack or timid in undertaking some of the more demanding Verdi works: *Forza, Don Carlo,* and *Otello* are offered. With the French repertory, in addition to *Carmen,* two rarely-heard operas: *Le Prophète* (in a concert version) and *Béatrice et Bénédict* are featured. Five operettas are in the current repertory and for the first time in many years no American musicals (*Gigi* was given in 1988–89 but is not repeated in the newer schedule).

The Graz company of singers is quite large but is made up of two groups: those who are under contract for the entire season and others who are brought in for specific rôles in specific operas. Many of the singers are young, but the quality of the voices is quite variable, with some among them very excellent and others, by "big-house" standards, barely acceptable. (The few Americans in the company can be counted among the very best of the singers.) There are also problems with the orchestra (to give it its official title:

the Grazer Philharmonisches Orchester), which even when playing under the direction of the chief house conductor sounds at times both anemic and tentative. When the orchestra is performing on a concert stage there are approximately 90 musicians, but the pit in the theater is small and can accommodate at most only around 60 people. For some of the big works in the repertory the sound is undernourished. As for the staging, sets, and costumes, the quality is more consistent. Graz has successfully brought off some unconventional stagings of standard works (their current *Ring* is a good example). The operetta productions are best described as lavish.

With operas, operettas, ballets, and (in other seasons) musicals sharing the stage, one can anticipate an average of twelve to fourteen opera performances each month. The theater is closed on Mondays, and even with the inclusion of the ballet schedule there are many other evenings when the theater is dark. Between Wednesday and Saturday one has the best chance to see a run of several different works on successive evenings, but there is no set pattern on which one can rely from one week to the next. In previous seasons performances of operettas and musicals matched in number those of operas, but that policy has now shifted, with more operas on the calendar.

The Box Office is at the back of the theater in the modern, new addition attached to the older building by the glass-walled "bridge." The address is 10 Kaiser-Josef-Platz, 8010 Graz. (This is just a few steps from the tram stop behind the opera house.) The hours are: Monday through Friday, from 0900 to 1400; Saturday, from 0800 to 1200; closed on Sundays and holidays. The Abendkasse is in the front lobby of the theater and opens one hour before each performance. The telephone number is: (0316) 82-74-22. Generally tickets can be ordered six weeks in advance when the schedule for the following month is published. No credit cards are accepted.

Prices are divided into several different categories (A, B, C, D), with the "C" category most often in effect and "D" reserved for premières. With "C," the eighteen rows of the *Parterre* (orchestra-level seating) range from S 380,- to S 210,-; the *Balkon,* from S 320,- in the first rows (1-3) to S 265,- (rows 4-6) and S 210,- in the last three rows; the *Galerie* from a high of S 210,- to S 75,- in the last four rows. *Stehplätze* are S 25,-. Prices in the *Logen* (the Boxes) start at S 380,- and at the low end cost S 210,-. The "B" category prices (*Carmen,* German comic operas, and some of the ballets) generally run 20% lower than the "C" prices. And the rarely-used "D" sequence of prices is about 60% more than what one pays for the "C" tickets.

Tourist information is available at the Hauptbahnhof in an office not off the main waiting room but with its entrance outside from the first platform, trainside, at the back of the station. They are open daily, Monday through Friday, from 0800 to 2000 and on Saturday and Sunday an hour later, from 0900 to 2000. They will make hotel reservations for you at no charge. Telephone: (0316) 91-68-37. There is a second office in the center of the city, at 16 Herrengasse, in the block just behind the Rathaus (which faces the Hauptplatz). They perform the same services as the office in the station and are open one hour later in the evening, daily, from 0900 to 2100. Their telephones are: (0316) 83-52-41 and 70-52-41; telex: (0) 31-17-85; and telefax: (0316) 83-79-87.

Two of the city's newest and most expensive hotels are just opposite the front of the station. One other, older and with more moderate prices, is a few hundred yards (around 250 meters) off to the right. There is not much to choose from within very close walking-distance of the opera house. The very helpful girls in the Informationsbüro at the station can best advise you according to your budget and your needs. With Graz's excellent trolley system connecting most parts of the city it is not necessary to be close to the center if you are planning on a stay of several days.

Money can be changed inside the Hauptbahnhof in an office to your left as you leave the train platforms. Their hours are as follows: Monday through Thursday from 0730 to 1330 and 1400 to 1830; Friday: from 0730 to 1330 and 1400 to 1930; Saturday: from 0730 to 1330; closed on Sundays and holidays. On Sundays money can be changed in the post office which is off to the left of the main doors of the station. The larger post office "downtown," close to Andreas-Hofer-Platz and one block from the river, will also perform this service. The entrance is at 11 Kalchberggasse. Neither American Express nor Cook's has an office in Graz.

INNSBRUCK

INNSBRUCK enjoys a picture-book setting, surrounded by steep Alpine peaks which during most of the year are capped with snow. Unless you happen to be a skier (Innsbruck has twice hosted the Winter Olympics and remains an important center for winter sports), you will discover that the most interesting part of the city is quite small and can be visited on foot in less than two hours. (Most of the old area is a pedestrian zone where one can walk and stop to look without having to worry about noisome vehicles.) On the perimeter of the old city and just a few steps across from Maria Theresa's palace, the Hofburg, is the Tiroler Landestheater. This complex serves as the "home" for the opera company, an active theater ensemble, and a modest ballet troupe.

What with extensive alterations and additions little remains of the original theater built in 1835. Though the auditorium has retained its horseshoe shape with three circles of balconies, during the last and most drastic sequence of renovations the partitions were stripped from between all the boxes. The overall seating-capacity was greatly reduced as well (the total is now around 800) with the removal along the side walls of the second-row box seats and all of the seats with poor sight-lines in the topmost-level, the *Galerie*. Each of the balcony tiers now has open rows of seating, with only single rows on the sides. The result is a modern and extremely efficient theater, with excellent, bright acoustics and no seats without a good view of the stage, but quite unfortunately, a theater with little warmth and no charm. The architects in attempting to relieve the starkness of the bare walls and ceiling added fussy ribbed designs to the plaster; this rather cheap-looking ornamentation may have had some good effect on the acoustics but does little, until one's attention is diverted to the stage, to change the cold "feel" of the auditorium.

The season in Innsbruck begins in late September and lasts until the end of June. The repertory is quite small, a total of eight operas, but most of them on the schedule for 1989–90 would hardly be labelled as "standard" even in the largest houses: Cornelius's *Der Barbier von Bagdad,* Boito's *Mefistofele,* Strauss's *Elektra,* Janácek's *Jenufa,* and Mozart's *Idomeneo.* Even the other three: *Fidelio, Così fan tutte,* and *Faust* (known in German-speaking countries as *Margarethe*) are not exactly "everyday fare." In other seasons a single Verdi or Puccini work has been included, but Innsbruck tends to avoid the nucleus of works seen so often in other theaters. Operettas and musicals are however the main staples of the company, and although only four different ones are offered during the 1989–90 season, they are each given very long runs, outnumbering the opera performances. As these lighter works make fewer demands on the voices, they are often repeated on several evenings in a row. Usually, once the season is well underway, only two operas are offered simultaneously, but the times are rare when the public is given the opportunity to see each of them together on successive nights. With plays regularly using the same stage (plus, on just a few occasions, a ballet) a visit to Innsbruck to see an opera requires some very careful planning. The theater is closed on both Mondays and Tuesdays, but on average six to eight times each month an opera is on the schedule. Due to the intricacies of scheduling sketched out above, I have yet to see an opera in this city, but I highly recommend the very polished operetta productions, which often play to sold-out houses.

The resident ensemble of singers is small, but Innsbruck, unlike the other small Austrian companies, occasionally invites a few internationally-acclaimed stars to assume major rôles in their productions. Also, as is the practice in Graz, a good number of other singers, most of them young and still unknown, are engaged for specific assignments as "guests," both in the operas and operettas. The pit orchestra is made up of members of the Innsbrucker Symphonieorchester, which throughout the year offers the city's major series of subscription concerts in an auditorium in the Kongresshaus. The reduced group of musicians used to accompany operettas produces a nice sound; if the full complement of players needed for operas can be trusted to perform with equal zest and precision, the Innsbrucker Symphonieorchester must be a very fine ensemble.

The Box Office is inside the theater, at 2 Rennweg, the street that begins at the archway connecting the Hofkirche with the Hofburg and then parallels the entire length of the Hofgarten. (Coming from the Hauptbahnhof by either of two ways the distance is about the same: 7/10th's of a mile (1.2 kilometers). From in front of the station, either go to the right to the end of Süd-Tiroler-Platz, turn left on Museumstrasse, and then right on Burg-graben; or go towards the left end of Süd-Tiroler-Platz, take the street, Saturner Strasse, that leads away from the station, and when you come to the Triumphal Arch on your left, turn right on Maria-Theresien-Strasse, and follow it to where it ends at Burggraben. Burggraben curves and by the side of the Hofkirche leads directly to Rennweg.) From Monday through Satur-day the Box Office hours are from 0830 to 2030; Sundays and holidays, only for tickets for that evening's performance, from 1830 to 2000. Advance sales for all events scheduled within an entire coming month begin eight days before the beginning of that month. No credit cards are accepted. Tele-phone: (05 12) 52-07-44; telefax: 52-074-333. The mailing address for inqui-ries is: Tiroler Landestheater, 2 Rennweg, 6020 Innsbruck

The directors of the Landestheater boast that their ticket prices are the lowest in all of Austria. The highest-priced seats, at S 300,-, are in the first four rows of the *Parkett* (the orchestra) and the center *Logen* (Boxes) on the first level *(I Rang)*. The next category at S 250,- applies to rows 5-9 in the orchestra, the few seats (14) in the Boxes close to the stage on the orchestra level, and the center-(called the *Balkon*) and first-row seats on the second level *(II Rang)*. In two more increments of S 50,- prices come down for orchestra seats as one moves towards the back of the theater (the 20 rows are split into five different categories!) and for seats in the upper levels. The seats in the third and top-most level (the *Galerie*), excellent for both sight-lines and acoustics, range from S 155,- on the front row to S 55,- on the back rows. Standing Room, located on the sides of the *Galerie,* costs S 40,-.

Tourist Information is available in two locations: off to the left as you come out of the Hauptbahnhof and "in town," on the edge of the old city, at a point close to where both Maria-Theresien-Strasse and Museumstrasse intersect with Burggraben (and not far from the opera house). The office in the station is small and often crowded with back-packers; here they mainly deal with hotel reservations, for which you pay a deposit which is then deducted from the hotel charges. They are open daily, between 0800 and 2200. The office at 3 Burggraben, known officially as the "Fremdenverkehrs-verband," is more spacious, but they keep shorter hours: daily, from 0800 to 1900. They also make hotel reservations. (In spite of what may be a long wait, it is certainly more convenient to leave the station with a hotel reservation in hand and where taxis are available, should you need one. The office on Burggraben is over 6/10th's of a mile away/1 kilometer, and if you have a lot of baggage would require two taxi rides.) Both offices have facilities for changing money.

Hotels are fairly plentiful in Innsbruck, but directly across from the station there is not the usual cluster offering a wide range of choices. Also, with the Landestheater bordered by a park and public buildings no hotels are in that immediate neighborhood. Innsbruck however is a pleasant city in which to walk, should you find yourself within a mile or so of the theater. The city is crisscrossed by tram and bus lines, and a 24-hour Tageskarte for unlimited rides may be bought at either of the Tourist Offices for S 45,-.

Money can be changed at both of the Tourist Offices at the hours given above. American Express and Cook's each maintain offices in Innsbruck; in fact they are across the street from each other on Brixnerstrasse.

LINZ is not on the usual tourist circuit, although admirers of Anton Bruckner know the city well because of the annual autumn festival given in his honor. The Abbey of St. Florian, where Bruckner received his early training and where he was later buried, is one of the largest in Austria. Its handsome baroque buildings, housing an extraordinary library, a rare collection of Altdorfer paintings, and sumptuous apartments, is located some eleven miles (eighteen kilometers) to the southeast. Linz itself is attractively laid-out, with its old section, now lovingly restored, huddled around the main bridge crossing the Danube. The city has no spectacular monuments with which to lure the visitor, and its most interesting museum, devoted to Austrian (and German) painters of the 19th and 20th centuries, lies across the river in the suburb of Urfahr, but both the old and new sections of the downtown area are appealing because of their compactness and simple elegance. The city fathers acted kindly towards those on foot by barring all vehicular traffic except trolleys from the main commercial street, the Landstrasse.

The opera house is in the Landestheater, a complex of three theaters not far from the Danube in the old city. From the Hauptbahnhof a #3 trolley goes directly to the Hauptplatz, the broad, irregular square sloping up from the river; a short distance away on foot is Kloster-Strasse (the last street away from the Danube on the southwest end of the square); it goes by the side of the Landhaus and then, after a few more paces, to the small park on which the theater faces. From the station to the theater (by way of the Hauptplatz) is well over a mile (approximately two kilometers).

Opera-goers in Linz are not happy with their small theater. A campaign is underway to replace the present building (which was put up in 1803) with a larger and more modern structure. Even though the theater was rebuilt in 1939 and enlarged between 1954 and 1958, it still seats only around 676 people with Standing Room for 80. Though perhaps ideal for intimate chamber opera, the main problem is that the auditorium is cramped and does not work well for large-scaled works: the stage and pit are quite small, and sight-lines are not good from many of the seats on the sides of the two steeply-raked balconies. (In both balconies all of the seats are in open rows, with traces of the old Boxes remaining only with a handful of seats near the stage and at the rear of the first balcony.) Furthermore, almost half of the seats in the parterre are spoiled acoustically by the ponderous overhang of the first balcony. The best seats in the house are in the center portions of the two balconies; seats on the sides are only good on the front rows.

The Landestheater opens in late September and closes in early July. In the course of a season between six and eight operas are offered, along with three or four operettas and musicals. Though all works are sung in German (even the Mozart-Da Ponte collaborations), the choices are interesting because an effort is made to maintain a balance with operas drawn from the German, Italian, French, and Russian repertories. Some rarely-performed works occasionally turn up on the schedule, such as in 1988–89 Auber's *La Muette de Portici* (here done as *Die Stumme von Portici*) and in 1989–90 Rossini's *Wilhelm Tell (sic)*. Linz sometimes has premiered new works by Austrian composers and has now joined those companies championning Zemlinsky. Although the stage of the Landestheater is occasionally "borrowed" for plays with large casts (the theater company has exclusive use of an adjacent and smaller auditorium), either an opera or an operetta (or musical) is on the schedule on an average of around eighteen times each month. (This impressive number becomes considerably reduced after one subtracts the performances that are reserved for special groups and therefore not open to the general public.) Usually two operas and one operetta (or musical) are presented within the same month, with no pattern as to when any of these are performed on successive evenings. There is also no set day on which the theater is regularly closed; this may occur midweek or just as often on a weekend night.

Linz currently has an excellent but small group of young singers under contract, with very few listed as making only guest appearances. (There is once again a sprinkling of Americans serving their "apprenticeship" with this company.) If a strongly cast *Rosenkavalier* heard in October 1989, with young singers in all the major rôles, is any measure of the standard of what one can usually hear, opera lovers in Linz have little reason to envy some of the larger houses elsewhere. The only problem is that many of these artists will probably be moving on soon to more prestigious companies. Linz does have its shortcomings however: a rather raw, loud, and blustery orchestra, the Bruckner-

Orchestra Linz, but some of the fault lies with the small dimensions of the theater where many in the audience are sitting almost on top of the pit. Also with this production of *Rosenkavalier* criticism could be levelled at some of the sets, which looked "provincial," but here again the designers can be excused in part because they have to cope with such a small stage. But if you go to the opera to hear good singing, I strongly recommend Linz. From following reviews and from second-hand reports I can also vouch for the quality of the operetta performances. There is unanimity that they are very well sung and sumptuously produced.

The Box Office is inside the theater to the left of the main doors. The hours are: Tuesday through Friday, from 1000 to 1230 and from 1600 until 1930; on Saturday, from 1000 to 1230; closed on Sunday, Monday, and holidays, but the Box Office opens at 1800 on these days if an evening performance is scheduled. The telephone number is: (0 732) 27-76-55 (which I found to my frustration is only answered during Box Office hours). Tickets go on sale eight days before each performance. No provisions are given for ordering and paying for individual tickets by mail, but tickets may be reserved by telephone, subject to the eight-day limit. The mailing address is: Landestheater, Promenade, A-4020 Linz.

Prices reflect the awkward shape of the theater, with the most expensive seats at S 330,- located in the middle section of the First Balcony *(I Rang)*. Next come the seats in the first seven rows of the Orchestra *(Parterre)*, priced at S 295,-, but the seats on the ends of each of these rows (because of poor sight-lines) fall into two lower pricing categories; also in this price-range a string of front-row seats once again in the First Balcony. The third category at S 240,- includes most of the balance of the Orchestra, a few off-center seats in the First Balcony, and front-row center in the Second Balcony *(II Rang)*. The seats priced at S 190,- include the rear of the Orchestra (far under the Balcony overhang), more off-center seats verging on the sides in the First Balcony, and some good seats, rows 2-3 center and front-row sides, in the Second Balcony. The only good seats priced at S 135,- are rows 4-5 in the Second Balcony; the others are too far to the sides in both Balconies. Finally, at S 95,- and S 65,- are the last three rows of the Second Balcony, good seats except for a limited view of action placed at the rear of the stage. Standing Room, located at an angle between the center and sides of the Second Balcony, costs S 20,- (for a view of the stage this position is better than many of the seats on the sides).

Tourist Information is available in the Hauptbahnhof off to the right of the main waiting room (as you come in from the train platforms) and down a long corridor, next to the more clearly marked flower shop. The "summer" hours, from 1 June to 30 September, are quite different from the "winter" hours. Summer, from Monday through Saturday, 0900 to 1200 and 1300 to 1900; Sundays and holidays, from 1400 to 1900. Winter (1 October through 31 May): Monday through Saturday, from 0900 to 1200 and 1300 to 1800; closed on Sundays and holidays. They will make telephone calls for hotel reservations at no charge. The telephone number: (0 732) 54-0-00. A second office is on the corner of Altstadt and Kloster-Strasse, the latter being the street you would take from the Hauptplatz to the Landestheater. This office does not deal with hotel reservations. Summer hours: Monday through Friday, from 0800 to 1800; on weekends and holidays, from 0900 to 1130 and from 1230 to 1830. The winter hours: Monday through Friday, from 0900 to 1800; closed on weekends and holidays. This is the office however to which you would write or call for general information about the city. The formal name and address: Städtische Fremdenverkehrsbüro, 17 Altstadt, A-4010 Linz, Postfach 310; the telephone number is: (0 732) 23-93-13-78 or 23-93-13-83 and the telex is: (02) 2407 touri a.

Hotels are to be found scattered throughout the city, including several that are quite close to the opera house. There is only one establishment immediately across from the Hauptbahnhof, but its prices, compared with others in Linz, are in the upper-middle range. Along the trolley line connecting the station with the Hauptplatz (the tracks follow Landstrasse) the hotels are all on the side streets. Unless you know the city and have reserved in advance your hotel, you would be well advised to consult the Tourist Information office in the station, rather than trying to find accommodations on your own.

Money can be changed in the Hauptbahnhof in a small banking office just next door to the Tourist office. The hours are: Monday through Friday, from 0800 to 1900; Saturday, from 0800 to 1200 and 1300 to 1700; on Sundays and holidays, from 0800 to 1200. The main post office on Domgasse also performs this service, but their hours are not as good as those of the bank at the station. Both Cook's and American Express have offices in Linz

SALZBURG would be a mecca for tourists even if it were not the

birthplace of Mozart. Oddly, there is nothing especially dramatic or eye-catching about the site: a low plateau crowned by a fortress-palace, a narrow valley crowded with buildings, and a small river, elements shared by many other cities and towns, but here it all somehow comes together in magical harmony. There are really two Salzburgs: the quaint baroque houses and shops of the burghers lining the narrow streets, and the more grandiose, partly Italianate monuments of the archbishop lords, usually fronting on open squares. Perhaps what delights the visitor is the gentle contrast between the two architectural styles, which are constantly in play each time one turns a corner. With new construction now strictly controlled in the heart of the old city there is a little bit the Disney-like atmosphere of a town frozen in time, but what came about in Salzburg came about slowly and with an enlightened human touch. One visit, and you will be captivated.

The "local" opera company, housed in the Landestheater, is obviously dwarfed by the high-powered (and expensive) forces brought in each year for both the brief Easter Festival and the much longer summer Festival (from late July through the end of August). At that later time the Landestheater too becomes an important component of the Festival, but it then is used only for plays. The big imported musical events—the operas, orchestral concerts, and recitals—take place across the river in the three buildings grouped together as the Festspiel Houses; at the Mozarteum, just behind the Landestheater and the Marionette Theater, festival-goers are offered a daily schedule of chamber music concerts.

The Landestheater (at 22 Schwarzstrasse) faces the Makartplatz where most of the city's main bus lines conveniently intersect. Immediately behind the theater are the formal gardens of the Schloss Mirabell; some 600 feet (200 meters) beyond the front of the theater is the main bridge leading across the Salzach into the center of the old city. The building, dating from 1893, is relatively small, seating only around 730. The orchestra section, only 15 rows deep and quite wide, is unlike most other theaters in Austria in following the German pattern of providing no center aisle (the German frontier lies just a few miles to the east). There are only two rings of raised seating: a circle of Boxes (three rows deep at the back and center of the theater, two rows deep on the sides) and a Balcony (seven rows deep at the back tapering to three rows on the sides). The auditorium is comfortable, but in spite of some rococo details in the architectural decoration it has a rather stolid, graceless appearance and little charm. Sight lines are good except on the far sides near the stage. The acoustics however are excellent: warm and intimate. For some productions, given the small dimensions of the pit, the orchestra spills over into the two proscenium boxes on the same level.

In comparison to Graz, Innsbruck, and Linz, all with much larger operating budgets, Salzburg's repertory is very modest, usually consisting of only five or six different works. During most of the year performances of musicals and operettas far exceed the number of operas. Also, as the Landestheater stage is shared with a drama and ballet company, operas are produced on an average of only about six to eight times within a single month. Two or three different works are usually performed concurrently, but it is quite rare for any two of them to be seen on successive dates. Each season at least two Mozart operas figure in the annual repertory, but in commemoration of the "Mozart Year" (1990–91) five of the "big" works and a program of one-acters are on the schedule, four of these presented as new productions. Supplementing its regular Landestheater series the company moves once a year to the other side of the Salzach and mounts an opera on the stage of either the Grosses or

Kleines Festspielhaus: *Otello* in October of 1990 and in the 1991–92 season *Lohengrin*. Within a two-week period these works are usually repeated four or five times. In March of the 1989–90 season the company in tandem with Graz completed its part in a joint year-by-year traversal of the *Ring*. Salzburg has yet to see the entire cycle brought together in a single season because of its expanded commitment to Mozart in 1990–91 (the Wagner operas have been given in the more commodious facilities of the Festival buildings in the old city). Filling out the repertory in recent seasons are works as diverse as Prokofiev's *Bethrothal in a Monastery* (1987–89), *Don Pasquale* (1988–89), *Eugene Onegin* (1989–90), and carried over to 1990–91 from the previous year, *Zar und Zimmermann*. On occasion the company has presented the world premières of new operas; usually these have been by composers affiliated in some way with the conservatory, the Mozarteum, next door.

The singers on Salzburg's roster are drawn from all over the world, many of them quite young. Some go on to international prominence after serving their "apprenticeship" years on the Landestheater stage. Salzburg has shaped the careers of many young Americans, a few of whom as distinguished "alumni" later return as guests to assume leading rôles. (Among all the singers under contract for 1990–91 the only names known to me are those of the visiting Americans.) The orchestra, even for the operettas and musicals, is made up of musicians drawn from a pool of instructors and advanced students at the Mozarteum. As this orchestra is extremely active on the concert platform, they play very well when in the pit of the theater.

The Landestheater season runs from mid-September to early June. Throughout the year an opera usually is scheduled for a Saturday evening, but there are enough exceptions to this pattern, when a play or ballet is listed instead, to warrant a close look at Salzburg's calendar before planning a visit. There are also occasional Sunday matinées. As a general rule the theater is closed on Mondays. The Box Office is inside the theater facing the small lobby at the front of the building and is open Tuesday through Friday from 1000 to 1300 and from 1730 to 1900; on Saturday from 1000 to 1300; closed on both Sunday and Monday. For the Sunday matinées (at 1500) and the Saturday performances (usually beginning at 1900 or 1930) the Box Office opens one hour before curtain time. Prices for most operas range from S 475,- to S 165,-. Tickets in the Orchestra section (the *Parterre*) are divided into five categories, beginning at S 475,- on the first row to S 280,- at the back in rows 13–15. In the Boxes (the *Logen*) front-row seats *(Vordersitze)* cost S 475,- in the center and S 460,- on the sides; second- and third-row seats *(Rücksitze)* in the same locations are respectively S 410,- and S 220,-. Balcony tickets in the center section start at S 355,- on the first row, S 280,- in rows 2–4, and S 220,- in rows 5–7; all seats on the sides are priced at S 165,-. Standing Room is not sold. Telephone reservations may be made by calling

(662) 71-5-12-0 during Box Office hours. There are no provisions for reserving and paying for tickets by mail. (To give a fair idea of how Festival prices in recent years have gotten out of hand, the most expensive tickets for a play in the Landestheater in August are priced at S 1400,-, more than $100 US; between September and June, during the theater's regular season, an opera ticket for one of the same seats usually costs between S 475,- and S 410,-. At Festival-time in any of the three Festspiel Houses opera tickets start at S 3300,-; black-market prices may be many more times that amount!)

Programs cost S 33,- and are of interest only if you are fluent in German. A mimeographed insert lists the cast and credits, and the only plot summary is given in German. The cloakroom charge is S 10,-.

Tourist Information is readily available in Salzburg at three different locations. The small office in the Hauptbahnhof is upstairs on the same level as the train platforms. It's open daily from 0800 to 2000, and will make hotel reservations. The service fee is S 10,- with a S 50,- deposit credited against the first night's charges. The telephone numbers are (662) 71-7-12 and 73-6-38. The city's main office is at 7 Auerspergstrasse, between Schwarzstrasse paralleling the river and Rainerstrasse, the principal street leading from the station to Mirabellplatz and Makartplatz (and the Landestheater). This office is open Monday through Friday from 0730 to 1800; closed on Saturday and Sunday. This office too makes hotel reservations. The mailing address is: Fremdenverkehrsbetriebe der Stadt Salzburg, 7 Auerspergstrasse, A-5020 Salzburg, and the telephone number is: (662) 80-72-0. The third office is at 5 Mozartplatz across the river in the old city. (Mozartplatz joins the Residenzplatz on the north side of the Dom; also American Express happens to be just next door.) This office is open daily from 0830 to 1800 and offers as well hotel reservation service.

Hotels are scattered throughout the city, with the highest concentration of both five-star luxury establishments and more modest accommodations found close to the Hauptbahnhof and the Landestheater. However, on weekends finding a room at the last minute may be difficult. At Festival time, when the city is jammed with visitors, you should not go near Salzburg without a confirmed reservation in hand.

Salzburg has a tourist bus ticket, good for unlimited trips for 24 hours. These tickets, costing S 20,-, are sold in Tabak shops, but there you can only buy them in units of five for S 100,-. Usually your hotel will have a supply of these, allowing you to buy at cost one or two according to your needs.

There are two facilities for changing money in the Hauptbahnhof: upstairs on the train platform level, daily, from 0800 to 2000, and downstairs, on street-level in the main entrance hall, daily, from 0700 to 2200. Everywhere in the city there are places offering to change your money, and during the summer Festival many banks arrange to have special Saturday and Sunday hours. At American Express, even when cashing their travelers checks, you will be charged a hefty commission (mandated by Austrian law). Cook's, with its affiliate Wagons-Lits, also has an office in Salzburg.

BELGIUM

For the art-lover Belgium's museums and churches contain a quite exhausting array of treasures, ranging from the exquisite detail of the Flemish primitives to the bold opulence of Rubens and his followers. Many of Belgium's small cities too are in themselves like museums: Bruges, Ghent, Mechelen, and Louvain, where time seems to have stopped many centuries ago. By USA-standards it is an extremely small country because in any direction, out from Brussels by train, in one hour (or less) you will have crossed the frontier to find yourself in either France, Luxembourg, Germany, Holland, or wetting your feet in the North Sea. If you have a Eurailpass, this means that you can make almost any city your "headquarters" for daytime trips for touring and still be back in time for an opera that night. However with most train service ending around 11 pm (2300 hours), and an opera ending not much earlier, it would be risky to try to combine an opera with your sightseeing and still make it back to your home base and hotel by the last train.

Opera played an important and unique rôle in the political history of Belgium by igniting a revolution that brought about the country's independence from the Dutch. In August of 1830 Auber's *La Muette de Portici* was being performed at Brussels' opera house, La Monnaie, a theater still much in existence today. Auber's plot revolves around an uprising in 1647 of the Neapolitans against their Spanish oppressors. In the second act there is a rousing patriotic duet between the two revolutionary heroes who vow to free their countrymen. At this moment in the opera many in the audience, filled with nationalistic fervor, rushed out of the theater and into the streets, setting in motion the events that within a few weeks had the Belgians breaking away from Holland and proclaiming their own constitutional monarchy. A model for some of the nearly bloodless revolutions we have thought unique to our own time? And an opera serving as the catalyst for a revolution? (To vindicate the Dutch: their administration had been benign and not particularly oppressive; also they governed Belgium not through conquest but by treaty after the fall of Napoleon. The unhappiness of the Belgians stemmed more from cultural incompatibility than from other causes, they being Catholic, their rulers Protestant.)

Until very recently the Belgian government was offering vigorous financial support to three separate opera companies: La Monnaie in Brussels, the Opéra Royal de Wallonie, based in Liège, and the Opera voor Vlaanderen, shared by both Antwerp and Ghent. Each of these by its geographic position, and the Liège company by frequent travels to nearby cities, made opera easily accessible to most of the country. In Belgium a special situation exists because of the fragile balance and relationship between the Belgian Flemish and the Belgian French, the Walloons.

Recent economic problems throughout the country have brought about severe cut-backs in the appropriations given to cultural organizations. The most severely affected has been the Flemish Opera (the Opera voor Vlaanderen). A strike in Antwerp in the spring of 1988 halted all activity by the company and led to the cancellation of the 1988–89 season. Adding to this confusion the Ghent opera house was closed after it was declared unsafe and badly in need of renovation; at the time it appeared that no funds could be found to make the needed repairs. Then in the winter of 1989 Gerard Mortier, director of Brussels' La Monnaie, agreed to take on in an advisory rôle the challenge of reviving the ailing Antwerp and Ghent companies. (More recently Mortier has accepted the position as director of the Salzburg Festival, beginning in October 1991; undoing Karajan's money-making empire and bringing the Festival back to its original purpose should prove to be a formidable task. Until Mortier leaves his post at La Monnaie in 1992 he remains one of the busiest opera managers in the world.) Money has finally been appropriated to renovate the Ghent theater, the work to be completed by the fall of 1991, and a newly-appointed director for the company was able to offer once more a full opera season in Antwerp beginning in October of 1989. By the time of the closing performances in June and July of 1990 it was clearly evident that in a single season the city for the first time in its history had become one of the major opera centers on the Continent.

As much for political as for economic reasons the subsidy for La Monnaie in Brussels has been reduced, and beginning with the 1989–1990 season they have had to economize on bringing in outside "name" singers and curtail plans for new productions. In Liège the situation is not yet very clear with respect to how the French Opéra Royal will cope with the crisis, but they enjoy two great advantages over the other two groups: first, by the fact that their geographic base in Belgium is somewhat wider, the cities where they perform (Liège, Charleroi, Verviers, and Mons) may help in supplementing the budget; second, they have strong ties (through co-productions) with opera companies in Italy, Germany, and France, so that for reasons of international prestige the Belgium government may be more reluctant to impose stringent budgetary cuts on a company highly visible beyond its own borders. These monetary problems are indeed very distressing for the current state of opera in Belgium, but everything could change very quickly if there is a marked improvement in the nation's economic health.

In both the Flemish and French parts of the country there is nothing very unusual or exotic about the terms used in describing seating in their theaters. Only in Liège could there be problems. In Brussels, where a kind of formal bi-lingualism is practiced, the seating arrangements are not complicated. A *loge* is a box, and a *balcon* will of course be a balcony. (For a description of the cavernous *fond de loge,* the seats in the rear of a box, and other terms defying easy translation I refer the reader to my more detailed description of seating arrangements given under "FRANCE.") In Liège the terms *rez de chaussée* are used to label what we in the USA call "orchestra seats" or, in somewhat pretentious imitation of the French, "the parterre." Also in Liège, *pair(e)(s)* and *impair(e)(s),* literally meaning "even" and "odd," are applied to "right" and "left" orchestra seating, as one looks towards the stage.

In describing the three companies below I follow alphabetical order in listing the cities where each is based. For those other cities where they may perform, I refer the reader back to either Antwerp, Brussels, or Liège for more details about the respective companies.

ANTWERP (Flemish: ANTWERPEN and French: ANVERS) Even the casual tourist knows how closely Peter Paul Rubens and his followers are associated with Antwerp. There is the artist's house (and studio), and scattered about the city in various churches and museums some of his most celebrated paintings. The ships which used to dock within a few hundred feet of the cathedral and the old town hall now call at the huge port which lies further down the river Scheldt, north of the city, but everywhere in Antwerp evidence still exists of the city's great and long importance as one of Europe's largest shipping centers. Though the city is criss-crossed by tram and bus lines, all but a few of the most interesting sights lie just to the east of the Centraal Station, concentrated within a mile, and easily accessible on foot.

The opera company based in Antwerp actually has two names, which could cause some confusion for visitors, and when the French equivalents are are added to their English translations, we end up with a total of six! As of

1989 the "parent" company shared by Antwerp and Ghent discarded its old name (Opera voor Vlaanderen) and took on a new one, De Vlaamse Opera ("Flemish Opera," and in French: "Opéra Flamand"). The second name, Koninklijke Vlaamse Opera ("Royal Flemish Opera"), parallels the name of the Liège company in the French-speaking part of Belgium; the Liège company calls itself the Opéra Royal de Wallonie (the Ghent division of the Flemish Opera uses the name: Koninklijke Opera Gent). To keep things simple I will use only the name "Flemish Opera" below.

The opera house is but a short distance from the train station, about ⅕ of a mile (350 meters), off to the east by either of two streets leading towards the center of the city. (One route: go to the far end of the Konigin Astridplein, the square just in front of the station, and turn left on Gemeentestraat; go four blocks to the second square where all of the busses are lined up, and go left again on Frankrijklei, the wide boulevard, and a few doors down is the opera house; or, from the main side entrance of the station, with the train platforms behind you upstairs, go downstairs to your left, take De Keyser Lei, the street lined with the many hotels and restaurants; go four blocks, and on your right, on Frankrijklei in the middle of the short block, is the opera house.)

The theater, built between 1904 and 1907, is in the traditional horseshoe shape with three levels of balcony seating. The style is best described as Victorian neo-classical, chaste and somewhat delicate rather than overly ornamented. The interior will probably take on a much warmer appearance when it is thoroughly cleaned and renovated (the upper walls and ceiling look quite shabby), but the money appropriated for repairs was used instead for modernizing the stage equipment, a matter of some urgency. The entrance and the ground-floor areas have been cleaned up, but much needs yet to be done to refurbish the seating in the upper levels. The figure of 979 for the total seating capacity in 1989–90 will undoubtedly change, up or down, when money is available for a complete refitting of the auditorium. Some seating space was sacrificed on the sides in each of the balconies when new lighting and technical devices were installed towards the front of the theater. Now almost all of the remaining seats command a very good view of the stage. Describing the various levels poses few problems, although some of the seats still given on the seating-plan have either been removed or are not being sold to the public. After the Orchestra (the *Parterre*) with fourteen rows split by a center aisle, the First Balcony *(Eerste Balkon)* at the front has three "open" rows of seats encircled at the back by a series of nineteen Boxes; these however are not true Boxes but what the French call *Corbeils,* groups of seats enclosed by low, waist-high partitions. Seven single front-row seats on each side extend towards the stage. The Second Balcony *(Tweede Balkon)* is made up of four rows extending across the center and the same number off to both sides. The Third Balcony *(Derde Balkon)* has five rows in the center and three rows on the sides; behind and above the middle portion of this level are seven rows of wooden seats, here broken into two sections of at first four rows and then three *(Eerste* and *Tweede Amfitheater)*. The acoustics are excellent in the upper parts of the house; I am assured they are equally good down below.

In the first months of his brief term as advisor, Gerard Mortier made some drastic changes in the way the Flemish Opera had traditionally operated. Until 1988 there had been separate choruses, orchestras, and technical personnel for both Antwerp and Ghent and often different repertories as well. Now there is a new and much leaner (and younger) single company, and when the Ghent theater reopens in 1991 the musicians and others will then move back and forth between the two cities. Until 1988 each city had also maintained a quite ambitious season, together presenting around a dozen operas, five or so operettas, and three or more musicals, some of these done in collaboration, others done independently. In Antwerp and then in Ghent most but not all of the works had been repeated four or five times. This is now to change, with the company concentrating solely on the production of opera. Eventually, beginning in 1991, a season will consist of ten different works, five to be done in Antwerp, five to be done in Ghent. Each opera will then be repeated some eight times in only one city, with the audiences, if they wish to see all ten works, making the trips back and forth to see them. The Belgian Railways have put into effect special tariffs for opera-goers between Ghent and Antwerp; there is a reduction of 40% for the first ticket holder and 60% for all others seated and traveling together, up to a maximum of six. (By local train the 39 miles/65 kilometers between Ghent and Antwerp normally takes between 45 minutes and an hour; if there is a special "opera train," it may be much faster.)

For a long time the repertory of the Flemish Opera has been quite ambitious: strong in German opera, particularly with Richard Strauss (who conducted in Antwerp), and with a distinguished history of presenting complete *Ring* cycles. For the inaugural season of 1989–90, beginning in middle October and ending in early July, nine works were chosen that ran the gamut from Monteverdi to a recent contemporary Belgian opera; also included were two Verdi operas, Haydn, Rossini, Tschaikovsky, and Richard Strauss. Each work, introduced at the rate of one per month, was repeated six or seven times (five times for the concert performance of Rossini's *Tancredi*). Except for *Orfeo,* scheduled mostly on successive nights, there was an interval of one to three days between each performance. With each opera there is at least one matinée, usually falling on a Sunday.

The same policy has continued of filling all of the leading rôles with singers brought in from "outside." The works are sung in the languages in which they were written (when the company was founded in the nineteenth century many of the operas were performed in Flemish). A number of Belgian musicians born in Flanders have been prominent all over Europe in the movement to revive baroque-era performing technics. With this new company Gerard Mortier wanted to produce more baroque operas and to give these musicians more frequent exposure in their own country. Except for these works, for which specialized and known ensembles are engaged, a regular house orchestra is in the pit accompanying the singers. It goes by the name of the Orkest van De Vlaamse Opera, and a monthly series of concerts (often with vocalists) was initiated during the 1989–90 season; a similar series was also planned for 1990–91.

The Box Office is located at sidewalk-level just to the left of the main steps and doors of the opera house. (A red neon sign marks the entrance.) The hours are Tuesday through Saturday from 1000 to 1800. They reopen one hour before each performance for last-minute sales. For some years prices for the Flemish Opera had been kept ridiculously cheap: a high of 500 FB (FB = francs belges) for the best seats, a low of 225 FB for all the seats in the Third Balcony. With the start of the 1989–90 season, prices are now much more realistic and more expensive, but tickets are still far less costly than comparable seats at La Monnaie in Brussels. Five categories are now in effect: 1400 FB for the Orchestra and the center of the First Balcony; 1100 FB for the Second Balcony center and the sides of the First Balcony; 800 FB for the center of the Third Balcony and sides of the Second Balcony; 400 FB for the sides of the Third Balcony and First Amphitheater; and finally, 200 FB in the Second Amphitheater. Premières are considerably higher in price in each of the categories, 1800 FB, 1500 FB, 1100 FB, 600 FB, and 300 FB respectively. There is no provision for Standing Room. Tickets go on sale one month before the first performance of each work and may be reserved by telephone; payment must be received ten days before the date of the performance. There are no other special instructions about ordering by mail. The telephone number for reservations and information is: (03) 233-66-85. The mailing address is: Koninklijke Vlaamse Opera, 3 Frankrijklei, 2000 Antwerpen. Credit cards, American Express or Visa, are accepted. One of La Monnaie's most felicitous innovations has been adopted by Antwerp: ten minutes before the performance is due to begin, all persons under 25 or over 65 may purchase any tickets left unsold at the set-rate of 150 FB. Those people having tickets in the Third Balcony or either of the two Amphitheaters are segregated and have a very long walk upstairs; the entrance at least is from one side of the main lobby and not outside through a deviously-hidden side door.

Programs are priced at 250 FB and are indeed quite handsome, but unless you are eager to own a libretto that includes the original text as well as a Flemish translation, there is no need to buy one. (Synopses of the plot are provided in Flemish, French, and English.) Detailed information about the performing artists is also available in a flyer that is printed for each opera and distributed free of charge. This too is written only in Flemish.

Tourist information is conveniently located in a small building just outside the Centraal Station in the square, the Koningin Astridplein, facing the main front exit from the station. Off-season, from November through April, the hours are Monday through Saturday, from 0900 to 1200 and from 1400 to 1700; closed on Sunday; in season, from May through October, the hours are Monday through Friday from 0830 to 2000; Saturday from 0900 to 1900; and Sunday from 0900 to 1700. Their telephone number is (03) 233-05-70. Hotel reservations can be made here at no charge. There is a second office "downtown," on the Groote Markt within a few steps of the cathedral and the town hall. Their hours are similar to those of the office next to the railroad station. For sale at both offices is a special pass with detachable coupons for 147 FB which permits you to take 8 tram or bus rides, with no limit on the length of time the pass is valid.

Hotels abound on the Koningin Astridplein, which you see right in front of you when you come out the main doors of the Centraal Station, and they can be found in all price categories. There are other hotels in the immediate vicinity of the station if you go out by the side door on the left and go down De Keyser Lei. Most of the hotels in this area tend to be more expensive, with some in the luxury class.

Money can be changed in a well-marked booth inside the station. The hours and days conform more or less to those of banks. When this booth is closed, as on weekends, holidays, or in the evening, money can be changed at one of the windows where railway tickets are sold, usually one of those marked "Buitenland." The exchange rate there will be the same as what you receive at a bank. Both American Express and Cook's have offices in Antwerp, and both happen to be on Frankrijklei, within a few short steps of the opera house. When cashing travelers checks in Belgium normally a costly surcharge is added to the exchange rate. You do not pay this fee when you cash your American Express checks at an American Express office or your Cook's checks at Cook's.

BRUSSELS (French: BRUXELLES and Flemish: BRUSSEL)

Though a very international city (the headquarters for the European Economic Community and for NATO) and boasting some of the best restaurants in Europe, central Brussels lacks a sense of overall unity with a distinctive character of its own. There are small areas that have kept something of their old charm, like the Grand' Place, and others, like a few blocks of the Rue Royale, that still retain their look of elegance, but many parts of the city are shabby and depressed, lacking any architectural distinction. Much of the problem can be blamed on developers, going back to the late 1800's, who were given a free hand to destroy large sections of the old city and who then replaced what they had levelled with structures that were either drab or pretentious. The brief building boom that followed after the last war scarcely improved the city's appearance. Only recently has this policy (or lack of one) been slowed, but the scars on the surface of Bruxelles still remain: behind and off to one side of the graceful proportions of the Grand' Place one finds boarded-up slums, and along the wide outer boulevards ugly new skyscrapers rise up right next to squalid, one-storey hovels. But the Bruxellois are a gracious people and are not to be chastized for the haphazard growth of their city. Enjoy Brussels' opera, one of the finest in all of Europe, eat well, and discover for yourself the many interesting sights that the city still has to offer!

THE THÉÂTRE ROYAL DE LA MONNAIE (in Flemish: Koninklijke Muntschouwburg, which in English I'll shorten to "The Mint") enjoys a solid reputation as one of the leading opera houses on the Continent. As with the other two companies in Belgium this company too has a sort of double identity and is known also by the title: Opéra National. It occupies a handsome neo-classical building, constructed in the 1790's, in the commercial center of the city, approximately 300 yards (300 meters) from the Grand' Place. In contrast to the chaste exterior, the inside of the theater, done over at some point in the nineteenth century, has the florid effulgence (on a smaller scale) of Garnier's Paris Opéra. The building was completely refurbished from top to bottom and its stage equipment modernized during the 1985–86 season. (The exquisite murals in the outer lobby were painted by Sam Francis.) La Monnaie is not a repertory company, and the eight to ten works mounted between late September and early July are scheduled on the block-system, meaning that only one work is repeated anywhere between five and ten times (usually with at least a one- or two-day interval between each performance). Productions brought in and performed by visiting opera companies may be repeated only two or three times. In most cases a new work is presented each month, but there is no over-lapping, with the last runs of one opera meshing with the beginning performances of a second one (as sometimes occurs at La Scala). If you are pressed for time and limited to one night of opera in Brussels, you will have to plan your schedule very carefully. Ballet programs, solo vocal recitals, and symphony concerts are also scheduled throughout the season on the stage of the theater.

Through the years La Monnaie gained much of its prestige because it introduced to French-speaking audiences much of the German repertory (beginning with Wagner and continuing with Richard Strauss) that was not being performed in Paris. The company also commissioned new works from many of the leading French composers writing around the turn of the century. In our own time it has been among the first houses on the Continent to champion the operas of Prokofiev, Berg, and Britten. Still true to this innovative spirit La Monnaie is currently exploring the nearly forgotten works of Franz Schreker. In Brussels they by no means neglect the standard repertory, but when they do produce a *Norma* or a *Traviata* or a *Parsifal* they try to engage the best available (and often young) singers. Since the last war most of the big, international stars of the singing world have at one time or another sung at La Monnaie, and this tradition continues today. Special mention should be made of the orchestra, a much admired ensemble, which supplements its appearances in the pit with concerts not only on the stage of the theater but with a large number of performances in other halls in and around Brussels.

Further evidence of La Monnaie's adventurous spirit can be seen in the fact that they were able to lure the American choreographer and dancer Mark Morris to move to Brussels, and beginning with the 1988–89 season this theater and city now are the "home base" for this remarkable artist and his company.

With its freshened gilt, restored ceiling murals, and new red plush the theater now radiates both elegance and warmth. Comfort has also been much improved (the building had become very shabby), but few of the sight-line problems in the boxes on the sides could be changed. Fortunately there are not many of these seats. In terms of size, with seating for 1134, this is one of the smallest of the important houses on the Continent, with a feeling of great intimacy (except perhaps from the back rows of the uppermost balconies). There are four tiers of seating above the large and wide orchestra area, with the boxes on each level placed above and behind the unobstructed, "open" rows of seats. In those rows of seats along the balcony edges, even on the sides, the view of the stage is still fairly good. At the back of the theater on the topmost levels additional rows of these open seats offer at very reasonable prices an excellent view of the stage. Acoustically La Monnaie ranks among the best, with singers especially favoring it because of the flattering sound they hear of themselves and of their colleagues. The only unusual seating term is for the *baignoires,* literally "bathtubs," clustered together on the second tier; these are like boxes except that the partitions between them come only up to waist-level. The seats to try to avoid are the *fonds de loges;* though priced very cheaply in Brussels and having reasonably good sound (much better than the comparable seats at Paris' Palais Garnier), you will see only a portion of the stage. For a fuller account of such seats see the section about seating arrangements under "FRANCE."

The Box Office is located to the right of the main lobby area, and if the main doors to the theater at the front should be closed, a door on the right side of the building remains unlocked. They are open, Monday through Saturday, from 1100 to 1800; closed on Sunday. The telephone numbers are: (02) 218-12-11 or (02) 219-63-41. The mailing address: T. R. M., 4 rue Léopold, 1000 Bruxelles. Reservations by telephone for tickets are accepted approximately 30 days before the date of each first performance of an opera; full payment, by check or postal money order, must be made within 10 days. Credit cards are now accepted. Prices range from a low of 200 FB (for boxes on the sides of the fourth level) to a high of 2000 FB (for seats orchestra-center, first balcony and first-level boxes facing the stage); good seats in the fourth balcony, center and facing the stage, cost 400 FB; the less desirable *fonds de loges* are priced between 150 FB and 600 FB. (Prices for the premières, the first performance of each opera, are different, ranging from a high of 3.200 FB to a low of 250 FB.) The Box Office is open one hour before curtain-time, with a bonanza for those 25 years old or younger and for all persons over 65 (the age that in French-speaking countries is happily called *"le troisième âge"*): all unsold tickets, no matter what the official price, go on sale five minutes before the beginning of the performance for 150 FB. One has to wonder how some elderly people might find their way from the box office to their seats and get settled in that short span of time. There is no Standing Room.

Programs are sold for 300 FB and are obviously the product of someone who has put some serious thought into compiling cogent comments about the work being performed, but you also are buying a libretto with a French translation. Small inserts provide synopses of the plot in English and German, but all the information about the artists is in French and Flemish.

On occasion La Monnaie moves some of its operas, ballets, recitals, and orchestral concerts to other locations within the city. The three places I describe are all most conveniently either on or just off the Rue Royale, the very fashionable long and straight avenue that begins at the side of the Royal Palace and goes north, running by the edge of the large public park and in the general direction of the Gare du Nord, the north railway station.

THE CIRQUE ROYAL (Flemish: Koninklijk Circus): This arena-like space proved most useful to La Monnaie during the period when the opera house was closed for renovations, and with great ingenuity opera was presented here almost "in the round," and as far as I could tell, without any trace of sound amplification. The space is now used for a number of the ballet programs, with at least one appearance annually by the Mark Morris Dance Group. Bleachers circle on three sides the orchestra "pit" (on floor level) and most of the stage (built up "behind" the orchestra). With a full house, the acoustics are amazingly good, probably owing to the fact that the ceiling is rather low and the spectators arranged in such a way as to prevent the sound from echoing off the masonry walls. The Cirque is at 81 Rue de l'Enseignement (Flemish: 81 Onderrichtstraat), the third and last of the three streets coming together on the Rue Royale just behind the ministries building opposite the Royal Palace, on the north side of the large Park bordering the

Rue Royale. The closest metro stop is at Parc (Flemish: Park), and you should continue up the Rue Royale with the Park to your right; busses from the center of the city leaving from De Brouckere would be #65 or #66; the #92, #93, #94 busses go in both directions down the Rue Royale from the Avenue Louise. Tickets bought in advance may be purchased either at the La Monnaie Box Office (see above) or at the Cirque. The Box Office at the Cirque is open Tuesday through Saturday and closed on Sunday and Monday; their hours are from 1100 to 1800. The Box Office here is also open one hour before each performance. The telephone number is: (02) 218-20-15.

THE PALAIS DES BEAUX-ARTS (Flemish: Paleis voor Schone Kunsten): This is a complex containing a number of small recital rooms and a large concert hall called the Grande Salle Henry le Boeuf. This last hall is called into service for most of the orchestra concerts using the forces of La Monnaie, sometimes joined as well by the opera chorus and special soloists. It is an attractive auditorium with very good acoustics and resembles somewhat Vienna's Musikverein with its rectangular shape and the deep balconies massed at the back. (The international competitions for the prestigious Queen Elizabeth awards also use this hall.) Although one side of the Palais borders the Rue Royale, the main entrances and the Box Office are at 23 Rue Ravenstein (Ravensteinstraat), the street that parallels the Rue Royale, down the hill, one block below the Park and Royal Palace. A #71 bus from De Brouckere goes in both directions on the Rue Ravenstein and will take you at the other end to the Porte de Namur (Naamspoort) stop of the metro; if you use the busses on the Rue Royale (see above for the Cirque Royal), you will want to get off at the Place Royale (Koningsplein). Ticket sales for events scheduled here involving La Monnaie may be bought at the opera house Box Office until the day before the performance. The Box Office in the Palais des Beaux-Arts is open Monday through Saturday from 1100 to 1900; they also open one hour before a performance. The telephone number for the Palais is: (02) 512-50-45.

THE HALLES DE SCHAERBEEK: A long run of Gluck's *Orfeo ed Euridice* was given here almost nightly towards the end of the 1987–88 season, while the opera house was booked for a Handel opera and a series of dance programs. Some people felt that the Halles, formerly a warehouse and public market now converted into a "performing space," was not suitable for presenting an intimate, small-scaled opera, and the venture was not deemed a success, but the opera may return here again in future seasons if the right work is chosen that will draw in the crowds and help balance the budget. (The last time the space was used was during the 1988–89 season for

a few ballet performances.) The public is seated on bleachers, and you are advised to bring your own cushion, although cushions may be rented upon payment of a deposit. The address is 22, Rue Royale Sainte-Marie, on the extension of the Rue Royale that runs behind and beyond the church of Ste. Marie (which stands in the middle of the avenue); the Halles are approximately 150 yards (150 meters) behind the church. The nearest metro stop is Jardin Botanique, a good 800 yards (800 meters) distant; the most convenient bus is the #93, which runs in both directions along the Rue Royale and then out the Avenue Louise.

The very excellent book shop in the opera house is well worth visiting if you are looking for the latest books or periodicals dealing with opera or if you simply want to browse. They have an exceptionally good selection of books and magazines in all languages, and you might be able to find something here that you thought had been out of print for many years. The hours are from 1100 to 2000, and they are open from Tuesday through Saturday; on Sundays, when a performance is scheduled, they open one hour before curtain-time and remain open for 30 minutes more after the curtain has come down. The entrance is on the left or north side of the theater as you face the front doors; or once inside the building you will find it at the opposite end of the hall that leads to the Box Office.

Tourist information, marked with an "i," is available at the Gare du Midi in a small booth on the ground floor near the restaurant area. (The city's other two stations have no such facilities.) They are open daily from 0900 to 1800 and can help with making hotel reservations. The charge for this service is 100 FB. Due to staffing problems you may find this office closed off and on during the day, but eventually someone appears and opens up again. Two other offices are located at subway stations (the Porte de Namur/ Naamsepoort and Rogier stops), but I have always found them closed when the posted hours said that they were supposed to be open. The most reliable source for tourist information is at the Brussels airport, open daily from 0800 until 2100; if you arrive by plane, take advantage of this more dependable office where they are equipped to provide information about the entire country.

For getting about the city the Brussels transportation system has a 24-hour ticket costing 140 FB. These may be bought at a ticket booth before entering the metro. Following the procedure in effect elsewhere in Europe, you insert the ticket into a stamping machine at the entrance to the subway or when you get on a bus, and from that time on, until the 24 hours are up, the ticket is valid for an unlimited number of trips.

Though Brussels appears to have an ample supply of hotels, most of the cleaner or newer ones are quite expensive (a minimum of $80 and up per night) and quite far from the "downtown" center; also, very few are conveniently located for either the train-traveler, the opera-goer, or the visitor wanting to be in or near the historic core of the city. I know of only one moderately priced hotel close to the Gare du Midi, and it always seems to be booked up. The other hotels in that area are quite forbidding and dingy and are only for the young and brave. Near La Monnaie, likewise, there is little to choose from, and the two nearby hotels that have somewhat reasonable rates are usually full. Since the theater is over a mile (1.6 kilometers) from the Gare du Midi, your best bet is to look for something in another part of the city. Unless you want to depend on taxis to move about, you will want a hotel very close to a subway stop, especially if your stay should fall on a Sunday when bus service is cut back. (The metro runs daily until 12 midnight, but most bus service ends between 8 and 9 pm.) It will require some careful planning, either with a branch of the Belgian Tourist Office here in the USA or with tourist information in Brussels, to make the right choice.

Money can be changed daily in the Gare du Midi from 0800 until 2000. A similar office, also open daily, is located in the Gare Centrale (Centraal) and is open one hour longer: 0800 to 2100. In the area around the Grand' Place there are a number of small, hole-in-the-wall agencies where you can change money, usually until 1900 on weekdays. The exchange rates are clearly marked in the windows, but it is always wise to check. Note than in Belgium a better rate prevails when changing cash rather than travelers' checks. Both American Express and Cook's have a number of branch offices in Brussels.

CHARLEROI is visited on the average of one evening a month by the Opéra Royal de Wallonie which performs in the Palais des Beaux-Arts. A Box Office there is open from Monday through Friday between 1030 and 1300 and again from 1430 to 1800. The telephone number is (071) 31-44-20. Ticket prices range from a low of 200 FB in the third balcony to a high of 800 FB in the center rows of the orchestra. (The term *corbeille* is used here for the seats in the rear of the orchestra.) The hall is very modern, with all seats downstairs and in the three upper levels having an excellent view of the stage (the three raised seating areas are squarely at the rear of the theater and not on the side walls). As for the city itself, it is "new" by Belgian standards, founded only in 1666 and often rebuilt after the devastation left by invading armies. It lies at the center of the now-depressed coal and steel industries. See LIÈGE for details about the Opéra Royal de Wallonie.

GHENT (Flemish: GENT; French: GAND) is a treasure-house of medieval art and architecture and should be on everyone's "must" list of places to visit. The "Adoration of the Lamb" by the van Eyck brothers in the

cathedral of St. Bavon (Sint Baafs) is usually where the tourist begins, but there are also many things that can be enjoyed just by wandering around without once going into a church or museum. A good guidebook (or guide-person) is indispensable. And something for USA-history buffs: on Veldstraat (Rue des Champs) you will see the building, now a shop, where the delegates from the United States were housed who were to sign the Treaty of Ghent in 1814; this marked England's belated recognition of American indepen-dence.

Not until 1991, unfortunately, will Ghent once again have a regular opera season. Its opera house, condemned as unsafe and closed, is now undergoing extensive repairs and is scheduled to reopen in the fall of 1991 with a season of five operas, spread out between October and the following July. The company that used to perform in the Ghent opera house, the Opera voor Vlaanderen, has been reorganized after a paralyzing strike in 1988. Under a new name, De Vlaamse Opera, the company resumed operations confined to Antwerp beginning in October of 1989. In the meantime no proposals have been made to find another venue for opera in Ghent before the old house reopens, although occasionally a few works in concert form are scheduled to be brought from Antwerp and performed in one of Ghent's auditoriums. Everything is being done to encourage opera-lovers in Ghent to come to Antwerp: a special subscription series is set aside for them, and the Belgian Railways have provided special train service and reduced fares (a 40% reduc-tion for the first ticket-holder and 60% for all others, up to six, seated and traveling together). (For more details about the company and future plans for Ghent, see under ANTWERP.)

The opera house is just off the main thoroughfare carrying the trolley line from the train station to the center of the city. (The distance from the station is roughly 1 2/5 miles or 2 kilometers; going backwards, from the city-center, it is approximately 500 yards or 1/2 kilometer.) Coming from the station by trolley, when you see the large and imposing law court building (the Gerechtshof/Palais de Justice) on your left, Schouwburgstraat (Rue du Théâtre) and the opera house will be on your right. Shortly beyond the theater this same street leads into an attractive square (in Flemish called the Kouter, meaning "the field," and in French, the Place d'Armes); this square was once considered the most fashionable and aristocratic residential area in all of Ghent. I have not been inside the opera house (dating from 1837–40), but photographs and a seating plan show it to be in the graceful Italian style with five tiers of balconies arranged in a horseshoe pattern. The theater ws inaugurated in 1840 with a recital by Franz Liszt. The renovations promise a change in some of the seating arrangements, reducing the capacity (for-merly holding 1300) in order to improve the sight-lines. Many of the seats on the sides, especially in the boxes on the first and second levels, have almost no view of the stage. One hopes that the architects charged with modifying the structure will have visited Zürich to see what can be done most successfully to adapt an old theater to fit modern demands.

Until 1991 the Box Office in Ghent will be selling tickets for performances in Antwerp, as the expanded schedule still anticipates many people continuing their allegiance to the company and traveling from Ghent. When the opera house reopens, and if the pre-1988 policy is reinstated, prices in Ghent will be exactly the same as those in Antwerp. The Box Office is located in the lobby of the opera house and is open from Tuesday through Friday from 1000 to 1600; closed on Saturday and Sunday. Ticket prices for Antwerp are obviously not discounted when bought in Ghent (See ANTWERP for details). The telephone number is: (091) 25-24-25. And the mailing address is: Koninklijke Opera Gent, 3 Schouwburgstraat, 9000 Gent.

Tourist information is not available in the train station (St. Pieters Staation) but some distance away in the heart of the city in the "crypt," actually the basement, of the Town Hall (Stadhuis/Hôtel de Ville). On foot this would be roughly 1½ miles (2.5 kilometers). From the trolley loop immediately in front of the station take the #1 tram to the Koornmarkt (Marché aux Grains), a 10- to 15-minute ride (be on the lookout for the opera house on your right just as you cross the canal). A one-way ticket costs 30 FB and can be bought from a machine. When you get off the trolley, the tourist information office will be on Botermarkt (Marché au Beurre) just off to your left in front of the free-standing belfry or clocktower. From November through the end of March they are open daily from 0900 to 1700; between April and the end of October from Sunday through Thursday: 0900 to 2000, and on Friday and Saturday: 0900 to 2100. The telephone number is: (091) 24-15-55.

Hotels are scattered about the city, with only a few in the vicinity of the train station. The latter are for the most part moderately expensive. This is one occasion when the tourist office can be of great help, and you can leave your bags at the station and retrieve them later after you know where you will be staying.

Money can be changed inside the station, off to the left in the main lobby, daily, between 0800 and 1200 and from 1400 until 1800. Cook's also maintains an office in the city.

LIÈGE,

LIÈGE, flanking the steep banks of the Meuse, is an extremely handsome city and the capital of the French-speaking or Walloon district of the country. Like almost all of Belgium it has suffered terribly from the ravages of invading armies, with one of its most painful moments occurring during the last war. After being liberated by Allied forces in the fall of 1944, Liège, like Antwerp, was still within range of German V-1 and V-2 "buzz bombs" and for two months was bombarded daily by these terrifying weapons. The city was rebuilt, and today one would never know, except after consulting historical records, the extent to which the city was damaged. Yet the survival of many different architectural styles gives Liège much of its special character, with each successive conquerer: the Franks, Germans, Burgundians, Spanish, Austrians, and French each leaving behind some trace of their influence.

The city has a rich and proud musical history. It was the birthplace of Grétry in 1714 and of César Franck a century later, in 1822. A special technique of violin playing was developed in its Conservatory, and this style of playing became known as the Belgian school, best exemplified by the famous virtuoso Eugène Ysaÿe

THE OPÉRA ROYAL DE WALLONIE of Liège is the French counterpart to Antwerp and Ghent's Flemish Opera. Between September and the end of June six to seven operas are produced alternating with a comparable number of operettas. All of these are scheduled on the block-system, with an opera (repeated four or five times) followed soon afterwards by an operetta (repeated five to seven times). Most of the singers making up the casts of the operettas are company "regulars," and often many of them assume small parts in the operas. Otherwise this cannot be called a true repertory company because the leading rôles in the operas are usually filled by guest artists, rarely with any returning to appear in a second work. Most of these singers are not familiar names, the majority of them being young Belgians with a scattering of Italians, French, British, and occasionally an American. According to most of the critics I have read, the sole weakness of this company, which has an excellent orchestra and imaginative designers and directors, is the unevenness of the singing. The repertory is fairly standard, running the gamut from Mozart to Puccini, with at least one work every season by Verdi, something by Wagner (or by another German composer), and usually a single romantic French work. Most operas are sung in the language in which they were written. Liège shies away from the avant-garde (the domain cultivated by La Monnaie), but they do try each season to present one work that is "safely" modern, often a contemporary opera that has been successfully performed elsewhere by another company; or they bring back for a second hearing a forgotten twentieth-century Belgian work. The Opéra Royal de Wallonie has toured extensively in Europe and has been seen in Canada and the USSR. They (or certain members of the company) are linked to opera centers in other countries (France, Germany, and Italy) through collaboration on new productions, and in July of 1989 they were involved in the staging at Versailles of *Traviata* and *André Chénier* during the bi-centennial festivities of the French Revolution.

The Théâtre Royal de Liège sits on one side of a large square, the Place de la République-Française, in the center of the city. It is approximately 1⅓ miles (2.2 kilometers) from the Gare des Guillemins, but either a #1 or #4 bus for a fare of 30 FB makes the trip in 10 to 20 minutes, depending on traffic, and the bus stop is right beside the theater. The building was originally modelled on Paris' Théâtre de l'Odéon, inaugurated in the 1820's, and twice, in 1864 and 1901, considerably modified inside; a thorough renovation was completed just a few years ago. The theater now has seating for 1051 people with the orchestra level (here called the *rez de chaussée*) and four tiers of ringed balconies. The names attached to each seating area "upstairs" are a bit confusing and should be sorted out to make them clearer: The first raised level is the *balcon* with two rows of seats circling the hall and behind them the *loges de balcon*. Second up, come the *premières loges* with no "open" rows of seats. The third level has a *galerie* of open rows of seating centered at the back of the theater with the two side areas consisting again of boxes called *deuxièmes loges*. On the fourth level the center section at the back is called the *amphithéâtre*, while on the sides a single row of seats still retains the label of *troisièmes loges*, even though the boxes were all ripped out during the last renovation. Though the acoustics of the theater are excellent, sight-lines from the seats on the sides still remain a problem.

The Box Office is just inside the doors that face the Place de la République-Française and is open Monday through Friday, from 1000 to 1300 and from 1400 to 1800; on Saturday from 1000 until 1300; closed on Sunday. The telephone numbers for information are: (041) 23-59-10 or 23-77-13. Prices range from a low of 250 FB to a high of 1000 FB. The Box Office is open one hour before each performance. Only American Express cards are accepted.

Tourist information is available just outside the Gare des Guillemins, a two-minute walk through and out the main doors of the station and then immediately left. They are open daily, Monday through Saturday, from 0930 to 1200 and from 1230 to 1800; on Sunday they keep the same hours but close earlier, at 1600. Hotel information is provided.

Finding a place to stay in Liège presents no problem because many of the city's hotels, in all price categories, are in the immediate vicinity of the Gare des Guillemins. The square in front of the station, the Place des Guillemins, contains a good number, and then the Rue des Guillemins, leading off from the square at an angle to the left, could be called "hotel row." This is the same route the busses follow heading north towards the center of the city.

Money can be changed inside the station off to the side of the main entrance. The hours are daily from 0900 to 1200 and from 1300 to 1800. Cook's has an office in Liège, but there is no American Express.

MONS is another of those ancient Belgian towns, many times devastated by invading armies, and many times rebuilt. The town is filled with numerous interesting vestiges of its past but is usually overlooked by the hurried tourist. Mons was also the birthplace of Orlandus Lassus, the great Renaissance master of polyphony. The Opéra Royal de Wallonie makes occasional visits, bringing each season three or four of its operas and operettas to the town's Théâtre Royal. Information about the performance dates and prices can be obtained either in Mons or in Liège.

VERVIERS, an industrial city of moderate size some 15 miles (25 kilometers) to the east of Liège, is included in the regular schedule of the Opéra Royal de Wallonie, but the company only brings their productions of operettas to the city, not the operas. The operettas are repeated three times in a row, on Friday and Saturday nights and on Sunday afternoons, beginning in October and continuing through June. All of these works are performed in the Grand-Théâtre de Verviers. For citizens of the city having opera subscriptions, free bus service is provided to Liège on certain specified nights throughout the season. Ticket information may be obtained by calling: (087) 33-44-94. There are no particular sights to attract the tourist to Verviers, but the surrounding area is extremely beautiful.

FRANCE

On 17 March 1990, following many years of controversy and several post-ponements, the new **Opéra-Bastille** finally presented its first opera: a brief run of Berlioz' *Les Troyens*. Until the curtain went up there had been fears that a last-minute strike might cancel the entire production. Except for a mishap when part of the scenery fell on one of the singers, the evening came off successfully. Those who had anticipated yet further problems with the opening-date of the new theater were for once proven wrong, but given the long record of previous disappointments, the pessimists were quite justified in their predictions of failure. After the last performance of *Les Troyens* in early April, the theater closed down once more to prepare for a revival in May of Janácek's *Katya Kabanova* using the sets of the Opéra production of a few years ago.

For almost two years, with the press and the public looking on, there has been serious and bitter dissension in the ranks of those who were to lead the opera. Firings, angry resignations, law suits, and threats of boycotts have made dramatic headlines in the newspapers, but no progress could be seen in organizing an initial season. The main auditorium of the building was finished on schedule for the inaugural concerts commemorating Bastille Day 1789–1989, and by January 1990 the stage equipment was in place, again by the appointed time, in anticipation of a season that by then was supposed to be fully underway.

Why a new opera house and opera company in the first place? Cynics would say: because of the vanity of President Mitterand who wanted to endow Paris with lasting monuments, as have many of his predecessors (Louis

XIV, Napoleon, and the late President Pompidou, among the best known, come to mind). Two other such projects initiated by Mitterand (they too were controversial when first begun) were the Musée d'Orsay and the vast underground additions to the Louvre; ridiculed at first, both quickly won the public's enthusiasm once they were finally completed. But the Bastille has been in trouble from the start. Mitterand is not an opera lover, and the story goes that the only time he ever went inside the old Opéra was for a ballet performance and that he left after the first act.

Everything concerning Paris' lyric theaters has been mired in politics for years, especially since the last war. As subsidized companies they steadily cost the government more and more money, and when performances were bad, the government was criticized as well as the theaters' administrators. Rolf Liebermann's tenure as director between 1971 and 1980 restored much glory to the old Paris Opéra, but not even he was able to subdue entrenched unions or placate a group of stubborn, chauvinistic subscribers (and others) who resented the presence of so many "foreigners" occupying a French stage. (With Liebermann the old repertory-scheduling was abandoned for good and replaced by far more infrequent but star-studded productions.) After Liebermann left, standards once again fell, and often, because of strikes or sudden cast changes, one never knew for sure until the curtain went up if the performance might be cancelled or at best postponed. In the 1980's there were some memorable evenings along with others that are best forgotten. Mitterand and his people, apparently without much practical knowledge of the workings of an opera organization, intended for the new Bastille to begin its first year as a full-fledged repertory company offering some 250 performances with a basic core of some 25 to 30 different works. Everyone seemed outwardly pleased with the appointment of Daniel Barenboim to head the new company. Then, however, it was discovered in late 1988 that Barenboim intended during his first season to "break in" the new company slowly with a kind of "festival" series, arranged as at the "old" Opéra on the block-system; for the first year he would have ended up with only a meagre 71 or 72 nights of opera, not the five- or six-nights-a-week schedule the government wanted. Also his decision to include *Carmen* and *Pelléas et Mélisande* showed no initiative or originality in exploring the French repertory. When it was revealed how much he was being paid, the press and the public expressed outrage, and he was summarily fired. Not until the summer of 1989, after many other personnel changes, was another musical director chosen: young Korean-born, American-trained Myung-Whun Chung (who doesn't speak French). This 37-year-old conductor, not very well-known, is still holding on to his title as Music Director, but no one knows if he will last. In conducting the opening series of *Les Troyens,* he survived one of the severest tests imaginable, but the critical response to his musicianship was only moderately enthusiastic. Most ominous is the fact that even after Myung-Whun Chung was appointed others very high up on the staff, thought to be invulnerable, have been sacked.

As for the new theater itself, from the technical angle of rehearsing and staging operas, it has been everywhere hailed as a major wonder, the most far-advanced such building ever built. With ten full-sized stages, each of which can be prepared with sets and then quickly moved into place, it is an opera manager's dream. Still more spaces behind and underneath the building are yet to be completed: ateliers for costumes and set-construction, and the notoriously-celebrated *Salle modulable,* the smaller theater with facilities for adjusting the dimensions of both its auditorium and stage. These components of the complex have had their own share of political problems after new elections forced the Socialists to share power with a rightest group under Chirac; in 1986 Chirac was able to halt construction on the project, a costly delay in itself, and work was not resumed until Mitterand's party won back more votes in the 1988 elections.

The exterior of the building has few admirers, but inside, in the auditorium (the *Grande salle*), so far the judgments have been favorable. Opinions about the acoustics have for the most part been good, but the Music Director has himself expressed unhappiness about what he feels is the "coldness" of the sound, with the voices too "remote"; in working closely with the set designers he has hoped to achieve a better balance between the stage and the pit and to add more warmth and intimacy to the sound. The hall is equipped with very elaborate devices for "tuning" the sound, should this prove necessary.

I confess to having a love-hate feeling about the old Opéra. In almost forty years of visiting the city I have witnessed some truly wonderful performances and others that were awful, unbelievably awful. I have no regrets at all in seeing the old theater closed or put to other uses. From the moment it was built it was not a good auditorium for either seeing or hearing opera because in so many of the seats one has a poor view of the stage (if one can see it at all!), and if not seated in the front row of one of the numerous boxes, the sound seems to be coming from several directions at the same time. It must be someone's idea of a sick joke that starting in the fall of 1989 the building was to become the exclusive home of the Paris ballet; that art, even more than opera, demands that one have a full, unobstructed view of the stage, and the Opéra, unless radically revamped, hardly qualifies. This building was designed primarily for people to stare at each other, both outside in the huge social halls and inside in the auditorium itself. During the fall of 1989 there were rumblings of discontent about other matters in the administration of the ballet, so perhaps the idea of housing a dance company at the Opéra may eventually be dropped as well. My own suggestion for the theater would be to tear out all of the partitions between the boxes, following the successful example of Zürich, but as this is a *monument historique,* very likely no such drastic changes would be permitted. If that is the case, close the Opéra and let the tourists pay to come in one by one and gape at this monument to the gaudy, pretentious taste of the Second Empire.

On the next few pages I give what I hope will be helpful information about attending an opera in France. Not that it is all that different from opera-going in other countries, but there are certain things, such as the French terms used for seating, the presence everywhere of the *ouvreuse* (the usherette), the Frenchman's disdain (unlike the German's) for the *vestiaire* (the cloakroom), and a few basic words for ordering tickets, things which may be of use in making you feel more at ease if you cannot speak French and want to avoid either embarrassing or unnecessarily costly mistakes.

Except for the Opéra-Bastille, which is to be a repertory company producing a group of several operas on consecutive nights, throughout all of France (and in Paris' other few opera-producing theaters) the *stagione* or block-system is in effect. This means that within any given time and in any single place you don't have much choice or variety as to what is available. Unlike Austria, England, Germany, and German Switzerland, where a number of different operas will be performed on the same stage within the same week, in Paris and the provinces the usual pattern is to repeat the same opera a number of times within a single month and to offer no alternatives other than ballets or perhaps concerts.

It is now the opera companies in the provinces, not in Paris, that have taken over the lead in championing new or neglected repertory, experimenting with new production technics, and most important for the future vitality of the lyric theater in France, providing opportunities for young singers. In short, the best and most interesting opera in France is now to be found outside of Paris. This does not make it easy for the traveler who is pushed for time. Distances between cities (and opera houses) are much greater than they are in Germany, and though direct service by train from Paris is always excellent, train connections between or among provincial cities are going to be slower and often less convenient. In Germany it is possible and quite easy to plan on seeing a different opera in a different city on each of several successive nights; in France in most instances you will find that you will need to allow yourself more time in getting between opera centers in the provinces. Also you will have to plan your itinerary more carefully to have it mesh with much leaner opera schedules. And you will want to allow yourself plenty of time to savor the great and varied scenic, cultural, and historical richness of this unbelievably beautiful country. With time out too for the superb food and wine, found everywhere, which normally cannot be fully appreciated on the same night when you plan to attend an opera.

The terms the French use for the seating arrangements in their theaters are for the most part easily recognized, as in many cases our own words are derived from theirs (parterre, parquet, etc.). The majority of the buildings date from the nineteenth century, with a ground-level orchestra section divided by one or two aisles and then three or more rings of boxes *(loges)*, horseshoe-fashion, circling the auditorium. Only three terms are likely to be completely unfamiliar: *baignoire, corbeille,* and *strapontin.* The exotically-labelled *baignoire* literally means "bathtub," but in theater parlance it is simply a box-seat in a slightly raised circle of boxes surrounding the seats on the orchestra-level. *Corbeille,* meaning "basket," is most notably used at the Théâtre des Champs-Elysées for groups of seats, enclosed usually at waist-height, circling the front edge of the first balcony; these seats must have been conceived by the architects as a kind of intermediate compromise between the closed-in box and "open" seating in a balcony. These seats, very choice and very expensive, are a marvelous example of conspicuous consumption because the ticket holders, "protected" by a low barrier, have a good view of the entire theater, and yet at the same time they are clearly seen by others. The third term, *strapontin,* represents a monstrously-conceived contraption designed to squeeze one more person (who has to be a masochist) into the space that would normally be left open in and for the aisle. Usually constructed of wood, with no padding at the back or on the bottom, a *strapontin* is supposed to fold back (by stiff spring action) flush against the outer side of an aisle seat; in theory the weight of the unlucky person sitting in a *strapontin* will prevent it from snapping back noisily into its folded position. Avoid at all costs these seats unless they happen to be the very last spaces available in an otherwise very special, sold-out performance!

The word *fauteuil* should be familiar to anyone who has labored through the first year of French: the dictionary meaning of "armchair" or "easy chair" is quite accurate, but in France these will be the seats (without all the plush) found in the orchestra and sometimes in the first rows of the first balcony ring. They usually are also the most comfortable and most expensive seats in the house. (In the Opéra-Comique in Paris the term *fauteuils* is also used for the center seats in the back of both the second and third balconies; here this is certainly a misnomer because the seats, though not expensive, are extremely cramped and painfully hard after ten minutes of sitting.) Strasbourg, Colmar, and Nice use the word *galerie* instead of *balcon* for the three upper tiers in their houses, where ordinarily we associate *galerie* with space only on the topmost level, as in Italy. Bordeaux labels the sides of its first tier with this term, while Toulouse reserves it just for its second balcony. Given the widely differing applications of *galerie,* be sure you know where it is before buying a ticket. Throughout most of France *amphithéâtre* is used to designate those seats on the highest level at the back of a theater, where both the acoustics and the sight-lines are excellent (though the seats themselves may be made of the hardest of woods). (At the old Opéra on both sides of the theater on this same level, the fourth and highest, two terms were in use which were misleading: their *loges de côté* were really not boxes at all because the partitions did not extend up to the ceiling; the *stalles,* contrary to British usage, were simply long rows of hard wooden seats, steeply raked, located behind the *loges de côté* and usually sold as *sans visibilité,* without a view of the stage. It is true, one could see just about half or a third of the stage, but the acoustics here were superb.) The Nice opera and Toulouse's Capitole borrow a beautiful euphemisim from theater slang (with echoes of the famous 1943 French movie, *Les Enfants du paradis*) when they designate a small area above and behind their *amphithéâtre* as the *paradis* (no translation necessary); in Nice one can hear perfectly, but the stage is visible only through slits in the wall; in Toulouse the *paradis* is simply the topmost section of the third balcony behind the *amphithéâtre.* Finally there are the notorious *fond de loge* "seats," all too numerous in many of France's older theaters and especially at the old Paris Opéra. Usually these tickets are not very expensive. These are the chairs in the second and third rows of each box which, depending on their position in the sweep of the curve of a balcony, have only a partial view of the stage. To see anything, you have to leave your chair and stand up, bending your body at an awkward and very uncomfortable angle. In many of these seats you also have the annoyance of hearing the music two or three times because it bounces off the side and back walls of your box. In many older French opera houses comfort and good sight-lines, unfortunately, sometimes come at a premium.

Program booklets in Europe are rarely free, but opera-goers at the Bastille can thank a political rivalry for the fact that when they go to their seats they are now handed a sheet listing the evening's cast along with other credits. Chirac, the conservative Mayor of Paris, whose administration controls the Théâtre du Châtelet, began the practice in 1988 of making available at no charge single-page programs for the operas and concerts given at the Châtelet (these sheets are found in small boxes attached to the walls in the corridors surrounding the auditorium). Mitterand's Opéra-Bastille took up the challenge and now follows Chirac's commendable example. In times past at the old Opéra in order to get a list of who was in the cast you had to pay upwards of 30 F for a glossy program filled mostly with large perfume ads and full-page photographs (liberally air-brushed) of the principal artists; this was a total rip-off because there was little information about what and where the singers had performed. A few years ago (at long last) the programs began to provide full biographies of the singers (with smaller photographs) along with a few essays about the opera, but to justify raising the price to 40 F the programs became bulkier by including a complete libretto in French. At the new Opéra-Bastille, where the price of the programs has now risen to 50 F, don't be coaxed into buying a program unless you want an expensive memento of the evening; a list giving the cast is available for free inside the auditorium. In the French provinces you can expect to pay between 10 and 15 F for a booklet giving you most of the information you will need.

In most theaters in France (and in movie houses as well) you are shown to your seat by a woman called an *ouvreuse* (usherette) who will expect a small tip for rendering this small service. One or two francs should be enough. For years some of the nationally-subsidized theaters have tried in vain to abolish this archaic institution. At the Opéra-Bastille they have at last succeeded. Tipping is disruptive because people often forget until the last minute to go through their pockets looking for the right coins, and if you have a coat over one arm and perhaps a program or newspaper in your hand, plus your ticket, it can be awkward trying to find the correct change. Should you neglect the tip you'll not be slaughtered on the spot, but the *ouvreuse* in her mind will put you down as another of those ungainly, stupid foreigners.

Unlike the Germans, who dutifully go to their seats unencumbered by coats and shopping bags (in most German theaters it is almost mandatory that they leave these things behind), the French rarely use the services of the *vestiaire* or cloakroom. French theaters usually have at least one *vestiaire* on each level, and if the theater is large, one will often be found on both the right *(côté droite)* and left sides *(côté gauche)*. The charges for this service are usually 3 to 6 F. If you are wearing a light coat or are dressed for winter cold it is not considered bad form to take your things with you to your seat, but most of the time heavy rain gear, if wet, is left in the *vestiaire*.

There is always bar service in French theaters, with a modest assortment of cold drinks and coffee, but nothing comparable to the vast spread of elegant hors d'oeuvres, salads, sandwiches, fruit desserts, and sweets that are seen in every German opera house. Even at the old Paris Opéra, where one might have expected to see fancy open-faced sandwiches, there was always the plebeian chunk of a *baguette,* sliced length-wise, containing the usual slim portion of cheeze, ham, or salami *(saucisson).* In the last years they began offering *croissant* sandwiches, which were at least more manageable and spread fewer crumbs on you and your neighbors. Be prepared however for a mob of people all trying to get served at the same time: the French have yet to learn that by standing in an orderly line they will be served more promptly.

Curtain-times differ widely in France as one goes from north to south. In Paris performances generally begin early, as they do in London, with 1930 the usual time. (Some of the longer Wagner operas are scheduled to start at 1700 or 1800.) Further south, in Strasbourg or Lyon for example, 2000 is the usual hour, but in the Midi and Bordeaux 2030, even for a long opera, is not at all unusual (Marseille, Nice, and Toulouse).

For most travelers a trip to France begins with Paris. For that reason I have not strictly followed alphabetical order in arranging the list of opera centers but begin with Paris. The other cities follow in the proper sequence.

Finally, a few words to help you in buying a ticket:

le billet, un billet, deux billets etc. are the words for ticket, one ticket, two tickets, etc.

le guichet is the ticket window
les heures d'ouverture are the times when the ticket office is open
une place is a seat
disponible when applied to a seat means "still available" or "unsold"
complet means sold-out but on occasion a few seats *sans visibilité* (with an obstructed view of the stage) may still be available.

PARIS in all its beauty and complexity defies description. It would be presumptuous on my part even to try.

In March of 1990 the curtain finally went up at the new **Opéra-Bastille,** with performances of Berlioz' *Les Troyens* marking the beginning of a time when Paris once again may take its place among the world's leading opera centers. Plans for the 1990–91 season are still vague and confused. It remains to be seen how the new Musical Director can cope with the government's earlier demand to provide some 250 performances in the course of the first season.

In spite of all of the confusion and uncertainty about the Opéra-Bastille, operas occasionally are still being presented in Paris, but in other theaters. The most notable of these are the Théâtre des Champs-Elysées and the Théâtre du Châtelet: the first of these was for a time loosely affiliated with the state-run lyric "consortium," while the second theater is owned and operated by the city of Paris. A brief description of both will follow. Nothing to do with opera in Paris, so it would seem, can occur without great storms of controversy: to wit, the on-again, off-again decisions about what to do with the old Opéra-Comique (the Salle Favart). The fate of this venerable old institution is still in the balance, although at the end of the spring season in 1988 the decision was made that it was to close and become a privately-operated playhouse. That idea has apparently been abandoned, for during the 1989–90 season visiting companies (a number from Eastern Europe) and pick-up groups were still offering operas with some frequency. (The resident Opéra-Comique troupe, a repertory ensemble performing every night, disappeared many years ago, in the early 1970's, but until 1988 the theater continued to be controlled by the administration of the Paris Opéra.) Then finally there is the old Opéra or the Palais Garnier as it is now more often called; supposedly it is to be used only for the presentation of ballets, but just as at the Opéra-Comique the theater in 1989–90 has been rented out on a few occasions to visiting opera companies.

To be informed about what is going on currently throughout France, look for a copy of *Opéra International* (now selling at 30 F), found in most street-side kiosks. The schedules, printed at the back of the magazine, are indispensable because they not only list dates and casts but where to telephone for tickets. The calendar is handy as well because it covers two months instead of just one (the coverage of other European countries is less complete). For Paris alone the schedule includes as well concerts involving vocal soloists in sacred music and in symphonies; for all of France solo vocal recitals are listed. If your stay is short and limited to Paris, you can probably get by with one of the weekly magazines giving all the schedules for opera, concerts, dance programs, theaters, and movie houses. *Pariscope* sells for 3 F, and *L'Officiel des spectacles* sells for 2 F; they are also available on newstands everywhere in the city. The schedule for the Opéra-Bastille is under the heading "théâtres" towards the front of both magazines, and as it is a subsidized theater among the other "théâtres nationaux," these are always placed at the beginning of the theater list (the old Opéra, the Opéra-Comique, and the Théâtre du Châtelet normally figure in this list as well). Both magazines appear in the morning on Tuesdays and cover events from Wednesday of that week through Tuesday of the following week. Under the section devoted to concerts and music you will also find information about other opera possibilities; sometimes there is a brief rubric for opera alone, but unless this format changes with the opening of Opéra-Bastille, schedules of the subsidized companies are given only once in the first pages of the magazines.

Getting to and from these theaters is easy because each of them is quite close to one or more Métro stations. (The Opéra-Comique is somewhat more difficult to find because it is located midway between two stops and is also off on a side street.) Both *Pariscope* and *L'Officiel* always indicate the nearest Métro station for theaters (the symbol after the street address is a large "M" followed by a smaller, raised "o"). For concert halls, where some operas may be scheduled, only *Pariscope* gives the Métro stops in a list of all addresses at the end of the week's concert announcements. The more high-toned *Opéra International* assumes that its readers will know how to find the theaters: no addresses are given.

L'OPÉRA-BASTILLE.

In 1982, when the international competition was announced for the designs of a new opera house, the government had already decided that the new structure would be built at the Place de la Bastille. The choice of this site may at first have seemed ill-advised, but one of President Mitterand's stated purposes was the creation of what was called an *"opéra populaire,"* an opera house catering to a larger, wider public, and the Place de la Bastille is located on the edge of a working-class district. There were several practical considerations as well: there were excellent transportation facilities already in place (eight bus routes converge here, and three Métro lines meet underneath the square, one of which, line #1, follows the

Rue de Rivoli-Champs-Elysées axis out to the affluent *arrondissements* on Paris' western side). Another advantage was a suitably large building site, an abandoned suburban railroad station long marked for demolition; few houses or shops had to be torn down and people displaced. Finally, just to the west and behind the drab buildings lining the far side of the Place de la Bastille is the Marais, a district not too long ago falling into ruin but rich in historic mansions, many of which date back to the sixteenth and seventeenth centuries (only the nearby, exquisitely-proportioned Place des Vosges had managed through the years to retain its respectability). Since the 1960's, when strict preservationist laws were put into effect, the Marais has slowly come back to life and now is dotted with elegantly restored town houses. The presence of an opera house in the vicinity has already boosted further restoration projects, pushing real-estate prices even higher. The neighborhood to the north and east of the new theater is a dull mix of houses, shops, several hospitals, apartment buildings, and small factories and is without much interest or character. Some evidence of gentrification in this district is now apparent as well.

After the notorious prison was razed some two centuries ago, the site it once occupied remained barren and somewhat depressing, flat and open, and the Place de la Bastille until recently was notable only for its heavy vehicular traffic. The buildings facing on it were quite ordinary, some of them even slum-like. Shortly after 1789 and at various intervals in later years proposals were put forth to construct a monument to commemorate the beginning of the Republic, but nothing ever came of the projects. Only the name of the square was left to recall the extraordinary events that had occurred there. (Bricks set into the pavement are supposed to trace part of the outer walls of the old prison, but you risk being run over if you try to look for them.) Even the column in the middle of the square honors not the capitulation of the Bastille but the martyrs of the Revolution of 1830. Mitterand has now endowed the square with an imposing monument that ostentatiously ties his Socialist government to its Revolutionary antecedents. (The new theater was inaugurated with a gala concert on 13 July 1989, the day before the two-hundredth anniversary of the date that has come to symbolize the founding of the French Republic.) But it is ironic that a building put up by Socialist leaders and now for the first time drawing visitors (other than history buffs) to the area should be dedicated to what is still an elitist art-form. Yet the government from the beginning has insisted that the new opera be a "popular" opera, "opera for the people." It remains to be seen if that goal will be fulfilled.

A young Canadian, Carlos Ott, born and schooled in Uruguay but given advanced training in the USA, was the winner among the more than 750 architects competing on the project. Not surprisingly the Opéra-Bastille looks quite out of scale heaped up against one side of the Place de la Bastille, but taking into account the very irregular dimensions of the square and the odd contours of the construction site, perhaps the architect should be credited with more success than some of his critics are willing to grant him. Although much glass is used in the facade, I think that even more glass would have toned down the theater's massiveness and also made it look less like a modern industrial plant. What appears to be the main entrance at the rounded front of the building, up the broad flight of steps, is not used except on special ceremonial occasions (the doors are opened only during intermissions and at the end of a performance). Ticketholders enter either at street-level, down a few steps from the sidewalk outside, or through the doors, clearly marked, leading from the subway tunnel. Inside, in the outer halls and many levels of corridors surrounding the auditorium, again the architect has been criticized, this time for the monotonous use of the same white and light-buff stone, stainless steel, and glass, nowhere relieved by any warm colors. Some critics have compared these spaces to the cold and sterile feel of a hospital hallway, but this is all in keeping with the "hi-tech" look which the French, slow to adopt, now seem to be using everywhere. One felicitous touch however is the presence on every level, tucked into the outer walls, of small areas with tables and comfortable chairs; before a performance or during intermissions these "conversation nooks" provide a pleasant escape from the milling crowds in the surrounding corridors.

Most successful however is the auditorium inside, called the *"Grande salle"* to distinguish it from the three other theaters in the same complex. For the first time opera-goers in Paris enjoy comfortable seating, excellent sight-lines, good acoustics throughout most of the hall, and as added bonuses, air conditioning and supertitles. The auditorium also has more warmth and simple elegance than one is led to anticipate after seeing the maze of stairways and corridors outside. The official figures for the seating capacity are 2716; this breaks down to just under 1600 in the Orchestra and slightly more than 1100 in the two Balconies and the four levels of slim, rectangular Boxes on each of the side walls. In spite of the overall size of the hall it has been designed so that the seats at the back are still not too far from the stage. (The center portion of the Orchestra has 32 rows; in the Balconies the number of rows varies from 8 up to 11.) Each level is quite steeply raked, with the Second Balcony more sharply angled than the slightly shallower Balcony below it. What gives the *"Grande salle"* its unique and boldly dramatic "look" is the way in which each of the Balconies is broken into five distinct rectangular sections; the center and widest section is the furthest back from the stage, with each parallel, outer pair that flanks it then extending some three yards (3 meters) forward. The seating in the orchestra is similarly split into five sections by four aisles. Unfortunately, towards the back of the auditorium someone saw the opportunity to place *strapontins* on the ends of the aisle seats. Some traditions do not disappear in France! The four levels of shallow

Boxes (the *Loges latérales*) on each of the side walls were designed mainly for the purpose of sound dispersion and not to increase the seating capacity of the hall (they are only one or two rows deep). Aesthetically they also add a decorative element to what would otherwise be a monotonous wall. Each set of Boxes seats a total of only 47 people; those who suffer from acrophobia should by all means avoid the two highest levels.

The largest and most important of the three other theaters in the Opéra-Bastille complex is the *Salle modulable,* best translated as the "adjustable theater"; it adjoins the back-stage area of the *"Grande salle"* off to the right of the Métro entrance on the sidewalk by the opera house. This space, in which the dimensions of the stage and the seating areas can be either expanded or made smaller, is one of the most innovative components of the new house. The walls because of their varied surfaces also can be shifted experimentally either to reflect or absorb sound. According to the use to which the theater is put (for ballets, "chamber" operas, film showings, concerts by small ensembles, etc.), the seating capacity ranges from around 600 up to 1200. As of May 1990 the outer walls and ceiling were in place, but otherwise the space was empty, a casualty of the budget cuts imposed by Chirac back in 1986. (In the original plans for the Opéra-Bastille this theater was to have been the first part of the complex to open; it was supposed to have begun full operation as early as 1987.) Work on the *Salle modulable* was due to start up again in the summer of 1990, with completion now slated for late in 1991.

Another but much smaller theater is located at the front of the opera house, one floor below ground-level (you can see into it through the glass panels opposite the Box Office). This is the *Amphithéâtre,* a cleanly-designed semi-circular space with the audience seated on seven concentric platforms constructed of stone; you bring your own cushion or rent one at the theater. The seating capacity, with no assigned places, may go as high as 500. The stage is wide and shallow and like the Greek and Roman forms on which it is modelled, framed in masonry at the back. The *Amphithéâtre* lends itself to a great variety of uses (recitals, lectures, chamber concerts, and plays), especially for events requiring little preparation of the stage.

The third and smallest of the theaters is the *Studio,* located above the restaurant that was rebuilt across the alley to the left of the main entrance to the opera house. This intimate hall was designed to duplicate in miniature (but without the balconies) many of the features of the *Grande salle.* Seating 246 people, this space is used most frequently for recitals and lectures.

In late spring of 1990, when the Opéra-Bastille authorities finally got around to announcing the schedule for the 1990–91 season, the news prompted much sarcastic criticism in the French press. Opera lovers reacted with keen disappointment at what appeared to be a policy of cautious retrenchment. Instead of the long-promised large repertory and frequent performances, only eight different works are to be presented in the course of the entire year. Beginning late in the fall Paris is to have: *Otello,* Berio's *Un Re in Ascolto, Manon Lescaut, The Magic Flute, Le Nozze di Figaro, The Queen of Spades, Samson et Dalila,* and finally Janácek's *Katia Kabanova* (a holdover from May of 1990, following the Berlioz opening, but a work also seen only a few years ago at the Opéra). Plácido Domingo is to sing in the first five presentations of the *Otello* that opens the season (13 November 1990), but in the succeeding performances and in the other operas to follow little excitement was generated by the details of what was known of the casts. Another complaint stirred up by this announcement was that all but one of the productions were either to be borrowed from other theaters or to come from sets prepared in past years for the old Opéra; *The Magic Flute* is the sole new and original production for 1990–91. It had been hoped and expected that more new productions would be created using the vaunted new facilities of this technically advanced stage. Of the eight works only one is drawn from the French repertory, and not by any reckoning is it a work long absent from French stages. In short, a season that except for the borrowed Berio is far less promising and ambitious than the repertory Barenboim had proposed for what would have been his first year, but he of course was fired in part because of what seemed at the time to be his excessive cautiousness. Upon seeing this schedule, Paris' opera lovers had every reason to react with disappointment, anger, and frustration.

The Box Office for the Opéra-Bastille is at street-level in the wide hallway at the front of the theater. It is open Monday through Saturday from 1100 to 1830; closed on Sunday and holidays. A computer screen by each window allows you to see exactly where your seats are located in the theater. At the Box Office tickets for each event go on sale 14 days in advance of the performance; for orders by telephone: (1) 40-01-16-16, tickets are available 13 days in advance (Monday through Saturday between 1100 and 1800). As all major credit are honored, no provisions are made for paying by check or money order. Tickets may also be obtained at branches of FNAC, the large discount department store. For information and schedules (access to a tape recording) the telephone number is: (1) 43-43-96-96; the mailing address is: Opéra-Bastille, Service Développement Public, 120 rue de Lyon, 75012 Paris.

Prices for most of the operas are placed into five categories, ranging between a high of 370 F and a low of 40 F. With the Orchestra and the two Balconies divided by aisles into five sections, ticket prices in each area are determined to a large extent by two axes: from the front of the theater to the back and from the center outwards to the sides. This system is easy to follow when you have a seating plan before your eyes but is far too compli-cated to attempt to transcribe here. I shall have to simplify. In the Orchestra, at the front in the middle sections, tickets are priced at 370 F; off to both sides and just to the rear of the center the prices are set at 270 F; in the last seven rows (under the First Balcony overhang) prices go down quickly: three rows at 170 F, two at 120 F, and finally two at 40 F. (Here the acoustics are variable, and the supertitles cannot be seen.) In the First Balcony, following somewhat the pattern of Orchestra prices, the first forward rows of the three center sections are priced at 370 F; on both far sides, beginning at the front and immediately behind the higher-priced center seats, prices are set at 270 F; at the back in all five sections: 120 F. (Though the acoustics are good under the overhang of the Second balcony, about half-way back the supertitles are no longer visible.) Prices in the Second Balcony to some extent repeat the configuration in the First Balcony but begin and end one notch lower on the pricing scale: the front and center rows at 270 F; the far sides, front, and two rows in the center sections behind the more expensive seats at 170 F; and finally, half (or more) of all the seats in the rear portions of each of the five balcony sections at 120 F. All of the tickets for the Boxes (the *Loges latérales*) are priced at 40 F.* Ticket prices for vocalists in recital and for orchestra concerts follow a different system and are grouped into four categories, not five; there are also two price scales in effect: 220 F to 50 F or 190 F to 50 F. The reputation of the artist(s) and ticket demand seem to determine which scale is to be used. There is no Standing Room. All prices in both the *Amphithéâtre* and the *Studio* are uniformly set at either 50 F or 80 F, depending on the type of event being offered.

Slick programs for the operas are sold at 50 F and are not worth the price unless you want a French translation of the libretto, essays about the work, and more detailed information about the singers. Thanks to the good example set by Chirac's rival Théâtre du Châtelet, the Opéra-Bastille attendants inside the auditorium now hand out a one-page sheet giving the names of all the performers. This costs nothing. A similar sheet is distributed at recitals and concerts. With these events the glossy programs sold for 30 F outside in the foyers are in most cases quite worthless; usually no texts are provided for song recitals, and the essays accompanying orchestral programs are a rehash of what can be found in the notes on the sleeves of your recordings at home.

Tours of the Opéra-Bastille costing 10 F are offered several times each

---

*At Pierre Bergé's press conference announcing the 1990–91 season, he had other news that caused howls of protest among Paris' opera-goers. For those performances when international stars are engaged to sing, tickets in the Orchestra, normally costing 370 F, will go up to 520 F; the 270 F tickets will also rise proportionately, leaving only about 1000 seats to be sold for less than 200 F. Though this may be a very realistic measure, designed to pay for first-class opera (if it can be assumed that the presence of big stars is any guarantee of a first-class performance!), sadly it marks the end of further illusions about this theater and its total dedication to "opera for the people."

week. These are especially interesting when you are taken backstage to see the new production facilities. Information about the schedule is available at the desk opposite the ground-level entrance where you would come in from the Métro exit. (Those who lead the tours are fluent in English, but it would be wise, if you know no French, to ask and be sure beforehand.)

THE PARIS OPÉRA (PALAIS GARNIER).

Designed by the young architect Charles Garnier and inaugurated in 1875, some six years after the Emperor Napoléon III had already fled into exile, the Opéra (or Palais Garnier as it is now often called) is a remarkable monument to the pomposity and extravagant opulence of Second-Empire taste. The building is huge: those parts not seen by the public, such as the stages, rehearsal rooms, the archives and office areas, are quite vast; the grand staircase and many large public rooms on the main upstairs level are not matched by any other theater in the world. (There is an amusing story, probably apocryphal, that during a performance not long ago the curtain had to be quickly lowered while several people rushed out to look for Pavarotti who had missed his cue; he had completely lost his way between his dressing room and the stage, and had ended up in full costume outside on the street.) In proportion to the over-all size of the structure the auditorium is quite small, with seating for around 2000 people (the "official" number is 1991), and of this number perhaps only at most a third sit in any comfort and enjoy a reasonably good view of the stage.

Not counting the *baignoires* almost on orchestra-level on the sides, there are four tiers of balconies circling the horseshoe-shaped auditorium. (The only time the term *balcon* is used is for labelling the eight rows of seats at the rear of the orchestra; this entire section is raised, and for my taste these are the best seats in the house, as well as the most expensive.) The first three rings of balconies consist solely of boxes *(loges)*, either center *(face)* or on the sides *(côté)*, and from long experience I can say that unless you are seated at the front of a box you can expect problems either with sight-lines or acoustics (or both); on the sides, about halfway towards the orchestra pit, even from a front-row seat you can forget about seeing very much of the stage. The fourth and highest level is made up of the *amphithéâtre*, dead-center at the back, with "open" rows of seats, and on the sides, *loges* along the front of the balcony and *stalles* behind them. Here the *loges* are not true boxes because the partitions between them come up only to one's waist; the *stalles* are rows of hard, wooden seats, ranging from a partial view of the stage to none at all. There is actually a fifth and last level above this tier, located in the corners between the center section and the sides; here, if you can tolerate the heat rising from below, you crowd around small openings in the walls for a view of about one-half of the action placed on the stage. Space for standing room is not sold as such, but in perhaps as many as one-third of the seats, in order to see anything, you end up standing anyway.

The acoustics of the Palais Garnier have been highly and rightly praised. For those sitting anywhere in the orchestra section, at the front of the boxes, and in any part of the open galleries on the topmost level, the sound is rich and clear and beautifully resonant. Elsewhere, especially in the back areas of the *loges,* those notorious *fond(s) de loge* where little of the stage is visible, the sound is marred by echoing off the partitions between the boxes.

Throughout the auditorium most of the upholstered seats, even those in the orchestra and *balcon,* are quite lumpy and worn by over-use. Many of them creak very loudly when one shifts one's weight ever so slightly. Even noisier are the hard seats on the fourth level which fly back into an upright position with a frightening crash whenever the occupant leans forward to try to glimpse some bit of the movement on stage; all too often a quiet or tender moment in a performance has been punctuated with these loud sounds that can be heard everywhere in the theater. Though there are many things that need to be changed or improved at the Palais Garnier, certainly the replacement of all the seats should be very near the top of the list.

Until things settle down in Paris it is useless to speculate about what will happen with the old Opéra building in the future. In addition to performances by the Ballet de l'Opéra, during the fall of 1989 and winter of 1990 the theater was host to visiting ballet companies and concerts by instrumental and choral groups brought in from "outside." Also scattered throughout the season there have been a few operas, mostly baroque works by touring ensembles. Prices for ballets always were about ⅗'s of what one paid for operas: 300 F for the best ballet seats, as opposed to 550 F for operas, but how this pricing-scale will be adjusted later is anyone's guess.

The Box Office is off to the far right (beyond the gift shop) after you enter the Palais Garnier through any of the main doors. The hours in effect (through January of 1990) were Monday through Saturday from 1100 to 1900; closed on Sunday. For the moment it is not likely these will change. Ticket reservations could always be made by telephone (47-42-53-71) between 1200 and 1800, Monday through Saturday. If the old stipulations remain in force, these requests are accepted 13 days in advance for performances scheduled between Monday and Friday; 12 days in advance for Saturday and Sunday performances; telephone orders are closed the day before the performance. Again under the old rules, mail orders may be sent to: Opéra de Paris, Service Location par Correspondance, 8 rue Scribe, 75009 Paris. If you are ordering from outside of France you must enclose a self-addressed envelope and an international reply coupon. You will receive in return a notice indicating that tickets are (or are not) being held for you. No money need be included with your order, but your tickets must be picked up and paid for no later than by 1500 on the day of the performance.

Again, assuming that no extensive renovation work is in progress, there still will be guided tours of parts of the Opéra, and if no rehearsals are taking place you will be admitted into the auditorium. Unfortunately you are not taken into any of the backstage areas. These tours are conducted seven days a week between 1100 and 1630, last about an hour, and cost 17 F per person. Groups assemble for these tours just inside the main doors at the base of the steps leading towards the grand staircase. Should you have a ticket to a performance at the Opéra, the tour will show you nothing that you can't explore on your own during the intermissions or before the curtain first goes up.

THE OPÉRA-COMIQUE.

Even more uncertainty surrounds the fate of the Opéra-Comique. (The theater is often called the Salle Favart, taking this name from the small street that borders the building on its east side; "Favart" is in other ways appropriate—he was not the architect—but an eighteenth-century composer whose light operas with spoken dialogue helped popularize the new *genre*.) In many respects this theater has a much more distinguished history than its grander counterpart several blocks away. Founded in the 1780's it was from the beginning dedicated to this lighter form of opera (not all *opéras comiques* necessarily have happy endings). Throughout most of the first half of the 1800's French composers (Adam, Auber, Boïeldieu, Delibes, Hérold, among many others) supplied by far the greatest share of what was seen at this theater, while the Opéra, except for Halévy and Meyerbeer (a transplanted German), was largely dominated by the Italians and mainly an international house. (It is ironic that by the time the Palais Garnier opened in 1875, although the public remained infatuated with the large-scale pageantry of "grand opera" as conceived by Meyerbeer, no major French musician was still composing works in this style that still hold the stage today. An interesting project for Opéra-Bastille would be to revive some of the many now-forgotten operas commissioned from French composers for Garnier's palatial Opéra.) Until the coming of Italian *verismo* the Opéra-Comique was essentially a "French" institution, and such mainstays of the repertory as *Carmen, Les Contes d'Hoffmann, Manon, Louise, Pelléas et Mélisande,* and Ravel's *L'Heure espagnole* were either commissioned by this company or given their first performances in this theater. After the last war it was still presenting operas six times a week, and for a long time the Comique (and less so the Opéra) encouraged young French singers to appear on its stage. Works from the Italian repertory (Donizetti, Verdi, Puccini) were usually done in French translation. Gradually, as the Opéra was then broadening its repertory, the larger house also took over some of the works that at one time had been in the exclusive domain of the Comique. The old and somewhat artificial distinction between "grand opera" and *opéra comique* was no longer honored, and some of the better singers (of which there were not many) also drifted away to be absorbed by the other theater. Severe budget cuts hurt the Comique more than they did the Opéra (where no matter what the program, crowds of tourists went anyway, paying outrageous prices for tickets), and they had no resident ballet company with which to prop up the schedule when operas were not being given. During the late 1960's and early 1970's, when many of Paris' other theaters also found themselves competing for the first time with TV, the public simply failed to come out and support this company. (I recall from this same period an excitingly-sung, Christmas-season performance of Puccini's *Fanciulla del West,* complete with one old white horse, when there were all of eighteen people sitting in the theater. Those who had bought tickets for upstairs were all told to move to the orchestra section so that the *ouvreuses* in the other parts of the house could go home! Obviously no enterprise could justify its government subsidies when operating like that.) At the end of 1972 the theater even lost its old name and became the Centre National d'Art Lyrique. After the repertory company was disbanded, there were longer and longer periods when the theater would remain closed. However what little was still offered at the Comique was usually of very high quality and painstakingly rehearsed. They had been the first in France to do *Lulu* (in French and in its two-act format, well before the three-act version was available), and I remember with particular delight an all-Satie evening of opera, pantomine, and dance. The company had embarked on a well-prepared Massenet-cycle when the announcement was made in the spring of 1988 that the theater would close and be handed over in the fall to a private group for the production of plays.

This news was met with consternation and anger, and petitions to keep the theater open were circulated even as far away as the Met in New York (and doubtless in other cities in the USA). Two years later no one yet knows for sure to what different use the theater may be put, with every few weeks a new rumor surfacing which totally contradicts what had been heard earlier. So far the doors have not been locked and no plays seen as yet. In the course of the 1989–90 season the Comique has served as host to a number of foreign companies, most notably groups from Warsaw and Prague, and several Paris-based ensembles have staged baroque works as well as French chamber operas. There are still occasional recitals and instrumental concerts. In comparison to other recent years the stage of the Comique in 1989–90 has in fact witnessed more activity than before, but no longer is there a regular resident company keeping before the public the many small-scaled gems of the French repertory.

The building one sees today dates from 1893–98 and is the third one on this site, fire having destroyed in 1838 and 1887 two earlier theaters. The atmosphere inside the auditorium is intimate rather than elegant or opulent, and in comparison to some other Paris theaters of this size (it seats 1200) it wouldn't be unfair to call the decorative style rather plain and dowdy. The acoustics throughout are good: dry and sharp without much warmth or resonance. Not counting the *Baignoires* (under the first balcony) that surround the orchestra-seating, there are five levels of semi-circular tiers: first a *Balcon*, next the *Premières loges*, then the *Fauteuils* of the *Deuxième* and *Troisième Étage(s)*, and finally at the top, the *Amphithéâtre*. The *Balcon* and the *Amphithéâtre* consist entirely of "open" rows of seats, while the three levels between them also have a generous number of seats lined up in rows in the center and facing the stage; Boxes are found only on each of the sides. (Most of these Box seats, even those on the front row, are to be avoided because of poor sight-lines). Like the worn seats at the Opéra, the seating in this theater needs to be torn out and replaced. Sadly, unless another theater takes up the slack (one of the goals of the Opéra-Bastille was to do this), there will be little opportunity to hear many of those less-often-played French works (from Auber, Bizet, Chabrier, Charpentier, Dukas, Fauré, d'Indy, Lalo, Massenet, Milhaud, Offenbach, Poulenc and many others) that from time to time used to be in the Opéra-Comique repertory.

The rules for ordering tickets used to be the same as those in force at the Opéra, but this may well have changed since there is now no regular pattern of scheduled events in the theater. The Ticket Windows are to your left in the main lobby when you come in from the front doors; often these are closed, with only the side doors on either the Rue Marivaux or the Rue Favart left open. The hours are Monday through Saturday from 1100 to 1830; closed on Sunday and holidays. The telephone number is: 42-96-06-01. Tickets for Standing Room have never been available in this theater.

THE THÉÂTRE DES CHAMPS-ÉLYSÉES. The centers of
gravity for opera in Paris have shifted in recent years to other theaters. The Théâtre des Champs-Elysées (TCE), a building quite famous in its own right, is over on the Avenue Montaigne, a few doors up from the Place de l'Alma. (It was here in 1913 in a first performance by Diaghilev's Ballets Russes that Stravinsky's *Le Sacre du printemps* shocked the musical world. The theater had opened only the year before, in 1912, and is much admired in architectural circles as an early example of construction using reinforced, poured concrete.) The Théâtre des Champs-Elysées is very versatile and functions as a concert hall for orchestras, for solo recitals, for opera and ballet, and at various times for plays. On several occasions in the past most of the government-subsidized companies have borrowed this stage when their own theaters

were closed to make way for renovations. This building too was extensively refurbished from top to bottom a few years ago and the comfort of the patrons much improved, but as the auditorium is basically round in shape, nothing could be done to improve the sight-lines on the sides close to the front; most of the other seats have a very good view of the stage. The seating capacity is figured at around 1500. The acoustics are noted for their dryness and sharpness.

In 1987 several of the people who used to be associated with managing the old Opéra-Comique started producing operas at the Théâtre des Champs-Elysées, for a time calling the company "Le Libre Opéra" when it still retained loose ties to the administration of the Palais Garnier (the Théâtre National de l'Opéra de Paris); in the fall of 1989 the former director himself of the Paris Opéra (who was never offered a position at the Bastille) also became associated with this group. To date they have made opera available in two ways: either by staging their own productions with internationally-known singers or by inviting companies to come in from the outside with a limited run of one or more works. The operas originating in the TCE have for the most part been staples of the repertory and usually have been repeated in a series of around six performances. The "guest" productions have offered much more diversity with rare, resurrected baroque scores (often not fully staged) and seldom-seen, neglected French operas, these last in productions often brought in directly from the French provinces. During January and February of 1990 the theater was hosting an extended visit by the Maly company of Leningrad in a nightly presentation of Russian masterpieces.

In the spring of 1990, when the director of the TCE resigned in order to join forces with the Opéra-Bastille, it was assumed that the TCE would reduce its rôle as one of the city's opera centers. The appointment of a new director, firmly committed to the policies of his predecessor, has quickly dispelled such fears. The 1990–91 season includes among other promising works concert performances of Mozart with outstanding casts, a return visit by the Maly company of Leningrad, Cavalli's *Giasone* brought in from Innsbruck's summer festival, and the Welsh Opera production of *Falstaff*. Beginning with the 1991–92 season the new director intends to put his own mark on the theater by staging operas by Lully, many of whose works have not been heard or seen since the 1600's. If the recent success of John Christie's production of *Atys* is any measure of Lully's appeal to modern audiences, these revivals, scheduled at the rate of one each year, should prove to be very exciting.

Tickets for productions at the Théâtre des Champs-Elysées (15 Avenue Montaigne) go on sale at the Box Office 14 days before each scheduled performance. The Box Office is inside the main doors of the theater and is open Monday through Saturday from 1100 to 1900; closed on Sundays and holidays. Telephone reservations may be made by calling 47-20-36-37 between 1400 and 1800; orders are honored 20 days in advance of the performance and close 3 days before it. Orders by mail should be accompanied by a check made out to the theater and must include as well a stamped, self-addressed envelope, sent to: Service Location, Théâtre des Champs-Elysées, 15 Avenue Montaigne, 75008 Paris. This service will be of little use unless you know well in advance the dates of what you want to see; mail orders must be received no later than 21 days before the performance. Ticket prices cost more than those at the Opéra-Bastille, with the best seats in the house selling for 450 F; other tickets start at 50 F and go up to 320 F. A surcharge of 10 F is levied on mail and telephone orders. Credit cards are now accepted.

Another organization, the Orchestre de Paris, periodically has scheduled operas at the Théâtre des Champs-Elysées. A few years ago this orchestra joined with the Washington, D. C. opera in mounting a Mozart cycle that moved back and forth across the Atlantic. The opera projects of the Orchestre de Paris vary from year to year, and in their "home," the Salle Pleyel on the Rue du Faubourg Saint-Honoré, they program opera in concert. Recently they have been performing much Wagner, usually one act at a time.

THE THÉÂTRE MUSICAL DE PARIS-CHÂTELET.

Another possibility for hearing opera in Paris is at the Théâtre Musical de Paris-Châtelet where, once the season is underway in mid- to late September, some form of music is offered almost daily until the end of June or early July (operas, orchestral and chamber concerts, recitals, ballets, jazz, and musicals). Better known by its shorter and simpler name, the Châtelet is located on the Right Bank facing the square called the Place du Châtelet, just across the Seine from the Conciergerie on the Ile de la Cité. The theater is subsidized and managed by the city of Paris, which means that it falls under the jurisdiction of Paris' conservative mayor, Jacques Chirac, who also happens to be one of the staunchest opponents of the French Socialist president, François Mitterand. On various occasions Paris' music lovers have been either the victims or beneficiaries of the sparring between these two rivals. During the late 1980's when the nationalized theaters (accountable to Mitterand) were mired in controversy, the Châtelet (also called "Chirac's theater") was attending to the business of presenting first-class operas. (It is only fair to note that two of the star-studded productions of the 1989–90 season, *Fidelio* and *Meistersinger,* though generally well sung, were judged to be total disasters from the point of view of the staging.) An ambitious Mozart cycle with "authentic" instruments was launched in this theater in 1990 and at the rate of a single new opera each year is to continue through 1994–95. At least one work is coproduced annually with the Grand Théâtre de Genève: Handel in 1990, Offenbach in 1991, and among the productions originating in the Châtelet in the 1990–91 season are Dukas' rarely seen *Ariane et Barbe-Bleue* and a staged version of Berlioz' *Damnation de Faust*. William Christie and his Arts Florissants, after winning much acclaim for their "discovery" of Charpentier's *Médée* in 1989, are to continue their exploration of rare French and Italian baroque opera in 1990–91 and into the following season. Unfortunately, these latter works, given in concert form, are scheduled for only one performance, as is the case with most of the operas done in collaboration with French Radio (three in 1990–91). The fully-staged productions are usually repeated between four and six times.

When the theater was inaugurated in 1862, it was one of the most technically-advanced theaters of its time. With its horseshoe shape and four tiers of balconies, the seating capacity is at around 2000. Three successive renovations since 1980 have done much to make the theater more comfortable and to improve most of the sightlines, all without marring in any way the old-fashioned appearance and pleasant charm of the interior.

The Box Office is in the main lobby off to the left and is open daily between 1100 and 1900. At the Box Office tickets go on sale two weeks before the date of the performance. By mail, however, tickets for the entire season are available starting from the moment when the booklet listing the calendar for the year is published, usually in late May or early June. This booklet may be requested by writing the Service des Relations du Public, le Châtelet, 2 rue Edouard Colonne, 75001 Paris; payments for tickets, either by money order or with a check drawn on a French bank, should be directed to this same address; a stamped, self-addressed envelope must accompany all orders. By telephone: (1) 40-28-28-40, between 1000 and 1900, Monday through Saturday, tickets may be ordered one month before the date of the performance; telephone sales are halted one week before the performance date to allow time for processing the check or money order (the rules determining payment are the same as those when ordering by mail). All major credit cards are accepted at the Box Office.

Prices for the operas generally are divided into two pricing scales: one for the staged productions ("A") and one for the performances given only in concert form ("C"). The "A" category starts at 395 F and goes down to 80 F; the "C" category ranges between 295 F and 70 F. Note that the first tier of seats, though still labelled as the *Corbeille,* now consists of open rows of seats (as a result of the last renovations in the theater); going up from this level the next tier is the First Balcony, then the Second Balcony, and finally the Amphitheater. Students with the proper identification, young people under twenty, and people 65 or older are entitled to a special price of 50 F for any seats left unsold 15 minutes before the start of each performance.

As noted in the introductory section to "France," programs are distributed free of charge to all ticket-holders. This practice, unheard of in France until it was begun by this theater, has now been copied at the Opéra-Bastille. For the operas at the Châtelet the cast is named along with a summary (in French) of the plot; for concerts and recitals there is simply a list of the composers and titles of the works to be performed.

An information desk is located in the outer part of the lobby, to the left just as you come in through the main doors. Its staff is very helpful in answering questions and very generous in handing out the booklets describing the many different series of concerts presented at both the Châtelet and its "subsidiary" space, the Auditorium. (This hall, located not too far away in the underground Forum des Halles, is not used for staged operas but has, among many other things, a wealth of programs featuring outstanding vocalists.) With the regular evening events, plus a series of recitals and concerts presented at noon and Sunday concerts at 1600, often in the course of the season the two theaters between them may be offering as many as three or four different programs on the same day.

If your taste runs to opera given on a big and spectacular scale, with casts numbering in the hundreds on the order of Verona's outdoor arena presentations in the summer, you may want to investigate what is scheduled at the **Palais Omnisports de Bercy,** a large, modern indoor sports stadium not far behind the Gare de Lyon on the Right Bank. These performances of one work usually occur in May and June and are given almost nightly, with different singers for the leading rôles filling in on alternate nights. A number of these singers are quite well-known, but all of the voices, because of the large space, are amplified. *Turandot, Nabucco,* and *Carmen* have been given in past seasons; *Faust* is due in 1991. The Box Office is open Monday through Saturday from 1100 to 1800. Telephone reservations may be made by calling 43-46-12-21; information may be obtained by calling 43-42-06-06. Tickets are also available through FNAC. Prices start at 100 F and have a top price of 350 F.

Opera productions on a slightly more modest scale than those at Bercy are occasionally scheduled in the **Palais des Congrès,** the huge auditorium in the convention center at the Porte Maillot (at the end of the Avenue de la Grande Armée, the extension of the Champs-Elysées beyond the Arc de Triomphe). The sound is amplified. Often opera (and dance) companies from other European countries settle into this theater for lengthy stays of at least two or three weeks. Tickets may be ordered by calling: 47-58-14-04; prices usually are about the same as those at Bercy.

A close check of *Opéra International* may reveal the existence of opera performances scheduled in many interesting historic sites scattered throughout the city. Churches are a preferred location. Also a number of theaters that ordinarily are used for plays have in the past few seasons gone into the business of renting their stages to small pick-up ensembles presenting "chamber" operas. Many of these productions are given only one or two performances, but the repertory is quite interesting.

Tourist information, providing hotel reservation service, is available in all of the four train stations in Paris that have international trains linking France with the countries lying beyond its borders to the east and to the south. A list with their hours is given below. These branch offices are closed on Sunday (except for the Gare du Nord "in season"), leaving only the main tourist office on the Champs-Elysées open daily the year 'round (this office is closed only on Christmas Day and New Years). Also, there is no such service at either of the two international Paris airports, Roissy/Charles de Gaulle and Orly. If from Roissy you take a train into the city (the RER line), you will want to get off at the Gare du Nord where there is a tourist office. If you take one of the airport busses from Roissy/Charles de Gaulle the last stop is at the Arc de Triomphe, not too far from the Champs-Elysées tourist office; from Orly by bus you will have to take a cab or the métro from the airport terminal at the Gare des Invalides.

The official name of the Paris tourist office needs no translating, l'Office de Tourisme de Paris, and is at 127 Avenue des Champs-Elysées, on the south side of the street (as you face the Arc de Triomphe with the Place de la Concorde behind you). The métro stop, George V, is conveniently nearby, but be sure that you follow the signs in the tunnels coming out of the subway that direct you to the *côté impair*-side (odd, not even, street numbers) of the Champs-Elysées; otherwise you will have to walk up the long block in order to cross back over. Their hours, seven days a week, are from 0900 to 2000; the telephone number is: 47-23-61-72.

The branch tourist offices in the railroad stations have the same hours "in season," which runs from Easter through the end of October, but the "off-season" hours, from 1 November until Easter, are all different. These offices, with the exception of the Gare du Nord in season, are not open on Sunday.

Gare du Nord: season: 0800 to 2200 and Sunday: 1300 to 2000; off-season: 0800 to 2000.

Gare de l'Est: season: 0800 to 2200; off-season: 0800 to 1300 and 1700 to 2000.

Gare de Lyon: season: 0800 to 2200; off-season: 0800 to 1300 and 1700 to 2000.

Gare d'Austerlitz: season: 0800 to 2200; off-season: 0800 to 1500. To find any of these offices look for the "i" sign and follow the arrows.

An abundance of hotels in all categories surrounds each of the above stations, except for the Gare d'Austerlitz (where you arrive coming from southwestern France and Spain); you can see the hotels clearly when you come out any of the main doors. However, you won't soak up much of Paris' unique atmosphere by staying in the vicinity of a railroad station. If you don't know the city well, you will get a much better feeling about it by choosing a hotel on the Left Bank, away from the swarms of tourists crowding the sidewalks and cafés on the Right Bank. The Paris Tourist Office issues a very handy booklet (free of charge) listing hotels in each of the twenty *arrondisse-*

ments (districts) of the city, giving their prices and the various types of accommodations available. Though no hotels in Paris can any longer be described as inexpensive, a number of small and quiet family-run hotels still exist on the Left Bank. In choosing the location only be sure that you are not too far from a métro line that will take you over to where you will be attending the opera. Paris' subway system is fast and efficient, and in all likelihood, even if you stay on the Left Bank, it will only take you ten minutes to get where you want to go on the other side of the Seine. Any of the tourist offices can be counted on to give you good advice.

Money can be changed at almost all hours at Paris' two airports. Inside the city, if you need to change money on a Saturday or Sunday or after banks are closed during the week, you will need to go to one of the Thomas Cook banking branches in either the Gare de Saint-Lazare or the Gare du Nord. (The exchange rate is always better there than at a hotel.) Their hours are from 0800 to 2100, seven days a week. Convenient métro lines link these stations with all parts of the city. During regular business hours money can be changed at any of the four branches of American Express (one of which, at 11 Rue Scribe, is the famous "home base" to so many Americans); Cook's has upwards of ten offices scattered throughout the city.

BORDEAUX, in France's southwestern corner, lies near the cen-

ter of one of the richest and most famous wine-growing areas in the world. The city's fortunes have always been closely linked to the extremely volatile and speculative wine business. Recently, by fostering a more diverse economy, Bordeaux and its huge river port now enjoy a steadier prosperity. This part of France has for centuries had close ties to England: Eleanor, daughter of the Duke of Aquitaine, brought to the English crown in her wedding dowry this and many other of the richest provinces in France. The English kings' claim to sovereignty over these lands led to the Hundred Years War, with Bordeaux remaining under English control until 1453. Because the city's former rulers retained their love of French wine, England held on to its Bordeaux-connection in taking the largest share of the region's wine, most of it exported on ships sailing from Bordeaux. (Only in the last few years has West Germany's wine-consumption exceeded what used to go to England.)

The city's core, laid out in the 18th century by men of ambitious vision, set the pattern for what the Baron Haussmann in the next century was to do for Paris: parts of the old city were demolished and then replaced by wide, tree-lined boulevards; new civic buildings were constructed following the designs of some of France's most eminent architects (the two Gabriels and

Victor Louis). In the middle of the city, as a kind of "centerpiece" dominating a central square, is the grandiose and very handsome Grand Théâtre, a huge colonnaded, neo-classical structure built between 1773 and 1780. (The same architect, Victor Louis, later conceived the plans for the buildings and galleries that surround the Palais-Royal gardens in Paris, and the similarity in styles is quite striking.)

From the Gare St.-Jean, the city's main train station, two bus lines, either #7 and #8, will take you right to the front steps of the **Grand Théâtre.** (On foot by any of the most direct routes it is just under 2 miles/around 3 kilometers; about half of that distance is through a very uninteresting and shabby section of the city.) To return by bus from the opera house to the Gare St.-Jean is more complicated: the bus going in the other direction stops at the far end of the Allées de Tourny, the broad, tree-lined park leading off diagonally from the front of the theater; the bus stop is across the traffic circle, the Place de Tourny, on the other side of the Cours de Verdun. A single ride bought from the bus driver costs 7 francs; a 24-hour ticket, bought in any *tabac,* costs 16 francs.

In spite of the Grand Théâtre's enormous exterior dimensions the auditorium inside is relatively small, with seating for only 1200 and Standing Room for around 50. (The stage area however, taking up about a third of the structure, is unusually generous with respect to the time when the building was constructed.) Though shaped in the usual horseshoe with four tiers of balcony seating, the architectural design is very unusual and severe: six massive, rounded columns, evenly spaced around the circle, tower up through the first three levels, interrupting the sweep of the curve. Between each of these columns the fronts of the balconies jut out with squarish, drawer-like projections. The effect (for me) is rather harsh and ungraceful, though some might praise the design for its classical restraint. Above the third level (here called the Second Balcony) and above the capitals of the columns, an unbroken band circling the auditorium marks the beginning of the *Amphithéâtre* and the *Paradis.* The many arches rising above this level to support the ceiling hinder from a number of angles the view of the stage. The theater has been hailed as an acoustical marvel, but some seats none the less are to be avoided because of either poor sight-lines or erratic sound.

Just now what the building most badly needs is a complete overhaul, inside and out. The elegantly decorated public rooms and lounges are in fairly good condition, but many other parts of the theater look sadly worn. I understand that conditions backstage are even worse. Closing the Grand Théâtre for renovations has been much talked about, but the excuses most often heard for delaying the project are as much a matter of money as the fact that suitable temporary quarters cannot be found. Apparently an opera season and several concert series would have to be cancelled for an entire year. Certainly with the Mai Musical festival, when many foreign visitors come to

Bordeaux, one would think that the Bordelais would want to project a more generous image of their patronage of the arts; their magnificent theater now appears to be a victim of benign neglect.

The opera season usually opens in early October and continues into late June. (Although an opera is presented in May, the two or three performances are included in the quite separate schedule of the Mai Musical and are not part of the regular subscription series.) Bordeaux is currently beset with two matters seriously affecting their repertory: a financial crisis and a vociferous group of subscribers who want more operettas and fewer operas. Failure to obtain a special subsidy meant that the 1989–90 season's first operatic production, *Aïda,* had to be done in concert-form and not staged. This city is now quite unique among the older, established companies in France in including such a large share of these lighter works in its regular schedule. In 1989–90 there were six different operettas as opposed to five operas. The company's director has made the claim, with considerable justification, that the operetta is also part of the national "cultural heritage"; five out of the six works chosen were French, with Offenbach and Messager the only composers well known outside of France. As for the operatic repertory from year to year there is both diversity and balance, with a good sampling of German and Italian works, and unlike the bias shown in selecting the operettas, only a modest proportion of French titles. The presence of operettas in the schedule should not be taken to mean that the company has shied away from presenting more challenging compositions: a new *Götterdämmerung* in 1989 finally completed a *Ring* begun much earlier, only a single part of the cycle offered by itself each season; Strauss's *Elektra* is on the calendar for 1989–90; and Bordeaux has participated in the revival of seldom-performed Rossini. The operas are presented at the rate of one each month, and most are repeated four or five times, usually over two successive weekends plus a Tuesday (with at least one or two matinée performances). The operettas are also introduced one per month and then repeated anywhere between three and nine times, usually on successive nights (also over weekends); matinées are often scheduled on the same date as an evening performance. Ballet programs take up the slack in the monthly calendar when no opera is to be given.

Bordeaux has no resident ensemble of singers other than the chorus. For each opera guests are recruited from outside, many of them French; a few of those taking on secondary rôles may be engaged however to sing later in the course of the same season. There appears to be no set policy about hiring internationally-known artists: some of the operas have almost stellar casts while others use singers who are virtually unknown. In the operettas (none of which I have seen) all of the names are unfamiliar to me; only very few of these singers are held over to perform in more than one work. The orchestra accompanying the operas is usually the Orchestre National Bordeaux Aquitaine, a symphony based in Bordeaux that tours extensively throughout the region. Under Alain Lombard's tutelage they have become a fine-sounding, firmly-disciplined organization. (Other guest conductors, not Lombard, lead the orchestra when they are heard in opera.) The musicians in the pit for the operettas are a different group, smaller in number, who call themselves the "Orchestre du Grand-Théâtre."

The Box Office is inside the theater on the right side of the main entrance hall. They are open Tuesday through Friday from 0900 to 1600; on Saturday from 1100 to 1600; closed on Sunday, Monday, and holidays. One scale of prices, divided into six categories (ranging from 190 F to 29 F), is in effect for operas; another (from 160 F to 23 F) is used for operettas. To break these figures down and to list each seating area to which they correspond is far too long and complicated. I will try only to give in a general way prices for the better seats (from the point of view of sight-lines and sound) and will not attempt a comparable run-down for the operetta tickets. For starters, Bordeaux has unusual labels for what in other theaters would simply be called the "First Balcony": here it is split between the *Loges-Salon* in the center and the *Galerie* on the outer-sides (but still with a good view of the stage). The second tier, which elsewhere would be the "Second Balcony," becomes here the *Premier Balcon,* with a center section called the *Loge Philharmonique;* the third level therefore is the *Deuxième Balcon.* In this theater the Orchestra seats, called *Fauteuils Orchestre,* are quite good because the floor is very steeply raked; all of these seats are classed with Category I (190 F), along with all of the desirable seats on the first level. (To be avoided in this category are the claustrophobia-inducing *Baignoires* and *Loges* that circle the theater at orchestra level.) In Category II (155 F) come the first two rows in the *Premier Balcon* and the first three rows of the *Loge Philharmonique.* Category III (128 F) includes the first and second rows of the *Deuxième Balcon;* to be shunned here are the *Strapontins* in the orchestra. In Category IV (80 F) are some good and inexpensive seats: the first three rows, dead-center, in the *Paradis;* less good are the rear seats in the *Loge Philharmonique* (rows 4–5); and to be avoided are the *Loges* at the back of the *Premier Balcon.* Category V (53 F) is a catch-all for most of the unsatisfactory seats throughout the theater, most of them on the sides, where one has a very limited view of the stage. Category VI (29 F) is for Standing Room in the *Paradis* (or for any seats at the top that should be unoccupied!).

Quite unique to Bordeaux is the practice of exacting a surcharge of two F on each ticket sold through the Box Office, whether it be "in person," by telephone, or by mail. (The only comparable fee that I know of anywhere on the Continent is La Scala's imposition of a 10 % charge to all returned tickets that are then re-sold through the Box Office. One can only hope that Bordeaux collects this money and puts it into a rehabilitation fund for the theater.) Also, when ordering by mail, even though a stamped, self-addressed envelope is to be included, 10 F per order is added to the cost of the tickets. The directions for ordering by mail are quite specific: all orders for tickets are honored one month before the date of the initial performance of that work; orders that are received prior to that time are discarded. Orders by telephone or in person begin on the Saturday preceding the date of the first performance; with telephone orders payment must be received no later than 24 hours before the day of the performance. The telephone number is: 56-48-58-59, and the mailing address is: Service Location Grand Théâtre, Place de la Comédie, 33074 Bordeaux-CEDEX.

Tourist Information is available both at the Gare St.-Jean and in the middle of the city, quite close to the Grand Théâtre. At the station the office is reached from outside, about midway between the *Arrivée* and *Départ* main doors. They will call at no charge to make arrangements for hotel reservations. The hours are daily, from 0900 to 1800; on Sunday and on holidays from 0930 to 1230. The telephone number is: 56-91-64-70. The office in the center of the city is on the Cours du XXX-Juillet, the street that runs by the front steps of the theater; the office is one block over, on the far corner, just before the Park (the Esplanade des Quinconces). They have the same hours as the office at the Gare St.-Jean. The telephone number is: 56-44-28-41, and the complete mailing address is: 12 Cours du XXX-Juillet, 33080 Bordeaux-CEDEX. This would be the address to use when writing or calling from outside the city.

Hotels in all categories (and some fairly good restaurants) abound in the square just across from the station and in the streets nearby. A wide choice of hotels is also to be found in the center of the city, quite close to the Grand Théâtre. There is almost nothing in the way of accommodations in the drab streets between the two areas. (See above in the second paragraph for information about bus transportation.)

Money can be changed inside the station, downstairs, in the below-ground-complex that is visible in the middle of the *Départ* section of the building. The Bank is not very clearly marked but is at the end, to the right, of a long corridor leading to the underground garage. They are open daily from 0800 to 2000. There are also branches of Cook's and American Express in Bordeaux. The main office of Cook's is in the Gare St.-Jean, with two other affiliated agencies only a few steps from the Grand Théâtre; the office for American Express is also in the heart of the city and within sight of the opera house.

COLMAR (see Strasbourg below)

LYON rivals Paris in the intensity of its commercial activity, but it has much more to offer than a preoccupation with business and making money. The Lyonnais have cultivated palettes, and many consider the city to be France's gastronomic capital, which would logically make it Europe's leading city for fine food and superb restaurants. (Some will argue that this distinction belongs to Brussels.) Lyon is also a very old city (Lugdunum in Roman times) and during the Renaissance was the center in France for book-printing and for liberal, Protestant thought. Unfortunately the average tourist only sees Lyon from a train window traveling between Paris and the Riviera, but the city offers much more over and above its superb cuisine. Combined with a night at the opera the visitor will be kept quite busy taking in Lyon's unique museums, its fascinating Roman ruins, and its handsome urban architecture.

The **Opéra de Lyon** is at the moment without a permanent home. The old opera building, located in the heart of the city on the Place de la Comédie next to the Hôtel de Ville, is now closed because of extensive renovations that were scheduled to have begun in 1987. The old seating plan of the theater shows that there was space for approximately 1200 people. Delays in the funding have meant that work began only in late 1988, and it is anticipated that at least four to five years will be required before the theater reopens, probably by late 1993. As a result operas are now given in some four different places scattered throughout the city, but most performances (staged or in concert form) are given in the modern Auditorium Maurice Ravel which seats 2036. In late June and July performances move outdoors to the splendid setting of the Roman theater in the section of Lyon known as la Fourvière, the steep hillside bordering the "downtown" center of the city on the western bank of the Saône. I give directions below only for finding the Auditorium Maurice Ravel.

The repertory for the Opéra de Lyon is wide-ranging and includes each year at least one "world première" of a new work. Critics have heaped praises on the company for the quality of the singing and the staging. Most of the singers, conductors, and directors appear as guest artists, many of them world-famous. Lyon does not yet operate as a resident or repertory company, but a number of their productions have acquired some sort of permanence by being recorded and released on disks. Nine or ten operas generally are presented in the course of a season, which runs from October to June. The concert performances are given on a single night; most of the other operas are repeated four to five times within a two-week period.

The Auditorium Maurice Ravel, in which the Lyon Opera performs, looks very much like an inverted flying saucer perched at a precarious angle. Inside, the same boldness of design prevails, but the hall is quite comfortable, the acoustics good, and all seats have a clear view of the stage. The easiest landmark in Lyon to look for when hunting for the hall is the tall, reddish-brown, cylindrical headquarters of the big banking establishment, the Crédit Lyonnais (the Crédit Lyonnais signs are prominent just below the cone-like top of the building). The Auditorium Maurice Ravel is just next door, on the bank's north side. This is in a totally rebuilt part of the city, adjacent to the main new railroad station, the Part-Dieu; the station is approximately a mile (1.4 kilometers) to the east of the center of the older city, and the Auditorium is about 1200 feet (400 meters) from the station, back again towards the west. A number of pedestrian ramps criss-cross the area outside the front of the station; to reach the Auditorium and, along the way, the Box Office (located in the Centre Commercial), you will want to take the stairs towards the left, with the Gare la Part-Dieu directly behind you (the Crédit Lyonnais cylinder will be almost directly in front of you); two modern hotels, the Athena and the Mercure, will be on your left at the top of the stairs. Continue some 600 feet (200 meters), and still on a ramp above street-level, you will pass by the side of an ugly brown-bronze block of a building, faced with diamond-shaped slabs, called the Centre Commercial, an indoor shopping mall. Two signs on the outside walls: "Euromarché" and, in yellow, "Jelmoli" will identify this as the part of the Centre Commercial where the opera Box Office is located. The ramp at this point will go by the corner of the building; turn sharply right, and then, at another 90 degree angle, back to the left. Continue on another 400 feet (130 meters) straight ahead, beyond this building, along a partially covered arcade, and at the end of the ramp the Crédit Lyonnais cylinder will be on your left and down the ramp, the Auditorium Maurice Ravel on your right. At street-level this is at the intersection of the rue Garibaldi and the rue Servient.

One of the Box Offices for the Opéra de Lyon is on the second level of the Centre Commercial, the enclosed, multi-storied shopping mall. This is on the same level as the pedestrian ramp. Inside the mall towards the back on your right, look for a small kiosk opposite the main information desk ("renseignements") for the shops. The hours are from Monday through Saturday: 1100 to 1800. Ticket prices are quite reasonable, with only two categories in effect for the performances in the Auditorium nearby: either 110 F or 170 F. The exit doors (look for the sign "Porte de l'Esplanade"), just beyond the back side of the Box Office kiosk, will take you outside again with the Crédit Lyonnais building straight ahead and the Auditorium around the corner off to your right.

A second Box Office is found across the Rhône in "downtown" Lyon on the Place de la Comédie opposite the site of the now-closed opera house. Again, this is a kiosk; they are open from Tuesday through Saturday from 1100 to 1800.

Telephone orders are taken by calling: 78-28-09-60 during the hours when the Box Offices elsewhere are open. Mail orders are honored for the entire season from 15 September on and should be addressed to: Opéra de Lyon, 9 quai Jean Moulin, 69001 Lyon. At the Box Offices most tickets can be bought approximately three to six weeks before each performance. This schedule for advance purchases varies but is published in late spring in the announcement of the coming season's program.

The one problem in arriving at Lyon at the Gare la Part-Dieu is the lack of any tourist information inside the station or even nearby. The only tourist office is in the older part of the city, but that is more than a mile away. Even if you take the subway from the train station, make your one transfer, and get off at the Hôtel de Ville stop (almost next door to the old opera house), you will still be a good distance (about a half-mile or 900 meters) north of the Place Bellecour and the tourist office. This is located in a kiosk on the Place Bellecour, the large and imposing square at the southern base of Lyon's two most important commercial streets, the Rue du Président Herriot and the Rue de la République; at the north end of these two streets are the Hôtel de Ville and the opera house. The Office du Tourisme will be the last building on the easternmost edge of the Place, on the Rhône side. They are open Monday through Friday from 0900 to 2000; on Saturdays from 0900 to 1400; closed on Sundays. They may be able to help you with hotel information and reservations if you call: 78-42-25-75.

Once again, in the neighborhood of the Part-Dieu station, hotels are a problem because there is so little choice. There are two very modern hotels attached to one side of the station (you will pass them on the ramp leading to the opera Box Office and the Auditorium Maurice Ravel), but these are moderately expensive and with their very sanitized American look, cater mostly to business groups. Two smaller, older, and reasonably-priced hotels are directly across the street on the far side of the Auditorium, but to reach them from the station you will probably need to use a taxi. A much wider choice of hotels (and restaurants) is to be found in the center of Lyon, across the bridges over the Rhône, but this will be about a mile away, though if you are going to the opera you lose the advantage of having the theater close by. Even in Lyon you should expect to pay a third to a half less than what is considered normal hotel fare in Paris. Your best bet is to leave your luggage in a locker at the train station and take the métro into the center of the city (6,50 F for one ticket), and there look around for a place to stay. Urban renewal in the Part-Dieu area has unfortunately given that section of Lyon a very sterile, lifeless appearance, quite untypical of the handsome city lying to the west.

It is possible to find at least the amenity of money-changing facilities inside the Part-Dieu station. A Thomas Cook's office, marked by an orange sign, is located in the middle of the tunnel (on ground level) off of which are the stairs leading up to the train platforms. They are open 365 days a year from 0930 to 1830; two other Cook's offices are in the center of the city. American Express also has a branch in Lyon.

MARSEILLE is an exciting, animated city, blending in unique fashion its historical and cultural ties to northern Europe with its importance as a major Mediterranean port facing towards southern Italy and Africa. It is also a proud city that traces its origins in 600 B. C. to Phoenecian traders who in turn were followed by Greek and Roman colonists. The natives claim with a certain degree of meridional braggadocio that their principal avenue, La Canebière, is more beautiful than Paris' Champs-Elysées. In some respects they are right because their street is set off by the dazzling blue of the Midi sky and the shimmering colors of the Mediterranean off in the distance. The natural setting of Marseille is magnificent, and once you have satisfied yourself that you have seen most of what the city has to offer, there are all the places to visit just to the north: Aix-en-Provence, Nîmes, Arles, Avignon, and Orange that no visitor to this part of southern France should under any circumstances miss seeing. And then of course off to Marseille's east, the Riviera.

The Opéra de Marseille has for two centuries been an important component in the city's cultural life. In the last fifteen years it has shed the provincialism that marked its post-war reputation and has now assumed a position in the front-rank of France's opera companies. Like Lyon and Nice (and unlike Paris) it appears to have the unstinting support of the city's political establishment and without budgetary worries seeks out for some of its productions the best available singers, conductors, and designers. Between October and early June some nine or ten different operas are presented, and each is now sung in the language in which it was composed. To Marseille belongs the honor (and courage) of being the first company in France to mount a complete and uncut version of Berlioz' *Les Troyens* (1978–1980), and this triumph was to be repeated again during the 1988–89 season. Marseille has shown a healthy instinct to stray from the "tried and true" and has not been afraid to put into its repertory works that other opera directors might think of as doomed to fail at the box office: Menotti, Britten, Janácek, Boïto, and so forth. And critics are almost unanimous in stating that alone among French companies Marseille keeps before the public a good share of the German repertory, which is sung in German. Operas are given on the block-system, and most are repeated between four and six times over a period of just under two weeks. Filling out the schedule are ballets and occasional concerts by the very capable Orchestre Philharmonique de Marseille, the same group that performs in the pit for the operas.

The opera house is easily and quickly reached by the métro from the Gare St.-Charles; the entrance to the métro is several escalator flights down, underneath the main exit from the station. You will want "Direction Castellane" and to get off after "Colbert" at the second stop: "Vieux Port," the picturesque old inner harbor of the city. Look for the signs pointing to the exit on "La Canebière". (In the opposite direction, going back to the Gare St.-Charles, you will want to choose the line marked "Direction La Rose.") One métro ticket costs 6,50 F; a *carnet* (booklet) of six costs 27,00 F. The theater will be just around the corner, up the Canebière just a few steps (and past the "downtown" tourist office); turn right on the first street, the rue Beauvau, and you will see the portico of the opera house directly in front of you. The Box Office, hidden from view, with no protruding sign, will be outside on the left as you face the main doors to the theater; it fronts on the street that parallels the building's north side.

The exterior of the opera is a nicely-proportioned neo-classical structure dating from near the end of the 1780's. The interior was destroyed by fire in 1919 and reopened in 1924. The best evidence of this date and period is to be found in the decoration of the stairways and public rooms which recall old photographs of the interiors of the public rooms on the S. S. Normandie. With the bas-reliefs, marble statues, mirrors, and murals this is a style somewhere between art nouveau and art deco; only the parquet floors remind one that this is an opera house, not a long-gone steamship, the pride of the French Line. The seating was rearranged in 1987 and now can accommodate 1832 spectators, with a very generous 450 seats in the *amphithéâtre* alone. Marseille is proud of the fact that its theater is the best attended in all of France and that its ticket-pricing policies allow so many to pay so little to see an opera. There is nothing very distinctive or memorable about the inside of the auditorium itself, an unadorned, rather plain hall that in many respects resembles Toulouse's Théâtre du Capitole. Very wisely, I would say, gratuitous atmosphere here has been sacrificed to give most of the seats an unobstructed view of the stage. The three balconies (the third and top one being called the *amphithéâtre*) are wide and spacious and tie into the side walls far enough back from the stage so that even the seats on the ends of each balcony are still reasonably well angled for seeing the stage. The acoustics are quite good, though exception should be made for the few rows of orchestra seats tucked in at the back under the first balcony.

The Box Office, as noted above, is outside, to the left, fronting on the side street. The hours they are open are somewhat complicated because on the first day that tickets go on sale, 15 days in advance of a performance, the Box Office remains open from 1000 to 1600; after that one day, the regular hours, from Tuesday through Saturday, are from 1000 to 1230 and from 1500 to 1800. The Box Office is always closed on Sunday and Monday. An exception is made for Sunday if there is an opera scheduled for that evening (the special Sunday hours are from 1000 to 1230). In the case of the 15-day limit for advance sales, when the first performance of the opera will fall on a weekend, the option is retained to move the opening date of sales back or forward by two or three days in keeping with the regular schedule of the Box Office. For most operas the ticket prices will have a top of either 120 F or 150 F; below this, grouping these two categories together, the prices are still more than reasonable: 115/145 F and 85/105 F. In the *amphithéâtre* the prices drop abruptly to 35/40 F (and there are 450 of these seats, all with an excellent view of the stage). The Box Office telephone number is: 91-55-21-22 or 91-55-21-23. Mail orders for tickets should be sent no more than one month in advance and accompanied by a check to: Trésor Public, and with a stamped, self-addressed envelope to: Opéra de Marseille, rue Beauvau, 13001 Marseille. In the evening, 45 minutes before a performance, last-minute tickets may be bought for seats in the *amphithéâtre;* look for an open doorway just a few feet beyond the Box Office.

There are two very convenient tourist offices in Marseille. The first, located in the Gare St.-Charles, is by one of the main doors leading to the outside terrace on the same level as the train platforms. Though the office is small, all of the services that are available "downtown" are also found here: hotel reservations and general information about the city. The only problem is that they are not open on weekends. The hours, from Monday through Friday, are: 0900 to 1230 and 1400 to 1800. The main office is located in the first block of La Canebière as you go up the avenue with the Vieux Port at your back (you will pass it on your way to the Marseille opera). This office is just a few feet from the "Vieux Port"/"La Canebière" exit of the métro line (Castellane-La Rose segment) which you would take from the Gare St.-Charles. Breaking with an almost universal custom of the Midi, here they do not close for a long lunch (except on Saturday). From Monday through Friday their hours are from 0900 to 1830; on Saturday from 0900 to 1200 and 1400 to 1800. No service is provided on Sunday.

A wide choice of hotels is clustered around the front and to the sides of the Gare St.-Charles. To reach them, if you are intimidated by the long and steep stairs that lead down from the front of the station to the Boulevard d'Athènes, you can take the escalators inside the station that descend to the level of the entrance to the métro; instead of stopping at the ticket windows on your right, continue straight ahead and follow a tunnel that comes out on the sidewalk at the base of the stairs. Going back up to the station, unless you want the exercise, the tunnel and escalators will be most convenient; as you face the stairs at the bottom, the tunnel entrance is off to your left. (The Gare St.-Charles sits on a high bluff above the city, and the lands drops off quite sharply from in front; the view of Marseille from the terrace circling the main entrance to the station is quite impressive.)

Money can be changed inside the station at a small bank located on the same level as the train platforms; at the head-end of the platforms it will be off to your right. They are open 365 days a year, from 0800 to 1800. Both American Express and Cook's have offices in Marseille.

MULHOUSE (See Strasbourg) (The second syllable of the city's name is pronounced like the English "ooze," with no resemblance or connection to the English word "house"!)

NICE is a delightful city, and even though a big tourist center, one is never really conscious of the presence of other tourists, except in the summer, when the opera season has ended. It is also two cities: the animated, quaint fishing village, squeezed around the base of the ramparts of the old fortress, and the more modern, spacious city that begins on the Promenade des Anglais and stretches back up into the hills overlooking the sea. The site is magnificent, which easily explains why so many painters, musicians, and writers have been attracted to the area (lured as well by the near-ideal climate). Nice serves as a convenient point from which to go out and visit the multitude of fascinating other towns in the vicinity. If you are interested in painting and want to explore some small museums closely associated with painters who lived nearby, you should not miss Antibes (Picasso and Cocteau), Cagnes (Renoir), St.-Paul (the Foundation Maeght), Vence (Matisse), Vallauris (Picasso), and in Nice itself the Chagall and Matisse museums. All of these towns lie within less than 20 miles of Nice, and you can visit them either on your own by train or by bus excursions. And off to the east, again within less than 20 miles, are the scenically spectacular cities of Monte-Carlo and Monaco, with the three famous Corniches linking them together. This is an incredibly beautiful part of the world which I find, on each visit, more and more difficult to leave.

The **Opéra de Nice** is another of those small, plucky companies in the provinces which have an adventurous repertory, attract many world-famous artists, and usually come through with almost unanimous praises from the public and the critics. During the 1987–88 season Nice scheduled the entire *Ring;* for 1988–89, in collaboration with three British companies, they offered Berlioz' *Les Troyens.* Their season begins in late September and continues through to the end of June. Nine or ten works are produced on the "block-system" and then repeated between four and eight times within the space of from ten days to two weeks. Throughout the season a number of matinées are scheduled. The operas are sung in the language in which they were written. Because of the great variety in the works presented each year, it would be easier to list each title rather than to try in several sentences to give an accurate, over-all description of the repertory, but suffice it to say that Nice succeeds in keeping a healthy balance between the "tried and true" and those other, rarer works that ought to be heard more often. To fill in on those nights when opera is not scheduled there are symphony concerts (the Nice Philharmonique also serves as the pit orchestra), ballets by the local company, chamber music, and solo recitals.

The Nice opera house is wedged into a small corner of the old part of the city but is very close to the newer Place Masséna and the elegant buildings that line the Promenade des Anglais. (The back of the theater actually fronts on the sea and the Promenade des Etats-Unis, which is the continuation of the Promenade des Anglais.) To find the theater, go down the steps on the Mediterranean-side of the Place, past the large fountain, and continue straight ahead on rue de l'Opéra about a hundred feet (30 meters) until this street ends, and you are now on the rue St.-François-de-Paule; turn left on this street, and a few doors down on your right (another hundred feet) will be the theater. From the outside, the building is very unassuming, and you could pass by it without ever knowing that it is an opera house. Inside, in addition to the orchestra seats, there are four tiers of balconies circling the theater; the first three tiers are divided into boxes (on the sides, near the stage, on the two upper levels, the name changes from *loges* to *galerie*). The fourth and top level, instead of being divided into boxes, consists of open rows of seats and is called the *amphithéâtre;* above and behind is a series of more hard benches called the *paradis.* The seats on this level are "segregated" from the other seating below, reminiscent of the "Family Circle" in the old Met on Broadway and 39th; access is by a separate entrance around the corner on the left side of the building, through a small door and many steps up, or by a small cage elevator holding at most two people. In the middle of the *amphithéâtre* the sight-lines are excellent, and many people claim that these seats have the best acoustics in the house. The theater seats 1200, but of that number most of those who are sitting in the side boxes, except on the front rows, will see very little of the stage. The acoustics are quite dry and clear, but I wonder, never having heard a Wagner or Strauss work in this theater, to what extent the conductor would have to hold down his forces in the pit to keep from shattering the eardrums of everyone in the audience. Nice possesses a very attractive house, but at the moment it badly needs a thorough cleaning and refurbishing. It looks drab and shabby, and this appearance is in marked contrast to what one sees (and hears) on the stage.

The Box Office is located just to the right of the main entrance to the theater and is open from Tuesday through Saturday from 1100 to 1900.

Though normally closed on both Sunday and Monday, if a performance is scheduled for one of those evenings, the Box Office maintains the hours in force during the rest of the week. The telephone number to use to call for information about tickets and such is: 93-85-67-31, but no reservations are taken by telephone. Mail orders, accompanied by a check made out to the "Opéra de Nice" and a self-addressed envelope, with postage for registered mail, should be sent to: Théâtre de l'Opéra de Nice, 4 rue St.-François-de-Paule, 06300 Nice. Advance sales (in person at the Box Office or by mail) are grouped into three separate booking periods, an unusual but most convenient and simplified system for avoiding the confusion about what constitutes so-and-so-many days before a certain date. For performances scheduled between September and December, sales begin on 5 September; for January through March performances, on 2 November; and for April through June dates, on 1 March (from year to year, because of holidays, these times may vary by one or two days). The Box Office opens one hour before a performance.

Nice follows a curious policy of charging less for *opéras comiques* than for *opéras* (I suppose there must be considerable debate among the authorities when it comes to deciding how to classify a Mozart *singspiel!*), but in any case both price categories are extremely reasonable. The higher level starts at 90 F and goes up to 220 F; the lower price scale begins at 70 F and goes up only to 170 F. Prices in the *paradis* are either a modest 50 F or 40 F.

Tickets for the Nice opera can also be bought in selected stores in other cities strung out along the Riviera (and in Turin, Italy, as well). In alphabetical order: in Antibes: at Cote Ouest, Boulevard Wilson; in Cannes: at Rhapsodie, 26 rue Jean Jaurès; in Marseille: at FNAC, Centre Bourse; in Menton: at Photo-Post, 23 rue Partouneaux; in Monaco: at S. E. S., 15 rue Princesse Caroline; in Vence: at Vidéo Musique, 37 rue Marcellin Maurel; and in Turin, Italy: at Musica Viaggi, Corso Novarro, 45154 Torino, Italy.

Back to Nice: it is possible to take a bus from the Gare to a stop fairly close to the opera house, but you will still have to walk across most of the Place Masséna to the two streets (given above) that lead to the theater. From across the Avenue Thiers, directly in front of the Gare, the #5 bus goes to the north end of the Place Masséna. The #12 bus goes almost to the Place but turns off from the Avenue Jean Médecin; the Place Masséna is one block south, towards the Mediterranean. Bus tickets may be bought at the "Change" office across the street from the Gare, off to the right at the corner of the rue Auber and the Avenue Thiers; they are open daily from 0700 to 2400. A day or tourist ticket costs 16 F (good for 24 hours); single tickets costing 7 F may be bought on the bus from the driver.

The Office du Tourisme is just outside the train station, off to the left as you come out the main doors. They can be very helpful in providing reservations for hotels and information about the opera. There are two schedules for their hours: from October through May they are open between Monday and Saturday, 0845 to 1230 and from 1400 to 1800; their summer hours (which are relevant only for the end and the very beginning of the opera season) are as follows: from June through September, open seven days a week, including holidays, from 0800 to 1900.

In some parts of Nice, and especially across and down from the railroad station, almost every building you encounter is a hotel or pension. Most of them are quite reasonable. As you get closer to the Mediterranean, and on the sea itself, the prices go up. It is quite pleasant to walk in the city because of the generally mild climate during most of the year. From the neighborhood around the station, where you find so many hotels, it is no more than 25 minutes on foot to the opera house (a distance of about a mile or 1.4 kilometers).

A Thomas Cook office for changing money, open seven days a week, is off to your far right as you come out of the Gare. Off-season (from October to the end of May), they are open from 0800 to 1800; during the summer (June through September), they remain open until 2100. There is another establishment, marked "Change," almost directly across the street on the corner of the rue Auber and the Avenue Thiers, open seven days a week between 0700 and 2400; at this same place you can buy bus tickets. Cook's has another office in the city, and there is an American Express branch as well.

STRASBOURG is an elegant and unusual city, reflecting both its French and German past. Since World War II, as the seat of the Council of Europe and the European Parliament, the city has assumed yet a third identity as the new capital of what, one hopes, will soon be a united continent. Strasbourg is deservedly famous for its magnificent Gothic cathedral, unique in the fact that only one of its towers, capped by a lace-like steeple, soars above the city. One might think that the huge church with its sole, off-center tower would appear lop-sided or about to capsize, but the genius of its architects was such that the proportions are quite perfect as they are, and the building calmly stands over the city as a constant reminder of a once-dynamic and self-confident faith.

Strasbourg's opera, the **Opéra du Rhin,** is unusual because it is shared among three cities. Strasbourg serves as the "home" and administrative base and usually will have the same opera repeated four or five times; then the same production moves to Mulhouse, which is allotted two or three performances; Colmar will see the same opera only once or twice (it is the smallest city). The singers are all invited artists from the outside, but two orchestras: l'Orchestre Philharmonique de Strasbourg and the Orchestre Symphonique du Rhin-Mulhouse provide the accompaniment; the same chorus moves among the three cities. Because of the smaller dimensions of the stages in both Mulhouse and Colmar not every opera is taken outside of Strasbourg. (A few more details about Mulhouse and Colmar are provided below, after the section on Strasbourg.) The repertory is especially interesting because of the attention given each year to first performances of full-length operas by young, not well-known composers. Also, among the nine or so works presented each season (usually one each month), apart from those belonging to the standard repertory (Mozart, Verdi, Puccini, Wagner, Bizet, etc.), there is at least one opera (and sometimes two) that is rarely produced today, such as, in recent seasons, a work by Rameau, Handel, Gluck, Cimarosa, or Rabaud. A lighter work too, like an operetta by Offenbach, Strauss, or Lehar, often is included in the annual fare. With but few exceptions, even though many of the singers are French and quite young, the works are not performed in French translation. There will often be a gap of at least one or two days between dates for performances. Generally the lighter works and operettas are presented without a break on successive days. A good number of the operas are also scheduled for matinée hours, and many of these occur on Sundays. This company also works closely with the Karlsruhe opera across the Rhine: during the 1988–89 season Karlsruhe brought over their production of Strauss' *Die schweigsame Frau,* and Strasbourg took their new *Mignon* to Germany. Much to the credit of the Opéra du Rhin many of their performances are available on widely-distributed disks.

Strasbourg's **Théâtre Municipal,** rebuilt in the 1870's using the plans of the original, classical 1821 structure, is on the Place de Broglie, near the eastern side of the city's center. On foot from the station, depending on traffic, it is about a 20- to 25-minute walk. A #15 bus makes the trip in about half that time; single tickets for 4,20 F may be purchased from the bus driver, while a *carnet* (a booklet of 5 tickets) is for sale for 21 F inside the station in an office right next to the small bank (see the directions for finding the bank below). The theater seats 1143; four shallow levels of balconies (here called *galeries*) circle the interior, and with none of them cluttered by box-partitions or supporting columns, the sight-lines are excellent except for the seats on the sides approaching the stage. With good acoustics, this is a pleasantly comfortable ambiance in which to see and hear opera. The Opéra du Rhin also uses on occasion the much larger auditorium of the Palais de la Musique et des Congrès, a modern structure, dating from the mid-1970's, out from the center of the city; it is near the site of the buildings of the European Council and Parliament. Apparently the hall was originally designed mainly for meetings and for orchestral concerts and is not ideally suited to opera. (For some years the Opéra du Rhin has wanted to have its own theater near the new city administrative center in the southern section of the city.) The Palais can seat 1984 people. I have not visited the hall and can say nothing about the seating arrangements and the acoustics, but when the company has performed there in the past, they have usually been able to play to a sold-out house. A #20 bus goes from the Gare to the Palais.

The Box Office is inside the theater on the Place de Broglie, just to the left of the main doors. They are open, Monday through Friday, from 1000 to 1230 and from 1600 to 1900; closed on Saturday and Sunday. If a performance is scheduled for either Saturday or Sunday, they open ¾ of an hour before the curtain goes up; in the case of weekday performances, they open again ½ hour before curtain-time. A very complicated system is in effect for determining ticket costs, but in all cases for the higher-priced tickets, an opening or première performance in Strasbourg moves up by one notch on the pricing scale; subsequent performances are always cheaper. Rather than making the orchestra seats the most expensive in the house, Strasbourg puts a higher premium on all of the seats in the first-level balcony. The top prices will generally range between 170 and 200 F, which still remains a very reasonable sum. At the low end of the scale, a good number of tickets are pegged at 30 and 40 F, which includes everything on the fourth level and on the sides of the third level. Tickets in advance for performances scheduled at the Palais de la Musique are sold only at the opera Box Office; if any remain unsold, they are available at the Palais ¾ hour before curtain-time. For information from the Box Office the telephone number is: 88-36-43-41. Another telephone number can be used for reserving tickets six days in advance of the first performance of a work (88-36-71-12). Mail orders are accepted one month before the initial date of a performance of a work and for 15 days thereafter; write: Service des locations, Opéra du Rhin, 19 Place de Broglie, 67008 Strasbourg CEDEX. If tickets are available, your order will be confirmed by return mail within 15 days, at which point you must send back a check in payment.

A tourist office is located just across from the Gare, off to the right, on an "island" about 100 feet (30 meters) from the station's main entrance. (If car and bus traffic is heavy, use the escalator taking you down to the tunnel underneath the Place de la Gare in front of the station; turn right at the first stairs, and go back up to street-level.) The hours at the tourist office vary according to the season: from October through May, they are open, Monday through Friday, from 0900 to 1230 and from 1345 to 1800; closed on both Saturday and Sunday; from June through the end of September, they are open seven days a week, including holidays, from 0800 to 1900. Their telephone number is: 88-32-51-49. A second tourist office is "downtown," two blocks from the cathedral at 10 Place Gutenberg; with the main doors of the cathedral at your back, go directly away from it, west, and you will be in the square with the tourist office off to your right. Out of season this office is open on Saturdays, in addition to the Monday through Friday schedule; the hours are otherwise the same in both offices. The telephone for this office is: 88-32-57-07. Two more offices, useful mostly to people traveling by car, are in the outskirts of the city: one is close to the Pont de l'Europe, the bridge over the Rhine connecting France with Germany; the second is in the Palais de la Musique et des Congrès, not too far from the buildings housing the European Council and Parliament.

A number of hotels, ranging in price from the moderate to the very expensive, can be found on the Place de la Gare, the semi-circular square just in front of the station. There are many other good hotels scattered throughout the center of the city, but they are difficult to find without a map and clear directions; there are none in the immediate vicinity of the opera house. Consult the tourist office in front of the station or on the Place Gutenberg about prices and reservations.

Banking facilities are available in the railroad station, 365 days a year, between the hours of 0900 and 2000. As you face the station from the outside, this office is located inside the doors to the far left; if you are getting off a train and following the signs marked "Sortie," this office will be on your right just as you come out of the tunnel (still inside the station) from underneath the tracks. The office where you buy your bus tickets is next door, and their hours daily are from 0615 to 1900. No American Express, but Cook's has four branches in Strasbourg.

STRASBOURG/COLMAR (42 miles/71 kilometers south of Strasbourg) Colmar is a beautiful small city, full of quaint Alsatian charm. Its celebrated Unterlinden Museum contains among many other treasures the famous Matthias Grünewald altarpiece. Its streets, criss-crossed by canals, are lined with meticulously-maintained half-timbered houses, many of them dating back to the 1500's. If you put any stock in the conservative evaluations of the Michelin *Guide*, you will see that Colmar rates three stars, one of only three places in Alsace-Lorraine to merit such a distinction. If your visit to Colmar doesn't coincide with a performance by the Opéra du Rhin, you should still try to make the trip.

The Colmar opera house, the **Théâtre Municipal,** abuts on one side the Musée Unterlinden. (Coming out of the Colmar Gare, go across the Place de la Gare and one more block, out to the Avenue de la République and turn left on this main artery: the theater and the museum will be straight ahead, just over ⅗ of a mile/1 kilometer on your right.) The theater is quite small, with only 707 seats, but it is a little gem, built in the Italian style and opened in 1849.

Before you leave Strasbourg you can inquire about the opera schedule for Colmar. But tickets for individual performances are available only in the latter city. The Box Office (inside the theater) is open at the following times: Monday through Friday, from 1000 to 1200 and from 1600 to 1830; they are open on Saturday, from 1600 to 1800, only if there is a performance that day or on Sunday. Telephone reservations are accepted by calling: 89-41-29-82 between 1430 and 1600. On the Colmar schedule are a number of matinées, most of them on Sunday; for these and for the evening perform-ances the Box Office opens 30 minutes before curtain-time. The ticket prices are much lower than in Strasbourg, with the best seats in the house costing between 110 and 140 F and the lowest ranging between 20 and 30 F. The mailing address of the theater is: Théâtre Municipal, Rue des Unterlinden, 68000 Colmar. Advance sales begin five days before the date of a perform-ance.

There is a tourist office at 4 Rue des Unterlinden, across the square and opposite the theater and the museum; the tourist office, as with these other buildings, is ⅗ of a mile away from the Gare.

There are several hotels immediately in front of the station and several off to your left, two blocks away, on the street paralleling the train tracks. Not many are to be found in the oldest part of the city.

No facilities for changing money are provided in the Gare. Cook's has an affiliated agent in Colmar, but be prepared to change money during normal business hours or at a regular bank.

STRASBOURG/MULHOUSE (67 miles /113 kilome-ters south of Strasbourg and 24 miles/42 kilometers south of Colmar) Mul-house, a large textile and chemical center, has not much within the city itself to attract the busy tourist, but for train- and car-buffs there are two famous museums in the city's outskirts that draw visitors from the world-over: the Musée Français du Chemin de Fer and the Musée de l'Automobile. And for those interested in the history and development of printed designs on cloth, tracing an industry that grew up in Mulhouse, the Musée de l'Impression sur Etoffes, which is just to the right of the Gare after the main post office.

The Mulhouse opera house, the **Théâtre Municipal,** is approximately ⅕ of a mile (400 meters) straight out from the front of the Gare, around a large circular block of buildings, one more block still in a straight line from the station, and then directly opposite, on the far side of the Rue de la Sinne. It is an attractive theater, remodeled several times since its construction in the 1860's; it has seating for 822, but from many of the seats close to the proscenium, especially on the upper levels, the view of the stage is poor.

There are three tiers of balconies, and in both the second and third balcony there are a generous number of seats grouped at the center, where sight-lines are excellent. Acoustically the theater is quite good.

The Box Office is off the lobby inside the theater and is open from Monday through Saturday, from 1000 until 1200 and from 1630 to 1830; tickets may also be bought 30 minutes before curtain-time. Advance sales begin only three days before the date of each performance, and reservations may be made by calling: 89-45-20-04, between the hours of 1500 and 1630. For mail orders, write 15 days before a performance, describing what you want, and the Box Office will reply to confirm or deny your reservation. Address all correspondance to: Caisse du Théâtre Municipal, 39 rue de la Sinne, 68100 Mulhouse. Prices range from a high of 140 F (for seats in the first balcony) to a low of between 30 and 50 F for seats on the sides of the second balcony and for all of the seats in the third, top-most balcony.

A tourist office is located very close to the Gare, at 9 Avenue Maréchal-Foch, a street that runs off at an angle to the right as you come out the doors to the station; cross the Place du Général de Gaulle, with the post office on your immediate right, and the Avenue will be directly in front of you. They are open Monday through Friday, from 0900 to 1230 and from 1400 to 1800; on Saturday, from 0900 to 1200, and closed on Sunday.

There are hotels facing the station on the other side of the Place du Général de Gaulle, and quite a number, in the vicinity of the tourist office, can be found in the streets leading into the center of Mulhouse.

Money can be changed inside the Gare, daily, between 0800 and 2000. Cook's has an affiliated agent in Mulhouse, but there is no branch of American Express.

TOULOUSE, long the capital of Haut-Languedoc in southern France, rarely figures in the itinerary of most tourists visiting Europe. At present it is witnessing a boom as the main center of France's aerospace and aircraft industry. It is a lively city, tracing its origin back to a Celtic village that later became one of the most important commercial crossroads of Roman Gaul. The Michelin guide tells us that between the 9th and 13th centuries the court of the Counts Raymond was the "most magnificent" in all of Europe. The early 1300's saw the founding of the *Académie des Jeux-Floraux,* a literary academy that awarded prizes in an annual competition for the best compositions in verse; it is thought to be the oldest such institution in Europe. The vigorous cultivation in Toulouse of all the arts has continued down to modern times. Students of romanesque architecture and sculpture

know the city quite well because of its wealth of churches and museums, just as opera-lovers are aware that Toulouse's Théâtre du Capitole has for many years led the nation in reviving long-neglected masterpieces in the French repertory. Sound engineers too from several major recording labels have put on tape a good number of these productions, making them available to yet larger audiences.

The city itself is quite interesting. The most common material used in constructing both houses and religious monuments is pink-colored brick, seen throughout much of the region because stone is not readily available. The architects who designed Toulouse's medieval churches were amazingly ingenious in using brick to form intricate patterns and also to go skyward with graceful towers. Many of these buildings possess a genial warmth often missing from those built solely of stone. Unfortunately the traffic authorities have yet to act in banning automobiles from the city's more picturesque but very narrow streets; negociating a two-foot-wide sidewalk and dodging cars is hazardous when you are trying to view the sights. But after battling traffic one suddenly comes on pleasant, tree-shaded squares where one can sit quietly at a sidewalk café and regain one's composure.

In the center of Toulouse, flanking one entire side of the Place du Capitole, is the town hall (the Capitole) with its stylish mid-18th-century façade of brick and limestone; its symmetrical proportions conceal a mix of much older buildings behind it. ("Capitole," it should be explained, is a modern adaptation of the Provençal or *languedoc* word for "capitouls," the council of twelve men who until the Revolution directed the city's affairs.) At the corner on the far right and facing the square is the opera house, the **Théâtre du Capitole,** taking its name from the structure to which it is joined on the front. The theater is relatively small, seating only around 1035 (no provision is made for Standing Room), but it is good acoustically, and after the last renovations in the 1970's most of the seats with a poor view of the stage were removed. The design is quite basic: a semi-circle with three balconies, each of which has open rows of seating at the front; the relatively few boxes in the upper levels are on the sides, behind the "open" rows. Unfortunately few people have kind words to say about the auditorium's appearance; it looks a bit as if someone had intended to convert it into a movie house showing grade-B pictures. When all of the old ornamentation was stripped from the balcony facings and the walls, the smooth, bare surfaces were then painted a dark, institutional brown. When I once asked an elderly attendant why the choice of such an unpleasant color, his begrudging answer, without offering any explanation, was simply: *"Oui, c'est vilain!"* ("Yes, it's ugly"). The auditorium however is comfortable, and once the curtain is raised one can leave these other aesthetic considerations aside.

Toulouse's season begins in mid-October and ends in early June. Between five and seven operas are presented, along with four or five operettas, each on the block-system. Four ballet programs usually fill out the calendar. The repertory balances French with Italian and German works, each sung in its original language. Unique to Toulouse is the rediscovery of many French operas and operettas that have disappeared from the active repertory; usually one such work is given each season. The general practice is to plan the schedule so as to alternate operas with operettas. A run of performances of an opera, spread out over two weeks, is followed by a gap of some ten days to two weeks, and then an operetta is staged. The operas are usually repeated four to six times, the operettas anywhere between six to ten times. Other than a regular Tuesday series and an occasional Thursday performance the majority of performances are clustered around weekends, with matinées scheduled on Sundays. The operettas are given without a break on successive weekend days, again with matinées due on Sundays. Many of the productions seen in Toulouse are done in coordination with other opera companies in both France and other countries throughout Europe.

The singers invited to appear in Toulouse are a mixed group, many of them young, drawn from all over Europe and with great frequency from the United States. Though the operettas are almost entirely cast with French artists, including on occasion "stars" of the genre, one doesn't find a preponderant number of native singers taking on the principal rôles of the operas. Even in the French works one usually finds Americans, Roumanians, and/or Italians singing the leading parts. (Through the years both Toulouse and Marseille have boasted that most of France's best singers have come from their respective regions. This claim is largely true, but since the war there are unfortunately still very few French voices good enough to merit lasting international attention.) The chorus in Toulouse, the only singers under permanent contract, is often cited for producing good, rich sound. In the pit are members of the Orchestre National du Capitole de Toulouse, a group which some critics have singled out as now the best orchestra in all of France. The regular conductor, Michel Plasson, usually directs two of the operas, with eminent guest conductors brought in for the other works. With the operettas a smaller ensemble of musicians is used which goes simply by the name of the "Orchestre du Capitole."

The Box Office is located inside the small lobby of the theater. (If the main doors facing the Place du Capitole are closed, the first door a few feet just around the corner is open.) The schedule is Tuesday through Sunday from 0900 to 1230 and 1430 to 1800; closed on Sunday and Monday. Ticket prices are relatively easy to describe because there are only four different categories (operetta tickets cost slightly less than those for operas). Payment must be either in cash or by check; credit cards are not yet accepted. The arrangement of the seats requires no need of a translation from French to English. Category I (180 F) begins with the fairly steeply raked *Orchestre,* the single largest seating area with some 395 seats. Also in this same category is the entire first raised level, the *Balcon;* in the center facing the stage it is quite deep with nine rows; on the sides there are between one and three rows of open seats and behind them eight *Loges* (Boxes). The next price category (II at 135 F) includes all of the second level, the *Galerie,* which is eight rows deep in the center; the only irregular part of the theater's shape occurs here where on the sides the *Galerie* splits into two shallow tiers, first the *Galerie Côté* and then above it, the *Galerie Bis,* with again on each level some Boxes behind the open rows at the front. Category III (80 F) is for most of the third and topmost level, the *Amphithéâtre,* six rows deep in the middle and then thinning down from four rows to one on the sides. Apparently to conform to usage in other theaters the last five rows of seats of the *Amphithéâtre,* in the center at the back, have been called the *Paradis.* The 82 seats here fall into Category IV (55 F). In these otherwise excellent seats one is however at the mercy of the director who may want too often to move the singers out of sight towards the rear of the stage.

There are three booking periods, and at the beginning of each trimester, always a Tuesday, tickets may be ordered for any performances announced for within that period. (The opening date of each trimester changes by a few days from one year to the next, depending on slight shifts in the performance schedule but is always the nearest Tuesday to the start-up of the new season. To simplify I use an educated guess in giving each beginning date.) For the first booking period: around 16 October for the fall, through the end of December; for the second trimester: 2 January for the winter, ending towards the last of March; for the third: 1 April through the end of the season. Telephone reservations (61-22-80-22) are taken on a different schedule from the regular Box Office hours: Monday through Saturday, 0900 to 1200 and 1400 to 1800. Full payment must be received six days before the date of the performance. When ordering by mail, one should wait for confirmation of the space requested (somewhat precarious when writing from abroad); again payment must be received no later than six days before the date of the performance. Tickets may either be sent to the person making the order (with a stamped, self-addressed envelope) or held at the Box Office. The mailing address is: Théâtre du Capitole, Service Location, Place du Capitole, 3100 Toulouse. Information about the schedule may be obtained by writing: Service Relations Publiques (the same mailing address as above) or by telephone: 61-23-21-35, Ext. 407 or 457; open daily, except Sunday, from 0900 to 1200 and 1400 to 1800.

On rare occasions operas are performed in the Halle aux Grains, a six-sided building which once served as a storage and market facility for corn and wheat. The arena-like structure has been cleverly converted into a very modern and up-to-date concert hall and is now the main auditorium used by the Orchestre National du Capitole de Toulouse. During its 1989–90 season the Théâtre du Capitole scheduled *Il Trovatore* for a sequence of five non-subscription performances in the Halle; tickets, broken down into three categories, cost more than those in the "home" theater (250 F, 185 F, and 110 F). Also the Symphony in its regular monthly concert series sometimes presents a single performance of an opera in concert-form. Poulenc's *Dialogues des Carmélites* figured in their schedule for 1989–90. The Halle aux Grains is about 6/10's of a mile (1 kilometer) to the southeast of the Place du Capitole. The easiest (but not most direct) route to follow is the Rue d'Alsace-Lorraine, south from behind the Capitole, then left at the Musée des Augustins on the Rue de Metz; cross the wide Boulevard Lazare Carnot, with the Monument aux Morts on your right, and the Halle is directly in front of you. Tickets for operas and other musical events in the Halle may be bought at the Box Office in the opera house.

Tourist Information is no longer available in the railroad station but is found very close to the opera house, in the small landscaped square behind it. The two bus lines from the station, #2 and #26, stop on the Rue d'Alsace-Lorraine, the street bordering this square. (Or from the more central Place du Capitole there is a wide passageway cutting through the middle doors of the 18th-century façade. This leads into an inner court surrounded by the Renaissance portion of the town hall. Continuing straight through and under another archway, the Tourist Office is in the *Donjon* across the small street at the back. The stage doors at the back of the theater will be on your right.) This office has a "summer" and "off-season" schedule: from 1 May to 30 September they are open daily from 0900 to 1900; between 1 October and 30 April from 0900 to 1800 but closed on Sundays and holidays. They will make hotel reservations free of charge. During the "summer" hours they also offer money-changing services daily and on weekends and holidays when banks are closed. The telephone number is: 61-23-32-00, and the mailing address is: Office de Tourisme de Toulouse, Donjon du Capitole, 31000 Toulouse; telex: 531-508.

Hotels in every possible price category are found opposite the main entrance to the station. A long row of them is visible just across the square and over the bridge covering the Canal du Midi. There are two much more expensive hotels on the Place du Capitole, one of which is directly across the street from the side of the opera house.

Money-changing services including weekends and holidays are available only during the "summer" hours of the Tourist Office in the Donjon du Capitole. A 24-hour service for *"le change"* is offered at one of the ticket counters in the railroad station. This is located in the *Départ* section of the station and will be the last ticket window on the far right (the position shifts up and down the line of windows during the day and night according to the amount of ticket-selling traffic). Cook's through Wagons-Lits, has three agents who represent them in Toulouse. There is no branch of American Express.

For public transportation a single bus ticket bought from the driver costs 5 F. A *carnet* or cluster of ten tickets may be bought in any tobacco shop or at a window (poorly marked) near the center of the arcade on the Place du Capitole, directly opposite the Capitole and the opera house. (This window is to the left of a "store" with many video games.)

GERMANY

The richness and diversity of opera in Germany is quite unbelievable. No other nation in the world comes close to matching Germany's generous support of its musical establishments. It is conceivable that on one given night, let us say a Thursday, some forty or even fifty theaters throughout the country will be presenting an opera, and, to take this mind-boggling idea one step further, no two houses will be performing the same work at the same time. This gives the visitor an extraordinary range of choices, and because the country is relatively small and its railway service fast, clean, and reliable, it would be possible to spend a month traveling back and forth seeing a different opera every night. The quality of the performances will of course not be on the same level, but nowhere else on this earth is the opera lover offered such an extravagant range of choices.

Attending an opera in Germany is in one respect quite unlike going to the theater in any other country: German audiences are utterly and completely quiet. They do not talk, they do not rustle or drop their programs, nor do they squirm and wiggle in their seats, even during the longest of Wagner performances. The only time in Germany I have ever been bothered by conversation blocking out the music was in Munich, and the rude noise-makers were two portly Englishmen, not Americans. Moreover, the seats in almost all the German opera houses are extremely comfortable, with ample legroom for those people with long limbs. In rebuilding their theaters after the war, when all but a handful were totally destroyed or left as shells, one of the first considerations of those in charge of reconstruction must have been the comfort of opera patrons. Almost everywhere the sight-lines are excellent, and because the theaters, by most American standards, are on the small side, the seating capacity is on average between 1000 and at most 1600. Some people contend that most of the post-war theaters in Germany look more like modern movie houses than temples to the lyric arts, but if one goes to the opera to hear and see what is taking place on stage, not to be stared at by other patrons, I think the German architects have succeeded admirably in designing the new buildings. My only quibble is sometimes with the lack of warmth to the sound, but there is certainly no problem with being able to see and hear well, even in those seats furthest removed from the stage.

Seating arrangements: The words the Germans use to describe the different seating areas in their theaters can be misleading to an American. And not all theaters use the same terms for the same parts of the house. Briefly, the orchestra section normally runs the entire width of the building, with no center or side aisles. One enters one's row, even for center seats, from the far side, right *(rechts)* or left *(links),* and it is customary to remain standing at one's seat until most of the row has been filled. In some theaters the seating area towards the front nearest the stage is made up of *Orchestersessel,* but others, such as Munich, use the term *Parkett* for all of the orchestra seats. Yet another term, *Sperrsitz,* is sometimes used (as in Dortmund and Hanover) to designate the seating area in the orchestra about mid-way back, but in Stuttgart the word is used to single out the choicest seats in the first rows of the first balcony or ring. *Parkett* is also sometimes used for those raised seats at the rear of the orchestra section. Next come the *Logen* or *Ränge* (the balconies), the *erste* (first), *zweite* (second), *dritte* (third), with the top-most level sometimes called the *Galerie.* (For Munich, instead of the term *Rang* or balcony, *Balkon* is the next level up, with prices there comparable and sometimes even higher than the best center seats in the *Parkett.*) For someone fresh from France arriving in Germany, the term *Rang* will be confusing because in French *rang* means "row." (The German word for "row" is *Reihe.*) And unlike some theaters in France you never tip the usher who points you in the direction of your seat.

Programs: These are never distributed free of charge and are only worth the price (ranging from 1,50 DM to 5 DM) if you read German, want a souvenir of your evening, and require background on the opera as well as the director's justification for his staging (the latter can be very tedious reading!). The cast and credits are usually listed on a single sheet of paper inserted into the program, hardly by itself something you need pay for. All of the information you might want about the evening's performance can be found on posters prominently displayed throughout the theater or at the least in the lobby.

Cloakroom *(Garderobe* or *Vestiaire):* With splendid German thoroughness and efficiency this service is convenient, prompt, and courteous. A numbered hook or space is allotted to every seat in the house. Although in the USA many of us carry our coats with us into the theater, in Germany this is rarely done, and with German weather generally on the wet side, this means the added burden of umbrellas, which are not allowed to be taken inside. Follow the example of the natives and use this service. In many cases your ticket number on the level and side of the theater on which you are seated serves as your check-stub for coats and other articles left at the cloakroom. Sometimes a minimal charge of 0,50 or 1,00 DM is made (a sign usually tells you), but in many theaters checking is free. In other theaters each ticket-holder finds a locker on the ground level (near where you enter), you insert one or two DM coins, and you keep the key.

Food and drink: Germans love to eat and drink during intermissions, and the bar/buffet services are very busy between the acts. There are salad plates, open-faced sandwiches, pastries, fruit concoctions, all at very reasonable prices. There is also a wide choice of beverages, ranging from coffee and Cokes to beer and champagne. Watching so many people eating and drinking, and noting how much they enjoy themselves in the process, I often wonder how some of the opera-goers manage to stay awake and alert when they return to their seats. But many of them are back after the next break in the performance to eat and drink all over again. Tipping is not expected, as the service charges are included in the prices.

A few useful terms are given here which may facilitate your buying a ticket if you are not fluent in German:

Karte is the word for ticket

Kasse is the box office (*Kassa* in Austria)

Tageskasse is the ticket window for regular ticket sales

Vorverkauf is advanced sales

Abendkasse is the box office opening one hour (generally) before the performance begins, restricted to sales for that opera

Erfrischungsraum is where drinks, sandwiches, and other food items are sold. Smoking is permitted, but not usually in rooms with carpeted floors.

AACHEN (French name: Aix-la-Chapelle) is a charming city of moderate size, an important center for technical studies and research, just over the Belgian border. Since Roman times Aachen has been admired for its thermal springs, and its history is rich with the legacy of Charlemagne who made the city the capital of his empire. Aachen is graced with handsome parks and numerous, sometimes whimsical fountains. Lovingly rebuilt after the devastation of the last war the city has yet to be discovered by American tourists.

The opera house, known as the **Stadttheater** (plays and ballets during certain intervals also share the stage), is a short ten minute walk from the station, directly in one's path if one is headed toward the center of the old city. This is the place where Karajan began his career in the beginning years of World War II. The theater is small and intimate, and when it was rebuilt after the war the two balconies were redesigned so as to provide an unobstructed view of the stage. Even in the last row of seats in the second balcony one is still very close to the proscenium. These very good seats, it should be noted, are priced at only DM 12.

The repertory of this ensemble company is quite varied: among the seven or so works presented every season there will be at least one "contemporary" opera (Britten, Henze, Stravinsky in recent seasons), several Italian works, perhaps at least one Mozart title, often a single Strauss opera, and another German stand-by, as well as an operetta or musical comedy. If one times one's stay in Aachen very carefully it is possible to see two or perhaps three different works on two or three successive nights. Be cautioned however about those occasions when the stage is used for plays. The season opens in September and extends into June.

The Box Office is open Mondays through Saturdays from 1100 to 1300 and from 1700 to 1900; closed on Sundays. Telephone reservations, six days in advance of the performance, at 2-20-06 are accepted between 1130 and 1300, 1400 to 1600, and 1730 to 1900; on Saturdays no calls are taken between 1400 and 1600. The telephone number to use for ticket reservations or information is (0241) 2-20-06. Prices range from DM 34 for the most expensive seats to DM 10 for the back rows on the sides, upstairs. There are no performances on Sunday nights.

Tourist information is available directly across the street from the station, at the corner at an angle to the left, Bahnhofplatz 4. Their hours are Mondays through Fridays 0800 to 1800; on Saturdays from 0830 to 1200 noon. Closed on Sundays.

A number of small, good hotels, all in the moderate price range, are clustered right across the street from the station. With the opera house a brief walk away there is little reason to seek out a hotel in another part of the city.

Money can be changed inside the station at the following times: Monday through Saturday: 0800 to 2000; Sundays and holidays: 0900 to 1300. Neither American Express nor Cook's maintains an office in Aachen.

BERLIN (WEST) is a fascinating city: vigorous, restless, innovative, and at times very vulgar. Living now less "on the edge," as was true just a few years ago when East-West tensions were extreme, it is a city where the

arts are thriving while it still searches for its soul. Berlin was never beautiful, most of it built during the apogee of the Industrial Revolution (older Germans tell me it was the ugliest capital on the Continent), but the "new" city that has sprung up from the ruins shows in some places an architectural boldness that reflects its lively and youthful spirit.

East Berlin contains most of what was before the war the heart of the old city, and the DDR government in recent years has gone to great lengths to restore some sections of Unter den Linden to what they looked like before being reduced to rubble. For me only two buildings stand out as gems: the lovely Staatsoper and the nearby Schauspielhaus, the latter a sumptuously decorated hall now used mostly for concerts. Elsewhere in both West and East Berlin, when the Prussian kings and later Emperors tried to build monuments to themselves in the "French" style, something always went wrong with the proportions: a dome is either too high and narrow or too squat, or a portico has too many columns or the columns are too tall or too thin.

An excellent and succinct account of Berlin's operatic history was put together by James Helme Sutcliffe on the occasion of the city's celebration of its 750th birthday. I highly recommend this two-part article to anyone curious to learn more about Berlin's important rôle in the evolution of operatic production in Germany, especially during the time when the Kroll Oper was flourishing in the 1920's and, more recently, when Walter Felsenstein was directing the Komische Oper. These two articles appeared in *Opera News* under the title "Birthdays in Berlin": Part I in the 14 Feb. 1987 issue (pp. 32–35) and Part II in the 28 March 1987 issue (pp. 32–35 and p. 45). Mr. Sutcliffe writes frequently for *Opera News* and the British monthly *Opera* (and other periodicals as well) with incisive reviews of new productions both in Berlin and elsewhere in Germany.

THE DEUTSCHE OPER BERLIN on Bismarckstrasse is by common consent ranked beside Munich and Hamburg for the quality and size of its productions. It occupies the site of the 1912 theater, the "Charlottenburger Oper" destroyed in World War II, that was closely linked with the careers of artists such as Bruno Walter, Lotte Lehmann, Wilhelm Furtwängler, and many others of similar fame. It is a large house by German standards, seating just under 2000 (1970 to be exact), and its modified rectangular shape, wide at the stage and narrowing towards the rear, much like Hamburg, means that from most positions in the theater the sight-lines are excellent. There are two large balconies at the back and on the sides two levels of squared-off boxes, angled in such a way as to have all of the seats directly facing the stage. Acoustically all of the "upstairs" seats are superb, but in a few spots in the large orchestra section I am told that there are some problems with the sound. It is a handsome, elegant theater with several levels of large and attractive public rooms. In comparing Berlin with Hamburg, Berlin seems much more spacious and the sound brighter, but some of that is due to the fact that unlike Hamburg the architects of the new house had a much larger site on which to build.

The Deutsche Oper Berlin is quite easy to get to because it is served by one of the city's main subway lines with a station just a few feet from its front doors. Unlike Karajan's Philharmonie complex off to the east which nudges against the Berlin Wall, the rebuilt opera lies closer to the geographic center of West Berlin on the city's wide main east-west axis, this segment of which is called Bismarckstrasse. From the Zoo Bahnhof and subway your train will take you first to Ernst-Reuter-Platz, and then the second stop will be Deutsche Oper. A single one-way fare costs DM 1,70; a ticket valid for two hours, allowing you to go (for buying your tickets) and return, costs DM 2,70. You will want the U-1 line, direction Ruhleben, from the Zoo station; for returning, direction Schlesisches Tor. On foot, a distance of a long mile or approximately 1 ³⁄₅ kilometers, you will follow above-ground the route of the subway: from the Zoo Station up Hardenberg-Strasse and then to the left, at Ernst-Reuter-Platz, four long blocks on Bismarckstrasse to the theater. Allow at least 45 minutes because of the traffic at intersections.

Berlin's repertory is now enormous, probably almost on a par with Vienna, with some 50 operas presented in the course of a single season. There seem to be no marked gaps in the variety of what is offered outside the German staples, and the company prides itself on the large number of contemporary and newly-commissioned works kept before the public. Its roster of well-known singers is also quite large, with many names familiar to audiences attending the big houses in the USA. Since the war Berlin (like Hamburg) has fostered as well the careers of many Americans who have later gone on to international fame, and the company still follows this practice today. With but very few exceptions all operas are performed in the languages in which they were written. A notable deviation from this policy was a recent and very brilliant *Die Hugenotten,* sung in German, because in their updated version of the 16th century Protestant-Catholic dispute the producers wanted to draw a parallel with the rivalry between East and West; the final scene depicting the massacre of St. Bartholomew takes place beside a barrier modelled on the notorious Berlin Wall.

The season in Berlin begins in late August and continues into early July. With a few ballets, occasional concerts, and solo recitals sometimes sharing the stage with lyric works, the theater rarely closes its doors during the entire season. On an average between four and five different operas will be offered within a single week. There seems to be no consistent pattern as to the few (and rare) nights when the theater is dark, but most of these appear to occur only in December. During many other months something is scheduled for every single evening.

The Box Office is open, Monday through Friday, from 1400 to 2000; on Saturdays and Sundays, from 1000 to 1400. Ticket sales begin on Sunday for performances scheduled over the next ten days. Information about tickets can be obtained by calling: (030) 3-41-02-40; ticket orders may be made by calling: (030) 34-38-1 during Box Office hours (but not on Sundays and holidays). The mailing address is: Kartenbüro der Deutschen Oper Berlin, Richard-Wagner-Strasse 10,1000 Berlin 10. The Box Office is open one hour before each evening's performance for last-minute sales. The ticket price-scale most often in effect begins at DM 12 and goes up to DM 91; some events, such as recitals, begin at DM 10 with the top prices around DM 40; galas and operas with very special casts will command a much higher price range, beginning at DM 16 and going up to DM 125.

Tourist information is available inside the Zoo Station (because of building renovations the inside door is closed and you must go out to the street to find the entrance); they can be very helpful in finding room accommodations. Their hours, 7 days a week, are from 0800 to 2300.

Hotels and pensions in all categories are located both in the area surrounding the Zoo Station and, over a mile away, in the neighborhood of the Deutsche Oper, but few of these, except the luxury hotels, are very evident or visible when you are on the main thoroughfares (maybe encumbered with baggage) in either part of the city. Unless you know already of a hotel suitable to your budget, it is best to use the Tourist Office in finding a place to stay.

Money can be changed at the Zoo Station. The yellow signs will direct you back out to the street (once more, construction work has moved the bank to a temporary location), but the office is still under the Zoo Station roof. Their hours are: Monday through Saturday, 0800 to 2100; Sundays and holidays, 1000 to 1800. Both American Express and Cook's have offices in Berlin.

West Berlin's **THEATER DES WESTENS** since the mid-1980's has been managed by the same administration that controls the Deutsche Oper. On Kant-Strasse, one block and a half due west from the Zoo Station, this theater now serves as one of Berlin's stages for extended runs of musicals and operettas. Touring companies calling this their "home" have been taking musical comedies "on the road" to other parts of West Germany and to other cities in Europe. On occasion smaller operatic productions with simplified sets move from the large theater on Bismarckstrasse to the stage of the

Theater des Westens; Mozart's *Così fan tutte* was moved there in the spring of 1989.

The Theater des Westens survived the war bombardments without too much damage and briefly functioned after 1945 as the city's only opera house. A gaudy relic of the late 19th century, the theater in many ways resembles Munich's Theater am Gärntnerplatz, Munich's own equivalent of Vienna's Volksoper or (in some respects) Paris' Opéra-Comique. In its very old-fashioned way the theater is quite attractive, squeezing some 1250 seats into a small horseshoe on three levels. There is no problem with the acoustics, and only a few seats on the sides nearest the stage have poor sight-lines.

The Box Office for the Theater des Westens is across Kant-Strasse in a small pavilion, directly opposite the theater. Their hours are: Mondays through Saturdays, 1000 to 1800, and on Sundays from 1500 to 1800. The Abendkasse, opening one hour before an evening's performance, moves back into the theater itself. The telephone numbers are: (0 30) 312-10-22 and 312-50-15. Prices by Broadway-standards are quite reasonable: a low of DM 12,20 to a high of DM 59,20.

While in West Berlin you will undoubtedly want to hear the Berlin Philharmonic Orchestra perform in its "home," the **Philharmonie**. Unless the orchestra is on tour their season parallels that of the Deutsche Oper Berlin, with between 10 and 12 concerts every month. The strikingly modern hall is not easy to get to by subway; getting on at the Zoo Station and taking the U-1 line, direction Schlesisches Tor, the nearest stop is at Kurfürsten-strasse (not K'damm!), about one kilometer south from Matthäikirchstrasse. Slower but better is the #29 bus which goes up and down Kurfürstendamm; in the neighborhood of the Philharmonie get off on Potsdamer-Strasse. The bus at this point straddles the canal, eastward on the south, back to the Zoo area on the north. The Box Office at the Philharmonie is open Monday through Friday from 1530 to 1800; on Saturday, Sunday, and holidays from 1100 to 1400. Their telephone number is 2-54-88-0. Advance ticket selling times vary, but two weeks on average is in effect for most concerts.

BERLIN (EAST) was the capital of East Germany (the DDR or Deutsche Demokratische Republik), and in recent years with vast rebuilding programs it had begun to look more and more like a flourishing capital city. For the opera lover, visits to the Deutsche Staatsoper on Unter den Linden and the Komische Oper on Behren-Strasse (one block over, paralleling Unter den Linden) are mandatory, but with more people now crossing over into the eastern part of the city, tickets to both theaters are in great demand.

Even though the Berlin Wall has been breached, this still does not mean (as of May 1990) that people, especially non-Germans, are free to come and go as they please. Strict rules governing travel into the Eastern Zone may probably remain in effect until the two Germanies are completely reunited. For whatever restrictions are in force, you are advised to consult your travel agent, the West German Embassy in Washington, D. C., or travel bureaux in West Berlin.

Before the recent changes in East-West relations it was very difficult in West Berlin (and in Western Europe as well) to find out anything about the opera houses in the Eastern Sector of the city. Just to learn if tickets were available and if there had been schedule changes usually required a long and tedious trip across the border. The West Berlin papers gave no current news about theaters on the other side of the Wall. Only the *Berlin Programm Magazin,* a monthly guide selling for DM 2,50 and readily available on newsstands, provided some sketchy information about schedules, but you were never quite sure of their accuracy. Now things are quite different, and some of the newspapers in West Berlin regularly print all of the details you will need about schedules, casts, and curtain-times. (*Das Opernglas,* which for so long omitted Staatsoper schedules from their calendar, in the winter of 1990 began to publish them.) Also, when you now ask in a West Berlin booking agency about tickets in the East, you're no longer greeted by a blank stare or a look of impatient anger. They are only too happy to sell you tickets, should any be available.

The most convenient way to reach East Berlin's two opera houses is by the S-3 elevated railway trains that leave frequently from the Zoo Station. Get off the train at the Friedrichstrasse Station where if border restrictions are still in effect you go through passport/visa control; then continue south on Friedrichstrasse to Unter den Linden. Three blocks off to your left from the corner you will see the portico of the Staatsoper. For the Komische Oper, cross Unter den Linden (still on Friedrichstrasse) and go one block further to Behren-Strasse and turn right; the Komische Oper will be on the next corner on your right.

THE STAATSOPER is a beautifully proportioned building, both inside and out. Designed by the architect Knobelsdorff and inaugurated late in 1742, it was one of the first structures to go up on Unter den Linden in keeping with Frederick the Great's wish to redesign his capital in a more noble, neo-classical style. The theater burned in 1843 and was quickly rebuilt, but the bombings in the Second World War reduced it to rubble. After the War the East German government undertook the reconstruction using the original plans, and the building reopened in the mid-1950's; it was closed for a full year in the mid-1980's for renovations mainly of the stage equipment.

Since the resumption of performances beginning with the 1986 season, the interior of the theater still sparkles, as though the painters and upholsterers had finished their work much more recently.

The auditorium is semi-circular in shape, with a seating capacity of around 1400, but from almost any vantage-point the theater appears to be much smaller. The Orchestra (called the *Parkett*) holds about 600 people in 17 rows averaging some 35 seats across (the 18th row is short and split into two parts). In what marks a radical departure from Knobelsdorff's original plans, the three rings of balconies and their open rows of seating are broken only by aisles, not partitions. The rings are also quite shallow and steeply raked: five rows deep in the First Balcony *(I. Rang)*, seating approximately 290, and only four rows deep in each of the higher balconies *(II.* and *III. Rang)*, seating in each approximately 265. In the center of the First Balcony is what used to be the Royal Box, now the *Mittelloge,* where if your memory of old photographs is good, you should be able to conjure up Hitler seated with his entourage. The acoustics are excellent, but there are sightline problems with many of the rear seats on the sides nearest the stage.

The repertory of the Staatsoper is quite large, usually averaging around 40 or more different works each season, with strong emphasis on the standard German staples, from Handel and Gluck to Wagner and Strauss. A few contemporary operas figure in the repertory, as well as commissions and first performances of works by East German composers. Except for *Tosca* and *Aïda* and some but not all of Mozart's Italian-language works, everything is done in German translation. (Bizet, Offenbach, and Verdi do sound very odd when sung in German, but this an old tradition in this house.) When *Così fan tutte* in 1987–88 was presented in the Apollo-Saal, the large and sumptuously designed hall extending across the front of the building upstairs, it was given as a chamber opera and in Italian; in an alternate and new production in the main auditorium two years later it was sung again in German. At least for some works the matter of translation is somewhat flexible. The season opens in September and ends in early July.

A few of the singers under contract to the Staatsoper appear with some regularity in German rôles at the Met and elsewhere in the USA; others have so far confined their guest appearances to other stages within Eastern Europe. All three of East Germany's major houses: Berlin's Staatsoper and Komische Oper and Dresden's Semper Opera frequently draw on each others' roster of singers in scheduling their performances. (Most of the "exchanges" are arranged between the Staatsoper and Dresden.) Unless one has attended many performances in Berlin or listened to a good number of broadcast tapes, the majority of the singers cast in leading rôles will not be familiar names. This in no way reflects on the quality of what one will hear and see: this is a superb repertory company where every stage gesture has been honed to perfection. And the productions, in spite of the intimate "feel" of the house, are often quite big and lavish. A ballet company shares the stage with the opera, but outside of holiday time, when the big Tschaikovsky works are presented, the ballet evenings are limited to one or at most two per week. On very rare occasions there are recitals. There is no regular pattern as to the two to four nights each month when the theater is dark, but at least one or two of the days will be a Monday. Sometimes when no opera is scheduled, a chamber music concert is given in the handsome Apollo-Saal on the second floor, on the same level as the First Balcony seats; this large room, restored to its baroque-neo-classical splendor, is frequently used for concerts and occasionally for opera with scaled-down forces.

The Box Office, found inside the front lobby to your left, is open from Monday through Saturday, 1200 to 1800; on Sundays and holidays, from 1600 to 1800. An Abendkasse opens one hour before curtain-time. The telephone number for the Box Office in effect in May of 1990 (but perhaps to change with reunification of the two Berlins) is: (from West Berlin) (0372) or from other points in West Germany (00372) 2-07-13-62, between 1200 and 1800, Tuesday through Saturday. With monetary unity now in force in the East and West, prices have gone up and are comparable to what one pays in West Berlin. The prices that one used to pay for tickets, before the Wall came down, were truly astonishing . . . and good cause for some East Germans to wonder about the consequences of reunification: DDR marks 15,00 for the best seats in the house and DDR marks 3,00 for the least expensive. (West Germans in the 1980's, when their DM's could be exchanged for ten to twelve DDR marks in West Berlin banks, often smuggled East German currency across the border and treated themselves to extravagant meals and first-class opera. The official and legal exchange rate in the DDR was still one Eastern mark for one DM from the West.)

You need not worry about missing your train from Friedrichstrasse back to West Berlin: it takes about 20 minutes at most to walk from the Staatsoper to the station. Most of the operas begin around 1900 or 1930 or even earlier, and most of them end by 2200 or thereabouts; one notable exception from this past season was a *Marriage of Figaro* that ended at 2300, but this still leaves you time to catch a train well before midnight.

THE KOMISCHE OPER on Behren-Strasse occupies a theater made famous by the director Walter Felsenstein, who revolutionized operatic production by stressing the dramatic and theatrical elements in the scores he chose to perform. Though Felsenstein died in 1975, his many disciples and associates have kept his ideas alive through their work on the stages of many other opera houses all over Europe. It must have been exhilarating some years ago to witness a Felsenstein production when it was new. Let me quote from James Helme Sutcliffe: "Scores were restudied . . . doubtful traditions were expunged . . . with rehearsals lasting six months or more until singers, down to the last chorister, could visibly motivate every movement to create a feeling that the dramatic situation was unfolding for the first time." ("Birthdays in Berlin-II," *Opera News,* 28 March 1987, pp. 32–33). Since Felsenstein's time the repertory has shifted somewhat from mostly operettas and operas with spoken dialogue; now the company performs more works out of the Italian *verismo* period along with operas such as *Eugene Onegin* and Gluck's *Orpheus and Eurydice,* titles one might expect to see announced instead for the Staats- oper. They have continued their new Mozart cycle, which still generates much controversy. During the 1989–90 season, which began in September and ended in mid-July, seventeen different operas were scheduled for per- formance; of this number three were new productions. (These figures for 1989–90 are quite close to the average of what one can expect from one year to the next.) The only musical given to date by this company is *Fiddler on the Roof,* first presented in 1971 and last revived during the 1987–88 season when it again proved to be very popular. Everything is sung in German. Of all the singers currently on the roster I recognize the name of only one who is fairly well known and on her way towards gaining an international reputa- tion; a few others, whose names would not be very familiar outside of East Germany, are occasionally engaged as guests to perform specific rôles at the Staatsoper in Berlin and at the Semper Opera in Dresden. The demands of this highly disciplined repertory company, where so much time and energy are still required by long rehearsals, preclude the use of big-name stars who might appear for only a few performances and then vanish.

The stage is shared with the Komische Oper's ballet troupe which on average is scheduled for one or two performances each week. These dancers usually maintain in their active repertory five full-length ballets along with a small cluster of short works. Once a month throughout the year the pit orchestra is scheduled to present a concert from the stage; this series often features vocal soloists drawn from the company's roster or engages instrumen- tal soloists from outside. The Komische Oper's season begins in mid-Septem- ber and ends in June. The theater is closed two or three nights each month but on no particular or regular evening.

For first-time visitors the interior of the Komische Oper is a most wel- come and pleasant surprise. The unprepossessing, somewhat cold modern façade that one sees from the street gives no hint of what is hidden behind it: a very charming neo-baroque theater painstakingly restored to what it looked like (almost) when it was put up in 1892. (The site is also of some historical interest because it was once occupied by Berlin's first commercial theater; in the late 1700's plays by Goethe and Lessing were here given their first performances.) The new theater was constructed on Behren- Strasse first and somewhat incongruously bore the name Theater Unter den Linden because it was linked to other buildings being erected behind it facing on that other street. The architects were members of a Viennese firm that specialized in theater design, and the Austrian influence is quite apparent. (One of the partners credited with the design of the Berlin building, Ferdinand Fellner, was also the architect who conceived the plans a few years later for Wiesbaden's new opera house, inspired as well by Austrian baroque.) After several management shifts, in 1898 the theater was renamed the Metropol, which it retained until 1947 when it became the home of the Komische Oper. For some fifty years the Metropol, though remembered mainly for operettas and musical revues, offered other forms of entertainment as well: operas, dance programs, plays, and variety shows; for a brief period in 1917 the Max Reinhardt company presented Ibsen and Nestroy, and later, in the mid-1920's, Bruno Walter conducted a performance of *Don Pasquale*. Just a few weeks before the end of the War the building was badly damaged during a bombing raid, but enough of the structure survived to warrant a reconstruction. The Russian occupation authorities granted permission to rebuild, and the work was underway by early 1946. The gala reopening of the theater, now to be known as the Komische Oper, took place on 23 December 1947, with a Felsenstein-directed, rousing production of *Die Fledermaus*. The theater was again closed during the 1965–66 season when the interior and stage areas were renovated, and to replace the damaged portions of the building removed in 1946, the modern sections fronting on Behren-Strasse were added.

The auditorium is roughly semi-circular in shape, but the proscenium arch cuts off both lines of the circle before they reach what would be the diagonal. This gives a more gentle sweep at the back to the two Balconies and provides better sightlines, except on the far ends nearest the stage. (In some productions the stage directors and designers integrate the Balcony seats closest to the stage into their sets.) In spite of the intimate "feel" of the theater, it has a seating capacity of 1208. The Orchestra (the *Parkett*) seats 770 in twenty-one rows (the last four of which are under the overhang of the Balcony); towards the middle of this section, where it is widest, there are as many as forty-four seats in a single row. The First Balcony *(1. Rang),* in most places only three rows deep, seats only 178, fewer than the topmost tier because the seats have more space between them; when the partitions separating them into boxes were removed, the seats were arranged so as not to be blocked by the columns supporting the Second Balcony. The Second Balcony *(2. Rang),* seating 260, consists of four parallel rows circling the theater almost to the stage (where the rows shrink first from three, then to two). The seats on this level, except for those noted, are highly recommended. The acoustics in all parts of the theater are warm and bright, and especially kind to the speaking voice.

What gives the auditorium its unique appearance is the height of the ceiling supported by the wall circling the theater above and behind the

Second Balcony. Two more tiers of seating could have been fitted in above this level, but the dimensions were probably determined by what the architects wanted for the acoustics; they chose instead to leave this space open and to decorate it with a handsome series of alternating tall and short arches. Reliefs, caryatids, medallions, and the inevitable putti, all in the Austrian baroque style, surround the arches and then ornament the wall where it gently curves to form the painted ceiling.

The Box Office for the Komische Oper is opposite the main doors to the theater, directly across Behren-Strasse. (This location is new, dating from the beginning of the 1989–90 season.) The Box Office is not open daily but only between Tuesday and Saturday, from 1200 to 1800. An Abendkasse opens one hour before curtain time. The telephone number (as of May 1990) is: 2-29-25-55; to call from West Berlin you may still need to use the area code prefix (0372) and from other points in West Germany (00372). On the last Saturday of every month tickets are put on sale for all of the events scheduled from the 7th day of the following month through the 6th day of the next (or second following) month. Up until 1 July 1990, when East German currency was merged with the West German DM, ticket prices for the Komische Oper (on a scale matching the prices at the Staatsoper) had been absurdly cheap, if and when you could find the tickets legally.

An information office for the Komische Oper has been opened at 41 Unter den Linden, immediately behind the stage of the theater, two storefronts short of the intersection with Glinka-Strasse. Here you can find schedules and brochures describing the opera house. Posters and programs are also for sale. The office is open Monday through Saturday from 0900 to 1800. It does not sell tickets but sometimes can tell you in advance what tickets might still be available.

The very handsome **Schauspielhaus**, totally reconstructed since the war, now functions as East Berlin's most prestigious concert and recital hall. Here you can attend concerts by the excellent Staatskapelle Orchestra (the same group that performs almost nightly in the pit of the Staatsoper) and by a multitude of fine orchestras brought in from all over the world. You will find the Schauspielhaus three blocks south, behind the Staatsoper, on what is now called Platz der Akademie (formerly Gendarmenplatz). The Box Office is open from Monday through Saturday during the following times: 1300 to 1530 and 1600 to 1800; they are also open one hour before each evening's performance. The telephone number to call (from West Berlin) is: (0372) 2-27-21-29.

BONN, the capital of West Germany, has retained its small-town atmosphere and used to be much criticized for the provincial style of its musical offerings. There have been some very drastic changes recently, and with the arrival on the scene of Dennis Russell Davies, who earlier directed Stuttgart's opera and is now chief conductor of Bonn's Beethovenhalle Orchestra (the same group that performs at the opera), the city is often praised for the world-class excellence of its productions. With most of its operas sold out, tickets are not easy to come by, except at the last minute, a few minutes before the curtain goes up.

All of the center of Bonn, itself quite small, has been made into a pedestrian area. The Hauptbahnhof is at the edge of the heart of the city, and the opera house a pleasant walk of less than a half-mile away. Unfortunately only expensive hotels are in the immediate vicinity of both the train station and the opera house, so unless you are familiar with the city and know the location of your hotel, it is best to check your baggage at the station before hauling it over to the tourist information office and then going off to look for a hotel.

The **OPERBONN** occupies a very modern structure beautifully situated in a small park on the banks of the Rhine. A small house, holding approximately 900, all of the seats have excellent sight-lines. The acoustics are superb. This theater gives one the illusion of being in a much larger auditorium, but at the same time it retains a special and quite remarkable intimacy. My impressions of Bonn are very favorable because I have seen some superb productions in that city . . . and with tickets bought within minutes of the starting time.

The repertory in Bonn is wide-ranging, with an average of some 12 operas scheduled annually, together with 2 or 3 ballet evenings. World-famous singers are brought in for the leading roles in many of the productions, but from my experience Bonn appears to demand from its "guests" sufficient time for rehearsals. There is no consistent pattern of evenings when the theater is dark. There may be three or four nights consecutively, during any part of the week, when performances are scheduled; then, for the following one or two evenings, nothing is staged, not even a ballet. No musical comedies or light operettas are on the roster. For squeezing in as many opera nights as possible during your stay in Bonn you should carefully consult the schedule beforehand.

The season begins in September and continues through June.

The Box Office is not at the theater but across town, on Mulheimer Platz, quite near the station and close to the tourist information office. To find the Box Office follow the signs leading from the station to the tourist office, but instead of turning left and going into the arcade where that office is located, continue on, straight ahead, and after a few more steps you are in Mulheimer Platz. Their hours are as follows: Mondays through Fridays: 0900 to 1300 and 1400 to 1800; Saturdays from 0900 to 1200. This office is closed on Sundays and holidays. Tickets for other musical events may be purchased here as well. Telephone orders: (02-28) 77-36-66-7, are accepted between 1300 and 1530, Mondays through Fridays, for performances 14 days in advance.

At the theater the Box Office opens one hour before the performance. Be warned, however: for popular operas the lines form early in the afternoon. If you should arrive in Bonn on a Sunday or a holiday this is the only likely way you will be able to get a ticket. Your best bet in buying a ticket is watching out for someone who comes into the lobby wanting to sell an extra seat. Prices range from a low of DM 26 to a high of DM 60.

Tourist information can be found at 20 Münsterstrasse, directly across the street from the station, one block on Poststrasse and then to the left. (The entrance may be obscured by scaffolding for new construction, but if you look closely you can make out arrows in the "i" sign.) Their hours are: Mondays through Saturdays, 0800 to 2100; Sundays, from 0930 to 1230.

Only high-priced hotels are in the immediate vicinity of the station. Good and very moderately priced accommodations can be found throughout the city, situated within the pedestrian zones. In any case no lodgings within this area are more than a ten-minute walk from the opera. But be forewarned: if your stay in Bonn extends over a weekend or a holiday ask for a room that does not face on the street. Around midnight and long afterward, into the early morning hours, the streets of Bonn are very noisy with the crowds coming out of the bars.

Money can be changed in the station. Cook's has an office in the Bonn suburb of Bad Godesberg, just to the south of the main part of the city. There is no branch of American Express.

COLOGNE (in German: Köln) With over a million inhabitants Cologne possesses one of the most important opera companies on the Continent. But the city itself, like its massive, mostly nineteenth-century cathedral, lacks both warmth and charm. The drabness of most of the new buildings is accentuated by the maze of busy thruways, Los Angeles-style, slicing up its heart. There are some good museums to enjoy in Cologne, their treasures elegantly displayed, but it is not a place I enjoy visiting for itself, other than for its excellent opera.

THE COLOGNE OPERA is located almost at the geographic center of the old, walled city, a short ten-minute walk from both the Hauptbahnhof and the Dom. A severe, trapezoidal structure on the outside, the interior of the theater is marked by sweeping balcony sections that seem to unfurl and then stop dramatically as they descend towards the *Parkett* (the orchestra level). Though of moderate size, with some 1400 seats, the house has a feeling of great intimacy, and the acoustics are excellent, especially in the blending between the orchestra and the singers. There are no poor seats in the entire house, even at the back of the *Parkett* (orchestra), underneath the protruding balcony units. A perverse historical note: Cologne's "new" opera house occupies the site of the city's main synagogue, destroyed by Hitler's SS on the eve of World War II. Jacques Offenbach's father was at one time a cantor in this synagogue, and the small, austere park in front of the theater now is called Offenbachplatz.

Cologne's repertory is quite large and varied, with between twenty and twenty-five works figuring in the course of one season. For the most part the handsome productions follow traditional lines, eschewing some of the "far-out" interpretations one is likely to see in some of the other smaller German houses. Throughout the year there are special solo recitals by prominent singers, and from time to time ballets are offered. No musical comedies fill out the roster of performances, but on some evenings of the week, when new works are in rehearsal, the theater is dark. Note that on occasion matinées are scheduled. A look in advance at the schedule will let you avoid those infrequent times when the theater may be closed for one or even for several days in a row.

Many of the lead-singers, among whom are a number of Americans, have international reputations. The company "regulars" and those who are cast in the smaller roles should be familiar names to anyone who keeps up with newer recordings and broadcasts of operas "live" from throughout Germany. Cologne has often served in the past as a spring-board for singers and conductors making their first American appearances at the Met.

Usually the season opens in September and closes in June.

The Box Office is open, Mondays through Fridays, from 1100 to 1400 and from 1600 to 1800; on Saturdays only from 1100 to 1400. It is closed on Sundays. The telephone number is: (221) 21-25-81. For tickets at the last minute before an evening or matinée performance the Box Office opens one hour before curtain time. For certain very popular operas or when a well-known singer is scheduled to perform, if you do not have a ticket in advance, join the line that begins to form early in the afternoon. The telephone number to use for the Abendkasse is 221-8248. Tickets may be ordered by mail 14 days in advance, addressed to Bühnen der Stadt Köln, Postfach 180241, 5000 Köln 1. Telephone orders are honored for ticket requests 10 days in advance of the performance. Ticket prices start at DM 15 and go up to DM 88.

Tourist information is handily accessible in an office very close to the Hauptbahnhof, directly in front of the cathedral (Dom). The office is open daily from 0800 to 2230; on Sundays and holidays from 0900 to 2230. The hours for making hotel or room reservations are shorter, closing at 1600 Mondays through Thursdays, and at 1230 on Fridays.

A few small, moderately-priced hotels are tucked away in the side streets quite close to the train station. Most of these hotels are still only a quick ten-minute walk from the opera house. Closer to the opera and nearer the commercial center of the city one finds only much more expensive, luxury accommodations.

Money can be changed inside the Hauptbahnhof and until 1900 daily in an office around the corner from the Tourist Information Office. Both American Express and Cook's have offices in Cologne.

DORTMUND, like Cologne, is not an attractive city, but it can

boast of having an excellent resident opera company. Except for a very fine museum of contemporary art, there is little by day to see or do in the city, unless one happens to be a stalwart beer-drinker. Six large and famous breweries are headquartered in Dortmund, but the visitor is cautioned against over-indulgence if a night at the opera is to follow. Visits to the breweries may be arranged at the Verband Dortmunder Bierbrauer, Markt 1, found in the center of the "old" city. Within less than an hour's train ride from Dortmund are many interesting smaller towns, each of which is very worth a visit.

With respect to the train station, which lies at the northern edge of the old city, the opera house is directly south of it, on the opposite rim of the southern limit of the inner city. It is two quick stops away by Dortmund's efficient, new subway system; on foot it is about one kilometer south, right through the heart of the main downtown business district. The **Dortmund Oper** is striking both outside and inside. When you first see it, you might think you were looking at a smaller version of Eero Saarinen's TWA terminal at Kennedy in New York. A small bronze plate, just to the left of the main entrance to the theater, records the fact that until 1938 and its destruction by the Nazis a Jewish synagogue had occupied this site.

Inside the building one finds an extremely comfortable theater, clean in its design but generating an atmosphere of great warmth. Once again, as with most of the new opera houses in Germany, every seat has an unobstructed view of the stage. The acoustics are excellent, but the best seats, I believe, are to be found on one of the many small balcony levels (here called *Logen*). The house is of modest size, seating some 1160 persons. The repertory of the Dortmund opera is small but quite varied. (It should be noted that within less than an hour's train ride from the city some seven other opera companies are competing for patrons, but Dortmund too draws its share of this nearby audience.) A minimum of ten lyric works are presented in the course of a season, which begins in late September and ends in late June. Concerts by the Dortmund Philharmonic Orchestra also share the stage of the opera house, as do evenings of ballet and one or two operettas.

Dortmund is basically a repertory company, and a very fine one at that. Rarely are "name" singers brought in from the outside, so that one can be assured of the pleasure of watching a performance where every detail in the singing and staging has been carefully rehearsed over and over.

The Box Office is open only five days a week from 1100 to 1300 and from 1600 until 1800; it remains closed for advance sales on both Sundays and Mondays and on holidays. Tickets may be purchased 8 days before a scheduled performance, 9 or 10 days in advance for a Monday or Tuesday date. Three telephone lines are available for calling: (231) 54-22-24-44/or 45/or 46. One hour before curtain-time the Abendkasse is open. Ticket prices, even for the most expensive seats in the house, are quite low: they start at DM 10 and go up to only DM 40; for first-night performances the price scale advances only slightly, from DM 12 to DM 50.

Tourist information may be found in a glass-walled pavilion located directly across the wide street, up the terrace-like steps off to the right, in front of the Hauptbahnhof. Someone is in the office between 0900 and 1800 on Mondays through Fridays; on Saturdays between 0900 and 1300; closed on Sundays. There is also a small information office next to the city hall in the park, the Stadtgarten, where you would come out if you had taken the subway from the station to the stop across from the opera house. This office, at Südwall 6, is open on Mondays through Fridays from 0730 to 1600; closed on weekends.

Finding a reasonably-priced hotel near the opera house or close to the Hauptbahnhof is a problem in Dortmund. There are very few hotels near or even in the inner city, and all of them are either expensive or moderately so. If you do not already know the city, it is advisable to arrive at a time when the tourist office across from the station is open. Someone there can be very helpful in arranging your stay.

Money can be changed in the station. Neither American Express nor Cook's has an office in Dortmund.

DRESDEN used to be hailed as one of Germany's most beautiful cities, "the Florence of the north," the poet Herder called it, but today, except for the Semper Opera (home of the Dresden Staatsoper), the Zwinger (a courtyard surrounded by exquisite baroque pavilions), and an elusive art collection, the city has very little to offer. In an action similar to the German raid on Rotterdam in May of 1940, when a terrible fire storm swept through that city, Allied bombers in February of 1945 destroyed most of Dresden and, as in the Dutch city, incinerated thousands of civilians. Unlike Rotterdam, however, which quickly swept away the ruins to rebuild (and for the past few years has been replacing the first generation of post-war structures with more substantial, more attractive buildings), much of central Dresden, some forty-five years after the War, is still dotted with piles of rubble and forlorn, barren lots. Many parts of the Electors' Palace, directly across from the opera house, are still roofless and a jumble of broken walls. In areas where the East German authorities did remove the ruins, they replaced the once-animated streets with wide pedestrian malls (which lack for people) or pretentious boulevards (which have little traffic) and then lined these empty spaces with monotonous, lifeless buildings. The few things that have been carefully restored, like the Semper Opera, the Zwinger, and parts of the Hofkirche, on the outside have turned gray and dingy from pollution and now are badly in need of yet another restoration. Since the War the city's famed picture collection has been moved back and forth between the Semper Gallery of the Zwinger and temporary quarters in the Albertinum, where only part of the collection can be exhibited. Due to capriciously maintained hours at the Albertinum (the excuse being that there, too, remodeling is underway), success in seeing all of the art treasures is doubtful.

Dresden has an old and proud musical history. It claims to have been the birthplace of German opera when, for a prince's wedding, Heinrich Schütz composed his *Dafne* there in 1627. After Vienna and Munich, it was the third city in German-speaking territory to erect an opera house, in 1667. Then we come to the three composers whose names remain so closely associated with Dresden: Weber, Wagner, and Richard Strauss. In 1817 Weber was engaged as music director of the court opera and held that post until his death in London in 1826; his major works were all composed in Dresden, and though they were premièred in other cities, it was the productions of his operas by the Dresden company that established his reputation and secured the spread of his influence. Wagner was appointed Kapellmeister of the opera in 1843 but in 1849 was forced to flee after his participation in the Revolution of 1848. *Rienzi, Der fliegende Holländer,* and *Tannhäuser* all were given their first performances in Dresden, and while still living in the city Wagner composed most of the music for *Lohengrin* and made the first sketches for *Die Meistersinger*. In 1901 Richard Strauss began an almost forty-year-long (and mutually happy) association with Dresden, where some nine of his fifteen operas were given their premières. After *Feuersnot,* even though it was not a success, the Semper Opera remained the scene of Strauss' great early triumphs: *Salome* (1905), *Elektra* (1909), and *Der Rosenkavalier* (1911); *Daphne* in 1938 was the last of the composer's operas to receive its first performance in the city. The names of four conductors whose careers were linked to Dresden should be mentioned as well. Fritz Reiner, after the death of Ernst von Schuch, served as Kapellmeister between 1914 and 1921; Schuch's long relationship with the company had begun in 1872, and it was he who not only fostered the connection with Strauss but also did much in Germany to promote Verdi and Puccini. Fritz Busch, in 1922 succeeding Reiner, continued Dresden's affiliation with Strauss and increased the city's importance as a center for contemporary opera with premières of works by composers such as Busoni, Hindemith, Othmar Schoeck, and Krenek. When the Nazis came to power, a rowdy demonstration in 1933 during a Busch-led performance of *Rigoletto* made him decide to resign and seek asylum in England. Karl Böhm, who a few months earlier had made his first conducting appearance in Dresden, apparently had no problems in accommodating his political views with the Nazis; in 1934 he was asked to take on the position vacated by Busch, and he remained with the company until going to Vienna in 1943.

Since 1841 Dresden's opera, now officially called the **Dresdner Staatsoper** (or sometimes, with the adjective reversed, **Staatsoper Dresden**), has occupied a theater conceived by the architect Gottfried Semper. Sentimental feelings about the building itself are so intense—pride is a factor as well—the company now often calls itself and is called by others the **Semperoper**, without any reference to the city. The opera house one sees today is actually the third building based on Semper's designs. After its destruction in 1945, the theater lay in ruins for many years with only the exterior walls intact. Not until well into the 1970's was the decision made to rebuild. The restoration was slow and meticulous, conscientiously preserving the very "old-fashioned" look of the original building but unobtrusively (wherever possible) making the house more comfortable for seeing and hearing opera. When the theater reopened in 1985, a symbolic date was chosen for the ceremonies: the fortieth anniversary of the aerial bombardment of 13 February 1945.

Semper's first theater, completed in 1841, had burned to the ground in 1869. When the time came to choose an architect for a new building, both the opera managers and the patrons of the house insisted on hiring Semper, but as he, like Wagner, had participated in the abortive uprising of 1848 he was still subject to arrest and punishment if he returned to the city. The government adamantly refused to grant him a pardon, but a compromise was worked out by which the architect from exile would send his drawings to Dresden while his son Manfred (untainted by his father's liberalism) was allowed to be on hand to supervise the construction. The plans for the larger second theater, inaugurated in 1878, incorporated many changes from the designs of 1841, including more improved machinery for the stage, but both buildings were conceived in the same exuberant, eclectic spirit. Semper claimed that his first theater was inspired by Early Renaissance models, his second one by High Renaissance examples, but both structures, in spite of all the well-meaning claims about influences, remain very German, not Italian; in the reconstructed theater this is quite apparent in the smallest decorative details in the interior and, outside, by the structure's sheer massiveness. For the third Semper Opera the backstage area was greatly expanded, but these additions are skillfully concealed to look like parts of the original building; more space for offices, in an unashamedly modern wing, was appended to the rear, but this in no way harms the appearance of the theater viewed from the front or the sides.

In the auditorium the most important change that the post-war rebuilders permitted themselves was the removal of almost all of the seats that had poor sight-lines, reducing the seating capacity from 1600 to 1326. Boxes built around the edge of the Orchestra-level and seats along the far sides of each of the four Balconies were taken out; judging from photographs of the old house it also appears that more than two-thirds of the seats on the fourth and top-most level were not included in the restoration plans. The Orchestra seating area (the *Parkett*) consists of nineteen rows and is basically oval-shaped (with both long ends cut off); the rows are shorter both at the front near the pit and at the back, while those in the middle bulge out to more than forty seats across. There is no center aisle. The first three Balcony rings (the *Range*) are quite shallow, only two rows deep and tapering to a single row near the stage; the fourth and topmost Balcony has three rows of seats which, closer to the stage, shrink gradually, first to two rows and finally to one. The seating capacity of the Orchestra is approximately 750; in the first two Balconies, because the columns marking off the Royal Box occupy space that otherwise would be used for seats, the seating on each level is limited to around 125; higher up, again giving rough figures, the Third Balcony holds 166, and the Fourth Balcony 160. The new seats everywhere, I should add, are both wide and most comfortable. There is Standing Room (behind the last seats in the Fourth Balcony) for about 30 people; these tickets go on sale one hour before curtain time.

The repertory of the Dresden Staatsoper is fairly large, with around twenty-five different works presented each season. In comparison to other opera companies in Germany, in Dresden the German staples take up quite a large proportion of the repertory. Italian and Russian operas are not by any means neglected (those that were presented in the three seasons between 1986 and 1989 were frequently repeated), but the company is not especially adventurous in exploring nonstandard fare. Almost without exception everything is performed in German. Recently no French works have been staged (they rarely are), but, crossing another national boundary, occasionally a Benjamin Britten opera is included in the schedule. One or two other contemporary or near contemporary operas (Matthus and Berg in recent years) also make up part of each annual season. In any case, Dresden is where one goes for Mozart, Weber, Wagner, and Richard Strauss. Every year Weber is usually represented by at least one work, and since 1986 there have been annual productions of at least four different operas by Mozart, five by Wagner, and five by Strauss. The season begins in late August and ends on the last of June. On average each month, with ten to twelve different works offered, there are between fifteen and nineteen performances, but the schedule is too irregular to anticipate on which nights an opera is to be presented. Ballets and concerts are also given in the opera house, and on at least five nights scattered at random throughout every month the theater is closed. (I have had my own problems with Dresden: the unexpected cancellation of two performances, for which nothing else in the repertory could be substituted, caused the theater to close its doors and remain dark.)

Among the repertory singers under contract to the Dresden Staatsoper a very high proportion of them are natives of the city. I am unable to name a single one who is well known outside of East Germany, as most of their guest appearances are limited to either East Berlin or Leipzig. Apparently Dresden, like Vienna, inspires many of its young citizens to pursue careers in opera and as students they pass through the local conservatory, the Hochschule für Musik Carl Maria von Weber. The majority of the guest artists invited to assume specific major rôles with the company are under contract either to the Berlin Staatsoper or the Komische Oper, and in some cases those attached to the Staatsoper are known internationally. (Interestingly a number of the East German singers now associated with Berlin began their careers in Dresden.) Among the other nationalities represented as guests, other than Poles, Czechs, and Bulgarians, it is curious that there are more Americans (eight) than West Germans (four); apart from one singer from Norway no singers from other Western European nations, including England, are on the roster. Though Dresden may not have suffered artistically by being politically isolated, the reunification of Germany should bring about a welcome opportunity for more of the city's own singers to appear in other countries and to become better known.

The opera house, located on Theater-Platz near the banks of the Elbe River, is a long distance (just under a mile/1.7 kilometers) from the Hauptbahnhof and the conspicuous cluster of hotels lined up across from the station. For transportation the trolley lines that intersect near the station are of little help because none of them comes close to the theater. You will have to walk to the theater, and on foot from the hotel area, if you follow the pedestrian mall (Prager-Strasse) and continue in the same direction, it should take about 40 minutes. If you can recognize the lantern and onion-shaped finial on top of the tower of the Hofkirche, that should serve as your signpost. The Semper Opera is just off to the left of the church. (Do not confuse the stubbier, more massive tower of the Rathaus with the church belfrey; the Rathaus tower has clocks on its four faces and is topped by a gold statue. If you are still headed in the right direction this building should be to your right, about halfway to the theater.)

The Box Office is not in the opera house but in a small building, the Wache, across the square (the Theater-Platz) to your left as you face the front of the theater. It is not clearly marked on the outside. If you succeed in finding the building, once inside you will see that there are separate windows for each of the city's main theaters. The extremely limited days (only four out of seven), times (different each day), and rules (totally byzantine) for buying tickets when the Box Office is open should frighten away all but the most determined opera lovers: Monday from 1400 to 1800 (restricted to advance sales for the week beginning on the following Monday, with no tickets sold to performances during the "current" week); Tuesday from 1000 to 1200 and from 1300 to 1700; closed on Wednesday; Thursday from 1300 to 1700; Friday from 1300 to 1500; closed on both Saturday and Sunday. Take note of the fact that on Mondays tickets go on sale for all the performances scheduled for the following week; also on Mondays no other tickets, other than those for the following week, are to be sold. (They will tell you on Mondays what is still available and what you can buy for later that week when you return Tuesday morning.) A Box Office inside the opera house opens one hour before curtain time. There are provisions for ordering tickets by mail, beginning on the date when the newest monthly schedule is printed, but this requires paying by check and enclosing a stamped, self-addressed card; otherwise all ticket purchases must be paid in cash, no credit cards. (In May of 1990 the prices, like those in East Berlin, were quoted in East German marks and were absurdly cheap: between 3 M and 18 M, plus a 5 pfennig surcharge for a "Culture Fund"; with reunification these prices obviously are no longer valid.) The mailing address: Staatsoper Dresden, Postfach 8, Dresden 8012, DDR/Germany; the telephone number for calling the Box Office locally: 4-84-20. Tours of the Semper Opera house are offered a few mornings every week. Usually these begin at 1100 or 1130, and information about the schedule may be found at the Box Office in the Wache (when you can find it open!).

A large office for Tourist Information is located on Prager-Strasse, the wide, mall-like area that stretches out for well over a half-mile (1 kilometer) directly across the open square in front of the Hauptbahnhof. The tourist office is to the right, near the end of the first low building past the high-rise Newa Hotel. The hours are Monday through Saturday, from 0900 to 2000; Sundays and holidays, from 0900 to 1400. Maps and brochures are available, most of them not free.

East Germany is still quite ill-equipped to receive many tourists from the West. Even after reunification, it may be a long time before enough new

hotels are built, private restaurants go into business, and many other amenities are provided to attract tourists and guarantee their comfort. The rules
restricting travel into East Germany have been changing very quickly, but
while tourists from the West may soon be allowed to cross the border freely,
there are simply not yet enough places where they can sleep and eat. Dresden
has only six large hotels, all state-owned and operated, and the only restaurants that I know of in the city are in those same hotels.

For the benefit of those who might want to go to Dresden "on their
own," I give below instructions that proved successful (in part) in May of
1990. With the reunification of Germany many of the rules are likely to
change soon, but other travel conditions may take longer to show improvement.

In May of 1990 I went to the DDR Reisebüro on Alexanderplatz in East
Berlin to reserve hotel space in Dresden and was given a voucher, as was the
practice then, after paying for the room in West German DM's charged on
a credit card. I bought my round-trip, 2nd-class rail ticket at the Alexanderplatz station, paying for it in East German marks. Two days later, with my
hotel voucher in hand, I went through the East German border control at
the Friedrichstrasse station (downstairs), showed the hotel voucher and explained that I was going on through East Berlin to Dresden. The visa cost
15 DM for the trip into East Germany. (Had I wanted to stay longer after
arriving in Dresden, I could have paid for the extra days at the hotel, and the
hotel would then have arranged with the local police to extend the visa. As
I understand it, there would have been no additional fee for an extension.)
At Friedrichstrasse, after finishing with the police, I went back upstairs, now
on the "other" side of the border, to catch one of the Berlin transit-system
trains to the Lichtenberg station. This station, on the eastern edge of the city,
is where the trains to Dresden originate. (Earlier, when I bought my train
ticket, they gave me a small map of East Berlin's transit network and warned
me to be sure to choose one of the trains from Friedrichstrasse that does not
branch off on to another line before it reaches Lichtenberg. This segment of
the trip was made easier too by the fact that a few days earlier the East and
West Berlin systems had been consolidated: a ticket bought in the West was
now valid in the Eastern zone of the city.) The train ride to Dresden was
uneventful, though the cars were crowded because of a school holiday scheduled in East Germany, a holiday not on the calendar in the West. Finding
my hotel was easy enough because it could be only one of the four high-rises
visible from the station. The room they gave me on the sixth floor was fine,
but it was like turning back the clock to the 1950's: it resembled the hotel
rooms in the buildings the West Germans had hastily put up in their ruined
cities some forty years earlier. What was depressing outside was the dirt and
the pollution. This wasn't helped by the ugliness of the new buildings, the
rubble still present after forty-five years, and the joyless results of inept city

planners who had designed the new city as if they hated or feared people. Except at the opera house where everyone was very friendly and helpful, most of the "natives" on the streets or lined up waiting for service at cafés looked tired and glum. A substantial evening meal proved to be a problem because I had chosen to eat late, not early, and the restaurants in all of the hotels closed their kitchens at ten. Nowhere in the center of the city after that hour was it possible to find anything to eat, not even a box of crackers or a package of nuts from a vending machine. Such things simply do not exist in East Germany. After discovering that the opera performances I wanted to attend were cancelled, and angered by not being able to see some of Dresden's fine art collection (the rooms were "temporarily" closed), I had had quite enough of Dresden. I don't plan to return until the West Germans in their buyout of the East have cleaned up the air and the streets (maybe knocking down some of the new buildings in the process). And perhaps the West Germans also can put some life back into both the city and its people—not an enviable task.

DUISBURG, though a large and rich industrial city of the Ruhr,

appears more like a tranquil town of moderate size when one sees only that part of the city in the immediate vicinity of the Hauptbahnhof and the opera house. Elegant and carefully tended parks spread out in front of you when you leave the main entrance of the train station. A tram line, stopping at the far right corner of the station (to the right as you come out), will deliver you after one stop to the edge of the handsome park that surrounds the complex of public theaters and the concert hall. On foot the opera house is approximately a fifteen-minute walk from the Hauptbahnhof and the tourist information office, by the side of which runs the tram line.

Duisburg has the odd distinction of sharing with Düsseldorf the large and very prestigious **Deutsche Oper am Rhein,** a company that moves its productions (singers, sets, and all) back and forth between the two cities. Its opera house, reconstructed after the last war, is smaller (approximately 1050 seats) and more traditional in concept than Düsseldorf's modern building. It's a very pleasant, warm theater. With almost half of the seating located upstairs in two deep balconies, there are virtually no problems in having a full view of the stage; only the very few seats closest to the proscenium are to be avoided. And acoustically the sound is very good. Duisburg also offers fewer nights of opera than Düsseldorf. Its monthly calendar is filled out instead with plays and ballets, but by carefully studying the schedules of both cities one conceivably could go back and forth between the two and see six or seven different operas in as many nights. As with Düsseldorf the season begins in September and extends through the end of June.

For more details about the repertory and the singers of the Deutsche Oper am Rhein see the entry for DUSSELDORF that follows.

At Duisburg the Box Office is open Mondays through Fridays from 0900 to 1830; Saturdays from 0900 to 1300; Sundays and holidays from 1100 to 1300. One hour before curtain time the Box Office opens for last-minute sales. Prices are quite reasonable, starting at DM 8 and going only up to DM 35 for the most expensive seats. For the opening night of a new production prices are higher, ranging from a low of DM 12 to a high of DM 46. The telephone number is: (203) 39-041.

Tourist information may be found at an office outside of the Hauptbahnhof, off to the right and past the Ibis Hotel, which adjoins the station building. It is at the corner by the tram stop that goes by the opera house. They are open, Mondays through Fridays, from 0900 to 1830; on Saturdays from 0900 to 1400; closed on Sundays.

There are a number of hotels in the immediate vicinity of the station, but none of them could be called inexpensive. For accommodations at more moderate cost you are advised to consult the tourist information office.

Money can be changed at the station. Neither American Express nor Cook's has a branch office in Duisburg.

DÜSSELDORF, with over a half-million inhabitants, is still slightly smaller than either Duisburg and Dortmund, but as an important banking and administrative center it has the look and feel of a city two or three times the size of its "neighbors." Its site on the Rhine with the restored *Altstadt* and the clever integration of parks and neatly framed bodies of water into the core of the "new" city combine to give modern Düsseldorf a special character that is sadly lacking in many other rebuilt, post-Hitler German cities.

The opera house is more than one kilometer, almost a mile, from the Hauptbahnhof or at least thirty minutes on foot. A ticket costing DM 1,50 and a direct line of the city's brand-new subway (the U-Bahn) will take you in five minutes from the train station almost to the front of the theater on Heinrich-Heine-Allee (also the name of the station where you should get off the train). This is the third stop after you leave the station. (Older maps of the city will show several trolley lines that once linked the theater with the Hauptbahnhof; the tracks are being dismantled and will soon be gone.)

THE DEUTSCHE OPER AM RHEIN, which Düsseldorf (with 70%) shares with Duisburg (30%), is a large repertory company which many critics would rank as nearly equal to the best in all of Germany. Never afraid of novelty or bold experimentation, this superbly rehearsed ensemble has always managed to attract many fine singers, among them a good number of young Americans. Only a very few names on the artists' roster can be said to have "star-status," but that is one of this company's strong points: the stress that has been put on training all those on stage to interact with one another. The repertory of some forty works is extremely large and varied, with an unusually strong representation of both French and Italian works, along with a solid share of German staples. Also, to the Deutsche Oper's credit, contemporary opera is an important component in their repertory. Most of the works are performed in the languages in which they were written, but on occasion a director wanting to make a particular "point" with his audience will insist that the work be done in German translation. Interestingly there are two different orchestras that may on different nights be accompanying the singers. The better of the two is the Düsseldorfer Symphoniker which on some dates may be giving an all-orchestral concert in the Tonhalle; on those evenings the Duisburger Sinfoniker is brought in to replace them. Düsseldorf schedules an opera for almost every night of the week; the only exceptions are the very rare evenings of ballet. The season extends from September through June.

The theater, which seats just over 1350, is a kind of compromise between two styles, the old and the modern. There are three levels of balcony seating, but the balcony rings on the sides do not reach forward as far as the stage, and where they begin to curve towards the back of the theater they are only one or two rows deep—not suitable for those people suffering from acrophobia! Except for some of those seats nearest the proscenium the sight-lines throughout the theater are excellent. Acoustically the blend of sound is quite good "upstairs," but I am told that in some parts of the *Parkett* there are some odd distortions. Düsseldorf, like Dortmund and Hanover, uses the term *Orchestersessel* for those seats in the *Parkett* that are closest to the stage.

The Box Office is open Mondays through Fridays from 1100 to 1300 and from 1700 to 1830; on Saturdays, Sundays, and holidays, from 1100 to 1300. The price scale for tickets is the same as in Duisburg: DM 8 to DM 35, with a small boost for the opening nights of new productions, from DM 12 to DM 46. One hour before the evening's performance the Box Office is open for last-minute sales. The telephone numbers to use to call for tickets are: (02-11) 13-39-40 or 13-39-49. Reservations begin on Monday for all of the performances coming up during the following week. Written orders should be addressed to: Deutsche Oper am Rhein, 24 Heinrich-Heine-Allee, 4000 Düsseldorf 1.

Tourist information is available inside the Hauptbahnhof, but it is not clearly marked. Look for the stairway leading to *Gleis* (track) 13, towards the middle of the "tunnel" through the central portion of the station. Just to the right of those stairs there is an office *(Verkehrsverein)* that also serves as the place where you can obtain tickets for the new subway and maps of the city. Their hours are seven days a week, including holidays, from 0900 to 1230 and from 1300 to 1800. Just in front of this office is a small orange-colored separate "pavilion" where you can obtain information about hotels. Their hours are: Monday through Saturday, 1000 to 2200; Sundays and holidays, 1600 to 2200.

There a number of hotels in all price categories in the streets around the Hauptbahnhof. Also on Heinrich-Heine-Allee there are a few hotels almost directly across the street from the opera house.

Money can be changed inside the Hauptbahnhof from Monday through Saturday between 0800 and 2200, and on Sundays and holidays between 0900 and 1300. American Express has an office on Heinrich-Heine-Allee, only a few doors away from the opera house; the Cook's office is on the street called Am Wehrhahn.

ESSEN, in the heart of the industrial Ruhr Valley, is no longer the
grimy coal- and steel-producing center that it was before the War. The rebuilt city now has an air of spaciousness, with the few restored buildings that survived the Hitler-era blending handsomely with many well-conceived modern structures.

THE ESSEN OPERA. Essen does not possess a long-standing reputation for its patronage of the lyric arts. In part this could be because so many other smaller cities in the vicinity have syphoned off much of the audience that would support opera in Essen itself. But in September of 1988 the city proudly inaugurated with *Die Meistersinger von Nürnberg* its boldly contemporary new opera house, designed by the late Finnish architect Alvar Aalto. Until the unveiling of this new theater, almost thirty years after it was first proposed, Essen had had to be content with its much-too-small, old opera house. That structure, rebuilt after the war, seated only 607 people.

When the theater first opened, the German press was full of speculation as to whether or not Essen, with no long-standing opera tradition, would be able to find the money to justify the building and maintenance of a much larger theater. (The new theater seats 1125, almost double the space available before.) Was the city then willing, the critics and skeptics asked, to spend the necessary money to finance more operatic productions worthy of its new house? The opening season was quite ambitious: ten operas, including two operettas, and a goodly number of ballet evenings, but the question had been posed: would Essen in future years, after the "extravagance" of its inaugural season, commit itself to winning and to sustaining a solid reputation for its company? The directors of Essen's opera wanted to see the city gradually establish a repertory company. Apparently this has happened more quickly than first anticipated. From the opening season, when only one lyric work on the block-system was introduced each month, four different operas (on average) are now given within the same period. Usually this comes to a total of between eight and thirteen performances each month, greatly increasing the number offered in 1988–89. It is now sometimes possible in Essen to attend three different operas within four to five days. Also using the new theater are a repertory acting company and the very fine Essen Philharmonic.

While the old opera house was a pleasant eight-minute walk into the main part of the city from the front of the Hauptbahnhof, the new house is just a few steps further in the opposite direction, in the "newer" part of Essen, out the *back* entrance of the station going under the railroad tracks. The theater is about ten minutes away, one block down either Rellinghauserstrasse or Huyssenallee, where these streets intersect with the busy Kruppstrasse traffic circle behind the station. It is indeed a handsome structure and breathtakingly beautiful when you step inside. Both in the lobbies and the theater itself one is immediately aware of the painstaking attention to fine detail, but most striking is the contrast and interplay between the pure white of the sculpted three balconies and the deep indigo blue of the walls, the ceiling, and the upholstery on the seats. Most of the acoustical problems of the new theater have been solved: though the sounds from the orchestra reach all parts of the hall, there were problems when the singers moved about while they sang because in certain places from the stage their voices would suddenly become inaudible. The inaugural *Meistersinger* in a dreary production performed mostly on a large and bare stage put the acoustics to a very severe test; other and later productions with more scenery to "catch" the voices and project them better to the audience have avoided this acoustical problem.

Most of the seating is in the orchestra section, but it is steeply raked and the sight-lines are excellent. The two irregularly shaped balconies at the back (the third balcony houses the theater's technical equipment) are actually very shallow and have seats for only 335 people. Once again, even in the 28 seats hugging the side walls, care has been taken to assure excellent visibility of the stage. Essen has broken with a long-standing German tradition and has one long off-center aisle splitting the wide orchestra section into two parts.

The Box Office hours are quite different from those in effect at most other theaters: Tuesdays through Fridays, from 1500 to 1930; Saturdays, from 1000 to 1330; closed on Sundays and holidays. One hour before curtain-time the Box Office is open for last-minute sales. Prices for tickets have risen considerably since the move to the new theater, but they still remain quite reasonable: DM 15 to DM 50, but for premières, higher, from DM 18 to DM 60. The telephone number for the Box Office is: (02-01) 81-22-1-00. A different telephone is in service for ticket orders in advance of a performance, with four weeks allowed prior to the performance date; from Monday through Friday, between 0900 and 1500, call (02-01) 81-22-2-00. Orders by mail should be addressed to: Theater & Philharmonie Essen GmbH, Abonnementbüro, Ill. Hagen 2, 4300 Essen 1.

Tourist information, though available in the Hauptbahnhof, is not easy to find because it is badly marked. Instead of following the exit signs leading to the inner city or central-downtown area, go in the opposite direction, towards the back of the station, the same way as you would go to the new Aalto-Theater. The office is located outside, just to your right, down a few steps, at the corner by the wide underpass going under the train tracks above. They are open 0900 to 2000, Mondays through Fridays; Saturdays, from 1000 to 2000; and on Sundays, from 1000 to 1200.

A number of reasonably-priced hotels are in the immediate vicinity of both the Hauptbahnhof and the Aalto-Theater. According to what is available at the time, you can choose which area is more convenient for your needs.

Money can be changed inside the station on the main level, two flights down from the train platforms. The bank is to be found almost in the middle of this passageway on the side near the InterCity Restaurant, and their hours are as follows: Monday through Friday: 0730 to 1900; Saturday: 0730 to 1500; and on Sunday and holidays: 1000 to 1300. Neither American Express nor Cook's maintains an office in Essen.

FRANKFURT has become the rich, post-war banking and commercial center of West Germany, and its opera, until some recent set-backs, matched in its own way the brashly enterprising spirit of the city. Parts of the old city-center have been lovingly restored, and some interesting new construction has been skillfully blended in with what was saved or rebuilt in the rubble left after the war. Other parts of the city are not of much interest, but the first-time visitor to Frankfurt should not miss a concert in what is now called the **Alte Oper,** the shell of the building that before the war served as the main opera house. Very cleverly the architects saved and restored the exterior walls of the bombed-out theater and inside, after removing all traces of the former balconies and upper circles of loges, created a large, double-tiered orchestra hall. Along with regular appearances of the fine Frankfurt Radio Orchestra, concert performances of opera are now presented in the Alte Oper (see below for details).

THE FRANKFURT OPERA. In the fall of 1987 disaster struck the "new" house of the Frankfurt opera when someone, identified as an East German terrorist, fire-bombed the theater and forced a halt in the opera season. The company at the same time was adjusting to a major shake-up in its artistic direction with the departure the year before of its popular but controversial musical director, Michael Gielen. After a brief interruption performances were resumed but now in the smaller quarters that had been used exclusively by the resident theater company. This space adjoins the opera and fortunately was not damaged during the fire, but, being small, only certain, more intimate works can be fit into the structure. To fill out its repertory the Frankfurt opera regularly goes back to its pre-war quarters in the Alte Oper for performances of opera in concert. To compound its problems it was discovered soon after the fire that asbestos had been used extensively in constructing the building it was to occupy after the war. This has complicated the reconstruction schedule, meaning that more time and more money will be required before the company can move back into its home. The latest word is that not until 1992 will the work be finished.

The complex of buildings housing the Frankfurt opera is just beyond the end of Münchener Strasse, at Theaterplatz, approximately a half-mile (or ¾ of a kilometer) from the huge Hauptbahnhof. Münchener Strasse, lined with large and small hotels, is found directly in front when you leave the station on the right side (facing away from the train platforms). It is quicker (and safer) to cross the network of roads in front of the station by using the underground passageway. The theater is also the first stop on the U-4 subway line, and tram-line 11 traces the same path at street-level.

The present theater used by the opera was not built for that purpose, and though the voices on stage come through clearly, the sounds from the small orchestra pit have no "bloom," and some of the instruments either blare too loudly or are muffled. The conductor can do little to remedy this. The ceiling throughout is quite low, designed to favor the spoken voice and not the lyric theater. There are approximately 900 seats in 22 wide rows in a gradually-raked area that in an opera house would be called the orchestra or *Parkett*. One must admire this company for its pluck in coping so well with a very difficult situation.

Assuming that the opera will be rebuilt in much the same form it had before the fire, it contains seating for around 1400. It was quite unusual among post-war theaters because the architects retained the "horseshoe" shape for the three upper levels. All of those seats, except for the ones on the sides very close to the stage, had a good view of the stage. Perhaps it is useless to mention the acoustical properties of the hall because some drastic changes may occur during the reconstruction, but the sound one heard was extremely bright and clear, maybe for some ears even unduly harsh. Under Michael Gielen's direction it was a sound that corresponded very interestingly with the "style" of Frankfurt's stagings: revealing and clinical detail from the orchestra and the singers, opening up in the score things that one had not heard before in other performances.

Frankfurt's repertory, presenting on an average some twenty-five operas in a single season, places the company among the most ambitious and innovative on the Continent. They have also to a large extent taken over the reputation once held by the Hamburg opera under Rolf Liebermann in commissioning and staging new works. (Add to this the performances by the Frankfurt ballet, a lively company under William Forsythe's leadership, quite famous in its own right.) Many world-famous singers assume the leading roles, and a number of Americans, now known internationally after launching their careers in Frankfurt, still return regularly to the city. Be prepared however for some rather "far-out" productions: some of the stagings "work," but others, in my opinion, do not. If you do not like what is taking place on the stage, close your eyes and listen: you will hear none the less an exciting performance!

As of this writing it is uncertain just when Frankfurt will schedule the start and the end of their 1990–91 season. 1986–87 was the last time when they opened in September and closed at the end of June. In 1987–88 they scheduled their opening dates for October and ever since have continued the season into the middle of July. Again, because of the uncertainties surrounding the reconstruction of the theater, it is impossible to establish a pattern as to when the theater is dark. During the Gielen administration usually there were performances of opera and ballet throughout the week except on Tuesday evenings. The new management varied that pattern, and then the devastating fire changed things even more drastically.

Box Office hours from Monday through Friday are from 1000 to 1800; on Saturdays from 1000 to 1400. Tickets may also be bought at an office in the Hauptwache station of the U-Bahn where the hours are longer: Mondays through Fridays, from 0800 to 1830 and on Saturdays from 0800 until 1400; on the first Saturday of each month tickets will be sold until 1800. Telephone orders (25-62-334) as well as orders by mail will be accepted 20 days in advance of a performance in care of: Städtische Bühnen, Oper, Untermainanlage 11, 6000 Frankfurt 1. The Box Office also opens one hour before the start of the evening's performance. Prices range from a low of DM 12 to a high of DM 48 for the best seats in the house.

The **Alte Oper**, which serves as Frankfurt's main concert and recital hall, now has also become the second theater for performances of the opera, but opera in concert-form. The brochure listing the month's programs (for the Frankfurt Radio Symphony, visiting orchestras, solo recitals, and such) can usually be found (for free) in the lobby of the opera house, but tickets for events other than the opera will have to be bought at the Alte Oper itself. From the Hauptbahnhof the theater is a good distance, well over a kilometer, perhaps as much as a thirty-minute walk. There is a way of getting there by the U-Bahn, but it requires three separate trains or two transfers. By the S-Bahn you will have to get off at the Taunusanlage stop, still several hundred yards or meters from the Alte Oper, which should be visible at the end of the park. Their Box Office hours are as follows: Mondays through Fridays from 1000 to 1400 and 1600 to 1900; they are closed on other days but open one hour before the evening's event. Tickets may also be purchased at the ticket kiosk in the passageway of the Hauptwache U-Bahn station (see above).

Tourist information, along with hotel information and reservations, may be found in the Hauptbahnhof, opposite track *(Gleis)* 23, to the far left with your back to the train platforms. They are open every day of the year, Mondays through Saturdays, from November through March from 0800 to 2100, and from April through the end of October from 0800 until 2200; on Sundays and holidays (throughout the year) from 0930 to 2000. A second tourist information office, with no hotel reservation facilities, is located closer to the heart of the city in the underground passageway of the Hauptwache U-Bahn station. They keep shorter hours: Mondays through Fridays, 0900 to 1800, and on Saturdays, 0900 to 1400, but they could be useful if you are lost and need directions.

In the area surrounding the Hauptbahnhof there are many hotels in every conceivable price category. Because from this area it is only at most a fifteen-minute walk straight down Münchener Strasse to the opera house, there is little reason to seek out lodgings where they are much more expensive, in the center of the city or very close to the theater.

Money can be changed inside the station between 0630 and 2200. The bank is off to the far right, with your back to the trains and looking towards the front towards the many shops and food establishments at the "head" of the platform. It is also very close to the exit you will take to get to Münchener Strasse and the opera house, at the opposite end of the platform from the tourist office. Both American Express and Cook's have branch-offices in Frankfurt (Cook's actually has several).

HAMBURG is for me the handsomest city in all of Germany.
Though almost completely devastated by bombing, it has been beautifully rebuilt by exploiting to the utmost the open parks and bodies of water that break the city up into smaller, more intimate units. It is a pleasant city in which to walk about, and even on the notorious Reeperbahn, the center of the "red-light" district, one is reminded of the great diversity of Hamburg's maritime heritage and wealth.

THE HAMBURG OPERA. Hamburg's opera soon after the war gained great prominence for the excellence of its ensemble work. Under the spirited direction of its exceptional and gifted director, Rolf Liebermann, the company attracted many young singers who later became quite famous after having learned their "trade" in that city. Liebermann was in the vanguard as well in championing new operas and in mounting neglected works. With his recent retirement it remains to be seen what new direction Hamburg will take, but the Liebermann legacy at present still remains quite solid and strong.

The opera house is over a mile away from the Hauptbahnhof, an interesting walk if you have the time, but until you know the city better it is advisable to take the U-Bahn, line U-2 or the Red Line, and to get off at Gänsemarkt, the second stop beyond Jungfernstieg after leaving the train station. This line leaves from the north end of the Hauptbahnhof (near the tourist office and InterCity restaurant) and should not be confused with the U-1 line at the opposite, south end of the long station. If you happen to miss the signs pointing to the opera house, you may need to ask directions for Dammtorstrasse which comes off the north corner of the Gänsemarkt square. The opera house, not easily recognized until you are standing almost right in front of it, will be on your right at 28 Dammtorstrasse, about two hundred or so feet up the street. A single ticket on the U-Bahn costs DM 2; a *Tageskarte* or one-day ticket is a bargain at DM 6, and both may be bought from machines.

The Hamburg opera can hold approximately 1685 people, plus a small number of standees admitted to the topmost level of the series of rear, center balconies. There are four levels of seats hugging the side and rear walls, somewhat in the fashion of the older style of theater, but with the loge seats jutting out from the side walls (these spaces look a bit like tilted shoe-boxes!) the architects had the good sense to slant or angle them towards the stage. Only two to three seats in each of the 40 *Logen* on the sides are partially blocked by the partitions separating each loge, but they are marked as such when you buy them and are specially priced. Nearly half of the seats in the theater are on the upper levels: 520 in the boxes and 280 in the shallow balconies at the back, and here the acoustics are excellent. I am told that in the *Parkett* the sound is almost as good.

While the house-lights are still up, this is not an especially attractive or warm-feeling theater, perhaps because the side-walls of plain and unpainted wood give (to me at least) the impression of heaviness and of being somewhat cramped. But when the lights go out and the curtains part, one can appreciate the fact that the architects put function before looks: even from the rear-most seat in the top balcony the stage seems to have moved very close. And the sound, thanks in good measure to a fine orchestra, is superb. Very much like the atmosphere in the auditorium the public rooms in the Hamburg opera were designed more for function than for visual delight.

Looking over the casts of singers in Hamburg one could often imagine oneself at the Met but for the names of those playing the smaller rôles! More Italian opera is performed here (and sung in Italian) than in other city in Germany . . . and perhaps in Italy as well.

During the 1988–89 season Hamburg could boast of having some 40 operas in its active repertory, although for a gala evening, with "superstars" scheduled to perform, the opera might be heard only once. Also some of the works are given in concert-form at the nearby Musikhalle. Ballets are also presented but not on any regular basis, such as on one particular evening of the week. (The Hamburg ballet is famous in its own right, often featuring the work of its director and choreographer John Neumeier.) In general there are no performances on Mondays, but once again there are occasional exceptions to this pattern. Hamburg begins its season earlier than any other that I know of in Germany: after the middle of August, and they continue well into the month of July, often near the end of their season presenting operas by guest ensembles or in concert versions. All works are presented in the language in which they were written, and with some of the Czech and Russian operas Hamburg has pioneered in the use of supertitles.

The Box Office is to be found at 35 Grosse Theaterstrasse, across the street opposite the left side of the theater as you face it on Dammtorstrasse. They are unusually accommodating by keeping long, uninterrupted hours, and they even remain open on weekends and holidays, though for the latter the hours are much shorter. From Mondays through Fridays the schedule is from 1000 until 1830; on Saturdays, Sundays, and holidays, from 1000 until 1300. Telephone reservations (at (040) 35-15-55) are accepted after 1100. Advance sales begin 14 days before the performance, and mail orders should be addressed to: Tageskasse der Hamburgischen Staatsoper, Postfach 30-24-48, 2000 Hamburg 36. Orders from foreign visitors are especially welcomed; be sure that your request includes a blank check (in German marks) and a pre-stamped envelope. Hamburg like many other companies uses a graduated pricing scale with seven different categories, each depending to a large extent on what is being performed and by whom. Their gala prices constitute even an eighth category, with prices going up as high as DM 180, but for most opera performances one can count on the "C" scale of prices, which begin at DM 4 for standing room and go up (in this category) as high as DM 80. There are a large number of very good seats, selling at between DM 10 and DM 35, in the higher reaches of the theater, both at the back and on the sides. Credit cards are accepted for charges over DM 50.

The Abendkasse is also located on Grosse Theaterstrasse and not in the opera house itself. If you are waiting for a last-minute ticket do not be confused by the crowd of young students standing around who act as if they do not know how to wait in an orderly line. Many days earlier they put their names on a list for turned-in tickets, sold at a student discount, and their names will be called out one by one as tickets become available. A good system!

A cautionary note: before you haul your coat and umbrella up to the fourth level expecting to find a cloakroom there, go downstairs to the basement of the theater where all of the cloakrooms are located. You won't see them when you first come into the theater from the outside. In Hamburg you need only look for the sign that corresponds to the general area in which you will be sitting (3rd level=*dritte Rang* and left=*links,* and right=*rechts,* and so forth).

Tourist information for hotel reservations is available inside the Hauptbahnhof, off to the far left as you come out either of the main Kirchenallee exits. Hamburg's train station can be puzzling because of its immensity and odd floor-plan. It straddles the train platforms which are well below street-level, while only two passenger "bridges" cross over the tracks above and are not connected one to the other from inside the station. You have a choice of either going down long stairways to the train platforms and then up again by escalator, or you may go outside the station at street-level and come back inside by the other entrance. One side of the station paralleling the tracks faces the inner part or center of the city towards the Mönckebergstrasse exit and is made up of only blank tunnels and pedestrian passageways. The other side, on Kirchenallee, is away from the main downtown area: this is where you find tourist information, change money, and may very well discover a hotel to your liking. All of the essential station services: restaurants, a post office, and train information are located on the "back" or Kirchenallee side. The main tourist office in the station is across the corridor from the post office (marked in yellow) and is open seven days a week, including holidays, from 0700 to 2300. Another office in "Bieberhaus" on Hachmannplatz, further off to the left outside the Kirchenallee side of the station, serves principally the needs of business travelers. This office also keeps shorter hours: Mondays through Fridays from 0730 to 1800, and on Saturdays from 0800 to 1500; closed on Sundays and holidays. Two other tourist offices might be of some help if you find yourself stranded in other parts of the city: at dockside, St.-Pauli and Landungsbrücken, an office remains open daily, including all holidays, from 0900 until 1800; another office, just off Mönckebergstrasse in the center of the business district, on Gerhart-Hauptmann-Platz, is open Mondays through Fridays from 0900 until 1800, and on Saturdays from 0900 until 1400.

Hotels in all price categories abound in the area adjacent to the Kirchenallee side of the Hauptbahnhof, the same side where you find tourist information. In fact all of Kirchenallee (and the streets off and behind it) could be called "hotel row" because of the great number of establishments strung out along its entire length. Nearer the opera house (two or four stops away from the station by subway, depending on which line you take) there are a few moderately-priced hotels, as well as many of the city's most expensive ones, but late in the evening after the opera and on weekends and holidays you have little choice in restaurants. For that reason and for many other services available at all hours I prefer to stay in the vicinity of the station.

Money can be changed at two banks inside the Hauptbahnhof. The larger of the banks is near the tourist office, the InterCity restaurant, and the large room where one goes for train information, but it is hard to spot because it is on an upper level up a steep flight of stairs. They remain open seven days a week between 0730 and 2200. The other bank, much smaller, is on the ramp at the other end of the station where one finds all of the small shops selling everything from beer and pastries to souvenirs. Their hours are Mondays through Saturdays from 0730 to 1500 and 1545 to 2000; on Sundays from 1000 to 1300 and 1345 to 1800. Outside, at the intersection of Kirchenallee and Adenauerallee (streets), directly across from the station, a tiny exchange office is located on the corner. They remain open one hour later at night and are open for business 365 days a year; their rate of exchange has been marginally better than what one finds inside the station. Cook's maintains three offices in Hamburg, and American Express has one.

HANOVER (the German spelling: HANNOVER) was a great surprise to me: I had expected to find a drab commercial and manufacturing city bent solely on boosting the merits of its famous industrial fair (its *Messe*). Instead I found a lively "new" city with much adventurous urban planning, richly rewarding museums, and a flourishing opera company. There is much to see of interest within the city, especially the way in which the reconstructed "old" has been blended with the "new." And also there is much to see and enjoy just outside Hanover in the small towns that surround it.

The opera house is a quick five to ten minute walk from the station. Follow Luisenstrasse which runs by the side of the Tourist Office, slightly angled off to the left directly in front of the station. The **Niedersächsische Staatstheater** is an imposing structure, a gutted relic of the German Imperial style, but thoroughly rebuilt and modernized on the inside after being severely damaged in the last war. It is a spacious, comfortable theater, seating almost 1300, and all of the seats are good except for those few in the side balconies closest to the stage. The sound-quality is excellent, although some may find that the orchestra and voices come through with almost too much brightness. You should allow time to explore the many stairways, corridors, landings, and refreshment rooms scattered throughout the building. Everywhere you will find fascinating costume displays, mock-ups of old and new set designs, and photographs and memorabilia of former singers. Hanover in no way resembles a movie house! With its succession of grand staircases and finely proportioned public rooms—and a most comfortable hall for seeing and hearing opera—Hanover is a kind of unique monument in Germany to the nineteenth-century, heroic style of opera-house construction. Only Stuttgart and Wiesbaden evoke similar associations.

For the size and variety of its repertory Hanover ranks just after Munich and Hamburg. Some twenty-five different works are usually offered in the course of a season; this figure does not include five or more operettas and musicals. Evenings of ballet are also presented; these tend to be very traditional in concept. The choice of opera repertory retains a good balance and variety, with no single nationality too dominant, but some of the French and Italian works are sung in German translation. Among the specialties of Hanover in recent years have been Weber and the less-often-performed German romantic comic operas. Few of the singers are well-known outside Germany, which in part explains why Hanover lacks the prestige of Munich and Hamburg, but this in no way implies that they are not very good. A small group of young Americans is "based" in Hanover, and in recent years some of them have gained attention with sensational appearances in the United States.

The opera opens in Hanover in early September and closes in late June. Be careful with the performances scheduled for Sundays: check to be sure if they are or are not matinées. During most of the season something is scheduled in the opera house every night of the week, but one or two Monday nights each month the theater may be closed.

The Box Office is in the front lobby of the theater. To buy your tickets, when you are coming from the Hauptbahnhof, you will have to walk around the entire building, which faces away from the station. The weekday hours of the Box Office are from 1000 until 1300 and from 1500 until 1730; on Saturdays, from 1000 to 1300; and on Sundays from 1100 until 1300. The Abendkasse in the lobby is open one hour before the curtain goes up. Prices for tickets start at DM 12 and go up to DM 52. The Box Office telephone number is (511) 1-68-69-99; for the Abendkasse: (511) 1-68-61-40.

Tourist information may be found opposite the Hauptbahnhof, across the street on Ernst-August-Platz and slightly off to your left on the corner of Luisenstrasse, the street that will lead you to the back of the opera house, one block away. The hours are weekdays from 0830 to 1800; on Saturdays from 0830 until 1200. Should you arrive in Hanover after that office has closed, hotel and other information may be obtained from the City Air Terminal, located on the opposite, back side of the Hauptbahnhof. They remain open on week nights as well as on Saturdays until 2000. Both offices are closed on Sundays and holidays.

A good number of hotels surround the immediate area of the Hauptbahnhof, which also puts you within easy distance of the opera. Many of these hotels tend to be expensive, but persistence will reward you with accommodations that are quite good and very reasonably priced. Don't be put off by facades that are less than elegant!

Hanover offers a 24-hour transportation ticket for DM 6; this will allow you to visit readily all of the museums and gardens that lie at some distance from the city's center.

Money can be changed at the bank inside the Hauptbahnhof at the following hours: weekdays, from 0730 to 2100; Saturdays, from 0830 to 2000; and on Sundays, 1000 to 1230. Both American Express and Cook's have branches in Hanover.

KARLSRUHE, a city of almost 300,000 inhabitants, is virtually

new. Severely damaged in the last war, only the Palace *(Schloss)* and a few of the buildings around it were left as reminders of the "new" Karlsruhe that had been founded in 1715. Like Mannheim it was laid out in a geometric pattern, but instead of following rectangles the streets radiate like spokes from the park in front of the palace. For my taste the most interesting buildings in the city are those that have been constructed since the war, and at the top of the list I would put the Karlsruhe opera complex, the **Badisches Staatstheater**, an imposing structure that must in part have served as a model for Essen's new Aalto-Theater. Other than its opera and a fine museum housing a strong collection of German primitives *(Staatliche Kunsthalle)* the city offers little to the tourist, but using Karlsruhe as your base you are at the center of a very interesting part of Germany where there is the possibility of taking many short day-long trips to neighboring sights outside the city.

The Karlsruhe opera is another of those remarkable small ensemble companies that for lack of snob-appeal is usually bypassed by foreign visitors who think that opera in Germany is only found in Munich. Karlsruhe has led in the revival of Handel, each year since 1979 adding another Handel title to its repertory. Their productions of other works have been borrowed by the Paris Opera, Lyon, Toulouse, and in recent years a solid partnership has grown up between Karlsruhe and Strasbourg's Opéra du Rhin who now co-produce at least one work annually. Not many of the singers' names on the roster will be recognized, but this has little to do with their competence: most of them are young and just beginning their careers (including a number of Americans). Others working in Karlsruhe, the older "regulars," show the mastery of their craft the moment they appear on stage.

In recent years between 20 and 25 different operas have been scheduled; a few operettas and musicals have filled out the lyric portion of each season. Ballets and a few plays also use the stage of the *Grosses Haus,* and on occasion the opera will move some of its smaller productions to the more intimate *Kleines Haus.* There is no predicting on which nights an opera rather than a play (or rarely a ballet) will be presented, but in general one can expect to see three or four operas within the same week. The season begins in September and ends in middle July. Most works are performed in the languages in which they were composed.

As a theater building the Badisches Staatstheater dating from the late 1970's deserves special mention for its architectural boldness. (It combines two auditoriums, the large one seating 1002 and the smaller one 330.) Constructed out of reinforced concrete, the architects have allowed the walls to retain the uneven grain of the wooden boards that formed the moulds into which the cement was poured. More important, in the *Grosses Haus* the seating on the three different levels is totally asymmetrical, with first the *Balkon* projecting deeply into one side of the *Parkett;* then, behind a wider section of the *Parkett,* there is the third level, the *Rang,* which runs across only two-thirds of the back of the theater. The effect is very powerful and dramatic, anticipating to some degree what Alvar Aalto designed for Essen. Quite unlike Aalto's building, the outer lobby in Karlsruhe is quite drab, but once inside the auditorium and upstairs on the ramps I had the feeling that I was walking about on the inside of a very forceful piece of sculpture. Every seat in the house commands an excellent view of the stage. Good acoustics are assured by the use of much wood. And one last point: almost a decade before the completion of the new theater in Essen, Karlsruhe had already broken with the old German tradition of not dividing the seating in the orchestra section; there is an off-center aisle that makes access to the seats at the front of the *Parkett* much easier.

Box Office times are as follows: Monday through Friday from 1000 to 1300 and 1600 to 1830; Saturday from 1000 to 1400; closed on Sunday and holidays. The Abendkasse opens one hour before each performance. The telephone number for ticket orders is (07-21) 6-02-02. Tickets go on sale for the following week's performances on the preceding Saturday. The price scale for most tickets begins at DM 8,50 and goes up to DM 34; the very highest scale in effect runs from a low of DM 18,50 to DM 64 (for galas and other very special events), with four other pricing categories falling between the two extremes. Orders by mail should be addressed to: Badisches Staatstheater Karlsruhe, Baumeisterstrasse 11, Postfach 1449, 7500 Karlsruhe 1.

There are two trolley lines leading from the Hauptbahnhof to the opera house: Line 3, marked "Rintheim," and Line A, marked "Neureut." The trip by trolley takes less than ten minutes, and you will want to get off at the stop marked Ettlinger Tor/Staatstheater, the fourth stop after leaving the station.

You can clearly see the opera house off to your right. A *Tageskarte* or day-ticket costs DM 5 in Karlsruhe. On foot you can follow the same route taken by the trolley lines which use Ettlinger Strasse between the train station and the center of the city. Roughly, the opera house is a good long mile or 1 ⅗ kilometers from the station.

Tourist information (marked this time with an "i" on a black background) is not inside the station but outside, across the wide Bahnhofplatz directly in front. Take the escalator down just at the station entrance/exit and go straight through the tunnel, choosing either one of the last two escalators up on your right. The tourist office occupies a corner of the Hotel am Tiergarten and also serves as the public transit bureau for the city *(Verkehrs-verein)*. Their hours are Monday through Friday: 0800 to 1900; Saturday: 0800 to 1300; closed on Sundays and holidays. If you have need to call the tourist office their number is (0721) 35-53-0.

There are a few hotels in the immediate area of the Hauptbahnhof, but these are moderately expensive. Other hotels, in all price categories, are scattered throughout the city, and a number are located on side streets not too far from the opera house. To save time in finding these you will probably need the help of the tourist office.

Banking facilities may be found inside the station, just to the left before you go out the main doors. Their hours are as follows: Monday through Saturday: 0700 to 2000, and on Sundays and holidays: 0900 to 1300. There are no offices of either American Express or Cook's in Karlsruhe.

KREFELD

KREFELD, if its name is recognized at all outside Germany, is at least quite familiar to both textile manufacturers and those who closely follow interesting developments in the field of opera. Shortly after World War II Krefeld and its neighbor to the southwest, Mönchengladbach, joined to-gether to form a single opera, theater, and ballet company which moves its productions (including the orchestra) back and forth between these two small industrial cities. (This link-up served as a model for the later fusion of the companies of Düsseldorf and Duisburg, due east across the river, in forming the Deutsche Oper am Rhein.) Faithful readers of *Opera News, Opera,* and the German magazines see at least one or two reports annually about unusual revivals of either old or more contemporary works put on by this company. Otherwise the repertory is quite modest in number and until recently fairly conservative as to the choices: generally only eight or nine works, including operettas and sometimes musicals, make up the total of a season's fare. However the rarer works that draw the critics (either to Krefeld or Mönchengladbach) are usually awarded with high praise.

In describing the two cities, because they share the same forces, I shan't repeat with MÖNCHENGLADBACH what I write here about this company, whose official name is **Vereinigte Städtische Bühnen Krefeld und Mönchengladbach**. But it will be necessary of course to go into some detail about the cities and their respective theaters and to provide information about tourist office facilities, hotels, and so forth. The two cities, about 15 miles apart (24 kilometers), are linked by frequent suburban rail service, a trip that normally takes between 16 and 20 minutes; holders of Eurailpasses need not buy additional tickets.

This entire part of Germany is amazing because of all the fine opera houses that are found within such a short distance of each other. I mention this here because on a recent trip, by making Mönchengladbach my "headquarters," it was possible to travel easily to Aachen, Köln, and Krefeld and then just over the Rhine to Duisburg and Düsseldorf. Had I started from either Dortmund or Essen, it would have been possible to take in most of the other cities. For starters there are the four big houses presenting operas almost nightly: Köln, Düsseldorf, Duisburg, and Dortmund, some within twenty minutes (by train) of each other, the furthest apart around an hour or less from each other. Then when one begins to include the smaller companies or those that perform only on the block-system (with all of these, very careful planning of dates is required in order to catch a performance), the list becomes almost endless: Aachen, Bonn, Essen, Krefeld, Mönchengladbach, and Wuppertal and then several not described in this book: Bielefeld, Gelsenkirchen, and Hagen. One need shift one's "home base" only once in order to put all of these companies within easy range (by returning to one's hotel by a late train or in some cases the last train). The only nagging problems occur when one has to decide on just one among several tempting choices, vacation time is limited, and there is no opportunity to catch again on a later night what one had to pass up.

Back to Krefeld. As the crow flies it is 32 miles (53 kilometers) north-northwest of Köln (about 45 minutes by train through Neuss), 12.6 miles (21 kilometers) on the west bank of the Rhine southwest of Duisburg (20 minutes by train) and finally (again) 15 miles (24 kilometers) north-northeast of Mönchengladbach (16 to 20 minutes by train). It is a pleasant and quite sophisticated small city. Its older inner district, now mostly a pedestrian zone, is bordered by four spacious, tree-lined avenues forming a large rectangle built on the site of the old walls. A jumble of railroad tracks closes off the main part of the city on its bottom or southern end. The opera house (constructed in 1962–63), used as well for plays, ballets, and concerts, is in a handsome civic complex built off to one side of the broad avenue, Ostwall; this attractive street goes north straight out from the front doors of the station. Though the theater is about ¾'s of a mile (1.2 kilometers) from the station, walking that distance may be slow because of several busy intersections. Both busses and trolleys go the length of Ostwall (the stop you will want is at either St. Anton-Strasse or Gartenstrasse).

The season begins in late September and ends in middle to late June. Obviously, since there is only one company, the honor of hosting the opening of the new lyric season moves from Krefeld to Mönchengladbach in alternate years. Following the same pattern, each of the cities usually sees only two of the four new productions on the schedule, which then the next year are given in both houses. (Allowing no favoritism towards either city must be a scheduling nightmare!) In the course of a year both cities during the 1989–90 season had seven operas (the single operetta, *The Merry Widow*, is included) out of the total of nine presented by the company. Dance programs (a total of five, old and new productions) fill in some of the gaps when a new opera production is being prepared. The repertory during the 1989–90 season was surprisingly eclectic for a company of this size: Rameau, Beethoven, Donizetti, Verdi, Tschaikovsky, Lehár, Massenet (his rarely-seen *Thérèse* was given in commemoration of the French Revolution), Janácek, and Henze. A contemporary work almost always appears in the schedule; Henze's *Elegie für junge Liebende* was the choice for 1989–90, Aribert Reimann's *Troades* the previous year. There is speculation that this company, as seen in the choices for 1989–90, is moving away from some of the hackneyed staples of the repertory they have often presented in previous seasons; this was the first year too in which there was only one operetta, not two plus a musical.

Most of the works are sung in German translation, although I understand that whenever *La Traviata* is offered it is done in Italian, one of the few exceptions.

The regular singers, very few in number, are for the most part young, an international mix drawn from both Europe and North America. Particularly outstanding and talented is a group from Belgium and the Netherlands (the frontiers of both countries are just a few miles to the west of this part of Germany). The productions I have seen were imaginative and intelligent without the contrived artiness one sometimes encounters in German theaters. The orchestra in the pit is made up of members of the Niederrheinische Sinfoniker, a better-than-average ensemble that also gives a series of monthly concerts in both Krefeld and Mönchengladbach. Concerts in Krefeld are staged in the Seidenweberhaus, also known as the Stadthalle, across the plaza from the Stadttheater (the opera house).

Given the fact that singers have to rest between performances (and these singers work quite hard) it is impossible to attend a sequence of two operas on successive nights by this company. Even by shuttling back and forth between Krefeld and Mönchengladbach this remains impossible. On occasion the lone operetta may be scheduled on an evening before or following an opera, but then there will be an interval of at least one or two days before the next opera performance. By combining what is in the current repertory with the new productions, there are rarely more than four different works (seldom five) presented within the same month; these works are repeated in the two theaters together somewhere around fifteen times. (If you are curious about investigating all four operas, you may have to wait two or more weeks to catch them all.)

The relatively new **Stadttheater Krefeld** has a capacity of 832, and all of the seats, except for the last two rows of the Orchestra, are quite good both for excellent sight-lines and clean, bright sound. (The problem with the back-row seats is merely a matter of being seated under the narrow overhang of the balcony.) The auditorium is shaped like a shortened or squarish rectangular box with a slight bulge in the side walls about a third of the way back from the stage. Both the Orchestra seating area, made up of nineteen long rows, and the one Balcony are steeply raked and without center aisles. The Balcony is quite shallow, only four rows deep across the back of the theater; on both ends two small angular projections, hugging the side walls, offer six more short rows of seats, somewhat like boxes without partitions. This is a good theater, comfortable and efficient, where one is not inclined to lament the absence of nineteenth-century charm.

The Box Office is inside the theater, just to the right of the main doors. They are open: Monday through Friday, from 1000 to 1300 and from 1700 to 1900; Saturday, from 1000 to 1300; Sundays and holidays, from 1100 to 1300. The Box Office reopens one hour before a performance (most operas are scheduled to begin at 2000). There are five price categories, all of them quite modest by USA-standards, with an additional charge (ranging from DM 7 down to DM 3) for the first-night performances of each opera. The most expensive seats are comprised of the first four rows of the Orchestra and the first row of the Balcony (Group A at DM 28). Next, in Group B at DM 24, are rows five through ten of the Orchestra, here called *Sperrsitz;* also in this category are the second row of the Balcony and a few seats in the box-like rows on the sides. Group C at DM 18 is rows eleven through fifteen of the Orchestra, again called *Sperrsitz,* as well as the third row in the Balcony and a few seats on the far ends of rows one and two. Group D at DM 14 is made up of rows sixteen and seventeen of the Orchestra, now dubbed *I. Parkett* and the last row of the Balcony. The final category, Group E at DM 11, consists of only the last two rows in the Orchestra, here labelled *II. Parkett.* There is no provision for Standing Room.

Tickets may be purchased three weeks before each performance. No formal arrangements are provided for ordering in advance by mail, but usually a telephone call will suffice to reserve a seat. The telephone number is: (0 21 51) 2-39-02. The address for mailing is: Stadttheater Krefeld, 3 Theaterplatz, 4150 Krefeld 1.

As with Mönchengladbach, there is no Tourist Information Office inside the station. Quite by luck for opera-goers, the city's sole source for such information is in the Seidenweberhaus just across the paved square in front of the opera house, the Stadttheater, but this is still very inconvenient and a very long distance to go from the Hauptbahnhof should you arrive in Krefeld without hotel reservations. (The directions given above for finding the Stadttheater apply as well to the Seidenweberhaus.) The hours are as follows: Monday through Friday from 0800 to 1830; Saturday from 0800 to 1300; closed on Sunday and holidays. This office will make calls to hotels free of charge. The telephone numbers are: (0 21 51) 292-90 and 292-93. The formal name of the office is somewhat long: Informationszentrum Seidenweberhaus Verkehrsverein Krefeld, and their mailing address is: 1 Theaterplatz, 4150 Krefeld 1.

The city has an adequate number of hotels, several of which, in all price categories, are very close to the station. A few others with moderate prices are fairly close to the opera house. A warning however: whenever there are trade fairs *(Messen)* or large conferences in Düsseldorf, hotel space in Krefeld becomes impossibly tight. Businessmen with reservations made long in advance spill out into all the suburbs of Düsseldorf. Krefeld is especially convenient because the *Schnellbahn* provides an easy and quick connection (20 minutes) between the centers of the two cities.

There are no facilities for changing money in the Hauptbahnhof. This service is offered at the Informationszentrum, but their hours, except for Saturday, are not too different from regular banking hours. Neither Cook's nor American Express maintains a branch in Krefeld, but they both do have offices in nearby Düsseldorf.

MANNHEIM, faithful to a strong musical heritage created in the 1700's, supports one of the best small opera companies in Germany. Natives of Munich, Stuttgart, and Frankfurt have "confessed" to me that they often go to Mannheim to find the operatic excitement and innovation which they feel they cannot find "at home." Whether these stories are true or not, Mannheim's company, to borrow a term from horseracing, is still the "sleeper" of the moment. An historical note: during the long rule of the Elector Palatine, Duke Karl Theodor (1724–1799), an ardent patron of all the arts, Mannheim attracted musicians from Austria and Bohemia who developed a new and dynamic style of orchestral playing. The so-called Mannheim School, admired and imitated throughout Western Europe, had an enormous influence on the evolving symphony, an influence perceived even as late as in Beethoven. Mozart twice paid prolonged visits to Mannheim (in 1777 and 1778) where he knew and respected many of the court musicians.

Alas, today in the city itself, except for its opera, there is very little to attract the casual visitor. Mannheim is laid out in a grid-pattern for its principal streets, and perhaps before the Industrial Revolution it was still a charming, small baroque town. But one can see from pre-Hitler photographs that very little of the old city survived the ravages of pompously ambitious nineteenth- and twentieth-century German merchants. The Second World War left in rubble almost everything these men had built, which was no great aesthetic loss, but in rebuilding the present city, with little left of note worth saving, the new" Mannheim is drab and ugly. Let me quickly add that in spite of their harsh urban environment the Mannheimers are extremely friendly and warm people. Go there to enjoy the opera and the people, but don't expect to find much else of interest in the city.

The Mannheim opera, called the **Nationaltheater**, is about one mile or 1.35 kilometers from the Hauptbahnhof, but it is very easy to find: when you come out of the station it lies straight ahead, following either of the only two streets leading directly into the city from the front of the station. It is a very modern, stylish hall, accommodating about 1100 and sharing a large lobby and refreshment area with the smaller theater (for plays) housed under the same roof on the other side. The seating arrangements give everyone the same unobstructed view of the entire stage; all of the raised seating areas are at the back of the theater and not along the sides. The acoustics are excellent, though some people may find that the orchestra is too loud "upstairs," tending occasionally to cover the singers. Some of that problem may be due to the conductor or to the fact that at those performances I attended only half the theater was filled, with not enough human bodies to absorb some of the excess sound.

In 1988–89 Mannheim was prepared to perform 17 different operas, including a complete Ring cycle. This number did not include several operettas and ten different ballet programs which also filled out the season. This series of 17, drawn this time only from the standard German and Italian repertory, was conceived as a special memorial to the opera's director who had died just before the end of the previous season. Normally Mannheim would have a better or wider representation of both French and Russian works and at least one or two contemporary compositions. But one of this theater's strongest drawing-points has always been its remarkable roster of leading singers and conductors, almost all of whom are known and respected on both sides of the Atlantic. The season begins usually in late August and goes into the first week of July. There are not many nights when the theater is closed, but it is advisable to consult a calendar before planning a visit. Generally one can find a grouping of three or four different operas performed together on successive nights.

The Box Office for advanced sales is not located in the theater but in a nearby-building at 26 Collinistrasse, one block over and one street back from the street bordering the banks of the Neckar River. The entrance to the Box Office is on the side of that building facing the river and not visible when you leave the front of the opera. Their hours are a bit odd: from Tuesdays through Fridays they are open from 1100 to 1300 and from 1400 until 1600; on Mondays, Saturdays, Sundays, and holidays they are open from 1100 until 1300. Telephone orders (06-21) 2-48-44/45/46/47 are accepted between 0900 and 1700 on those days when the Box Office is open longer; between 0900 and 1100 for those days having shorter hours. A ticket window at the opera house, not at Collinistrasse, is open one hour before curtain time. Prices for tickets seem shockingly low even when Mannheim's highest pricing category is in effect. Tickets for approximately a third of the operas range from DM 13 up to a high of DM 44; the majority will cost between DM 12 and DM 35.

Tourist information is to be found in a small glass pavilion across the street in front of the Hauptbahnhof. They can supply you with what you need in choosing a hotel. Their hours are much shorter than what one finds in larger cities, so be sure, if you do now know the city, to arrive before they close. They are open Mondays through Fridays from 0800 to 1800 and on Saturdays from 0830 until 1200. Closed on Sundays and holidays.

Quite a large number of hotels in all price-categories are off to the right and towards the downtown area, directly in front of you as you leave the Hauptbahnhof by the main exit. There are no hotels in the immediate vicinity of the Nationaltheater.

Money can be changed in the station at a bank located to the right of the main entrance. Their hours are: Monday through Friday: 0700 to 2000; Sundays and holidays: 0900 to 1300. Cook's maintains an office in Mannheim, but there is no local representative of American Express.

MÖNCHENGLADBACH (For more basic and detailed information about the opera company shared with Krefeld, the Vereinigte Städtische Bühnen Krefeld und Mönchengladbach, see above under KREFELD.) This very nondescript, small industrial city has acquired at least with many opera-lovers an enviable international reputation because of its adventurous opera productions. With Krefeld as an equal partner their jointly-subsidized company has shown great resourcefulness in exploring neglected repertory and in doing it well with both skillful singers and imaginative staging. Whether one sees the same opera performed in Krefeld or in Mönchengladbach, the production, the singers (usually), and the orchestra are identical. Each season two of the four new productions for that year are performed in only one city. This explains why critics in submitting their reviews sometimes use the date-line of one city rather than the other (the next year the one-year-old productions are then seen in both cities).

I should first try to situate Mönchengladbach with respect to cities that are better known (hereafter, following local custom, I shorten the name to "MG" whenever possible). On most maps of Germany this part of the country is a veritable scramble of large and small cities with very indistinct borders. MG lies about 21 miles (28 kilometers) due west of Düsseldorf, inland some distance from the west bank of the Rhine (about a 22-minute trip by the *Schnellbahn*); 34 miles (57 kilometers) northwest of Köln (a 40- to 50-minute trip by train); and finally 15 miles (24 kilometers) southwest of Krefeld (16 to 20 minutes by train). Aachen, almost at the Belgian border, is some 35 miles (57 kilometers) to the southwest (about 45 minutes away by train).

Though the people of Mönchengladbach are both gracious and kind, their urban environment is an unattractive and messy sprawl with little architectural or natural distinction. At least the main commercial street, Hindenburgstrasse, has been converted into a pedestrian zone (only slow-moving busses are allowed access), and at the far end is the city's large Stadttheater, a modern building (1959) used exclusively for plays. This can be a source of some confusion because MG actually has the luxury of operating two municipal theaters: the Stadttheater on Hindenburgstrasse only for plays (the Schauspielhaus) and the theater in Rheydt, a suburb, for both operas and concerts. This building is called both the **Stadthalle Rheydt** and the **Opernhaus**. Compounding the problem are logistic difficulties in getting to Rheydt, which is considered both a suburb and at the same time a district within MG. By train from MG to Rheydt, a distance of 2 miles (3 kilometers), the trip is easy and quick because the station in Rheydt is just behind the opera house; by bus takes much longer (I would not suggest trying to walk this route unless you are a superb map-reader and not bothered by intense, speeding traffic). Train service is fairly frequent (this is the busy line linking Köln, MG and either Krefeld or Aachen); Eurailpass holders need not buy additional tickets.

Even with its two theaters MG does not provide a fuller schedule than its neighbor Krefeld using its single stage for both operas and plays. Both cities offer essentially the same events but on different dates. In the course of a month the nights are very few when an opera is scheduled in Rheydt and a play in MG; on most evenings either one or the other of the theaters is dark.

To find the opera house from the Rheydt Hauptbahnhof go out the main doors, cross the parking lot, and take Moses-Stern-Strasse (on the left) one block to the first corner; on the right, facing Odenkirchener Strasse (number 78), is the main entrance to the theater. The original building, constructed of red brick, goes back to the late 1920's; in the early 1980's it was completely overhauled and reopened in 1984. The seating capacity is now at 811, only 21 fewer seats than the theater in Krefeld. There are other similarities as well between the two halls: a large orchestra seating-area, quite wide with no center aisle, and seventeen rows deep; a single balcony, six rows deep, across the back wall; and no side or rear boxes or other concessions to out-of-date snobbery. The hall is clean and efficient, with all seats up and down having an unobstructed view of the stage. The acoustics are clear and bright and to my ears a bit warmer, more mellow than the acoustics in the Krefeld theater.

For opera tickets in MG there are two Box Offices: one in "downtown" MG at the Schauspielhaus and another in Rheydt at the opera house. Both keep the same schedules: Monday through Friday, from 1000 to 1300 and from 1700 to 1900; Saturday, from 1000 to 1300; and Sundays and holidays from 1100 to 1300. The Box Office at the opera house opens one hour before the curtain goes up (which can be especially convenient for weekend and holiday performances). Oddly all of the ticket prices are consistently a few DM cheaper than in Krefeld, with even the "first-night" seats in MG costing less than those on the "regular" price scale in the neighboring city. MG also simplifies the labelling-system of the seats in the Orchestra by using the single term *Parkett* from the front to the back. With four (not five) pricing-scales, Category A at DM 22 includes the first eight rows of the Orchestra and rows one and two of the Balcony; Category B at DM 18 is Orchestra rows nine through fourteen and in the Balcony the third row; Category C at DM 14 is for the fifteenth and sixteenth rows of the Orchestra and the fourth row of the Balcony; and finally Category D is for row seventeen in the Orchestra and row five in the Balcony. First-night tickets have a "surcharge" ranging from DM 4 in Category A to DM 2 in Category D. There is no Standing Room.

Advance sales of tickets begin four weeks before the date of a performance when the words *"Freier Verkauf"* indicate that all seats have not been taken by subscribers; if a few seats should be available for a performance normally reserved only for subscribers, sales begin ten days in advance. As with Krefeld no provision is made for ordering tickets by mail, but as I am told that few performances in either city are ever totally sold out, usually a telephone call will hold a ticket. There are telephone numbers for each of the Box Offices: for the Schauspielhaus in MG: (0 21 61) 18-20-83, and for the opera house in Rheydt: (0 21 66) 4-43-05. There are two mailing addresses as well: for "downtown" MG: Schauspielhaus, 73 Hindenburgstrasse, 4050 Mönchengladbach 1, and for Rheydt: Opernhaus, 78 Odenkirchener Strasse, 4050 Mönchengladbach 2. Tickets for Krefeld may not be bought in MG (and vice versa).

Obtaining tourist information presents the same difficulties in MG that it does in Krefeld. There are no facilities in the Hauptbahnhof, although in the tiny cubicle in one corner of the station where one goes for train information (marked by an "i") they have on hand and distribute the booklet listing hotels in MG. This office however closes down early in the evening at 2000 and is not equipped to make telephone calls or offer other advice. The nominal office for tourist information for MG is with a privately-operated travel bureau about five minutes away on foot, one door to the left from the corner of Hindenburgstrasse and Bismarckstrasse (the first street is the main commercial artery of the city leading off to the left from in front of the station, limited to pedestrians and busses; Bismarckstrasse is the first large street that crosses it). The signs outside are marked "First Reisebüro" and "DB Reisebüro," and their hours are: Monday through Friday, from 0915 to 1800 and Saturday, from 0930 to 1230. They are closed on Sundays and holidays. They make calls for hotel reservations, and their own telephone number is: (0 21 61) 27-40; the mailing address is: 23–27 Bismarckstrasse, 4050 Mönchengladbach 1.

Hotels can be a problem in MG because you have to juggle some conveniences against certain other disadvantages. There are only two small hotels within sight of the front doors of the Hauptbahnhof; all but one of the others, large and small, are a good distance away (at least 30 minutes or more on foot). In Rheydt there are several hotels quite close to the opera house (and the Rheydt train station) but few restaurants to choose from in the vicinity, an advantage one has by staying in "downtown" MG. (There is no strong reason for staying the night in Rheydt and near the opera if after consulting the train schedules you see that you can return to MG without too long a wait. The times when operas begin and end are clearly legible on the flyers announcing the month's schedule.) A repeat of a warning given with Krefeld: when there are trade fairs or conferences in Düsseldorf, hotels throughout this region will be jammed to capacity. If possible, reserve your space well in advance or avoid the times when you will have competition from businessmen looking for accommodations.

There are no facilities for changing money in the MG station. As there are no Cook's or American Express offices in the city, for a favorable exchange rate you will have to use the local banks during their somewhat restrictive weekday hours.

MUNICH (in German: MÜNCHEN) deserves its reputation as the one city in Germany all tourists feel they must visit, and for most of them a trip to the opera is mandatory. However, a basic premise of this guide is that many other cities throughout Germany have opera companies capable of rivaling Munich, maybe not always every night of the week but certainly often enough to justify the fact that this city has no monopoly on quality and excitement. Munich does attract the singers, conductors, and stage designers and directors with the familiar "big" names, but this does not always guarantee an unforgettable evening in the opera house. And Munich's ticket prices

run generally at twice or three times the amount one has to pay elsewhere for tickets. Then there is the ever-present fact that with hordes of tourists (and others) scrambling for seats it is often very difficult to gain entry into the theater. In most other cities finding a ticket is quite simple, and it will be a good one at that, and for a very reasonable price. But with that out of the way, now Munich . . .

From the front of the Hauptbahnhof, where many tram lines converge, it is approximately a mile to the **Bayerische Staatsoper** in its "home," the **Nationaltheater**. There is now only one trolley line (number 19) to deliver you to Max-Joseph-Platz, where you will see the colonnade of the opera house facing the square. (Going in the other direction, back to the station, the trolley stop is right by the side of the theater near the door where many of the performers you have just seen or heard will be coming out.) By tram it is at most a fifteen-minute trip; on foot you should allow at least 45 minutes or more because of traffic congestion.

When the opera house was rebuilt after the war the basic seating arrangements were retained: a wide and deep orchestra section downstairs (with no center aisle), the *Parkett,* and five tiers upstairs, the first of which is called the *Balkon;* then three more shallow balconies to follow, here called *Rang* (plural: *Ränge*), and finally at the top, on the fifth level, the *Galerie.* All seats have an unobstructed view of the stage except upstairs on the sides nearest the stage. Acoustically the sound is bright and clear from every position in the house. The theater is larger than it looks, accommodating approximately 1780 people, not counting the 235 standees.

Munich's season runs from September through the end of June. (The annual Richard Strauss festival follows during the month of July; for information about the festival see Appendix I.) Though the number of different operas varies from year to year, generally there are upwards of thirty presented in the course of a single season. All are performed in the language in which they were written, with the exception of Czech and Russian works. Most of the artists appearing in major roles in Munich are known throughout the operatic world. The productions on the whole, with the exception of a recent *Ring* cycle, are extremely conservative but meticulously (and lovingly) detailed. Munich leaves bold innovation in stage design and interpretation to other companies in Germany. Special mention should be made of the playing of the orchestra which has been shaped by many of the world's finest conductors.

The Box Office for advanced sales is in a separate building at 11 Maximilianstrasse, on the corner just behind the back of the opera house. They are open on Mondays through Fridays from 1000 until 1300 and later, from 1530 until 1730; on Saturdays from 1000 until 1230; closed on Sundays and holidays. Tickets may be bought here seven days in advance of the date of a performance. By mail, orders are accepted four weeks in advance if you live outside the immediate Munich area. Write: Eintrittskartenkasse der Bayer-ischen Staatsoper, Maximilianstrasse 11, D-8000 München 22. The telephone number is: (89) 22-13-16, and they can be very helpful in telling you what is available for the next seven days or even for that evening. Prices for tickets follow several scales that seem determined mostly by the popularity of the opera and the reputation of the cast. Generally the lowest prices start at DM 7,50 and then go as high as DM 102,50.

The Abendkasse, opening one hour before curtain-time, is not where you might expect it to be. Instead of going up the broad stairs to the doors at the front of the theater, stay on the sidewalk to the right of the entrance, and a few paces down Maximilianstrasse you will see a modest door on your left. Inside is the famous Abendkasse where on many an evening an otherwise dignified or reserved opera lover has had to assume an unaccustomed bold-ness in accosting strangers, asking if they have extra tickets to sell. If it is a popular opera or famous singers are to perform, there will be masses of people waiting in line and others rushing about trying to spot someone with an extra ticket. Before you try your luck, be sure that you have a good supply of Deutschemark notes in small denominations. If in the rush to get inside the theater you hold someone up because you expect change for a 200 mark note, the person next to you with the right change will beat you out for that ticket. As far as I know no tickets are exchanged for more than the printed price. Near one of the ticket windows a uniformed guard, not known for his smiles, will be surveying the scene. He has always appeared to me as though he were monitoring every transaction. And beware of the line against the outside wall on the far left: that is the line only for young students who get special rates. Good luck!

About fifteen or more times during the annual opera season an organiza-tion called the Theatergemeinde offers its members tickets to performances that are closed to the general public. These are not special student or second-ary-cast performances, but the same productions with first-rate casts that are available to subscribers and the public on other nights (or afternoons). Tickets for these operas are not sold at the Staatsoper Box Office. The operas reserved for the Theatergemeinde are listed in the theater's monthly booklet with an asterisk and the brief notation: "Vorstellung für Besucherorganisa-tionen," meaning crudely: "For members only." Some of these performances are on Sundays, matinées or evenings, while others are scheduled on weekday or weekend nights. (Note that matinées usually are scheduled to begin at 1300.) Unused tickets from members are returned to the Gemeinde office and are priced at a slight discount from the going-rate for regular seats bought at the theater Box Office. A DM 2,00 charge is added to the price of each ticket, but there is usually a wide choice of prices and seating options. Although I list their telephone number: (89) 53-08-88, it is best to go in person to the office and ask about tickets there. You will find the staff very friendly and helpful. The Theatergemeinde office is very close to Munich's Hauptbahnhof, at the corner of Goethestrasse and Landwehrstrasse, only two blocks from the side entrance of the station facing Bayerstrasse (by the side of the Tourist Information Office). The street address is listed as 24 Goethestrasse, but the entrance is immediately around the corner on Landwehrstrasse. The office hours are Monday through Thursday from 0830 to 1800 and on Friday from 0830 to 1600; they are closed on both Saturday and Sunday. The mailing address is: Theatergemeinde e. V., 24 Goethestrasse, 8000 Munich 2. If you visit Munich frequently, it would be worth your while to look into joining this group.

Another last-minute source for tickets is the music store of Max Hieber at 1 Liebfrauenstrasse, the short street that connects the south side of the Frauenkirche (Munich's most famous church) with Kaufingerstrasse, the main pedestrian mall that runs west of Marienplatz towards Karlsplatz in the direction of the train station. At Max Hieber they often have tickets put up for sale by long-time Staatsoper subscribers, which means that these will be good seats but not necessarily very expensive ones. They will also try to get you tickets at the Box Office if for some reason you cannot go yourself. There is a modest broker's fee for their service. They do not deal with orders mailed or called in from abroad. The telephone number is: (89) 22-65-71, and the complete mailing address is: Max Hieber Musikalischer Instrument, 1 Liebfrauenstrasse, 8000 Munich 2.

Under no circumstances should you miss the opportunity, if possible, to attend a performance in the famous **Altes-Residenztheater** or **Cuvilliés-Theater**, the eighteenth-century baroque gem that was dismantled piece by piece and saved from destruction in the Second World War. This small court theater is hidden away in the old palace (the Residenz) that adjoins off to the left the Nationaltheater on the right. The Cuvilliés has space for 453 people and is only open a few times each month during the regular season of the opera. Plays, chamber music concerts, ballets, and occasionally an opera will be scheduled for the Cuvilliés, but there is no way of predicting in advance when something interesting has been planned. Walking tours of the Residenz usually include a quick look inside the theater. Tickets for a musical event or ballet may be bought at the Box Office for the opera at 11 Maximilianstrasse.

Another theater worth investigating in Munich is the old **Staatstheater am Gärtnerplatz** which puts on an odd collection of operas, operetta, ballets, and musical comedies. The season runs from October through July. Everything is sung in German, including the Mozart Italian operas and a host of Italian favorites such as *Rigoletto* and *La Bohème*. In many ways this house is the Munich-equivalent of Vienna's Volksoper: maybe the musical and production standards are variable, but there are no snobbish pretensions—all at popular prices. Here one can find some of the "slighter" but delightful works in the German repertory that are disdained by the larger companies (Flotow, Marschner, Humperdinck, and so forth). The theater is mid-sized, seating around 800. It looks a bit dingy inside, especially in the upper tiers of balconies, but that might be said to be part of its Biedermeier charm, as though the light fixtures were all fueled by gas. Gärtnerplatz, on which the theater fronts, is about an hour-long walk from the Hauptbahnhof. Neither the U-1 or U-8 subway lines, getting off at the Fraunhoferstrasse station, nor trams 20 or 27 will take you directly to Gärtnerplatz. Each of these lines still puts you a long block away from the theater. You will have to ask directions unless you know the city well or are good at map reading.

Tickets for the Staatstheater am Gärtnerplatz are available at the Box Office in the lobby at the front of the theater. The hours are Mondays through Fridays from 1000 until 1300, and in the afternoons from 1530 to 1730; on Saturdays they are open from 1000 until 1230. Advance sales begin on Saturday for the period between the following Wednesday through the Tuesday of the next week (instructions you will have to read twice in order to understand!). There is an Abendkasse opening one hour before the performance (telephone: (89) 20-24-11), and questions about other, subsequent events will be cheerfully answered by calling: 2-01-67-67. Prices start for most tickets at DM 17 and go up to DM 65; Standing Room is usually priced at DM 8. The mailing address: Staatstheater am Gärtnerplatz, Postfach 140 569, 8000 München 5.

Tourist information for Munich is found in the Hauptbahnhof, clearly marked with the usual "i"-sign, off to the far right as you approach the main part of the station with your back to the train platforms. There is also an entrance from Bayerstrasse which runs along the south side of the station. They are open daily, including Saturdays, Sundays, and holidays, from 0800 until 2300. The shorter winter hours, from 0930 to 1230, apply only to the weekends and holidays. You can buy at this office the 24-hour transit ticket (DM 7) if you are wary of using the automatic machines or the windows in the S- and U-Bahn stations. During the height of the tourist season there may be long lines of tired and impatient knapsack-enveloped visitors waiting to ask their questions, but the attitude behind the information counter is generally quite friendly and forgiving.

Hotels in every conceivable category are crowded together around the Hauptbahnhof on its south side in all of the streets leading off Bayerstrasse. Unless you want to find lodgings in another part of the city, there is little reason to wait in line and to pay the small fee for the tourist office to make your reservation.

Money is changed inside the station (just to the right as you come in the main entrance from the front or to your left as you leave); they are open every day of the year, including weekends and holidays, from 0600 until 2330. Cook's also has an office in the Hauptbahnhof as well as two others elsewhere in the city, one of which is on Lenbachplatz, about half-way between the station and the opera house on the trolley line that connects them. The American Express Office is on the same trolley line, about 700 feet (250 meters) from Lenbachplatz on Promenadeplatz (and a bit closer to the theater).

MÜNSTER is an attractive university center of some 260,000 inhabitants, but the core of the old city has the look and feel of a community of perhaps one-fifth that size. Münster was heavily damaged in the last war, but the city-fathers decided to reconstruct it much as it had been before the Allied bombings in 1944. Without indulging in excessive quaintness the city has adapted itself well to the twentieth century but retained many charming elements of its medieval and Renaissance past. The tourist brochures can claim very rightly that Münster sums up in its architecture just what one thinks a typical old-fashioned German city should look like.

The new building housing the opera and a separate, smaller theater, together called **Die Städtische Bühnen**, lies at some distance from the Hauptbahnhof, more than a generous kilometer on foot or by car because of the many angles and turns in the streets. From in front of the station Bus Line 9 (off to the far left at position A-3) will take you to the theater, and you get off a few feet from the Box Office; to go back to the station, the stop is behind the theater on Hörsterstrasse. More frequent service is offered by other bus lines (Numbers 1, 5, and 6 stopping at position A-2), and you get off at Spiekerhof; this will put you fairly close to the theater. You will have to go back one block from the bus stop and turn left at the first street, and the theater will be in front of you on the next corner. Going in the other direction, back to the station, you will find the stops for Lines 1, 5, and 6 one block off to your right, up Vossgasse which then becomes Apostelkirche-Strasse and finally Berg-Strasse (this street changes its name at each corner!). Bus tickets may be bought from machines and are priced as follows: one trip: DM 1,90 and the 24-hour ticket: DM 6. On foot, if you can find your way to the Domplatz in the heart of the city, the theaters are off to the northeast, at the corner of Vossgasse and Neubrückenstrasse, a distance of some 600 feet (or 200 meters). Even with a map in my hand, I have lost my way in Münster every time I have walked between the station and the opera house; the streets meet each other at odd angles, and it is very easy to miss the correct turn.

The theater holds approximately 990, with more than half of the seats in three tiers at the back and the sides. It would be an attractive theater were it not for some hundreds of differently-shaped, small white paper lanterns suspended from the ceiling. This gives a feeling of unnecessary clutter. Then there is the harsh purple upholstery used in covering the seats. All of the seats except for those in the balconies nearest the stage have unobstructed sight-lines, but on the two uppermost levels one's view of the stage may be hindered in part by the railing that goes across the front of each balcony. Acoustically there are no problems, as this is an intimate theater with no seats placed very far from the proscenium.

I would like to be able to report good things about Münster's opera, but the one performance I attended there of Humperdinck's *Königskinder* (on its opening night) was very disappointing. The singing, but for one excellent baritone, was mediocre; the orchestra very scrappy; and the sets, costumes, and direction not as good as one could find in any amateur high-school production in the USA. A pity, because *Königskinder* is a lovely work. On one other occasion I had gone to Münster to see their *Vespri siciliani,* but they had cancelled the performance (because one of the lead-singers was sick) and had substituted a Telemann chamber work I did not want to see. For now I shan't make any final judgments about the quality of what one can hear and see in Münster. I may have been unlucky and encountered two unusually bad nights, but the strength of this theater appears to lie in its productions of plays, not of operas. Within a year or so all of this may change very drastically because the then-current director *(Generalintendant)* was to be leaving at the end of the 1988–89 season.

The repertory in Münster is quite modest when compared to what is available in many other slightly larger cities, but here the theater *(Grosses Haus)* is used far more often for plays than for opera. Also the auditorium serves at least twice a month as the concert hall for the local symphony, and on some evenings ballet performances occupy the stage. Chamber operas, plays, and ballets are also presented in the adjacent theater *(Kleines Haus).* Around a dozen operatic works (including operettas and musicals) figure in a usual season, with a sampling of Italian and French titles to balance out the German ones. Everything is performed in German translation. On an average two or three lyric works are given each week, and as a general policy the theater is closed on Monday nights. There are no "star" singers here with (as yet) international reputations, and the company is quite small. Normally the season begins in October and ends in late June.

The Box Office, located outside the theater, fronts on the street off to your left (Neubrückenstrasse) as you face the main entrance to the opera house at the corner. They are open from Tuesday through Friday from 1000 until 1330 and from 1530 until 1900; on Saturdays they are open from 0900 until 1330; and on Sundays and holidays from 1100 until 1230. On the first Saturday of the month the hours are from 0900 to 1900. An *Abendkasse* inside the main theater opens one hour before the curtain goes up. The telephone number of the Box Office is (02-51) 59-09-100. Ticket prices are very reasonable and for most performances start at a low of DM 5,50 and go up to a high of DM 28,50. The highest scale of prices, on a few special occasions, comes only to a few more DM and is in effect very rarely: a low of DM 7 and a high of DM 33. No provisions seem to be made for ordering tickets by mail.

The Tourist Information Office is difficult to find because it looks like just another shop across the street from the Hauptbahnhof, but take the escalator down at the entrance to the station, go through the tunnel, and come up on the other side, opposite the station. Turn immediately left and the Tourist Office will be about ten stores down at 22 Berlinerplatz. Their hours are as follows: Mondays through Fridays from 0900 until 2000; Saturdays from 0900 until 1300 (on the first Saturday of each month from 0900 until 1800); and on Sundays from 1030 until 1230. Tickets for the opera may be bought here if orders are placed before 1800. You can call the Tourist Office at (02-51) 4-04-95.

There are a good number of hotels in the immediate vicinity of the station, both in front and behind it. There also is a fair scattering of very reasonably-priced hotels close to the opera house and in the central part of the city. In all locations these range from the modest and simple to the most luxurious. It is advisable, before you leave the tourist office or the station, to have a confirmed reservation in your hand, as well as a small map of the city. It is all too easy in Münster, in my experience, to make a wrong turn and to end up where you started from!

No facilities, other than at your hotel, are provided for changing money in Münster if you should need to do so outside of the regular banking hours. There are signs in orange-yellow inside the Hauptbahnhof leading you to believe that a bank is nearby, but when you go the considerable distance down Bahnhofstrasse (off to your right) in order to find it, you will discover that the bank keeps regular banking hours and closes early on weekdays and is locked shut on weekends. There are no branches of either American Express or Cook's in Münster.

NUREMBERG (German spelling: Nürnberg), long exalted during Hitler's Third Reich as the symbol of Aryan superiority, was reduced to rubble during the Second World War. The new city, ingeniously evoking something of Nuremberg's past, has retained the pattern of the old and narrow streets. The site is picturesque: the River Pegnitz, which splits the city into two parts and also forms a number of small islands, lies at the bottom of the two steep hillsides on which the city is built. Automobiles are barred from much of the "old" town, which makes it pleasant for the sightseer to

wander about on foot, but after visiting Dürer's reconstructed house and a few patched-up churches there is not much else of the city itself to linger over. For art-lovers there are the primitives and the paintings of Dürer and his followers in the Germanisches Nationalmuseum; the history of Nuremberg's toy industry in the Spielzeugmuseum; and for train-lovers the splendid Verkehrsmuseum next door to the opera house. (The Nuremberg to Fürth rail line, dating from 1835, was the first in Germany.)

There is no problem in finding the **Städtische Bühnen**, the opera house: it is about a quarter of a mile (400 meters) off to the left of the main exit from the Hauptbahnhof, on Frauentorgraben, with one wall of the building almost touching the train tracks. Constructed in the massive "imperial" style before World War I (the natives of the city seem to think it a good example of Jugendstil!), enough of the theater's core survived the bombings to justify re-creating the structure on the outside as it had looked before. Inside, the auditorium is far more chaste in appearance (and atmosphere) than one would expect; if indeed it is faithful to Jugendstil, it is a rather bland and timid version of it. Long and narrow, the theater seats 1082. There are three balcony rings, deeper at the back where they directly face the stage. On the upper two levels the seating is reduced to a single row as the balconies come closer to the stage. The sight-lines throughout the theater are excellent except on the sides closest to the front. Acoustically the sound is very bright and clean.

Beginning with the 1988–89 season the Nuremberg opera had a new director who with his ambitious first production, Pfitzner's *Palestrina*, elicited mixed reviews: the musical elements were highly praised but the production and direction received less than favorable criticism. It remains to be seen what a new *Generalintendant* can do to bring Nuremberg out of several years of lethargic provincialism. Apparently the opera has had no serious financial problems because their repertory each season until now has been quite large and diverse (upwards of some twenty-five works, many of them big works, along with many operettas and musicals, but all performed in German). Yet the company simply has not been capable except on rare occasions of bringing off a convincing, competent performance of what has looked so inviting on paper. The singing was generally poor, though I felt that those cast in the secondary rôles were often far better than the leads; the sets, costumes, and direction were sloppy and haphazard; and even the orchestra sounded as though they were still in rehearsal. The chorus however always sang well, though they rarely knew what to do with themselves when on stage. Let us hope that all of this will change. For now, until the new director can leave his stamp on the company, when you are in Nuremberg choose an operetta or a musical if you want to visit the opera. Or choose a new production overseered by the new director and hope that he is fulfilling his promise. A footnote: a number of young Americans are singing small rôles in this company and doing them very well; perhaps now they will graduate to some of the bigger parts.

The Box Office is inside the opera house, just to the left of the main doors. They are open Mondays through Fridays from 9000 until 1300 and from 1600 until 1800; on Saturdays from 0830 until 1300; closed on Sundays and holidays. Ticket prices range from DM 8 up to DM 42; "premières" are priced only a few marks higher. The Abendkasse is open one hour before the curtain goes up. The weekday telephone number to use is: (09-11) 16-38-08; on weekends for information about the availability of tickets call: (09-11) 16-37-70 from 1300 until 1900. Mail orders, ten days in advance of a performance, may be sent to: Städtische Bühnen, Richard-Wagner-Platz 2-10, 8500 Nürnberg 70.

Tourist information is not well marked, but it is found in the Hauptbahnhof, towards the center and off to the right as you face the doors leading out of the station. Their hours are on Mondays through Saturdays from 0900 to 2000 (on Friday nights they remain open until 2100); closed on Sundays and holidays. A second tourist office, located in the Hauptmarkt in the center of the city (a good distance from the station however) has different hours: they are open Monday through Saturday from 0900 to 1300 and from 1400 to 1800; on Sundays and holidays from 1000 until 1300 and from 1400 until 1600.

Numerous hotels may be found in the area immediately to the front and off to both the left and right of the Hauptbahnhof. Those to the left will of course be very close to the opera house. There are a few more hotels behind the station, and those on Peter-Henlein-Strasse, reached by a tunnel under the train tracks, will be close to the opera from its back-side.

Money can be changed inside the Hauptbahnhof opposite the tourist office. The hours are: Mondays through Saturdays, from 0745 until 1945; on Sundays and holidays, from 0915 until 1230. Both American Express and Cook's have offices in the city.

STUTTGART enjoys a unique setting: parks, rolling hills, forests, and even vineyards intersect the city at many points, giving one the impression that it is much smaller than it really is. The "downtown" area is quite compact and made extremely hospitable by the fact that many of the streets are closed to vehicular traffic. Although Stuttgart possesses no imposing monuments of great historical interest (no great castles or interesting churches), it is a warm and friendly city. Not to be missed is a visit to the Staatsgalerie and its fine collection of contemporary painting.

The opera house, the **Grosses Haus,** rebuilt after a fire and reopened in 1912, was one of the very few in Germany to escape destruction in World War II. (It was here that on 6 Sept. 1946 Secretary of State James F. Byrnes proclaimed that the victorious Allies intended to foster the reconstruction of a strong and unified Germany.) The Stuttgart company was also among the very first to resume normal operations after the cessation of hostilities, and on its early roster were many of the young German singers who later in the 1950's and 1960's gained prominence throughout the operatic world. Many of the names associated with the great Bayreuth seasons of the 1950's were also linked to Stuttgart where they first came into prominence. A few years ago the opera house was closed in order to refurbish the interior from top to bottom: the nineteenth-century décor was to be faithfully respected and restored to its original appearance. Though a few minor acoustical problems have yet to be resolved, the theater is now much more comfortable and the sight-lines for a number of seats greatly improved. To revamp and modernize the stage equipment the opera ended its season earlier than usual in the spring of 1988 and postponed its re-opening until late in the following fall. Stuttgart now has a virtually "new" opera house with, inside and out, an "old" look. It is not an especially elegant or graceful theater: the brown-gold paint throughout, trimmed with silver, not gilt, and the purple curtain fronting the stage look as though they were inspired by the bad taste of late Biedermeier, but this somewhat "heavy" atmosphere is quickly forgotten the moment the house lights go out and one's attention is focussed on the stage.

The auditorium seats just short of 1400 people, more than half of the seats being in the wide but shallow *Parkett.* There are three rings of balconies, each with a very different arrangement of the seating. On the first level, where in the center the royal box has been retained, there are large formal parlors (as in Vienna) behind the loges and separated from the outer corridor; now rarely used except on gala nights, these rooms evoke the time when members of the royal court would assemble here during intermissions for conversation and refreshments.

The opera house is a five-minute walk from the Hauptbahnhof, through the tunnel downstairs in front of the station and then off to the left, coming back up to street-level near the entrance to the park. The building is clearly visible, once you enter the park, beyond the large reflecting pool. (You can take a short-cut up the driveway of the Hotel am Schlossgarten.) Next to the opera, to the left, is the smaller, contemporary playhouse.

Recent changes in the administration of Stuttgart's opera may mean in the future less innovation and fewer commissions of new works, but at least the company is now out of the slump in which it found itself in the late 1970's and early 80's. The repertory is quite large, in recent seasons averaging some thirty operas, all of which are sung in the language in which they were composed. Stuttgart's special pride has been their championing of new works; most of Philip Glass's new operas have been given either their world or European premières by this company. Mention should be made too of the fine Stuttgart ballet, organized by John Cranko and now under the tutelage of Marcia Haydée, still one of the foremost dance companies on the Continent. The ballet shares the stage with the opera, but generally when it performs, the schedule calls for one or two evenings of ballet followed by one or two nights of opera. During other times, when the ballet is on tour, an entire month may be devoted to opera with no ballet performances. Many distinguished singers are affiliated with Stuttgart, and among them one sees the names of many young Americans. The season usually begins in late September and continues through the end of June.

The Box Office is in the lobby of the opera house (called the *Grosses Haus* to avoid confusion with the *Kleines Haus* or playhouse which is next door). Their hours are from Monday through Friday, from 1000 to 1800; on Saturday from 0900 to 1300. Prices for most performances range from a low of DM 10 to between DM 70 and DM 80 on the high-side; a large number of seats in the third ring, where all have a clear view of the stage and excellent sound, are priced between DM 10 and at the most DM 26. Advance sales begin on Saturday for all of the performances scheduled from the Saturday of the following week through the Friday of the next week after that. The Abendkasse opens one hour prior to curtain-time. Telephone inquiries may be made by calling: (07-11) 20-32-220 or 20-32-414. Written orders should be addressed as follows: Staatstheater Stuttgart, Kartenbüro, Postfach 982, 7000 Stuttgart 1.

Tourist information is available in an office below street-level in the tunnel-area in front of the Hauptbahnhof. From the central main entrance to the station (there are three such exits; the one you want is in the middle), take the escalator downstairs to the first underground level. The office, enclosed in glass, will be directly in front of you. They are open Monday through Saturday from 0830 to 2200; on Sundays from 1100 until 1800 between 1 May and 31 October; from 1 Nov. through 30 April the Sunday hours are cut back to 1300 to 1800.

Close to the station and to the opera house there are only hotels in the more expensive categories. Unless you know the city well you would be well advised to use the tourist office for directions in finding a hotel best suited to your budget.

Money may be changed inside the Hauptbahnhof at the following times: Monday through Saturday from 0800 to 2030, and on Sundays from 0900 until 2000. American Express has an office in Stuttgart, as does Cook's (with three branches).

WIESBADEN has one of the few opera houses in Germany that survived the war unscathed, and the word "lovely" immediately comes to mind in describing it. Built between 1892 and 1894, the **Hessiches Staatstheater Wiesbaden** in its design and decoration is basically baroque in the Austrian manner with few elements of the ponderous, pre-1914 German-imperial style (the architect was the Viennese Ferdinand Fellner). No one I have asked seems to know how many times the theater has been renovated or the seating arrangements modified, but the unusual width of the horseshoe curve gives most of the seats in the three balconies an unobstructed view of the stage. The blend of sound from the singers and the orchestra is pleasantly warm and clear. It is a very attractive and comfortable theater. Unfortunately this company now seems to lack firm direction at the top, and much of their effort is marred by very uneven singing and tacky, overly-contrived staging. In spite of a finely-trained chorus and a good orchestra (which by themselves cannot hold a performance together), all of the productions I have seen or read about were consistently poor and, in short, "provincial" in the worst sense. Undoubtedly there must be some works in the current repertory that are done well, but I cannot name them. If you go to Wiesbaden, go without your expectations too high.

Since Roman times the city has been esteemed for the curative powers of its abundant thermal springs. It is spaciously laid out, with many attractive parks bordering both the commercial and residential quarters. Wiesbaden has no outstanding architectural monuments (new or old) in its center: the two tall nineteenth-century churches, one Protestant and one Catholic, dominating the skyline are rather austere and graceless. More successful architecturally (to my taste) is the finely-proportioned colonnade that marks off the park in front and to the sides of the opera house. The oldest part of Wiesbaden is quite small and without any special charm or distinction; most of it is now a pedestrian zone. If you are seeking out rustic quaintness, it can be found quite close to the city in the famous and picturesque Rheingau region on the eastern bank of the Rhine as far as Rüdesheim (on this stretch the river is flowing from east to west). The vineyards begin on the edge of Wiesbaden and extend for some 18 miles (30 kilometers); this excursion can be made quite easily by train.

The opera house is in a park in the heart of the city, about 1.2 miles (2 kilometers) north of the Hauptbahnhof. Wilhelmstrasse, the city's most elegant commercial avenue, runs by the side of the colonnade that leads to the main doors of the theater. From the station to Wilhelmstrasse there are two choices of routes: directly across from the station is Bahnhofstrasse (basically a residential street) which goes straight north to the center of town (an underground tunnel avoids the congested square in front of the station); after four long blocks north, turn right on Rheinstrasse, the wide street with the tree-lined median; then after one block turn left, and go north again; this is Wilhelmstrasse, and the theater will be on your right, about 4/10's of a mile ahead (700 meters). The other route is somewhat off to the right at an angle from the front of the station: Friedrich-Ebert-Allee (with at first a park on the left and public buildings set back from the street on the right); after a gentle bend this street with a tree-filled median becomes Wilhelmstrasse at the junction with Rheinstrasse, about half-way to the theater; continue straight on to the theater, as you would if you had come from Bahnhof-strasse. The main stop for busses is on the east corner of Bahnhofstrasse opposite the station. Bus lines #1, #8, and #16 all go north to the center of the city and stop on Wilhelmstrasse by the side of the theater. A single fare costs DM 2, and a *Tageskarte,* good for 24 hours, DM 7. These can be bought from machines at the bus stop.

The season in Wiesbaden opens in late September and closes at the end of June. The annual repertory usually includes a total of some fifteen different works, of which two or three may be operettas and in some years an American musical. Most of the operas are familiar fare, drawn from Mozart, Rossini, Donizetti, Verdi, Bizet, and Puccini. Both Wagner and Richard Strauss have been meagrely represented and not enthusiastically received when Wiesbaden has tried them. In one of its very rare incursions into quite unhackneyed repertory, the company mounted Franz Schrecker's *Das Spielwerk und die Prinzessin* during its 1987–88 season; from what I have heard and read, the staging was a total disaster and the singing varied from quite good to very bad. A *Samson et Dalila* I saw in October failed to come across for many of the same reasons: the staging was boorishly wrong-minded and those cast in the lesser rôles sang better than the principals. *Samson* was done in French, but unless I had read the program I would not have known it. Some of the Verdi and Puccini is done in Italian, as is some of the Mozart (*Don Giovanni* in Italian but *Le Nozze* in German).

The large stage of this theater (the *Grosses Haus*) is shared with both plays and dance programs, but on average there are around sixteen opera (or operetta/musical) performances each month. There is no pattern as to when these are scheduled, but if several are to be performed on successive nights there is usually something requiring lighter voices sandwiched between two "heavier" offerings. It is often possible to see four different works (one at least will be an operetta or musical) in a sequence of four nights, followed by a series of ballets or plays. If and when the theater does close, Monday is the night of choice, but there are infrequent exceptions.

The singers in the regular company are of many different nationalities and some of them quite young. Among these are a number of Americans, several of whom have garnered high praises from the public and critics. A persistent problem for Wiesbaden seems to be not so much the quality of the voices themselves but a management that too often mishandles the casting. The chorus however is consistently excellent and sings very well even when forced to strike awkward poses demanded by the stage directors. The orchestra too, the Staatstheater-Orchester, can be relied on for solid and good musicianship.

The Box Office is inside the theater in the main outer lobby and is open at the following times: from Tuesday through Friday, from 1100 to 1330 and from 1630 to 1800; Saturday, Sunday, and holidays, from 1100 to 1230; closed on Monday. The Box Office opens one hour before each performance. Prices range from a high of DM 40,50 to a low of DM 8,00. Orchestra seating in this theater is only thirteen rows deep, with the first seven rows called *Sessel* and the six rows behind them called *Parkett*. The First Balcony *(I Rang)* is more difficult to describe because behind the double row of "open" seats entirely circling this tier there are twenty small Boxes *(Logen)*, plus in the middle a large Box *(Grosse Loge)* seating twenty. Seats in the front rows of the Boxes are far forward, almost comparable to a seat without a bothersome overhang. Opposite the stage the Boxes have space for four; on the sides space for only two. The Second Balcony *(II Rang)* is fairly shallow with four rows of "open" seats in the center; near the stage these rows shrink to three. The Third Balcony *(III Rang)*, steeply raked, has a fairly large seating capacity and is quite deep; beginning in the center with eight rows, as one rounds the curve towards the stage the number of rows then is reduced to seven, then five, and finally one at the ends.

Orders for tickets in advance are taken by telephone three weeks before the performance. However in the monthly flyer announcing forthcoming programs Box Office management has inserted a notice to the effect that their single number: (0-61-21) 132-325 is scarcely adequate to take care of the demand; callers, it is implied, should be patient. Written requests for tickets are honored at any time, but the tickets should be called for within twenty-one days before the performance ("in principle" a reply is sent from the theater if the requested seats are not available). There are no stipulations about sending money when the order is first made, but tickets must be paid for no less than one day before the performance or they are put back on sale to the public. The mailing address for tickets is: Theaterkasse, Hessisches Staatstheater Wiesbaden, 47 Wilhelmstrasse, 6200 Wiesbaden.

Not to be left unseen in this theater is the sumptuous *Foyer* which is off to the far left side as you face the building. (It is easy to not know that the room exists because the only public entrances on both the Orchestra- and First Balcony-levels come off the corridors on the side of the theater.) Built in 1902 after the construction of the opera house it is the architect Fellner's unrestrained, self-indulgent homage to Austrian baroque at its most florid and exuberant. During intermissions the *Foyer* serves as a bar and smoking room. At other times it is used for chamber and choral concerts.

Tourist Information is available at both the Hauptbahnhof and on the corner of Rheinstrasse where it intersects with Wilhelmstrasse. The office in the station is to the far right in the first main hall after one leaves the train platforms. This office also has the more convenient hours: daily, from 0800 to 2100. The telephone number is: (0 61 21) 31-28-48. You pass right by the "downtown" office when you take either of the routes suggested for going from the station to the opera house (see above for precise directions). It is however open only on weekdays, Monday through Friday, from 0800 to 1830; closed on weekends and holidays; the telephone numbers are: (0 61 21) 31-28-47 or 31-43-53. The address for mailing: Verkehrsbüro, 15 Rheinstrasse, 6200 Wiesbaden. Both offices will make calls for hotels free of charge (no deposit is required).

Unless you know the city well it is best to consult the Tourist Information office before setting off in search of lodging. Unlike most other cities in Germany, here the area immediately across from the station has no hotels but is occupied by a park on one side and residential and business buildings on the other. There are a few hotels on Bahnhofstrasse within a short walk of the station, but all are in the moderate or upper price range (because of the trees lining the sidewalks they can't be seen from Bahnhofplatz). There are a number of hotels very close to the opera house and many on the side streets about half-way between the station and the theater.

A bank for changing money is located in the Hauptbahnhof on the right side of the outer main hall. They are open from Monday through Saturday, 0800 to 1200 and from 1230 to 1945; on Sundays and holidays from 0900 to 1200 and from 1230 to 1700. Both American Express (on Webergasse) and Cook's (on Rheinstrasse) maintain branches in the city.

WUPPERTAL, normally, is not a city that one's travel agent would

say is on the "don't-miss" list. But for someone seeking out superlative opera it is well worth a visit. The **Wuppertal Opera** is highly regarded for many reasons: an excellent and highly trained ensemble company, adventurous repertory, usually with at least one world première every year, and imaginative staging. When Wuppertal mounts a new production critics come from all over Europe to appraise it. Among German companies it enjoys a reputation quite out of proportion to its size. The only "provincial" aspect of its productions is that all are performed in German translation.

With its population of almost 400,000 Wuppertal is actually a grouping of several small towns (mainly Barmen and Elberfeld) that came together in the 1920's to form one large city. It has a certain charm and rustic flavor because it is strung out for almost ten miles along the long and narrow valley of the Wupper River and is a curious mixture of church steeples, factory smokestacks, and country houses set off in unspoiled woodlands that often reach into the heart of the city. For train buffs the city is known for its famous *Schwebebahn* or aerial railway, a transit system dating back to 1900 that runs the length of the valley and for most of the way is suspended over the river itself. Also of interest in Wuppertal is the Von der Heydt Museum which houses an outstanding collection of 19th- and 20th-century painting.

The Wuppertal opera house, showing elements of Jugendstil, is basically round in shape with a steeply raked *Parkett* and two balconies; only a few seats close to the stage are without good sight-lines. The auditorium has a kind of elegant simplicity and seats 850 people; the acoustics are excellent. Access to the seats on the top-most levels is "segregated" and is restricted to doors and stairs at the side of the theater; if you suffer from acrophobia you should ask to be admitted through the main doors serving the *Parkett* because the other narrow stairs circle somewhat precariously the bare walls of a hollow cylinder some 60 feet high. Looking directly down can be quite frightening.

Wuppertal's repertory is not large, with usually some fifteen different works scheduled during a single season. In 1988–89 they repeated their highly successful (and controversial) *Ring des Nibelungen,* an admittedly audacious but very typical undertaking by this company. Add to the operas a few musicals (such as *My Fair Lady* and *Candide*), a Lehár operetta, and occasional performances by the resident ballet company, and this represents a fair sampling of what Wuppertal offers from one year to the next. The season extends from September through the end of June, but there are times when the house will be closed for several nights in a row. Wuppertal takes its productions to other cities in the area, and on some occasions the theater may remain dark for as many as four or five nights in a row. There is no pattern as to those times when the theater is closed. As for the singers who make up this company I for one was not familiar with any of their names; apparently both the young and older members of the ensemble are given little time in which to develop reputations with some of the bigger houses. In seeing a performance in Wuppertal it is quite evident that this is a troupe that is highly trained to work together: the moment they appear on stage and begin to sing and act, their professionalism is quite obvious. Among those on the conducting staff there are several who are beginning to become known for their work with the orchestras of other theaters in Germany.

The Box Office is located in an annex just off to the right of the main entrance to the theater and is clearly marked from the outside. Their hours are as follows: on Monday, 1630 to 1930; Tuesday through Friday, 0930 to 1300 and 1730 to 1830; Saturday, from 0930 to 1300; closed on Sunday. Tickets may be bought ten days in advance of the performance, and from either the opera Box Office in Barmen or the playhouse *(Schauspielhaus)* Box Office in Elberfeld (see below for directions about Elberfeld). The telephone numbers (for Barmen) are: (02-02) 55-00-55 or 55-66-07 and are open to receive calls one-quarter hour after the regular Box Office hours begin. Prices are quite reasonable, from a low of DM 9 to a high of DM 35. Given the small size of the theater and the good sight-lines in almost all of the upstairs seats, where the ticket prices are very inexpensive, an enjoyable evening of opera in Wuppertal need not cost you very much.

Now for the problem of getting to Wuppertal! Finding the opera house is quite simple because I know of no other city in Germany where the theater is almost directly across the street from the railroad station, but this happens to be the station in Barmen, where only suburban trains stop, not the station in Elberfeld where all the through trains on the main line either from Cologne or Düsseldorf will stop. All of this goes back to the fact that two towns joined together to form Wuppertal, and though both have large train stations, only one, the station in Elberfeld, is now served by express trains. The Barmen station is basically un-manned and has no facilities for buying tickets or for seeking information; you find out about train times from what you can see posted on the station walls.

It is quite easy however to reach the Barmen part of Wuppertal by using either the extensive suburban train service (called the *Nah Verkehr*) of the German National Railway (the *DB*), the *Schwebebahn,* or the bus network. (Eurailpasses are valid on the suburban trains in all directions but not on the other systems.) All of the suburban trains stop at Wuppertal-Barmen, and there is a train every few minutes between there and the Elberfeld station. Frequent service exists as well on this line connecting Wuppertal with Essen, Hagen, and Düsseldorf. One last caution: be sure that you get off at the Barmen stop, not at Oberbarmen, which is yet another suburban part of Wuppertal some two miles from where you want to be (if you want to be near the opera house).

Wuppertal-Elberfeld is now the main railway station for express trains serving the entire area. It has a full complement of services but no bank on the premises for exchanging money "out of hours." Tourist information for Wuppertal can be found at the end of the long tunnel sloping down the hill from the station into the center of Elberfeld. Look for a glass pavilion at street level called the Pavillon Döppersberg (a *Schwebebahn* station is next door). The Tourist Information Office hours are as follows: Monday to Friday, 0900 to 1800; Saturday, 0900 to 1300; closed on Sundays and holidays. Telephone: (02-02) 563-22-70.

Hotels in both Barmen and Elberfeld are within easy walking-distance of both stations, but as far as I can tell there is not a wide range of choices. When you come out of the main doors of the Elberfeld station at the top of the hill at least one hotel will be visible on your right. In Barmen when you leave the station it will look as though there were no hotels in that part of the city, but if you go immediately to your right and follow Friedrich-Engels Allee (a distinguished native son) some 500 feet to the Alter Markt (a very modern station for the *Schwebebahn* sets off the spot), you will see a number of hotels off to your right and to your left across the Wupper.

As noted above, no facilities exist for changing money in either the Elberfeld or Barmen station. There are as well no local branches of either American Express or Cook's.

GREAT BRITAIN

LONDON. Since the 1970's the British have witnessed a remarkable increase in the public's enthusiasm for opera. Regional companies outside London have been flourishing, although budgetary problems brought on by Thatcher economies have caused one group, Kent Opera, to disband. In the capital itself both Covent Garden (The Royal Opera) and the Coliseum (The English National Opera) usually play to full houses. Occasionally some of the city's major orchestras—no other city can boast of having so many!—schedule concert or semi-staged versions of opera. Many smaller groups, using "pick-up" singers and instrumentalists, produce opera rarities throughout the year; these groups appear in halls ranging from the Royal Festival Hall and Barbican Centre to pocket-sized theaters and spaces arranged in converted warehouses. To add to this mix there are frequent visits by touring companies, both English and foreign, as well as visiting orchestras from abroad doing operas in concert form. Though I cannot provide specific numbers, London in the course of a single season seems to have more opera, and operas from a wider choice of styles and periods, than any city in the world.

Details are given below for both Covent Garden and the English National Opera at the Coliseum. Finding tickets for some performances at Covent Garden can at times be difficult, but the information I provide should get you inside the theater (except on the most unusual gala occasions). I also describe London's major concert halls where with some frequency there are performances of opera in semi-staged or concert form. At the Royal Albert Hall, for example, the exclusive Glyndebourne Festival brings into the city in late summer one of the operas that figured in its just-finished season. With so many fine orchestras based in London: the BBC Symphony, the London Philharmonic, the London Symphony, the Philharmonia, the Royal Philharmonic, and many equally noted chamber ensembles, you might choose on some nights to forego the lyric theater and to sample London's concert fare. It is excellent.

Following the description of London I list the regional opera companies. Most of these groups continually move about while touring within a fixed area of the country. Their schedules are usually given in full-page advertisements in the English monthly magazines *Opera* and *Opera Now*. Ticket information and reservations are available by calling numbers outside of London. These telephone numbers are always listed along with the schedules.

Note: In describing the seating in their theaters the English use the word "stalls" to designate what we in the USA call "seats." Generally this term in most theaters is confined to the seats on the orchestra-level, but at Covent Garden it is also used in describing the seats on the third tier, the "Balcony Stalls." Though to an American the word suggests a small, enclosed cubicle for housing a horse, there is nothing unusual or animal-like about the construction of the seat. It is a seat like any other and, what is more, often sold at a premium price.

THE ROYAL OPERA HOUSE, COVENT GARDEN is a beautiful theater, both inside and out. It has a feeling of great warmth and elegance, the rich, deep red of the stage curtain and seat upholstery set off by the ivory white and gold of the walls and bands separating the upper seating levels. In spite of the horseshoe shape most of the seats, except those closest to the stage, have good sight-lines. The acoustics are a marvel of richness and clarity, even in those seats under an overhang, but the blend of voices and orchestra is at its best on the uppermost levels at the back of the theater.

When full, Covent Garden can accommodate 2113 people, plus 43 in standing room, confined to the aisle behind the Stalls Circle. (Standing room is sold only when the performance is otherwise sold out and even then at the discretion of the manager.) If the Stalls Circle seats are included (these are the raised rows of seats under the Grand Tier wrapped around the Orchestra Stalls at the back and on the sides), there are four levels of rings above the "ground" level: first, from bottom to top, the Stalls Circle, then the Grand Tier, the Balcony Stalls, and finally the Amphitheatre. Except in the Stalls Circle (three to four rows deep) and the Amphitheatre, each of these rings is quite shallow; the Amphitheatre, quite steeply raked at the top and back of the hall, has seventeen rows of seats. On the Amphitheatre-level Covent Garden uses two rather quaint terms to label the seating with poor sight-lines (but excellent sound) on the sides and near the stage: these are the Lower and Upper Slips. This area is not for those who are afraid of heights, for in order to see anything at all of the action on stage one must stand and lean out very perilously into the auditorium. Spaces here are almost always sold out by subscription because the prices are so cheap: £9 in the Lower Slips (only 36 seats) and £2.50 in the Upper Slips (143).

It is almost impossible to appreciate the handsome façade of the opera house because it is jammed against narrow Bow Street with a police precinct station just opposite. In recent years the market area to the side and behind the theater has been slicked up and is now filled with fancy specialty shops. To reach the theater by the Underground is quite easy: the station (on the Piccadilly Line) is just a few steps from the Box Office and the back of the theater, and signs from either the Long Acre or James Street exits clearly point you in the direction of Floral Street which runs along the right flank of the theater. By bus, getting off at Leicester Square on Charing Cross Road, Covent Garden is less than a ten-minute walk by Cranbourn Street, across St. Martin's, and then Long Acre to the tube station mentioned above. Or by bus, stopping at Aldwych and the Strand, follow either Wellington Street (the only major street in this area that crosses the Strand) that soon becomes Bow Street and goes in front of the theater or take Catherine Street, then left for a few steps on Russell Street, and then right on Bow Street.

The repertory at Covent Garden is extremely varied, very strong in both the Italian and German camps and balanced with a few Slavic works. At least one English opera, sometimes more, is on the annual schedule. Another strong point is the company's policy of keeping before the public neglected masterpieces from the 18th century (Handel, Gluck, etc.). If there are any notable gaps, in contrast to previous seasons, French composers are now somewhat neglected. Between 18 and 20 operas are presented annually, and a large proportion of these (at least in recent years) have been new productions (9 in 1988–89 and 8 in 1989–90). Surtitles are used for all the foreign-language works.

The singers' roster looks in part very much like that of the Met, with many of the same international stars who jet back and forth among the world's major houses. There are also a good number of very fine English, Italian, Scandanavian, and French singers whose names will not be as familiar. These are the singers who day-in, day-out provide the strength of this superbly honed company. The orchestra, heard on so many recordings that have come from this theater, is one of London's finest. Almost all of the conductors are well-known exemplars of their profession.

The stage at Covent Garden is shared with both the Royal Ballet and (in name only) with the Sadler's Wells Royal Ballet. (This last company is now principally a touring group, almost never performing in London; it will soon sever ties with this theater and settle into a new home in the English Midlands.) Although Covent Garden generally "operates" six nights in a row,

Monday through Saturday, in any given week it is impossible to predict how many operas, as opposed to ballets, will be on the schedule. In one week, for example, only one or two different operas may be presented on as few as two evenings; the other dates will be filled out with ballets. The following week however may be given over only to opera, with on rare occasions as many as four different works given in succession. Another quite unpredictable variable will be the scattering of evenings throughout the year when the theater is closed. This is because of rehearsals or scheduling problems, but Covent Garden's bi-monthly booklet announcing the upcoming programs always lists in advance the "no-performance" dates. If you want your visit to London to coincide with an opera night it is prudent to know the schedule in advance (see below under ordering tickets from the USA). Also note that the curtain goes up at 7:30 pm (1930) for most performances; Wagner and longer Strauss operas begin much earlier.

The combined opera and ballet seasons run from mid-September through mid-August. The late summer months may often include visits by opera or dance companies from abroad.

The Box Office is on Floral Street, opposite the north side of the theater and quite close to the tube station; if you are approaching the theater from the front on Bow Street, it will be the first street on the right side of the building. The hours are Monday through Saturday from 1000 to 2000; closed on Sundays and most holidays. All major credit cards (American Express, Access/MasterCard, Visa, and Diners Club) are accepted for orders given either in person or by telephone. Two numbers are listed for reaching the Box Office: (01) 240-1066 and (01) 240-1911. Tickets for Covent Garden are not cheap by any measure. Three price-scales are in effect for operas (ballets generally are set at about half these amounts): the lowest prices are for operas that are not especially popular or "sell-outs" with the public; the second is for most of the standard works in the repertory; and the third and highest category is reserved for galas and "blockbuster" performances, such as a *Trovatore* with Domingo. Seats in the Grand Tier, the most expensive in the house, sell for £64, £82, and £98 respectively; seats in the first eleven rows of the Amphitheatre, center, are priced at £19, £19, and £30 respectively. Fairly good seats elsewhere in the house will average between £43 and £70. Sixty-five rear Amphitheatre seats (called "Day Seats") go on sale at the Box Office at 10 am (1000) on the day of each performance and are priced at £12 at the lowest two ends of the pricing scale and at £20 at the highest end. Management however reserves the right not to make these available (as with the 43 Standing Room spaces) when TV cameras are in the house and on certain gala and other special evenings. Standing Room, for £6.50, is sold only when the rest of the house is booked and even then at the discretion of management; the times vary when these tickets can be bought, but generally it will be one hour before the curtain goes up. Prices in 1990-91 are due to rise sharply.

The program for each Covent Garden performance costs £2, but the folded insert, giving the night's cast, is duplicated within the program itself. Often you will see copies of this insert stacked up near where an attendant has been selling the programs, and you can pick it up for free.

Buying tickets by mail cannot be guaranteed, even if one strictly follows the "rules," because of the great number of seats that are held by regular subscribers. The season is divided into some ten booking periods, with each period for reservations by mail beginning on the 10th day of the month for all of the performances falling within the following third month. An example: beginning 10 October reservations by mail will be accepted for all works scheduled throughout December. Telephone reservations begin later, on the 2nd day of the next month for the following month. Another example: on 2 November telephone orders are accepted for all performances scheduled in December. If you are buying tickets from outside Great Britain payment may be made by credit card or with a check in sterling drawn on the branch of any London bank. The mailing address is: Royal Opera House, London, WC2E 9DD. From overseas, credit card purchases may also be made by Telex (27988 COVGAR G).

If you are prepared to spend between $130 and $160 for a Covent Garden seat, two of London's largest ticket agencies have branches in New York City that can probably find something for you. Edwards and Edwards and Keith Prowse maintain toll-free numbers and large staffs in New York. Usually they can tell you the schedule for Covent Garden from the bi-monthly brochure that is distributed free of charge at the Box Office in London. These agencies will only bother with the most expensive seats, which means that on top of a ticket price of somewhere between £59 and £75, translated into USA dollars, there will also be a fee of 24 %. Edwards and Edwards' toll-free number is (800-223-6108); in New York State dial (212-944-0290); they accept only American Express on credit charges. For Keith Prowse the numbers are (800-669-7469, new since May of 1989) and within New York State: (212-398-1430); they take American Express, Visa, and MasterCard.

When you find yourself in London and still without a ticket, the first step is of course to check with the Box Office on Floral Street. If they have nothing for the performance you want to attend, and you don't mind the uncertainty and risk of waiting until the last minute, people always turn up before curtain-time with tickets they cannot use and want to sell. The best place to stand and wait, about an hour before the curtain goes up, is by the side-door entrance on Floral Street, almost opposite the Box Office across the way. For some performances greatly in demand a few scalpers may be in the crowd. I understand that it is not against the law in England to buy a ticket from a scalper; scalpers are arrested on occasion, not for their business dealings, but only because they are guilty of "obstructing a public way."

The majority of ticket booking agents in London want nothing to do with selling Covent Garden tickets. They claim that with seats in such short supply (which is simply not true for many performances), it is not worth their time to call the Box Office and to be put on hold, waiting for a negative answer. However the London office of Edwards and Edwards may prove to be very helpful, though once again you will be offered only the higher-priced seats, plus a fee. Their London address is at 156 Shaftesbury Avenue, London WC2H 8PP (this is just a few doors up, northeast, from Cambridge Circus). Their telephone number is (01) 379-5822; all payments in cash, no credit cards. Though Keith Prowse in New York can promise you Covent Garden tickets, it is quite a different story when you approach their many branches scattered throughout London. The answer is "no" for Covent Garden in all but one: the office in the eastern part of Mayfair, close to New Bond Street, at 8 Grosvenor Street, London W1X 0AE; telephone (01) 629-4775.

If you visit London frequently, it would be to your advantage to become a member of the Friends of Covent Garden. The annual fee is £23, and this gives you priority notice of the schedule as well as priority booking privileges. The address is: Royal Opera House, London WC2E 9DD. For less money but without the special priority booking features of Friends membership you can be put on the mailing list to receive the bi-monthly announcements of programs. This also gives you the opportunity to write or call for tickets early. There are three subscription rates: for residents of Great Britain, £4.25; for Europe (and by airmail), £6.75; for the rest of the world (also by air), £12.75. The address is the same as above.

THE ENGLISH NATIONAL OPERA is London's second repertory company, offering 18 to 20 works each season, all performed in English with mostly native-born singers. What best characterizes productions at the ENO is their vitality and freshness, which usually does not mean novelty for its own sake. The ticket prices are about one-third the cost of comparable seats at Covent Garden, with many good seats available at between £12.50 and £19.50. The ENO's "home" is the London Coliseum, an enormous and ugly barn of a theater which won its name, when it was built in 1904, because it was the city's largest. Though the word "Coliseum" evokes a Roman-style arena, this is not some kind of sports palace but very much a theater and one of the few where all of the seats have excellent sight-lines. With a 2358 seating capacity it still remains London's largest.

The London Coliseum is quite close to Trafalgar Square, just a few steps up St. Martin's Lane on the right side of the National Gallery. Or from another angle, a few doors up the hill past the church of St. Martin's-in-the-

Fields. The nearest Underground stop is at Charing Cross (both the Metropolitan and Northern lines serve this station); busses stop in front of the National Gallery and on the southeast corner of Trafalgar Square. If you are using the Piccadilly line of the Underground the nearest station is at Leicester Square and a short walk downhill on Charing Cross Road.

In embellishing the interior (and exterior) of the Coliseum the designers must have thought they were giving us a comprehensive lesson in the history of architecture, from East to West, but lingering long in Imperial India. In achieving this awful eclectic wonder just about the only thing omitted is a trace of the Gothic, but more practiced eyes than mine, I am sure, would know how to find even something Gothic folded somehow into the Oriental baldaquins or the huge Byzantine-like dome overhead. Leaving aside the unfortunate décor of the building, it is a theater that serves its purposes fairly well: the width of the structure allows for an extremely large stage. Three deep and steeply raked balconies, almost parallel with the stage area (not wrapped or turned into the side walls), provide excellent sight-lines from nearly all parts of the auditorium. These are labelled first as the Dress Circle, then the Upper Circle, and finally at the top, the Balcony. The voices from the stage come through very clearly, but there are some odd problems with the sound from the orchestra pit. There seem to be many spots in the hall where not all of the orchestra comes through as a blend: some instruments are too loud, others barely audible. This is not the fault of the conductor and may be due to the gigantic, hollow dome in the ceiling over the stalls seating area where the sound is partially lost and perhaps re-mixed. I am told that the acoustics are excellent in the Balcony where the seats are made of wood and very hard—but very reasonable in cost: between £2.50 and £6.00.

The 18 to 20 operas presented annually usually include some 6 new productions, these last, sometimes in conjunction with other companies. Italian, German, French, Russian, and English works figure in the repertory. All are performed in English, a tradition faithfully upheld since the founding of the company in 1931. Important also with the ENO is the attention given to contemporary opera, and the company has given the première performances in England and in Europe of many works, such as Britten's *Peter Grimes* and more recently some of Philip Glass'. With the 1988-89 season the company embarked on a project of commissioning a new work each year from a young English composer. At least one Gilbert and Sullivan operetta is included in the annual repertory. Like the recent ENO version of *Rigoletto* set in New York City among Mafia-types, the G & S productions break with tradition, discarding many time-worn conventions and adding refreshing new vigor to the music and the plots. Innovative staging has become a kind of hallmark of this company, which can count many more successes than failures in its effort to shake the dust off some of the tired old war-horses of the standard repertory.

The singers with the ENO may include a dozen or so familiar names, but most of them will not be known to the average USA opera-goer. The majority come from the British Isles. Some are young and just beginning their careers. Others, who have sometimes "filled in" at the Met or been engaged to sing in houses such as San Francisco and Seattle, have not been bent on pursuing international "stardom"; they seem content with the exposure they receive at ENO and with occasional appearances with Britain's regional companies. A few go back and forth to Covent Garden, while still others are under contract to smaller opera companies on the Continent. The ENO is in many ways comparable to the New York City Opera (or as the latter once was in its early days) because of its mission in fostering young, native talent. Even though ENO has no big international stars, with all the attendant glamour and excessive hype, the quality of its singers is indeed very high.

The conductors' roster does contain a good number of familiar names. The orchestra of the ENO, a splendid ensemble, offers proof in nearly every performance that they have been shaped by some very fine leaders.

The season at the London Coliseum begins in late August and ends in mid-June. Performances are normally scheduled for five evenings a week, from Tuesday through Saturday. Sometimes around a holiday time the Tuesday performances are omitted; on rare occasions during other parts of the season Monday evenings will be added to the schedule. On average three different operas will be offered within the same week and then repeated on other nights during the second, following week. In the third week a new work is added and one is dropped. There are no ballets or other presentations competing for the stage.

The Box Office is inside the main doors to the theater, off to the left. They are open, Monday through Saturday, from 1000 to 2100; closed on Sundays and on certain weekdays preceding or following holidays. Given the size of the theater, no glamorous foreign stars, little snob appeal, and few tourists clamoring to get inside, there is no great problem in finding tickets. The rules for booking seats are less stringent than those in effect at Covent Garden because the season is divided into only three segments, each corresponding roughly to fall, winter, and spring. This means as well that the schedule is published well in advance of the time when you might expect to be visiting in London. For those with priority booking privileges (subscribers, Friends of ENO, and those on the company's mailing list) tickets may be ordered approximately five weeks before the start of each booking period; for the general public, three weeks before. All major credit cards are accepted. There is only one pricing scale for all performances: £26 for Orchestra Stalls (center) and in the Dress Circle, front center and the first few side rows; £19.50 for Orchestra Stalls (sides) and middle rows, center and sides, Dress Circle; £14 for rear of Dress Circle; £12.50 for about two thirds (middle and sides) of the Upper Circle; £10.50 for seats, rear Upper Circle; and in the

Balcony, the topmost level, £6 for front and middle, £5 front rows on the side, and finally £2.50 for the very back. For ordering by mail: ENO, London Coliseum, St. Martin's Lane, London WC2N 4ES. An assortment of telephone numbers is given for various needs. For charging tickets to a credit card: (01) 240-5258; for seat reservations that must be paid for and picked up within three days: (01) 836-3161; for recorded information about booking: (01) 836-7666; and for general inquiries about the schedule, etc.: (01) 836-0111. For £2.50, 100 seats in the rear of the Balcony go on sale each day beginning at 1000. Standing Room (at the back of the Dress Circle and Upper Circle) is available in principle, priced at £3.50, but is rarely offered. Ticket-holders for seats in the Balcony are "segregated" from the patrons in the rest of the theater; they must use a special door and stairs around the corner to the left of the main entrance, on the north side of the building.

Programs for the ENO cost £1, and if you are interested in knowing something about the artists involved, they are worth the modest price.

As with Covent Garden, there is a Friends of the English National Opera organization with a number of membership privileges, including priority booking for tickets. The annual individual membership price is £18 and must be paid either by check (in sterling) or by postal (or international) money order. The address is: Friends of the ENO Ltd., Registered Office: The London Coliseum, St. Martin's Lane, London WC2N 4ES. To be put on the ENO mailing list, which includes priority booking, three rates are in effect; within Great Britain and Ireland, £4.25; for Europe, £8.50; and for the rest of the world, by airmail, £12.50. For applicants within Great Britain and Ireland, credit cards may be used; for all others, payment must be made either by check in sterling or by international money order.

On the walls of the bars and lounges at the front of the theater, downstairs and on the upper levels, there are many interesting framed mementoes of earlier events that took place on the stage of the London Coliseum. Most notable are broadsheets announcing Sir Thomas Beecham's many performances of opera and appearances by some of the most famous actresses and actors of pre-World War I England.

An excellent book and record shop with items related to opera is located just to the right of the main doors to the theater, at 31 St. Martin's Lane. Most important for the readers of this Guide, they stock copies of the Hamburg-based magazine *Das Opernglas* which is so useful for finding opera schedules on the Continent.

CONCERT HALLS: A number of concert halls in London often serve as the venues for performances of opera in either concert form or semi-staged. Among these is the **Royal Festival Hall**, the first (1951) and largest of the buildings that have gone up to form a thriving arts complex on London's

South Bank. This is a very handsome and comfortable auditorium. Its "shoe box" shape permits an unobstructed view of the stage, with three terraced seating areas rising gracefully from the front of the hall to the back (Stalls, Terrace, and Grand Tier at the rear). The small boxes, which are clustered close to the stage, should be avoided because of their poor sight-lines. They were described by Sir Thomas Beecham, who had nothing kind to say about this hall, as looking like "sets of false teeth." (One wonders what Sir Thomas thought of the redundant opulence of that Edwardian atrocity, the London Coliseum!) From the back rows of the Royal Box, here called the "Ceremonial Box," often used by the Queen Mother and other members of the Royal Family, an orchestra playing on stage cannot be seen at all. For solo recitals the RFH can seat as many as 2931 when the area behind and on the sides of the stage is converted into additional tiers of seats. The London Philharmonic, the Philharmonia, the Royal Philharmonic, and the BBC Symphony regularly perform in the RFH. The London Symphony, though its "home" is the Barbican, also appears here, along with many notable ensembles from abroad and from other cities in the British Isles. While primarily designed as a concert and recital hall, ingenious machinery can transform the concert platform and first rows of the Stalls into a regular theater, complete with proscenium and orchestra pit. The English National Ballet (formerly called the London Festival Ballet) now has a month-long summer season in this hall.

Next door to the Royal Festival Hall and connected to it by ramps is the newer **Queen Elizabeth Hall** (1967), a smaller auditorium that is also often used for presentations of opera in concert. It is especially good for baroque works requiring reduced forces. The seating here is all on one level (Stalls and Rear Stalls) but raked so as to provide excellent sight-lines and good sound. Many well-known chamber groups regularly perform here, among them the London Bach Orchestra, the Academy of St. Martin's-in-the-Fields, and the London Mozart Players. The hall can hold as many as 1059 people at a solo recital when seats are placed on the stage.

Tickets for events in the Royal Festival Hall and Queen Elizabeth Hall are on sale at the Box Office in the RFH, daily, between 1000 and 2100. No space is provided for Standees. (Tickets may also be bought here for the **Purcell Room**, a much smaller space, seating 373, used primarily for lectures, solo recitals, and small ensembles.) Sales begin approximately three and a half weeks before all events scheduled for the entire following month. Purchases by mail from abroad are complicated by the fact that all orders must include a stamped, self-addressed envelope (with of course British stamps). It is easier to buy tickets using the number for credit card charges: (01) 928-8800. Major credit cards are accepted.

There is much to explore just within the RFH because of the many interesting exhibition areas tucked into the various levels of the building.

Much of this space was added in the mid-1960's when the RFH was closed and renovated and a large extension attached to the Thames-side of the building. There are also shops selling musical scores and recordings and a good bookshop. On every level one can find food and drink, ranging from a simple cup of coffee, beer, or a sandwich to a salad bar and an elegant restaurant overlooking the Thames. Free lunch-time concerts are given daily in the open areas near the food-catering facilities.

Outside and attached by ramps to the RFH are other buildings that make up this busy arts complex: the Hayward Gallery, for large traveling exhibitions; the National Film Theatre, exactly what its name implies; and the National Theatre, the newest component in the South Bank Centre, containing the Olivier, Lyttelton, and Cottesloe theaters. Busses crossing Waterloo Bridge stop nearby, and for the Underground both the Bakerloo and Northern Lines serve Waterloo station, behind the complex.

The **Barbican Centre**, opened in 1982, is a north-side-of-the-Thames (and somewhat more plebeian and commercial) counterpart to its older rival on the South Bank. Built in an area that was devastated by bombs during World War II, the Centre now serves as the "home" for the London Symphony in Barbican Hall and for the Royal Shakespeare Company in the Barbican Theatre and the Pit. The Centre also contains the Guildhall School of Music and Drama, one of London's largest public lending libraries, exhibition and conference halls, an art gallery, three film theaters, and many restaurants and informal cafés. Because of the vast size of the complex it is easy on one's first visit to get thoroughly lost. Finding the right floor for your seat in Barbican Hall can also be confusing because there are nine levels to choose from. Even finding the core of the building is complicated until you learn something of the layout. Both of the Underground stations, Moorgate and Barbican, are at some distance (likewise for the most convenient bus stops), and this requires a long walk (ten to fifteen minutes) following ramps that make their way through a maze of high-rise apartment towers and around the sides of parks and artificial "lakes."

Though primarily designed for orchestral concerts and conferences, the platform at Barbican Hall can be adapted for presentations of semi-staged opera. The London Symphony uses this hall rather than the Royal Festival Hall for such performances, though the orchestra does appear sometimes on the other stage. The London Savoyards also present Gilbert and Sullivan in full costume at the Barbican. This is a splendid hall, open and spacious, with a very pure quality to the sound. The sight-lines are all good except for a small group of seats (so-marked in the seating plan) foremost in the Orchestra Stalls off in each corner near the stage. Behind and above the Stalls are two wide Tiers or balconies, each of which barely overhangs the seats below. The seating capacity is just over two thousand (2026), with no provisions for Standing Room. The Box Office is on Level 7, open daily, including holidays, from 0900 to 2000. Tickets for all of the events scheduled during an entire month usually go on sale within the first few days of the preceding month. For orders by telephone call: (01) 638-8891. All major credit cards accepted.

As with the complex on the South Bank many free concerts are scheduled at various times throughout the day and night. Some are arranged in conjunction with special exhibits, while others may explore through popular or folk music some theme related to classical concerts being given in Barbican Hall. One of the most interesting events in April of 1989 was a three-day marathon, using a variety of well-known groups, playing all 84 string quartets by Haydn; the audience could contribute, if they wished, to a fund for famine relief in Africa.

Royal Albert Hall, a wonderful relic of Victoriana completed in 1871, joins this list of London's concert halls because of the famous Proms that take place every night for eight weeks from late July to mid-September. Sponsored by the BBC and featuring the BBC Symphony, many other world-famous orchestras perform as well, giving Londoners a rare opportunity to hear a great variety of stimulating programs at bargain-prices. Opera figures very often in the series with top-ranked singers doing either excerpts or complete works in concert form. At other times operas are presented semi- or fully-staged. One of the most eagerly-anticipated events is the presentation of a complete work from the Glyndebourne Festival (in 1988 *Falstaff* and in 1989 *Le Nozze di Figaro*).

When the performing forces do not take up much space, Royal Albert Hall will hold up to almost 8000 people. As might be expected, the acoustics are quite variable and can be very good or only adequate. With its semi-circular shape not all of the seats or areas reserved for Standees have good sight-lines, but tickets are priced accordingly, and all are quite inexpensive to begin with. Prices in the assigned seating sections vary very little (Glyndebourne is one exception, going from £20 down to £5), but the Standees pay the same price at the door no matter what event is on the schedule. The flat area in the center of the hall, elongated to meet the front of the stage, is the Arena Promenade (only for Standees: £2); surrounding this circle are the Stalls (£11–£14), sloping up to the base of the first ring, the Loggia Boxes (£9–£11.50); above them are the First Tier Boxes, not available to the general public; then above the First Tier, the Second Tier Boxes (£9–£11.-50); the Balcony (£5), and finally at the top of the hall, the Gallery Promenade, a second area reserved for Standees (£1.50).

Confirmed Proms-goers buy Season tickets and before each concert prepare a good picnic supper to eat on while they wait in line for the doors to open, then to stake out choice positions in the Arena and the Gallery. Arena Season tickets cost £70, a half season, £45; Gallery Season tickets are £50, a half season: £30. These must be ordered by mail, and the opening date falls in early May: write Promenade Concerts Box Office, Royal Albert Hall,

London SW7 2AP; only Access/MasterCard and Visa are honored unless paying by check in sterling. By telephone, with all credit cards accepted, orders begin towards the middle of June: (01) 589-8212 or (01) 589-9465, with telephone lines open from 1000 to 1800, Monday through Saturday. Ticketmaster orders (no booking fee) are taken from this same date, and orders may be placed 24 hours a day, again with all major credit cards accepted: (01) 379-4444. The program guide, a handsome booklet giving much information about the concerts and the artists, costs £2.

Proms audiences pride themselves on their good behavior, though on occasion, during breaks between the music, a good deal of wit can be heard coming from the Arena and the Gallery. "Last Night," the final concert of the season, presents the only true "pops" program of the entire series, and tickets in the seated sections go way up in cost, ranging from £36 (Stalls) to £24 (Balcony). The boisterous good spirits of this closing evening are capped by a performance of "Rule, Britannia!" and the audience joins in exuberantly with much flag-waving—this is not a time when an outsider sees any trace of the usual tight-upper-lip British reserve!

The London Tourist Board has a large office just outside Victoria Station, a glass and blue-walled structure (that looks a bit like a modern solarium) jutting out from the solid walls of the old station. With the station in front of you and the taxi-stand to your back, it will be off to your far right. They are open from 0900 to 2030 daily and offer a wealth of information about the city, sightseeing tours, and hotels (which you can reserve); you can change money and even order theater tickets (but not for Covent Garden!). A fee of £3 is charged for hotel reservations, along with the first night's bill paid in advance. Other branches of the London Tourist Board are found at Heathrow, Selfridges, Harrods, and, between April and October, the Tower of London.

A number of private, competing agencies deal as well with hotel reservations for London (all of them charge the same £3 fee), and their booths are quite visible around the inside walls in the main halls of Victoria Station. (An agency of this sort is also at Gatwick, just before the entrance to the hall where tickets are sold for the "Gatwick Express" trains to Victoria Station.) The only problem with these reservation agencies is that only a certain number of hotels are linked up to their computers. Many hundreds of other small (and sometimes cheaper) ones are not listed in their computers. Consumer Reports sells a special booklet giving the addresses and rates of a limited group of smaller London hotels; though they are reliable, they have only scratched the surface.

If you decide to stay near Victoria Station, a convenient neighborhood because so many services are available at late hours, plus good tube connections and numerous bus routes, there are perhaps as many as a hundred small hotels in the vicinity. In the area to the northwest, west, and south of the station (but not in front) some of the streets are lined end to end with small hotels. Within a ten-minute walk or less, Belgrave Road, Warwick Way, Ebury Street, and Eccleston Place are good places to look for reasonably-priced hotels. Most offer singles at around £25 and doubles at around £40. These prices always include the "full English breakfast."

Transportation in London is quite easy and convenient once you discover the subtle link-up between the Underground (subway) and the elaborate bus system. There are various passes for unlimited travel that are available in the USA through some travel agents, AAA branches, and British Rail in New York. (In other major cities throughout the world these passes are also supplied through British Rail offices.) They must be bought before you arrive in London. A 3-day pass costs $13; a four-day $17; and a 7-day $29. However, should you leave the country without one or should the $ US-to-£ rate be more favorable to the US dollar, one-day passes can be bought in London in any large Underground Station, from machines, or in an office of London Transport (there is one in Victoria Station adjacent to the left-side entrance, opposite the entrance where you find the Tourist office). In London a one-day pass costs £2.30, and its only disadvantage, as opposed to the pass bought abroad, is that it cannot be used during the morning rush period, before 0930. You can buy any number of these one-day passes and have them validated for each day that you use them. The other pass, good for 7 days, if bought in London costs £6.40 and is valid only within the central zone of the city (not Heathrow), which would be adequate for most tourists. The prices go up each time another travel-zone is added to the inner-city zone (two zones: £8.20; three: £11.20, etc.). A passport photo is required with these 7-day passes.

Changing money in London is no problem. Everywhere you will see bank offices competing for your USA $'s, and in all of the larger railway stations there is a Cook's office prepared to change money. Both Cook's and American Express have many branch offices scattered throughout the city. A money-changing service is also offered by many of the theater booking agencies around the city, not necessarily in conjunction with your purchase of a ticket.

THE "REGIONAL" OPERA COMPANIES OUTSIDE OF LONDON (in alphabetical order). The schedules for all of these companies are published in *Opera* and *Opera Now*, where you will find as well the telephone numbers to call when the company is on tour. (Welsh National Opera gives only one number for booking; the

other companies list a number for each of the cities where and when they will be on tour.) Some of the productions by these companies are well worth investigating; *Opera,* and not *Opera Now,* in its reviews can be a fairly reliable guide as to which ones to seek out.

KENT OPERA, which in December of 1989 lost its subsidy from the British Council, has ceased to exist. In 1989 the company had just celebrated its twentieth year of touring. Among the cities and towns regularly visited by Kent Opera were Bath, Canterbury, Dartford, Eastbourne, Northhampton, Norwich, Southsea, and Tunbridge Wells. As of June 1990 no plans had been announced about attempts to revive the company.

OPERA NORTH, Grand Theatre, 46 New Briggate, Leeds LS1 6NU. Box Office telephone (in Leeds): (0532) 459-351. Ticket prices from £4 to £18.75. Opera North generally limits the cities it visits to five (including its "home" city of Leeds): Hull, Nottingham, Manchester, and on a few occasions, York. The season begins in September and ends in July. Some works in English translation, others in the original language. This company is finishing its tenth season in 1989 and remains one of the most praised and admired of the "new" regional groups.

SCOTTISH OPERA, 39 Elmbank Crescent, Glasgow G2 4TP. Box Office telephone (in Glasgow): (041) 248-4567. Ticket prices run from £3 to £32. This company, like the Welsh National Opera, sometimes assembles better-known singers for some of its productions and often goes abroad in putting together a cast. The season extends from September through the end of June. Some works are performed in English but most in the original language. The Scottish Opera does not confine its touring to Scotland (Aberdeen, Bradford, Edinburgh, Inverness, and Newcastle) but also includes Liverpool in its visits.

WELSH NATIONAL OPERA, New Theatre, Park Place, Cardiff CF1 3LN. Box Office telephone (in Cardiff): (0222) 394-844. Ticket prices from £6.50 to £25. Some of the productions mounted by this company have been hailed by many critics as among the best being currently done in Great Britain. Unlike any of the other regional companies the WNO maintains a brave policy of exploring repertory that is often overlooked by many of the major houses. The casts are an interesting mix of both British and a few foreign singers. Some operas are performed in translation and others in the original language. The season begins in September and ends in the middle of July. The Welsh wander far afield from their "native" Wales in their touring because they include cities between the Midlands and the Channel coast. Among the cities visited are: Birmingham, Bristol, Cardiff, Liverpool, Oxford, Southampton, and Swansea.

HOLLAND

AMSTERDAM is still a delightful city, in spite of the hippies who arrived in the 1960's, stayed, and defaced much of it. A few of them are still around, old and tired by now, having left in their wake a city that still in some sections is shabby and shockingly dirty. And hotel and food prices, at least near the Centraal Station, have become astronomically high, but the good-hearted Dutch, resilient, civilized, and still tolerant, go about their business as though nothing had changed.

The new opera house (fall 1986), officially **Het Muziektheater,** is quite stark and uninteresting from the outside, although at night and at a distance, when its lights are reflected in the surrounding canals, it sparkles like a freshly-cut diamond. Inside however, the new theater is stunning, with a rich, deep red the predominant color. A wide and large fan-shaped orchestra section, gently sloped, is supplemented by two semi-circular balconies. The seating capacity comes to a total of 1600, with all but a few seats on the extreme ends of the balconies having an excellent view of the stage. The acoustics are quite good: a "dry" but very clear sound that, I understand, engineers can adjust when they wish (the latest technical devices were incorporated into the construction of the building, with the idea of being able to vary the sound quality). The ceiling, best seen from either of the two balconies, is a high-tech wonder of intricate tubes and cut-out shapes in metal, punctuated by rows of lights. It is a huge sculptural work that merits being seen from many angles (during the intermissions of the opera find time to look at it from every part of the theater). Comfort too must have been a priority of the theater's designers both in arranging the seating inside the auditorium and in planning the very handsome and spacious lobby areas outside.

The season in Amsterdam extends from early September through the end of June, when during this last month the opera works in conjunction with the annual Holland Festival. Eight or nine works are presented on the block-system, usually with a new work introduced each month and then repeated seven to nine times. Some scheduling adjustments may yet be made in future seasons because the opera in its new house has reduced by almost one half the number of works that were seen when the company occupied the old and much smaller Stadsschouwburg. The Netherlands Opera Company is not a repertory group, with only the chorus and the orchestra, the Netherlands Philharmonic, a "constant" from one production to the next; even the conductors are changed. Most of the singers as well, including those who are Dutch, are not carried over to a second opera. With but a few exceptions the casts for each performance have very few familiar names; those who are well known seem to be usually either Americans, English, or Dutch. The repertory is very wide-ranging, with the so-called standard works often given a very provocative (and sometimes outrageous) interpretation by an outstanding avant-garde director. Each opera is sung in the language in which it was composed, even to the extent of having the artists learn Czech in order to perform Janácek. This company is to be commended for putting before the public each season at least one contemporary or specially commissioned opera.

Unlike the old Stadsschouwburg, which was easily accessible, the Muziektheater will at first seem far out of the way, but on the new subway the trip from Centraal Station takes only a few minutes. With either a #9 tram (from in front of the station) or the subway (the entrance is inside the station) you will want to get off at Waterlooplein, which is at the side and back of the theater. Keeping the theater on your right, head towards the bridge over the nearest canal (you will have just crossed it if you took the trolley) and keep going as the building curves around with only the canal at its front. (If you go around in the other direction you will have to circle all of the new Amsterdam Town Hall, which adjoins the theater, and possibly get lost finding your way back over canals and through side streets.) The Box Office is inside through several doors, straight ahead off to your right. They are open from Monday through Saturday from 1000 to 1800; on Sunday from 1200 to 1800. Prices start (in guilders) at f 20, then f 40, f 60, and a high of f 80. The Box Office telephone number is: (020) 255-455. The mailing address is: De Nederlandse Opera, Postbus 950, 1000 AZ Amsterdam. The Box Office opens one hour before an evening performance.

Tickets may also be purchased at the VVV Tourist Information Office just in front of the railway station, but the "cut-off time" for a performance on the day you order your tickets is 1600. The hours there are: Monday through Friday, from 1000 to 1600.

Most of Amsterdam's operas are taken to The Hague for a single performance on a special subscription series. (There is fast train service between the two cities at 30-minute intervals throughout most of the day, and trains on this line run until well after midnight. The trip usually takes about 45 minutes.) Though I understand that tickets for most productions are extremely hard to get, there is no harm in trying. Tickets may be bought at any VVV Office throughout Holland (in Amsterdam, see above) or telephone the Box Office in The Hague at: (070) 60-49-30. Performances are given at the Danstheater ann't Spui which is not too far from the main railway station. The Box Office in The Hague is open from Monday through Saturday, 1000 to 1500. There are only two price categories: f 40 and f 60.

While in Amsterdam do not miss an opportunity to hear the splendid **Amsterdam Concertgebouw Orchestra** (**Concertgebouworkest**). In 1988–89 the orchestra celebrated its hundredth birthday, and another cause for celebration was the reopening of their hall, closed for three years for very extensive structural and cosmetic renovations. The Box Office is now located in a very strikingly modern pavilion (not admired by everyone!) added on to the building toward the back on its left side (as you face the front). They are open daily from 0930 to 1900 and reopen 75 minutes before each scheduled performance. Tickets for the orchestra are priced at f 45 and may be purchased as well at the VVV Office across from the Centraal Station (see above for hours). Trams #2, #5, and #16 go from the station to the concert hall (the #2 tram turns off one block short of the hall); and a #67 bus will also deliver you to the door. All credit cards are accepted.

Tourist information is available just outside the Centraal Station in a low building off to the left on the canal-side of the trolley tracks. Their hours, from Monday through Saturday, are from 0900 to 2345; on Sundays from 0900 to 2100. In a separate building next door to the right you can buy the special passes that allow you to take an unlimited number of trips on the trolleys and busses that criss-cross the city. This office is open daily until 2230. These tickets are valid for a calendar day, not for 24 hours from the time when they are first stamped, but they will be good on the few bus routes that run after midnight. Prices begin at f 8,65 for one day; f 11,60 for a two-day pass; f 14,20 for three days; and an additional f 2,70 for each day thereafter, up to a total of 7 days.

There are numerous hotels of all kinds scattered throughout the city, but those nearest the Centraal Station, which are so convenient for using the various transportation facilities, will be horrendously expensive or, even if quite modest and spartan, still not cheap. There are some small and attractive hotels in the southern part of Amsterdam, below or south of the Rijksmuseum, where the prices are much more reasonable; these require however a 20- to 25-minute tram or bus ride to and from the station, and you no longer have convenient connections in getting to the opera house. In any case the tourist information people can prove helpful in finding something suitable to your needs and your budget.

Money can be changed inside the station between 0800 and 2200 seven days a week. As you face the station, the bank is near the end of the long corridor leading off to your left from just inside the main doors. There are three branches of American Express and nine Cook's offices scattered throughout the city.

HUNGARY

BUDAPEST. Since the beginning of 1989 Eurailpasses are now valid for travel to and within Hungary. No supplemental charges are levied. Vienna is the logical "jumping-off" place for train travel to Budapest, with four trains daily in both directions connecting the two cities. The trip of 273 kilometers takes between three and four hours, and all trains have dining car facilities.

Budapest's two opera companies, the **State Opera** and the **Erkel Theater,** offer a rich and varied repertory. Some seldom-produced works, such as early Verdi and operas by Respighi, reached the West through much-praised recordings some years ago, and many of these are still being staged in Budapest as of May 1990. The opera season in both theaters begins in early October and continues through the end of May. Both theaters schedule performances throughout the week but usually are closed on Mondays (in general no concerts or recitals at all are given on that day). It is also worth noting that a number of Saturday and Sunday matinées are on the calendar, and these almost always begin at 1100. Evening performances generally begin at 1900.

Ticket prices by Western standards are still very cheap, but what you might expect to save on opera-prices will probably be used up when you pay for your hotel accommodations. There are arrangements for reserving tickets in advance through the Vienna office of IBUSZ, the state-controlled Hungarian Travel Company. This is convenient because you might want to plan your trip around seeing certain operas and then make your hotel reservations when you are sure of having tickets. Tickets may also be bought in Budapest from the Central Theater Booking Office, 18 Népköztársaság Road, District 6 or at the theaters themselves. A free booklet, published each month in German and English, is available in Vienna giving the schedules for all of the cultural events in both Budapest and outlying cities. (I have no accurate information about the times when the Box Offices are open.)

All hotel reservations must be made and paid for in advance before crossing the border into Hungary. A visa is also required, costing 250 Austrian schillings (approximately $18 USA). To obtain the visa you must surrender your passport and provide two passport-size photographs. The advantage to doing this in Vienna (through the Hungarian Travel Company, Kärtner Strasse) is that everything is returned within 24 hours. The visa for Hungary is valid for 6 months but does have a 30-day limit on the length of each stay. There is also a restriction on the amount of Hungarian money you can take with you into the country: normally 100 Forint (Ft.), which is less than $2 USA; for a month's visit, up to 200 Forint. There are no limits imposed on the amount of other currency you take with you into Hungary. I am assured that foreign money can be easily changed inside the country. As of January 1990 the American Express representatives in Budapest are still housed in the IBUSZ office at 3 Petofi Ter and still subject to certain government-imposed restrictions. Cook's has two offices in the city: the Wagons-Lits division at 3 Dorottya Utca and their second office, like that of American Express, in an IBUSZ branch at 5 Felszabadulas Ter.

Most of the above information comes from the Vienna office of IBUSZ, the official travel agency of the Hungarian government. They are located at 26 Kärtner Strasse, just a few blocks behind the Staatsoper (going towards St. Stephan's). Their telephone is (1) 515-55-0, and they are open Monday through Friday, 0900 to 1800; on Saturday, from 0900 to 1200. The mailing address for IBUSZ is 26 Kärtner Strasse, 1010 Wien 1.

The addresses for the two Budapest opera companies are as follows: the Hungarian State Opera, 22 Népköztársaság Road, District 6 and the Erkel Theater, 30 Köztársaság Square, District 8.

The New York address of IBUSZ is Rockefeller Center, Suite 2455, 630 Fifth Avenue, New York, New York 10111. The telephone in New York is: (212) 562-7412.

ITALY

Attending an opera in Italy is both very rewarding and great fun, but on too many occasions an adventure as well. Unfortunately, with strikes now such an important component of life in that country, you can never be quite sure that the curtain will go up on the work that you've traveled so many miles to see. A halt in train or plane traffic may mean that even though all is well in the opera house, you have absolutely no means of getting there. Or if a whole series of performances isn't cancelled because the chorus or the orchestra has walked out, the annulment of even just one performance may scramble the entire schedule, with dates then changed and artists replaced. This may sound like an unduly pessimistic description of conditions in today's Italy, but, sad to say, it is all too true. You should make your plans accordingly, with all of your options left open, and hope that *la buona fortuna* will be kind. When all goes well, the experience can be wonderfully exciting. If there is some hitch, there is little you can do.

I give below details about Florence, Milan, Naples, Rome, and Venice, in that order, assuming that most tourists will be visiting those cities, either on their own or on something like the Perillo or TWA tours that promise the "best of Italy" in ten days. There are many other exciting cities in Italy that offer on occasion excellent operatic fare: Bologna, Genoa, Palermo, Parma, Pesaro, Trieste, and Turin, but given the poor odds of having success in only Milan and Rome, I shan't push our luck by expanding the list beyond the first five. At least not for this edition of the *Guide*.

With Italy being the birthplace of opera, every one of its older theaters is linked in some way to most of the country's major and minor composers.

To me part of the thrill of seeing an opera in Italy is to be sitting in a theater that has witnessed so much musical history. Milan's La Scala and Venice's La Fenice, for example, are closely tied to every one of the great nineteenth-century masters, but before all others, Verdi's name comes first; Naples' San Carlo is steeped in the early successes of Rossini and of the bel canto composers; and Rome's opera, originally the Teatro Costanzi before Mussolini modified the exterior, saw the triumph of all of Mascagni's earliest works and then of *Tosca*. Only Florence is absent from this list, as its totally revamped Teatro Comunale is fairly modern, but its Teatro della Pergola, now used for recitals and chamber opera, is much older than any of these other theaters. La Pergola in its own right wins a place on any list of theaters because it was one of the first (in 1652) to be built in an oval shape with tiers of boxes, thus serving as a model for many of the Italian theaters that came later.

All of the opera houses in Italy, except La Scala and Naples' San Carlo, strictly follow the *stagione* system of scheduling. This means that only one opera is presented over a period that may vary from one to three weeks, and because the singers cannot be expected to be on stage two nights in a row, there will be a gap between performances of at least one or two days, sometimes many more. On those dates when no opera is on the schedule there might perhaps be an orchestral concert, a ballet, or a recital, but very often this is not the case, and the theater will be dark. La Scala manages to find an uneasy compromise between the *stagione* and repertory systems; they may have two different operas, never more than that, playing together on successive nights. In spite of its huge resources, on many days La Scala too will be closed. Likewise, San Carlo sometimes succeeds in presenting two works concurrently. This is during the height of its season, February and March, but during the rest of the year only one work at a time occupies the stage. For anyone accustomed to the full schedules in Vienna, in London, and throughout Germany, the paucity of choices in Italian cities will come at first as a shock. But with a careful matching of dates you can offer yourself a wider repertory by including several opera centers in your itinerary—trusting that no strikes disrupt your plans.

It is interesting to observe the great differences in opera audiences as you travel from north to south. The La Scala public is rude and noisy if they don't like what they hear and see, and in their total lack of mercy, perhaps justified by the prices they have to pay for tickets, they can bring the bravest of singers to tears. The Florentine and Venetian audiences tend to be stuffy and conservative, but at least they are polite. In Rome and Naples one finds an enthusiasm and generosity (indulgence perhaps?) that are totally lacking further north. These opera-goers don't take themselves too seriously and appear to be out for an evening of pleasure even if things aren't going all that well on stage.

The Italian vocabulary for buying tickets poses no great problem. In spite of other differences in local dialects, theater jargon remains fairly uniform. The words below should be ample:

un biglietto, due biglietti are "one ticket, two tickets."

la biglietteria is the Box Office.

un posto, due posti are "a seat, two seats" or *posto* may simply mean a "position" or "place," such as in a box where you may end up in a poorly positioned seat or on an upholstered bench and have to stand if you want to see the stage.

una poltrona, due poltrone di platea will be one, two orchestra seat(s), *poltrona* meaning "armchair" and *platea* is "orchestra level."

una poltroncina will be a "chair without arms," such as one finds in a box or loge or it can be a smaller seat in the orchestra section. At La Scala, when this term is applied to the Galleries, the two topmost tiers, this will be a seat on the front row.

il palco is a "box" or "loge" in a theater. Some theaters but not all will rank and price the tickets by whatever level this should be above the orchestra section. Naples uses the term *fila* and Rome the term *ordine* to indicate the appropriate level: *prima fila, 1° ordine,* etc.

la prima galleria, la seconda galleria are the first and second balconies. In Milan at La Scala these will be the open rows of seating (no partitions between them) on the fifth and sixth levels above the rings of boxes. In Florence at the Comunale these will be honest-to-goodness balconies (as we in the USA think of them), wide and deep rows of seats immediately above the orchestra-level.

la balconata is the term used in Naples for the two top tiers; in Rome this label is applied to the fourth level, just below the *Galleria* at the top.

(un posto) numerato is used for a "numbered seat," which at La Scala will be the second row in either of the two Galleries.

ingresso means "admittance" and applies to Standing Room.

prenotazioni are "reservations made in advance."

turno A would be the first cycle, A, in a subscription series.

fuori abbonamento is "non-subscription."

FLORENCE (Italian: Firenze), proud and aloof, somehow manages

to retain its equilibrium in spite of the hordes of eager, noisy tourists crowding its streets and monuments every day of the year. During the latter half of the nineteenth century Florence fell far behind other cities in Italy in vying for the privilege of hearing the premières of new works by Verdi and those who were to follow him. Only with the founding of the Maggio Musicale in the early 1930's, the first and oldest of Italy's annual festivals, did the city regain with patrons of opera some of the prestige it had lost to its earlier rivals.

Florence has what amounts in effect to two lyric seasons: one in the fall that begins in late September or October and ends in December, and a second season in May and June, held in conjunction with the Maggio Musicale Fiorentino. (Between early January and the middle of May there are only ballets and orchestral concerts, no opera.) The house is the **Teatro Comunale,** a building constructed as an arena in the 1880's and gutted by bombs in the Second World War. Shortly after it reopened some years after the war, this time rebuilt as a modern theater suitable for opera, it was devastated by the terrible floods of 1966 and closed again for extensive repairs. (A plaque about mid-way back on the right-hand side of the orchestra section grimly shows the level reached by the avalanche of water and mud.)

The Comunale is a handsome and comfortable theater throughout, especially in the two large balconies *(Galleria).* There is seating for 1800 and at present, no Standing Room. Even though the two balconies curve on the ends and wrap into the side walls, they are open and not partitioned into boxes. In the center they are quite deep and steeply raked, with excellent sight-lines. As a kind of token reminder that this is an Italian theater a single ring of wide boxes surrounds the seats in the orchestra section (the *Platea*). The acoustics in all parts of the theater are quite good: clean, clear, and efficient, but without much resonance.

In the fall, when the lyric season begins, in principle one opera is introduced each month and repeated between six and eight times. There is no overlapping, with one work being phased out when a second one is beginning. The gap between each performance may vary from between two or three days to as many as five. To illustrate how carefully you must plan in advance in order to see opera in Florence: in the fall of 1988 *Tristan* followed closely after *Simon Boccanegra,* which had initiated the season at the end of September. Through most of November there was a "hole" of some four weeks, without any opera until *Madama Butterfly* began its run in early December. To the three works presented in the fall the Maggio Musicale usually adds three or four more during May and June. This tightening of the spring schedule is accomplished in part by using the Pergola for at least one of the operas and by presenting each work only four or five times. Traditionally the Maggio Musicale is committed to mounting at least one twentieth-century opera, but the directors of the festival are discreet in their choices, and after a *Lulu* in one year they may find that without compromising their ideals a *Pelléas et Mélisande* will meet those demands in a subsequent year. In the two Florentine seasons, with a total of only six or seven operas, there is a healthy balance in matching Italian works with works drawn from the German, French, and Slavic repertories.

From year to year the only continuity is found in the orchestral and choral forces. Though Florence has its regular and favorite conductors, others are brought in as guests. This is true for the singers as well. A good number of these will be international stars with a surprisingly large number of Americans. With but rare exceptions all foreign-language works are performed in the language in which they were written. Surtitles are now being used, with translations of course in Italian.

A few notes about the Maggio Musicale Fiorentino: The festival began in 1933 under the impetus of Vittorio Gui and became an annual event in 1937. One of its original purposes was to dispel some of the provincialism that had settled over Italy's musical activities. The festival has remained faithful to this objective. Interspersed among the operas and concerts by visiting big-name foreign orchestras there are a good number of very interesting vocal and solo piano recitals. The schedule also includes several dance programs. The Maggio Musicale orchestra during the entire year is in the pit for the operas and ballets, and in the winter they are featured by themselves or with soloists in frequent concerts. This is a very fine group of musicians, and during the festival, when several world-famous conductors are invited to come direct them, they surpass themselves, both as a pit orchestra and when they are on the stage by themselves.

The Teatro Comunale is not far from the Stazione Centrale, less than a ten-minute walk from the southwest or left side of the station (as you face it from the front), one block up from the Arno. It is in a "new" or unhistoric part of the city, on the corner of the Corso Italia and the Via Magenta. The Box Office is on the Corso Italia, off to the right of the main front doors of the theater, in an office by itself not connected (for the public) to the lobby of the theater. They are open from 0900 to 1300, every day except Mondays and holidays, and then again, one hour before curtain-time. The telephone number is: (055) 277-9236. Two price-scales are in effect: one for each initial performance of an opera and a second price for all subsequent performances. (This scale is further complicated by the fact that the opening nights of both the fall season and the Maggio Musicale festival are priced yet even higher. I omit these in giving general estimates of ticket prices.) For the three operas in the fall (in Lire): L. 60.000 for the Orchestra *(Platea);* L. 40.000 in the First Balcony *(Prima Galleria);* L. 15.000 in the Second Balcony *(Seconda Galleria).* During the Maggio Musicale, when one can expect prices to be somewhat higher, the costs for the same seating categories come to L. 80.000, L. 50.000, and L. 20.000 (respectively).

The **Teatro della Pergola,** used for at least one opera and for recitals during the spring festival, is in a more interesting part of the city, off to the northeast behind the Duomo at 12-32 Via della Pergola. The theater has obviously been much modified and often restored since the original structure in wood was put up in 1652, but it is still a gem—if one can overlook some of the shabbiness. It seats 960 people, with an orchestra section 24 rows deep, three rings of boxes, and a fourth level, the *Galleria* or Balcony: here there are six to seven rows of steeply raked seats at the back of the theater and as the Balcony completes its circle close to the stage the double rows are narrowed to one. The acoustics are excellent, but the view of the stage improves in direct proportion to one's distance from it.

The Box Office at the Pergola is open Tuesday through Saturday from 0930 to 1300 and from 1545 to 1845; on Sunday from 1000 to 1300. They open as well one hour before the curtain goes up. Closed on Mondays and holidays. The telephone is: (055) 247-9651. Prices for the *Idomeneo* given during the 1989 Maggio Musicale started at L. 60.000 for seats in the orchestra section *(Platea)*; L. 40.000 in the Boxes *(Palchi)*; and L. 15.000 in the Balcony *(Galleria)*.

Ordering tickets by mail is complicated by the fact that the opening dates for sales are determined by the date of the first event in each segment of the annual season. These of course will change from one year to the next. And second, only those orders are accepted that conform to certain strict rules about the date of the postmark on your envelope, and this leads us back to the matter of "opening dates"! If you wish anyway to try ordering by mail, all correspondance should be addressed to: Biglietteria del Teatro Comunale, 15 Via Solferino, 50123 Firenze.

Tourist Information is found outside the Stazione Centrale in a small box-like structure propped up against the railing of the stairs leading down to an underground pedestrian mall under the square in front of the station. (With the train platforms behind you, go out the left side of the station, turn to your right and follow the walls of the station, and a few feet in front of you is the Tourist Office.) They are open daily from 0800 to 1930 (from April through October); off-season or winter hours may vary somewhat.

Hotel information and reservations may be made inside the station in an office in the large covered area opposite the train platforms. This will be to the left of the doors leading into the hall where tickets are sold. Their "winter" hours (November through March) are from 0830 to 2100; the "summer" hours are from 0815 to 2130, daily. Normally one pays in full for the first night's reservation plus a graduated fee (L. 1500 to L. 3500) based on the price of the room.

Transportation in Florence is best done on one's two feet because you see more and distances are short. But should you need a bus (which perhaps is safer!), there is a day ticket, available at a booth in the Stazione Centrale in the center of the area at the head of the train platforms. This ticket, good for unlimited travel until 0100, costs L. 2500; a single bus ride costs L. 600.

Changing money in Florence can be done almost everywhere and at almost any hour. (Remember that the Florentines were among Europe's first and richest bankers.) In the Stazione Centrale this can be done in the small office where you go for train schedules ("Informazione," marked with a large "i"), at the bank inside the hall where tickets are sold, and for 24-hour service, at window #19 in the line-up of windows selling train tickets. During business hours most of the travel agencies outside the station also offer this service (out the door to the left, as you would go to the Tourist Information Office). Both American Express and Cook's maintain offices in Florence.

MILAN (Italian: Milano) first appears to be a big and sprawling, no-nonsense, industrial city, maybe not of much interest to the tourist seeking out the picturesque or the monumental. After visiting the Duomo, the Galleria next door to it, and gazing sceptically at the outside of La Scala, the average tourist could say that he has "done" Milan and then move on to more interesting places. What the stranger does not appreciate is the fact that while the citizens of the city seem to be preoccupied with business and making money they also have an avid interest in the day-to-day affairs of their main opera house. For the average Milanesi the triumphs and scandals of La Scala can arouse as much passion as the battles fought out by their soccer teams.

THE TEATRO ALLA SCALA is located in the very heart of the city. One end of the Galleria Vittorio Emanuele II, often called the city's "parlor," the center of its social life, comes out on the square facing the theater. At the opposite end of the Galleria is the Piazza del Duomo, the square surrounding the cathedral. The neo-classical façade of La Scala is imposing, but it gives no hint of the splendors to be found inside. One of the most magic moments I know of in any theater occurs just after the main house lights have gone down. There is still no light on the curtain and the conductor is just about to appear in the pit. The theater is dark except for soft lights still burning in every one of the boxes and in the galleries above them. For a few seconds a pinkish, reddish glow silhouettes the forms of the spectators and brings into sharp focus the delicate outlines of each of the boxes. Then for a very brief instant the audience itself is gently highlighted and each box transformed into a miniature stage. Those lights then go out, the conductor makes his entrance, and a spotlight on the curtain makes one turn one's attention to the front of the theater. The magic has rightfully shifted from the auditorium to the stage.

La Scala was built between 1776 and 1778 and for many years was the largest opera house in the world. (The theater took its name from the church of S. Maria della Scala which had occupied the site since 1381. The church in turn had been identified with its benefactress, Beatrice della Scala, a daughter of the dynasty then ruling Verona and wife of the Visconti rulers of Milan.

The jumble of buildings that once crowded in on the theater at the front and sides were levelled in the 1860's to create an office wing, the Galleria Vittorio Emanuele II, and the Piazza that now bears the theater's name.) In addition to the wide and deep orchestra section there are six tiers or rings of balconies, the first four of which are the boxes (the *Palchi*) and the last two the galleries (the *Gallerie*) with open rows of fixed seats. Standing room for 150 is in the two galleries, behind the second or last circle of seats. Estimates vary widely as to how many people the theater will accommodate; older guidebooks make the claim that the seating capacity is at 3600, but that number is far off the mark. This is mainly because figures are vague about the number of places sold in the boxes on the sides and near the stage, but a rough estimate is around 2000. The acoustics of La Scala have been praised since it was first constructed. Even though the theater was bombed during the last part of the Second World War and left virtually as a shell, those who had known the theater before its destruction could perceive little difference in the quality of the sound after its meticulous restoration. (Photographs of La Scala in ruins are mounted on the walls in and around the Box Office.) As for the sight-lines, obviously in a theater with this shape they are excellent throughout the orchestra section and at the back and center of the hall, but as one approaches the stage they become less good.

One would think that with La Scala's prestige and the constant demand for tickets more operas would be in the annual repertory and performances more frequent. This however is not the case with the *stagione* system of scheduling. On average ten different operas are mounted in the course of one year, and generally it is the exception rather than the rule that two will be alternating on stage at the same time. Each opera is repeated anywhere from between six to ten times. Ballets and concerts are presented with some frequency, filling in some of the gaps, but on many nights the theater is dark. The repertory shows some diversity, usually with at least one German, French, and Russian (or Czech) work and often something new by an Italian composer, but for the most part La Scala sticks to what it does so well: the Italian repertory. The season starts towards the beginning of December (sometimes with much tense speculation as to whether or not a strike will cancel opening night) and ends in July.

The management chooses their singers with much caution—a début at La Scala still has some significance. Though most of the secondary roles are sung by Italians, in the major parts one finds singers drawn from all over the world. Most of their names will be familiar. This is true as well of the conductors and of many of the directors and designers.

The doors to the Box Office are on the left side of the theater, just after the corner of the main façade. You then go down a flight of steps to the basement. The hours are from 1000 to 1300 and from 1530 to 1730, daily except Mondays. (On Mondays, only if a performance is scheduled for that evening, the hours will be the same as on other days.) Also, when something is scheduled in the evening the Box Office does not close at 1730 but remains open until one half-hour after the curtain has gone up (these special times apply to Monday as well); tickets are sold for that performance alone (if available!).

Ordering tickets by mail is permitted only to those who live outside Milan. The procedures are quite complicated and probably not worth the effort. (I have stood close to the ticket windows and watched foreigners come in who expected after writing well in advance to have tickets waiting for them. In every case their letters were returned—and no tickets. All of this was done politely but with a knowing smile.) Advance sales begin approximately three months before the first performance of an opera, and orders are accepted at that time for any later performance of that same work. (A problem here is that the opening date for reservations is extremely variable.) One must then wait for a confirmation of one's request from the Box Office and if the order comes from within Italy, then return the proper amount in Lire by check or postal money order. If the order comes from another country, there is still the wait for a confirmation, but in this instance tickets must be paid for at the Box Office no earlier than two days before the performance. The costs of mailing the confirmation or sending it by telegram will be added to the price of the tickets. Questions about dates and booking should be directed to the following telephone number: (02) 80-70-41. The mailing address is: E. A. Teatro all Scala, Ufficio Biglietteria, 2 Via Filodrammatici, 20121 Milan.

The prices for seats at La Scala on all four of the subscription nights are always higher than any others: Orchestra *(Poltrona/platea)* L. 164.000; Boxes, on all four levels *(Poltroncina/palco)* L. 132.000; First Balcony *(Prima Galleria: poltroncina/numerato)* L. 38.000/L. 27.000; Second Balcony *(Poltroncina/numerato)* L. 30.000/L. 14.000. On non-subscription nights the prices are correspondingly lower (but still not cheap except upstairs): Orchestra L. 105.000; Boxes L. 85.000; First Balcony L. 30.000 and L. 24.000; and Second Balcony L. 30.000 and L. 14.000. Standing Room is priced at L. 4000. American Express, Diners Club, and Visa cards are accepted.

Let me suggest several ways to find tickets:

1. First, of course, is to try the Box Office early in the morning and see if anything is available for the date(s) you want. If you are told that everything is sold out *(esaurito),* be patient, stay close to one of the ticket windows, but let several people behind the ticket counter know what you want and that you will wait. Usually there will be cancellations, and if you have made your intentions known, someone will give you a discreet signal, you go to the window, and you have your tickets. (For tickets that have been turned back in through the Box Office expect to pay a 10% surcharge.)

2. Scalpers, who are prepared to deal with people like you, come in and

out of the Box Office throughout the day. (Apparently through some kind of arcane arrangement they are picking up tickets that have been released by subscribers, with the subscribers' understanding that a premium will be added to the price.) If you've been standing somewhere near the ticket windows you may be given a signal to follow someone upstairs, and off in a corner somewhere outside near the theater the bargaining begins. It's unlikely that you'll be offered a counterfeit ticket (if such exist), but it is wise to verify in some way the date and the position of the seat. It's up to you how much over the "official" price you are willing to pay (L. 10.000 is probably the average "surcharge" for a fairly good seat).

3. CIT, the government-owned Italian travel service (Compagnia Italiana Turismo), buys up tickets for non-subscription performances and sells them principally to tour groups from abroad. In the unlikely event that CIT in New York has some leftover tickets it is still worth your while to write or call: CIT, 350 Fifth Ave., New York, New York 10001 or telephone: (212) 971-0181.

4. The CIT office in Milan may be able to help you. They are in the center of the Galleria, prominently marked, just a few steps from La Scala and the Box Office. A very gracious gentleman, Signor Renato Ceriani, is in charge of filling orders for tickets from La Scala for CIT offices throughout the world. Sometimes he has cancellations from his group orders and may have a few to spare. These will usually be tickets in the highest price categories. His direct telephone line is: (02) 86-42-47 and his Telex is: 311-042; his office is two flights up, behind the travel bureau counters on the ground floor, but because he is back and forth to the theater during much of the day it is best to call him first.

5. 150 Standing Room tickets go on sale one hour before the performance, but usually the lines begin to form two to three hours in advance. Much depends of course on the popularity of the opera and the singers. The line forms in the corner to the left of the main entrance to the theater, beyond the door to the Box Office, in front of the La Scala Museum (Museo).

6. Finally there are the scalpers who hover around the main doors to the theater about an hour or so before curtain-time. There may also be a few people, not scalpers, who do have extra tickets and want to sell them. Do not be shocked if a sweet grandmotherly-type, clutching one or two tickets, comes shuffling up to you and indicates that she wants to sell her tickets at a premium. I suspect that some older people have kept their names for years on the priority subscription lists but rarely enter the theater. This is one way for them to pay their electricity bills and to buy a few extras.

The La Scala programs, selling for L. 20.000, are large, heavy, very slick and filled with photographs, many in color, of the sketches used in designing the sets and costumes. The programs also contain copies of the libretto, a few essays, and a great deal of superfluous information that can be found elsewhere, if you want it, at a much cheaper price. The inserted page listing the artists looks like a scaled-down version of the handsome La Scala posters. An obliging usher with an armful of unsold programs may be happy to pull out the insert at the end of the evening and give it to you.

Tourist Information for Milan is found in two locations: in the Stazione Centrale and downtown in the Piazza del Duomo. The railway station office is small but efficient. It is just to the side of the Cambio office in the huge hall, separated from the train platforms, where you find all the stands selling food, newspapers, and what-have-you. Their hours are daily from 0900 to 1230 and 1415 to 1800. The larger office in the center of the city is to the right of the Duomo, across the square directly opposite the entrance to the Galleria. They are open as follows: from 0930 to 1230 and from 1330 to 1800; closed on Sundays but open on holidays. (Often they have the large La Scala posters and are generous in giving them out to anyone who asks.) Neither office deals with making hotel reservations, but they will give you a brochure listing names, addresses, and prices.

There are hotels in all categories close to the train station off to the left side and down the long stairs (this is the left side with your back to the train platforms). In several of the streets here you will find moderately-priced hotels after you pass beyond the deluxe ones. Most of Milan's most expensive hotels happen to be in the neighborhood of La Scala on the Via Manzoni.

A one-day tourist ticket for unlimited use on busses, trams, and the subway is for sale for L. 3200 in the subway (Metropolitana) stations at either the Stazione Centrale or the Duomo. A ticket for a single ride costs L. 800 and can be bought from a machine—if the machine accepts your money.

Money can be changed inside the station next door to the Tourist Information Office in the large hall described above. Their hours are from 0800 to 2000, Monday through Saturday; 0900 to 1400 on Sundays and holidays. American Express and Cook's each have an office in Milan. Near La Scala, should you need money to buy a scalper's ticket, the CIT office in the Galleria has a money-changing service. There are also a number of other places, clearly marked, in the center of the city offering this service. Banks in Italy usually open at 0830 Monday through Friday and close at 1330; a few reopen in the afternoons, but not many.

NAPLES (Italian: Napoli) has one of the most beautiful physical settings of any city in the world and many of its buildings are extremely handsome, but in recent years much of the city has begun again to look rather shabby. Some of this can be blamed on the devastating earthquakes that shook the area a few years ago, straining the city's finances when it took in

thousands of homeless refugees. Another factor seems to be the pervasive influence of the Mafia, which apparently has scared away foreign capital. Naples has never enjoyed a particularly good reputation with tourists because of stories about pickpockets and street crime, but I've always wondered to what extent these tales are true. In spite of a sense that just now Naples is not looking its best, one visit should convince you why the city has inspired so many wonderful songs extolling its beauty.

THE SAN CARLO OPERA HOUSE has not suffered the neglect shown to other buildings in Naples. Some renovations to the theater were made in the summer of 1988, making even better its already superb acoustics. It is some 40 years older than La Scala, dating back to 1737, but numerous modifications through the years and a disastrous fire in the early 1800's have changed its appearance. Today it is still an extremely beautiful theater, more restrained in its decoration than La Scala but equally imposing with its six tiers of boxes. Figures for the seating are not precise because of vague estimates (like those for La Scala) about the number of seats sometimes sold in the boxes, but roughly 1800 for a total seems close. No provision is made for Standees.

The season at San Carlo begins in early December and ends in late June or early July. For 1988–89 two full-length ballets were included with six operas and an Offenbach operetta in making up the series offered to subscribers. Each item on the calendar was repeated five times on the cycles reserved for subscription-holders; for all the operas a total of only three non-subscription performances were added to the schedule. Except for the Offenbach, all of the works presented in that season were by Italian composers; in most years there is at least one opera by a German or a Frenchman. (San Carlo is unique in its social consciousness: everything on their program is repeated at least once, sometimes more, for the elderly of the city; the original casts are used, no substitutes, and the ticket costs are nominal. Obviously the general public is not admitted. Even the fact that these are matinées, not evening performances, is consistent with a policy of catering to old people.)

The singers are mostly Italian, ranging from the very famous to the not-so-famous. A number of the latter are young, recent graduates of the Naples Conservatory, one of Italy's oldest and most prestigious singing academies. A few foreigners appear occasionally in the casts. The orchestra is first-rate, as one would expect from a city where music is so highly revered. My impression of the San Carlo company is that because of a tight budget they owe much of their success to bold ingenuity, careful planning, and meticulous rehearsals. They tend to perform opera as subtle, polished theater and let other houses use their stages for singing contests.

San Carlo is in the center of Naples, with the Royal Palace just behind it and the city's famous Galleria Umberto I just opposite. The Box Office is inside the main doors of the theater, off to the left. They are open daily, except Monday, from 1000 to 1300 and from 1630 to 1800. On the days when a performance is scheduled they do not close at 1800 but remain open until the end of the first intermission. Four different pricing scales are in effect for the five cycles of subscription performances and the few that are "open" and listed as "non-subscription." This is further complicated by the fact that ticket costs do not gradually become lower as one goes from the bottom to the top of the six rings; boxes on the second level cost more than those on the first! I could cover an entire page if I gave every detail about the ticket costs, so will omit all of the intermediate prices between the highest and lowest figures in each of the four scales. The top prices are for seats in the Orchestra; the lowest are for seats on the sixth level in the Balconata, the only level where the seats are arranged in rows without partitions. Cycle A, for the first evening of each event: L. 130.000 to L. 25,000; Cycle B: L. 100.000 to 20.000; Cycles C and F: L. 80.000 to L. 15.000; and Cycle D and non-subscription: L. 70.000 to L. 12.000 (note that there is no Cycle "E"). The mailing address of the Teatro di San Carlo is: Via San Carlo, 80132 Napoli, but there is little point in writing in advance for tickets because the subscription performances are usually booked up. However at the last minute tickets do become available, and it is worth your while to call the Box Office: (081) 797-21-11. The program booklets sold at San Carlo contain essays about the opera but nothing about the artists; they are not worth the L. 7000 just to have the names of the singers.

Vocal recitals with orchestral accompaniment are sometimes scheduled for San Carlo. Also there are fairly frequent concerts by visiting orchestras. Information about these events can be found either at San Carlo or by consulting *Qui Napoli,* the free booklet describing each month's cultural calendar for the city. This booklet is available at most hotels or at any of the tourist information centers.

The **Teatro Mercadante** on the Piazza Municipio (opposite the Castel Nuovo or Maschio Angioino) hosts occasional visits by touring opera groups. Concerts and recitals as well are often given here. The Mercadante is a five-minute walk from San Carlo. Telephone: (081) 552-41-47.

For a special treat, in part because of the opulence of the setting, check to see what chamber music concerts or recitals are being given at the **Villa Pignatelli**. (That is its shorter title; the full name is: the Museo Principe di Aragona Pignatelli Cortes, a villa now housing a collection of furniture and porcelains.) This is located on the Riviera di Chiaia, facing the public gardens called the Villa Comunale to the west of the Via Partenope.

Tourist Information is found at Naples' two main railroad stations: Centrale to the east of the opera house and Mergellina, serving that area and the Santa Lucia district to the west of the theater. Both stations are approximately two miles (3 kilometers) from San Carlo. A third office for information is at 10/A Via Partenope, only about 6/10th's of a mile (1 kilometer) from the theater. (Plans are afoot to merge the separate administrations of these three offices and to change the hours and days when they are open, but no one is certain when this will take place. The times given below are in effect as of May 1989.) The Stazione Centrale office, Piazza Garibaldi, is inside the station in a "box" on the train-platform side of the building and off to the far left (with your back to the trains). They are open Monday through Saturday from 0900 to 2000; hours for Sunday are indefinite, but they are closed on all holidays. The telephone is: (081) 26-87-79. The Mergellina station office keeps the same hours but is for now closed on Sundays as well as on holidays. They are on the ground floor of the station, to the right of the main doors as you come out to the street. The telephone is: (081) 761-21-02. Both of these offices are very cooperative about booking hotels and will do so at no charge. They also accept such requests by telephone. The Via Partenope office, which also does hotel bookings, closes for lunch between 1200 and 1400 and is also closed on Sundays and holidays.

Most of Naples' moderately-priced hotels are concentrated around the Stazione Centrale area in the Piazza Garibaldi. Not many hotels of any sort are to be found near Mergellina. Some of the big luxury hotels, all with magnificent views of the bay, are clustered on the Via Partenope; these are within a ten- to fifteen-minute walk to San Carlo.

Transportation in Naples is mostly by bus; the only remaining tram line connects Mergellina with Santa Lucia. Naples' so-called "Metropolitana" is not a real subway but instead, the main railroad line tunneling under the city and linking Mergellina and suburbs further west with the Stazione Centrale (Eurailpasses are valid on this line). There are frequent trains, but it is not very useful for getting around the central portions of the city. Transportation tickets come in two segments and cost L. 1000 each: a "green" morning ticket, good for unlimited use between 0700 to 1400, and a "yellow" afternoon-evening ticket, from 1400 to 2400. After midnight single bus tickets may be bought from the driver or conductor for L. 600. The tickets in use during the day are found in tobacco shops, some bars, and wherever you see busses grouped at terminals. On Sundays and holidays, when most shops are closed, you will have to buy a single-trip ticket or find a bus terminal and the kiosk where day-tickets are sold.

Money can be changed in the Stazione Centrale in an office at the far left end of the main hall (you are facing the exit from the station and the train platforms are behind you). Their hours are, Monday through Saturday, from 0830 to 1230 and from 1330 to 2000. Sunday and holiday hours are from 0930 to 1400. There are no money-changing facilities at the Mergellina station. Both American Express and Cook's have offices in Naples.

ROME (Italian: Roma) Little needs to be said about Rome, without doubt one of the world's great cities, where the minute you step foot in it you feel its vibrancy and creative vigor. Rome also has a touch of madness which can be either endearing or exasperating depending on your own mood of the moment. Musically the city's past is extremely rich. At a time when Papal patronage was still important and powerful, many of Europe's most talented composers were drawn to Rome for training and to write for the city's churches. In the 1400's and 1500's the Papal court fostered a remarkable fusion of musical styles, combining Franco-Flemish polyphony with Italian expressivity and love of melody. Though Rome was only one of many influences in shaping the direction of the baroque, the city's music patrons, both ecclesiastic and secular, were among the earliest enthusiasts of that new and exciting Italian invention: opera.

Throughout the 1800's Rome saw a moderate number of important operatic premières, but the most sensational occurred in that century's last decade. The year 1816 however is remembered for the inauspicious and scandalous failure of Rossini's *Barber of Seville*. Rossini must have forgiven the Romans because he came back in 1817 with his highly successful *La Cenerentola*. (The *Barber* fiasco took place in the Teatro Argentina, a building that still exists but is no longer used for opera; *La Cenerentola* débuted in the Teatro Valle, another theater no longer in use.) Between 1844 and 1859 four of Verdi's operas were given their first performances in Rome (two at the Argentina and two at the now-destroyed Teatro Apollo), but after enjoying enthusiastic favor with his audiences in Rome, Verdi was soon writing for foreign houses and did not return with commissions within his native country until *Otello* and *Falstaff*.

THE TEATRO DELL' OPERA DI ROMA. Shortly after 1870, when Rome became the capital of the newly unified kingdom of Italy, a wealthy entrepreneur Domenico Costanzi decided that the city needed a larger and more elegant theater in which to stage opera. The building that was to bear his name became in time the city's principal opera house. First called the Teatro Costanzi, it was then officially named the Teatro Real, and finally under Mussolini the Teatro dell' Opera di Roma, by which it is known today. (Mussolini encased the façade with a ponderous layer of travertine marble, but little was done to modify the interior. He also levelled the other structures that were jammed up against the building, creating the small open space, now known as the Piazza Beniamino Gigli, fronting on the Via Viminale.) A measure of glory came to this theater when Mascagni's *Cavalleria rusticana* was performed for the first time in 1890, thus heralding the movement that became known as *verismo*. Two more operas by Mascagni followed in 1891 and 1898, *L'Amico Fritz* and *Iris*, but neither of these works was welcomed with the enthusiasm generated by *Cavalleria*. Puccini added further prestige to the Rome Opera with the triumph of his *Tosca*, premièred here in January of 1900. (I have often wondered about the authenticity of the first stage sets, as the Romans would have been quite familiar with all of them: San Andrea della Valle, the Palazzo Farnese, and the Castel San Angelo. Though almost certainly painted on a simple canvas backdrop, were they painstakingly realistic in the Zefferelli manner or merely suggestive in broad strokes of the sites they were to evoke?) Since the Second World War the Rome Opera has had its very good and bad moments, the occasional bad moments largely stemming from the fact that the politicians who determine the budget have too often been tempted to meddle in the artistic operations of the company. More than in any other theater in Italy Rome has had to suffer many administrative squabbles, dismissals, and sudden resignations, sometimes causing delays or cancellations to parts of its schedule. They seem to be on a most felicitous course at the moment, especially in their policy of presenting seldom-produced Rossini and other less-performed works of the other bel canto masters, but one dares make no predictions about the future.

The seating capacity of the Rome Opera is around 1475, once more only an approximate figure because of the variable number of places that can be sold in many of the boxes. The theater is almost round, creating a nice intimacy with the stage, but in the five tiers of seating there are also the inevitable sight-line problems on the sides. The orchestra seats about 500; next, three levels, all of boxes, have seating for around 450 (the first tier of boxes is considered as being on the "ground floor," with the second tier then counted as the "first" level "up"/1° *Ordine*); the fourth level, called the *Balconata*, is divided between boxes on the sides and a middle section with three rows of seats, the total coming to 190; and finally at the top and rear center of the theater is a large and open *Galleria* seating 335. (On this level the two "arms" that reach towards the stage were at one time used for Standing Room but are now left bare. In Rome, as in many other houses in Italy, with the exception of La Scala, Standees are now barred because they proved to be a nuisance.) The acoustics are very bright and alive, qualities that can be verified (to the extent that microphones can be trusted) by the many recordings RCA made in the late 1950's and early 60's using this house as its studio. Rome is unique among the five Italian theaters we are looking at here because each of the boxes and the supporting columns in the *Galleria* are topped by an arch rather than squared off; this gives a feeling of lightness and delicacy to the interior, hinting at something an Oriental might have designed. The only criticism I have to make with the theater is its general look of shabbiness (as of May 1989), quite a contrast with the sparkling appearance it had just a few years ago. The subtle "earthy pink" of the basic wall color is now more "earthy" than "pink." Perhaps once again this is the result of a quarrel over some budgetary matter.

Usually the Rome season begins sometime after the middle of November and ends in May or very early June. Seven or eight operas are presented during those months, and each is repeated between six and eight times. Five of each of those performances are for those who have subscriptions; any performances over and above that number are non-subscription. Though the repertory is largely Italian, one or two of the works will be German or French and sung in the original language. To fill out their subscription series there are usually three evenings of ballets (Rome is very proud of its distinguished company of dancers). The singers for the most part are well-known Italians, with a sprinkling on occasion of "foreign" stars. For the German operas a mostly German cast is brought in for all of the title rôles. The excellent orchestra is led by a number of conductors, some of whose names will be familiar, others not.

Finding the opera house is quite easy because it is so close to the Rome railroad station, Termini, and if traffic is not too heavy, only a six- to seven-minute walk. (If you go out the left side of the station, with the train platforms behind you, cross the street, Via Giovanni that parallels the side of the station, and go straight ahead two very short blocks; turn right on Via Principe Amadeo and go another two short blocks, and you run into Via Viminale. To your left, one block away, you will see the theater.) The Box Office is just to the left of the main doors to the opera house. Tuesday through Saturday the hours are from 1000 to 1300 and from 1700 to 1900; when a performance is scheduled they remain open after the usual closing-time until the hour when the curtain is supposed to go up. On Sundays the hours are from 1000 to 1300, and they reopen one hour before the start of the evening's performance. They are closed on Mondays and on all holidays. Ticket prices are arranged in three categories: the *Prime* or initial perform-ances of each work; the other four sold by subscription (not necessarily following in a linked sequence); and the non-subscription dates scattered among the later subscription ones. As there are 13 different prices quoted in each category, giving the entire list is far too long and complicated; I will give only a top, middle, and bottom price for each. For the *Prime:* Orchestra/ *Platea,* L. 80.000; Box in center/*Posto in palcho* on the Third Level/*2° Ordine,* L. 50.000; and finally, the top Gallery: L. 10.000. For the 2nd through 5th subscription performances (respectively): L. 55.000; L. 32.500; and L. 10.000. For all other (non-subscription) dates (again, respectively): L. 35.000; L. 23.000; and L. 8.500. Note that except for seats in the Gallery, all of the *Prime* ticket prices are more than double those for the non-subscrip-tion performances. Reserving tickets by mail may be tried, but the results are not guaranteed: No more than 40 days before the date of the performance, and no later than a week, send your request and a check or postal money order to: Teatro dell' Opera-Servizio Biglietteria, 1 Piazza B. Gigli, 00184 Rome. Normally you would be sent a receipt indicating that your order had been honored, but with requests from abroad this is quite doubtful. Present the receipt at the Box Office starting two days before the performance or right up to curtain-time. There are elaborate restrictions about the number of seats, never more than four, than can be ordered, and these vary according to the position of the seats and whether or not the order is for a subscription or non-subscription date. In any case you will be safe in restricting your request to two tickets. No reservations are taken by telephone, but if you need information, the Box Office number is: (06) 46-36-41.

Programs at the Opera cost L. 10.000 and are worth the price if you want a copy of the libretto of a lesser-known opera. At times these can be hefty little books with essays and documentation about the work. There are photographs of the artists in costume but no biographies.

Tourist Information is outside, about 100 feet (30 meters) from the front of the Stazione Termini in a small glassed-in booth, not very clearly marked. (This is found on the right-hand side beyond the loop where the taxis turn to come into the station.) The hours are daily from 0800 to 2000, November through March, and from 0800 to 2300, April through October. They will make hotel reservations for you, with a fee of L. 1000.

Hotels in all categories abound in the area around the Stazione Termini. On each side of the station, three blocks deep, there are any number of choices. Though the immediate surroundings are not particularly interesting, the area is very convenient because so many bus routes begin just in front of the station. A Metropolitana station as well connects here with the city's two main lines. The big disadvantage to staying in this section of Rome is that the historic sights (and sites) are not close by; on foot it will take you at least a half hour to reach the edge of the areas where older parts of the city begin.

A day-ticket for the city, valid on busses, trams, and the Metropolitana, costs L. 2800; a ticket good for a week costs L. 10.000 but is limited only to travel on busses. You can buy these at a kiosk inside the station or at a similar stand found at most bus terminals (such as the large one in front of the Stazione Termini).

Money changing facilities are found inside the station in the large, outer hall (separate from the train platforms). There are several tellers' windows in the middle of the wall opposite the front doors to the station. The hours are Monday through Saturday from 0830 to 1930, with sometimes a brief delay at 1400 when there is a shift change; on Sundays the hours are from 0800 to 1415; and on holidays: 0830 to 1630, with again a delay, as above, around 1230. American Express has an office in Rome, and Cook's has four.

For information about the Rome Opera's outdoor summer season in the Baths of Caracalla, see under "Rome" in the section "Opera Festivals" in Appendix II.

VENICE (Italian: Venezia) Many many people have tried to describe the strange and elusive magic of this wonderful city, but very few have succeeded in finding any single characteristic on which they can agree. It is a place of many moods, and in the course of a single day, not to mention several seasons, it has a way of escaping the grasp of words. If you don't yet know Venice, read up on it before you go (the literature is immense), and then experience its spell for yourself.

Modern opera owes much to the Venitians because it was they who took the infant art form out of the ducal courts and with the opening of commercial theaters made it for the first time a public entertainment, catering to popular tastes. Monteverdi, already quite famous for his *Orfeo,* was lured by the Venetians away from Mantua; he became the director of music at San Marco and for many years devoted his energies to the composition of brilliant and moving choral works. Some time after Monteverdi had withdrawn from public activity the Venetian's insatiable enthusiasm for opera convinced the ageing composer to come out of retirement and to write two more masterpieces: *Il Ritorno d'Ulisse* and *L'Incoronazione di Poppea,* two works that further changed the course of opera. Towards the end of the 1600's the Venetians were so infatuated with the new art form that every district of the city had its own opera house, and composers were steadily grinding out new works to satisfy public demands. By this time other cities as well in Italy were going through a kind of madness for opera, but Venice established the model that was quickly taken up throughout almost all of Europe.

THE GRAN TEATRO LA FENICE ("The Phoenix") is an exquisite jewel of a theater, its feeling of intimacy disguising the surprising fact that it can hold more than 1500 people. It opened in 1792 and was rebuilt after a fire partially destroyed it in 1836. The modest, almost plain façade facing the Campo S. Fantin gives no hint of the splendors to be found inside behind the doors. In addition to the seating on the orchestra level there are five tiers circling the hall, the first three consisting of boxes and the top two of shallow galleries with "open" rows of seats. The acoustics are excellent, but there are the inevitable problems with sight-lines as one approaches the stage.

Venice's season begins in late December, usually just before Christmas, and ends in the latter part of June. Normally seven or eight works are performed, with each being repeated between four and seven times. La Fenice has a long-established commitment to both contemporary opera and to older or unusual works quite rarely performed. More than other Italian houses they venture out more often beyond the national repertory and have a higher proportion of foreign works, usually at least two, sometimes more. It is difficult to classify the singers other than to say that most are Italian, the famous and the not-so-famous, with a handful of big-name foreign stars. When La Fenice schedules a German work they will usually import a good number of German singers. Throughout the year the theater is used for ballets, orchestral concerts, and recitals.

For once we encounter a relatively simple price-scale for tickets, with only two different categories: the initial performance and all subsequent ones; and inside the theater, a total of only four levels of prices. With the opening performance listed first *(Turno A)* and the following performances listed second (the *Repliche*), ticket costs are: Orchestra/*Platea:* L. 80.000 and L. 60.000; all Boxes/*Posto di palco:* L. 65.000 and L. 48.000; the First Gallery/*I° Galleria:* L. 35.000 and L. 25.000; and finally, the Second Gallery/*2° Galleria:* L. 25.000 and L. 17.000. There is no Standing Room.

To direct anyone to La Fenice and the Box Office from the Piazza San Marco can be quite hazardous because of the maze of small alleys that might lead you off the right path. Once you have discovered the way for yourself you will see that as directions go in Venice it is fairly easy. In any case if you start out from the Piazza San Marco, go to the far end, directly opposite St. Mark's, and go through the arcade or passageway on the left side; go straight ahead for about 150 yards (150 meters), cross over a wide canal and continue for another 75 feet (25 meters); then turn right at the second alley; you soon come to another bridge over a small canal, and there in front of you, to your left, is La Fenice. When at last you are in the Campo S. Fantin you may not realize that the humble building to your left is really an opera house. Only the posters announcing the program serve to reassure you. (There are a few signs along the way, high up on buildings, pointing to the theater, but they are rarely placed where you would normally look for them. The same problem exists with the street signs, when and if you can find them.)

The Box Office is inside the main doors of the theater, through another door to the left. They are open Monday through Saturday, but if there is a performance scheduled for Sunday (as there often is), they are closed on Monday. The hours are from 0930 to 1230 and from 1600 to 1800. The Box Office reopens one hour before the beginning of each performance and remains open until the curtain goes up. (In Venice opera patrons in theory are more punctual than elsewhere in Italy!) Reservations by mail may be made from abroad starting on the date when the programs for the entire season are announced, but payment in Italian lire by international money order must accompany the order. Tickets may be picked up two days before the performance and until one half-hour before it begins. The address is: Biglietteria del Teatro La Fenice, Campo S. Fantin, 30124 Venice. Telephone reservations are accepted no later than five days before a performance, by which time, no later, payment (by international money order) must as well be received by the Box Office. The numbers to call are: (041) 521-0161 or (041) 521-0336; Telex: 215647 I; and Telefax: (041) 522-1768.

Tourist Information is available in the Stazione in an office just to the right of the left-side main doors leading down to the steps that take you outside. (As the station is relatively small, you cannot get lost and miss it.) The hours are daily, from 0800 to 2100, and they will make hotel reservations for you. There is no fee for making the reservation, but a deposit of L. 10.000 is required which is then deducted from your hotel bill. There is also a Tourist Information office just off the Piazza San Marco on the left-hand side of the arcade at the far end of the square, opposite St. Mark's. You will go by it if you approach the opera house from this part of the city. They are open from 0900 until 1900. For those arriving in Venice by car, there is a Tourist Information office in the center of the Piazzale Roma, the large area for open-air parking just at the end of the causeway when you come into Venice. They have the same hours as the office at the Stazione and offer the same services.

Hotels are everywhere throughout the city, but you can waste a lot of time and energy setting off on your own without first having a reservation. Outside appearances often give no hint of the prices. And without a con-firmed reservation you never know when the hotel is booked up. The free service at the Tourist Offices is extremely efficient and highly recommended.

Transportation in Venice is of course by boat and your two feet. The *vaporetti,* for travel between the Stazione and the Piazza San Marco, are divided into two types: the *accellerato,* line 1, which makes all the stops along the Grand Canal (about ½ hour between the Stazione and San Marco), and the *diretto,* line 2, which follows a different route with no stops (and makes the trip in about ¼ hour). A single trip on Line 1 costs L. 1700; a day-ticket good for an unlimited number of trips costs L. 3600. On Line 2, a single trip is L. 2000; a day-ticket costs L. 5000. Tickets for the boats can be bought at all of the landing docks.

Money changing facilities are found in at least four offices inside the train station. There are a number outside as well. Most of these places open at 0800 and close at 1900; one of the ticket windows inside the station stays open until midnight. Both Cook's and American Express have branches in Venice in the heart of city, the former on St. Mark's Square and the latter on San Moise, the passage leading through the arcade (and eventually to La Fenice) at the end of the square opposite the Duomo.

SPAIN

Quite suddenly, a few years after the end of the Second World War, superb singers in incredible numbers began coming out of Spain, quickly establishing themselves on the world's opera stages as some of the most sought-after (and highest-paid) stars. As long ago as the early 1800's, steadily with each passing generation, a few singers of Spanish origin have won international acclaim, but there is no historical precedent for the fact that that country now seems to be producing extraordinary voices at a quite unbelievable rate. With each new season more new names come into prominence. This is all the more remarkable because until very recently there was only one full-time opera house in the entire country: the justly famous and highly reputed Liceu in Barcelona. Madrid's Teatro Real, built in 1850, had closed its doors in 1925, and except for a rare performance of opera on a concert platform, Madrileños had to content themselves with zarzuelas, a delightful, "native" lyric form somewhat like operetta or musical comedy but certainly not grand opera. The situation in Madrid has drastically changed now with the establishment (just a few years ago) of Spain's second professional opera company. Though the Teatro Lírico Nacional La Zarzuela currently has the name "Zarzuela" in its title (only because it temporarily uses the theater where zarzuelas are given in the fall), opera-goers should not be put off: the company offers no zarzuelas in its schedule and is totally committed to the production of opera. They hope to move to the renovated Teatro Real when by 1992 the repairs to the stage area are completed. Probably at that time their name will be both changed and shortened. In the meantime that theater is being used for the presentation each season of at least one or two operas in concert form. With the ambitious productions of Barcelona's Liceu continuing to win enthusiastic praises from the public and critics and Madrid's new company assured of a successful future, Spain is no longer an operatic "backwater": its finest singers can now be heard and seen more frequently on "home" stages. At the same time other, younger artists in greater numbers are being groomed for international careers.*

BARCELONA has long been recognized as Spain's cultural capital,

leaving to Madrid the management of the country's political affairs. In the post-Franco years Madrid has been doing very well in trying to "catch up" with its old rival (as evidenced by its newly-established opera company and its booming film industry), but Barcelona's outlook has always been international and progressive while Madrid, far inland and at the geographic center of the country, remained proudly isolated and shielded from many outside influences. Barcelona is an exciting and elegant Mediterranean port-city, rich in the variety of its modern buildings and retaining as well many traces of its Greek, Roman, and Gothic past. Unfortunately most visitors to Spain never see the city: its remote location in the northeast corner of the country puts it at some distance from the more popular, more "typically" Spanish cities well to the south. While Madrid has its Prado, filled with the old masters of Spanish (and other) painting, Barcelona has its superb Picasso and modern museums and a host of intriguing structures left by its master architect Gaudí. The robust Catalonian heritage of the city adds an interesting dimension to its Hispanic side, with even the street names given first in Catalan, and then in Spanish. Generating perhaps further confusion is the fact that Barcelona, steadfastly Loyalist in its feelings, was one of the first cities in Spain to try to erase bitter memories of the Franco-era by re-naming many streets that bore the Generalissimo's name as well as those of his henchmen and "heroes"; some recent maps of the city still show the old names and have not been corrected.

THE GRAN TEATRE DEL LICEU is easy to find: it lies almost

in the center of the city, at about the mid-point of Las Ramblas, Barcelona's most important and animated thoroughfare. (A subway station on the Green

---

*Some of the information about Spain given here comes indirectly from a number of different sources. For the account of Madrid's new company I wish to acknowledge the use of an excellent article by Frank Kinkaid, "Spell It M-A-D-R-I-D," that appeared in the May 1987 issue of *Opera News* (pp. 50–51).

Line, #3, is marked "Liceu" and is in the median of Las Ramblas.) The main façade of the building flanks La Ramblas, but another entrance and the Box Office for advance sales are on the narrow side street, the Carrer Sant Pau (in Spanish: the Calle de San Pablo). The Liceu is a sumptuously decorated theater and quite immense: it seats between 3000 to 3600 people, making it one of the largest opera houses in Europe. The orchestra section is quite wide and deep and around it, in a horseshoe pattern, are five tiers of balconies. The original theater was opened in 1848, but after a disastrous fire in 1861 it was promptly rebuilt. Although the acoustics are extremely good, there is the same old problem in theaters of this shape: poor sight-lines in the side balconies. The season at the Liceu runs from early September to the last of June or early July. Compared with what one can see elsewhere on the Continent and now in Madrid, the repertory is quite conservative, rarely including anything earlier than Mozart or later than Puccini and Richard Strauss. Within this fairly conventional time-span, which allows for much Verdi and Wagner, there are however on occasion some interesting forays into repertory not often seen on other stages: lesser-known Rossini, Donizetti, and Giordano, and in one recent season Weber's *Der Freischütz*, certainly an odd choice for a Spanish opera house! Barcelona has a long tradition of especially favoring the German classics, most notably Wagner, and when it casts these operas, it imports first-rate singers and conductors, usually from Germany and the USA. In fact when one looks at any recent season's roster, most of the singers' names will be quite familiar: these are the same artists most in demand in the "big" houses throughout the world.

At the Liceu the block- or stagione-system is in effect, with around ten to fourteen works scheduled in a single season; each work is performed in its original language. In many months between September and July two different operas are presented within the same month, but they never overlap; normally there is an interval of approximately a week between the end of the run of the first work and the start of the second. Most of the operas are now repeated five to eight times, usually with a gap of two days between each performance. (Indicative of the growing enthusiasm for opera in Spain is the fact that until 1985 each opera had been repeated only three times; gradually with each successive year the number has been increased.) It should be noted that true to Spanish custom the curtain goes up quite late: 2100 for most of the operas and no earlier than 2000 for even the long Wagner ones. Each opera also is allotted one Sunday "matinée" performance; the starting time is unusually late: 1700 or 5 pm.

Seating arrangements at the Liceu require a brief lesson in Catalan, not Spanish, and when tickets are in short supply you will probably have more success if you try to express your preferences in that charmingly exotic tongue rather than in Spanish (or English!). Beginning on the orchestra level, a seat is called a *Butaca,* just as in Spanish, but in Catalan the plural is *Butaques,* where the Spanish adds only an "s." Surrounding the orchestra section and on the same level are the *Llotges platea,* the "ground-level" Loges or Boxes. The first balcony is called the *Amfiteatre,* an unexpected seating designation because one would normally see it used in the uppermost balconies of the theater and not so far down; also unusual (though like the opera houses in Brussels and Antwerp) is the fact that the open rows of seats in the *Amfiteatre* have a circle of Boxes behind them; the prices here match those in the orchestra as the most expensive in the house. In the higher balconies, which are three rows deep, some are divided into both Boxes and open rows of seats (without low partitions between them). There are no *Llotges* or Boxes in the fifth and topmost balcony.

The Box Office for advance booking is at number1, Carrer Sant Pau (in Spanish: San Pablo), the small street bordering the north side of the theater. The hours are Monday through Friday from 0800 to 1500 and on Saturdays from 0900 to 1300; closed on Sundays. Shortly after the new schedule for the coming season is announced in late spring, subscribers have first choice (between late June and late July) in placing their orders. Beginning on 1 August all remaining tickets for the entire season are put on sale, but to buy a ticket you must go in person to the Box Office (the hours are different: Monday through Friday, from 0800 to 2000). Starting on 3 September, close to the time when the new season is already underway, orders by mail or by telephone are accepted, once again for any tickets still available for any performance on the year's schedule. If you order by mail, address your request to: Gran Teatre del Liceu, Departament d'Abonaments i Localitats, Rambla dels Caputxins, 65, 08001 Barcelona. Although the theater is supposed to reply by mail if the space you request is available, it is quicker and more efficient to telephone. Payment, addressed to the "Consorci del Gran Teatre del Liceu," must be sent in pesetas either by Eurocheque or by International Postal Money Order. Depending on the time left before the performance, the tickets will either be put in the mail or held at the Box Office. The telephone number for information is: (93) 318-92-77; for ticket reservations call: (93) 318-91-22. For buying tickets on the day of a performance, if seats are still to be had, the Box Office, in addition to the regular hours given above, reopens at 1600 and remains open until curtain-time.

Ticket prices for the 1990–91 season range from a high of 8.600 pesetas *(Platea/*Orchestra and seats in the *Amfiteatre)* to a low of 1.315 pesetas on the sides of the fifth level closest to the stage. For excellent sight-lines and balanced sound some of the best seats in the house are in the center sections of the third and fourth rings *(Tercer pis* and *Quart pis).* Each of the three rows of seats (from front to back) in each of these balconies is priced differently: in the third ring ranging from 7.645 pesetas to 5.735, and in the fourth ring from 3.465 to 2.630. Very few seats in the better-placed boxes are put on sale for single performances. Most of these spaces are retained by the families of long-time subscribers who are also members of the private consortium that still directs the affairs of the Liceu. On the day of a performance 250 seats close to the stage on the fourth and fifth levels (with a poor view of the stage but with excellent sound) are offered at the price of 540 pesetas; these tickets, in lieu of Standing Room, are like General Admission *(Entrada General),* but the spaces are numbered.

For all of the German and some of the less-familiar Italian operas the Liceu provides surtitles in Catalan. I would guess that the majority of the people in the audience are more fluent in Spanish than in the use of this exotic local tongue, but the appearance of Catalan, beamed out above the proscenium, serves as yet another reminder of Barcelona's proud and independent spirit.

Attractive programs are sold for 400 pesetas that provide useful biographies (written only in Catalan) as well as photographs of the artists. The essays about the opera are presented first in Catalan and then in a Spanish translation. At the back of the program is a brief summary of the plot in English.

Tours of the inside of the Liceu are offered Monday through Friday at 1130 and 1215. Larger groups (often made up of students) are taken through the theater between 1000 and 1300; for these latter tours it is necessary to call ahead for a reservation and confirmation (318-91-22). Those who wish to make the tour meet in the main lobby off Las Ramblas.

Tourist Information may be found at seven different locations scattered throughout the city. Both of Barcelona's principal railway stations (Sants and Término) have offices, but due to rebuilding (in preparation for the 1992 Olympics) Término is temporarily closed, and all trains from all directions now use Sants. The office there is in a corner near the front of the station (to the far right as you leave the main doors) and is open daily from 0800 to 2200. The telephone number is (93) 490-91-71. A different agency handles hotel reservations, and you will find them in the second cluster of small shops set apart near the front doors to the station, not too far from the tourist-office side of the main concourse (their sign advertising tours and excursions is more conspicuous than the notice indicating that they deal with local hotels). You make a deposit of 500 pesetas, credited to your first night's bill, and pay a modest 100 pesetas for the service. The main Tourist Office is at 658 Gran Vía de les Corts Catalanes, the wide east-west artery one block to the north of the Plaça de Catalunya. If you have followed Las Ramblas, going north from the port and beyond the opera house, turn to the right after the park, and the tourist office will be in the second block after you cross the wide and imposing Passeig de Gràcia. They are open Monday through Friday from 0900 to 1900; on Saturday from 0900 to 1400; closed on Sundays. The telephone number is (93) 301-74-43, and as with the Sants office they are not involved with making hotel reservations. The other tourist offices are useful for the most part in providing maps and general information and do not offer the hotel-finding service. The largest of these branches is down by the port at the base of Las Ramblas next to the column honoring Columbus; another office is to be found in the center of the Gothic quarter, behind the cathedral, on the Plaça Sant Jaume; another is two blocks to the south of Gaudí's Sagrada Familia on the Plaça de Pablo Neruda; and finally there is an office on Montjuic adjacent to the Palau de Congressos on the Plaça de l'Univers. The hours at these branches are not uniform, but generally you will find them closed between 1330 and 1530 for the lunch hour; most of them remain open until 1830, with only the office at the port staying open on Sunday.

There are only a few hotels in all categories close to the Sants station, but the elegant residential and business buildings in the area become rather somber after dark; furthermore, the station is some two miles from the heart of the city. A direct subway line connects Sants with the Liceu stop on Las Ramblas, and from there, up and down the entire length of the boulevard and on many of the side streets, there are many more choices among hotels. (Some of the city's most luxurious establishments are located in a three-block radius of the Plaça de Catalunya at the northern end of Las Ramblas.) In this animated center of Barcelona not only the opera house but many of the most interesting sites (and sights) are within easy walking-distance. Also, when the curtain at the opera comes down some time well after midnight you, like many of the natives, may want to find somewhere to catch a late snack. This poses no problem on or near Las Ramblas where many *tabernas* remain open until quite late into the early-morning hours.

Surprisingly there are no acceptable-looking hotels in the immediate area of the Término station and none along the boulevard that borders the port leading to the base of Las Ramblas. (After massive reconstruction in preparation for the 1992 Olympics, Término will once again provide the city's international rail service with the Talgo trains coming from Paris and Geneva. Perhaps by 1992 some of this now-shabby neighborhood will be transformed by urban renewal.) A word of caution: because of past terrorist bombings luggage can no longer be checked and held at a train station while you go outside, unencumbered, to look for a hotel. You now have to take your luggage with you, which is good reason to have in hand a firm hotel reservation before you venture out into the city.

For changing money there are facilities in the two main railroad stations in Barcelona. At Sants the hours are Monday through Saturday from 0830 to 2200; on Sunday from 0830 to 1400 and from 1630 to 2200. At Término (to reopen sometime in 1991) the hours are daily, Monday through Sunday, from 0730 to 2300. The American Express office is at 101 Passeig de Gràcia, one block beyond Gaudí's "La Pedrera" (Casa Milà) or, put another way, in the eighth block north of the intersection with the Gran Vía de les Corts

Catalanes, just before the Avinguda Diagonal. For mail service the Zip code is 08008 Barcelona. The telephone number is (93) 217-00-70. There are seven Cooks/Wagons-Lits offices, the most convenient of which is at 8 Passeig de Gràcia, between the Plaça de Catalunya and the Gran Vía de les Corts Catalanes. The telephone number is (93) 317-55-00. A small office is off the main lobby of the Hotel Diplomatic (three blocks north of the main Tourist Information office on the Gran Vía) at 122 Carrer Pau Claris; telephone (93) 317-31-00. A larger branch is at 578 bis Avinguda Diagonal, at some distance from Las Ramblas, about eight blocks north and off to the left, up the Avinguda Diagonal after its intersection with the Passeig de Gràcia. The telephone numbers are either (93) 200-53-65 or 200-51-44.

Two types of tickets are available for travel on Barcelona's efficient subway and bus systems; there is no time-limit restricting their use. The T-1 ticket, with 10 detachable coupons selling for 410 pesetas, may be used interchangeably on both the metro and bus lines. The T-2 ticket, selling for 365 pesetas, is good for 10 trips only on the metro. These may be bought at any metro station. With a good map in hand and a T-1 ticket you can set your own hours in exploring this exciting city and its major monuments (without the frustration of having to follow the schedule of a tour bus).

MADRID since the end of the Franco-era has been undergoing many tumultuous changes, as has the rest of Spain, and one of the most noteworthy differences is evident in the new-found and vigorous cultivation of the arts. At long last Madrid has a modern and new concert-hall complex where the city's main orchestra can perform, instead of in its make-shift quarters on the stage of the old Teatro Real. And even the city's chief treasure, the Prado, has finally undergone the necessary (and long-delayed) renovations to prevent the paintings from rotting off the walls. In spite of problems with automobile traffic, not unique to Madrid, and bad pollution, common to large cities the world over, from all reports there is a quite new spirit in the city which has already done much to remove the strait-laced image Spain's capital had until just a few years ago.

One of the most interesting and tangible developments has been the enthusiastic success of the new opera company, the **Teatro Lírico Nacional La Zarzuela.** Though the season does not begin until after Christmas, it runs from January through the middle of July. Eight or nine different works are given on the stagione- or block-system, usually one every month, and each is repeated five times: three on subscription and two non-subscription. Unlike Barcelona's Liceu, which is conservative in its repertory and imports most of its singers, directors, and designers, the Lírico is quite adventurous in its scheduling and unafraid to present world-premières by young Spanish composers and to feature other relatively modern works (Berg's *Lulu* has been given recently in the course of two different seasons, with *Wozzeck* appearing during the 1987 cycle). The singers in the leading rôles, depending on which opera is involved, are a mix of guests from abroad and Spaniards (for German operas, including Mozart, the company imports most of the artists), but in most of the Italian works one finds a scattering of young "local" singers in the secondary parts. Finally, except with the productions borrowed from other companies, most of the directors and designers are Spanish. Gradually a nucleus of young singers is being formed who could make this into a true repertory company. Operas are performed in the language in which they were written.

The Lírico is now playing its last years in the Teatro de la Zarzuela, anticipating its move in either 1991 or 1992 to the Teatro Real, if the renovations are completed on schedule. Its present "home" is located on the Calle Jovellanos just behind the Cortes, the old Spanish parliament building (and quite close to the Prado museum), in the middle of the triangle formed by the Paseo del Prado, the Carrera de San Jerónimo, and the Calle de Alcalá. This attractive theater is however relatively small, seating 1140, with three tiers of balconies. The Teatro Real, facing the Royal Palace from across the Plaza de Oriente, is more than twice as large (seating around 2400 people), although in the process of rehabilitating the stage area the seating arrangements may also be modified and either expanded or reduced. Judgment on that will have to wait until the theater is restored to its original purpose and inaugurated. From photographs it appears to be an extremely beautiful building, shaped more in a semi-circle without the horseshoe-like narrowing towards the stage. (This would indicate that sight-lines in the balconies on the side are not too severely affected by the curvature.) There are five rings of balconies, four made up of boxes, with a large and deep gallery of open seat rows in the fifth and topmost tier. There are plans underway, once the move has been made, to provide more performances of each opera and possibly to lengthen the season.

The Teatro de la Zarzuela is only six years "younger" than the Teatro Real, and when it was inaugurated in 1856, Rossini was among those invited to be among the audience. The building was often modified throughout the latter half of the century and was virtually rebuilt after a devastating fire in 1909. By 1955, when the theater was falling into disrepair and seldom used, it was threatened with demolition, but protests by a group of Spanish writers persuaded the authorities to spare the building and to renovate and modernize it. It reopened in 1956. Since that time the theater has periodically been refurbished and repainted, and at the end of the 1989–90 season the auditorium appeared quite bright and fresh. It may have to serve much longer than first anticipated as Madrid's only opera house: in May of 1990 I could see no evidence that work had even begun as yet on revamping the Teatro Real.

Finding the theater may be a bit difficult because the short street on which it faces, the Calle Jovellanos, is only one block long, connecting the Calle de Zorrilla with the Calle de los Madrazo, two narrow streets that bissect lengthwise the lower part of the "triangle" roughly formed by the Calle de Alcalá and San Jerónimo. (Most maps, if they even show the street, rarely name it.) The surest way to locate the theater is to take the short alley (the Calle de Fernanflor) to the right of the Cortes (also known as the Congreso de los Diputados) fronting on the Carrera de San Jerónimo; the main office of American Express is on the other corner to your right; turn left behind the Cortes, and then again right on Jovellanos; the theater, because it is set back from the street, is not clearly in sight until you are almost in front of it.

The Box Office is located in the main lobby, off to the right. The hours are Monday through Saturday, from 1200 to 1800; closed on Sundays and holidays. On those days when a performance is scheduled (each opera happens to be allotted one Sunday date), the Box Office hours run from 1200 to 2000. The main terms describing the various seating areas are similar to those used in Barcelona: *Butaca* for an individual seat, but a box is called a *Palco*, identical to the Italian. Seven different price categories are in effect: two for the *Platea* (the Orchestra), forward and rear, and two each for the *Primer Piso* (First Tier) and the *Segundo Piso* (Second Tier), here applied on both levels to the centers and the sides; only on the *Tercer Piso* (Third Tier) are there three price categories: center, "3/4's," and sides. This pricing system is further complicated by the fact that within each of the seven categories two different price-scales are used: for the first three performances of an opera, to which subscribers have first priority, tickets cost between 7.500 and 1500 pesetas; for the fourth and fifth performances, which are not sold to subscribers, tickets are much cheaper, ranging from a high of 4.000 down to 1000 pesetas. For these last performances there are no planned-in-advance cast changes that would in any way justify the lower prices. Tickets are in short supply for Madrid's opera, which to start with has a small seating capacity, and orders (for a maximum of two seats) are only taken by mail, not by telephone. It is possible however to call to find out if tickets are still available: (91) 429-82-25. The entire season is broken down into only two booking periods: in early January at the Box Office tickets may be bought for all of the performances scheduled for the first three months of the year, and in late March for the four operas coming up between April and July. Those who from outside Madrid (or from abroad) request tickets by mail enjoy the slight advantage of being able to place their orders one month in advance of the dates when the two booking periods normally begin (late December, instead of late January, and late February, instead of late March). There are problems however: a total of only 120 tickets is put aside for such sales, and each order must be accompanied by a stamped (in Spanish stamps!), self-addressed envelope. When you receive the reply that your order can be confirmed, you then send a check or money order in pesetas, plus a 750 pesetas service charge, in the name of the "Administrator Teatro Lírico Nacional La Zarzuela," with the address: 14 Calle de Los Madrazo, 28014 Madrid. It is probably easier to test your luck at the Box Office with a last-minute sale or turned-in ticket. A cautionary note: there are seven Boxes, front and close to the stage, paralleling each side of the first rows of the Orchestra seating area; though you will be sitting in full view of most of the spectators in the theater, you yourself will not be able to see much of the stage; avoid if possible these expensive seats, which happen to cost as much as the seats in the first 12 rows of the Orchestra and seats upstairs in the center of the *Primer Piso*. On the day of each performance the theater puts on sale 40 tickets, described as having "visibilidad reducida o nula" (no translation is necessary!); these are sold, one to a person, at 500 pesetas. Almost without exception performances in Madrid begin at 2000, an hour earlier than the usual curtain-time in Barcelona.

Programs are available at 600 pesetas, with the text of the opera, a Spanish translation, and essays and photographs.

In the fall, well before the beginning of the opera season, zarzuelas are presented in this same theater. It may be assumed, once the opera company moves to its other quarters, that zarzuelas once again will be produced in the winter and spring months, as was once the case before the opera company came into being and needed a house. The zarzuela is a delightful art-form, and if your visit to Madrid should come at a time when opera is not being given, treat yourself to a fun evening with Spain's "native" opera.

Tourist Information is available in several parts of the city. For most travelers by train the office in the Estación Chamartín, Madrid's busiest and most important station, will be the most convenient. (This station, on the northern perimeter of the city, is the last stop for international trains coming from both Paris to the north and Lisbon to the west. Chamartín is also the terminal for trains to and from Barcelona and for many cities in southern Spain. Madrid's second busiest station, Atocha, has no tourist information facilities.) The hours at Chamartín are Monday through Saturday from 0730 to 2230; on Sundays from 0930 to 1330 and 1630 to 1900. They don't make calls for hotel space. In the center of the city, some 4 miles (6 kilometers) to the south of Chamartín, there are three other main tourist offices, one of which is quite close to Teatro Lírico. This office, on the Calle del Duque de Medinaceli, #2, is right behind the Palace Hotel and a few steps from the Plaza de las Cortes and the Carrera de San Jerónimo; the Prado Museum is also nearby, across the wide Paseo del Prado, opposite the main front entrance to the Palace Hotel. The hours are Monday through Friday from 0900 to 1330 and from 1530 to 1900; Saturday from 0900 to 1430; closed on

Sunday. They make no calls for hotel reservations. The telephone numbers are: (1) 429-49-51 and 429-44-87. Another office is not far from the Royal Palace and the theater, the Teatro Real, which will soon house the Madrid opera. It is in the modern skyscraper known as the Torre de Madrid at the corner of the Plaza de España and the Calle de la Princesa, #1. They keep the same hours as the office on Duque de Medinaceli and make no calls for hotel reservations. The telephone number is: (1) 241-23-25. A third office, maintained by a different organization, is located at #3 in the Plaza Mayor, also not far from the Teatro Real but in the oldest part of the city. Their schedule is somewhat different from the two other "downtown" offices: Monday through Saturday from 0930 to 1830; Sundays from 1000 to 1700. At this office no calls are made for hotel reservations. The telephone numbers are: (1) 266-54-77 and 266-48-74.

As in Barcelona, the matter of making hotel reservations is now a privately-run business. If you face the front of the Chamartín station, the counter is next to the Hertz car-rental agency and the office of the Caja de Madrid. Someone is at the desk between 0800 and 2200. A deposit of 600 pesetas is paid, which is later deducted from your hotel bill, and a charge of 175 pesetas is added for the service.

Although there are a few modern hotels near the Chamartín station, that part of the city is fairly new and without much character. Also the station is at a considerable distance from "downtown" Madrid which lies almost 4 miles (6 kilometers) to the south. A subway line, requiring a change at the first stop, links Chamartín with line #1 which bisects the heart of the city. To be close to the Teatro Lírico it is not necessary to stay at the Palace or across the way at the Ritz (two of Madrid's most luxurious and expensive establishments) because many other hotels in all price categories are within easy walking-distance. In the heart of the old city, in the area around the Puerta del Sol and on two other streets, the Calle del Arenal and the Calle Mayor, you will find a great number of establishments of all types, ranging from refurbished older (and small) hotels to more modest pensions (these usually located on the upper floors of business or apartment buildings). Most of these are no more than a 15- to 20-minute walk from either the Teatro Lírico to the east or the Teatro Real to the west. By all means avoid all the motel-like hotels that have sprung up in the newer eastern and northern parts of the city. In most cases you will have to rely on either taxis or on long bus or subway rides to go back and forth to the center of the city.

Money can be changed at Chamartín daily, seven days a week, from 0830 to 2200. An office of American Express is within just a few steps of the Teatro Lírico de la Zarzuela on the Plaza de las Cortes at #2. The telephone, in order to check on their hours, is: (1) 429-57-75. The Zip code, in case you wish to avail yourself of their mail-forwarding service, is 28014. There are nine offices of Cook's/Wagons-Lits in Madrid, and most of them are open from

Monday through Friday between 0900 and 1300 and again from 1600 to 1900; on Saturday from 0900 to 1300. The branch closest to the Teatro Lírico is off the lobby of the Palace Hotel, opposite the Tourist Office on the Calle del Duque de Medinaceli. Another branch, also conveniently located near the opera, is at 23 Calle de Alcalá, close to where this street intersects with the Gran Vía. The other Cook's offices are found in the newer parts of the city, out in almost all directions from the old center of Madrid, and would only be useful if your hotel is in the immediate neighborhood.

Transportation to and from the Chamartín station and the center of the city is best done by metro, even though this in most cases will require at least one change to another line. A ticket, which you use for ten rides, costs 410 pesetas. This ticket, which is stamped each time you insert it into a machine, may be bought in any metro station. The bus system is more useful for travel outside the central section of the city. The "Bono-Bus" ticket has ten coupons and costs 350 pesetas. These may be bought in metro stations and above ground in the state-licensed tobacco shops.

SWITZERLAND

Ordinarily the tourist visiting Switzerland thinks only of Alps and skiing, ravishingly beautiful countryside, immaculate towns and cities, and perhaps to top it off a feast of chocolate bars. Maybe too a finely-made watch, a cluster of secretive bankers, and the inevitable cuckoo clock. But the average tourist seldom sees or knows about this country's remarkably active and diverse musical life. The Swiss can choose among three very fine opera companies: those of Zürich, Basel, and Geneva, and in addition there are the smaller groups based in Bern, Biel/Solothurn, Luzern, and St. Gallen. Smaller cities such as Schaffhausen, Winterthur, and Zug often host touring engagements by opera companies coming from other countries in Europe (such as Italy, France, Germany, Poland, Czechoslovakia, Hungary, and so forth), and there are visits back and forth within Switzerland by some of the Swiss-based groups.

In mid-July the Swiss National Tourist Office compiles a calendar of all the announced musical events for the coming season, a calendar that runs from August through June of the following year. From this exhaustive listing, which includes orchestra and recital schedules as well, one can see at a glance just how much there is to choose from: musical fare that is rich, varied, and extremely cosmopolitan. This calendar is available for the asking from any branch of the Tourist Office, but as noted above in the first part of this Guide, only the dates given for Geneva are useful. Those given for both the Basel and Zürich opera houses are limited to only the initial performances of new stagings and revivals; later performances and dates for other operas figuring in the repertory are omitted.

BASEL (in French: Bâle) is an extremely attractive small city, its rich cultural resources far surpassing those of many cities five times its size. The many times I had changed trains there, seeing only that part of the town visible from the main doors to the Hauptbahnhof/Gare, itself a rather seedy structure, I had assumed that what lay beyond was likewise of very little interest. But on the contrary, when I spent several days in Basel, I was very happily surprised. Though poised on the border with France, it is still largely a German-speaking community, but then that part of France it adjoins, Alsace, is itself of a split-heritage.

Be sure, when you are traveling to Basel from Germany, that you do not make the mistake of getting off the train at the Badischer Bahnhof, the first station you will come to in Basel. This station is on the wrong side of the Rhine and quite far from the center of the city. Be patient and continue on to the station marked "SBB" and shared with the French railroads (the SNCF) for all of the connections leading across the border to France. This is the final stop for all Swiss and German trains, leaving you with plenty of time to get off and putting you "downtown" in Basel.

The opera, called both the **Stadttheater** and the **Basler Theater,** is not far from the station (about ⅗ of a mile or 1 kilometer), but until you know the city don't proceed without a map. One intersection of five large streets can prove quite tricky! Three different trams, going by two different routes, will bring you close to the theater with approximately 300 feet (100 meters) yet to go on foot: from the Bahnhof, either tram #2, two stops to Bankverein (this stop is not clearly marked) and then left on foot at Steinenberg; or trams #1 or #8, two stops to Bankverein (a clearly marked divider in the middle of the street) and then to the five-street intersection and straight, at a left angle, to Steinenberg. To return to the station on tram #2 look for the stop, much further down the street from where you got off, on St. Alban-Graben. In front of the theater in the little park take note of the wonderfully playful fountains designed by Tinguely.

The interior of the recently-built Basel opera theater is of a very striking, bold design, beautifully blending a generous use of teak with stone, white plaster, and glass. The house has room for just under 1200 people, and except for a handful of places in the two balconies, those positioned at the very front of the theater, all of the seats have an unobstructed view of the stage. The acoustics are excellent, with more warmth than one would expect in a modern building of this moderate size.

The repertory is fairly standard: German, Italian, and French, all sung in the original languages, with very few incursions into the twentieth century. Basel has reserved its boldness for its productions of older works, having just completed a controversial Mozart-cycle under the direction of Jean-Claude Auvray. Armin Jordan, who had been the music director of the opera but now is tied to Geneva and Paris, still returns occasionally to conduct. The singers who make up this strong but small repertory company are superbly trained and rehearsed. They are for the most part quite young (a number of them are Americans), and many of them, I am sure, are at that point in their careers where very soon they will become quite well-known internationally. The opera shares this house with both a ballet company and a theater group, and on a average three to five different operas will be performed in the course of a single month. Usually twelve works comprise the total of the season's fare. During a visit to Basel it is sometimes possible to see two or three operas on successive evenings; at other times there may be a gap of as many as five days between opera performances. The season runs from September through June.

The Box Office is open Monday through Saturday from 1000 until 1300 and in the afternoons from 1530 until 1845; telephone: (061) 22-11-33; on Sundays the Box Office is closed but telephone orders may be made between 1000 and 1700 by calling (061) 22-11-30. No written orders for tickets are accepted. An Abendkasse opens 45 minutes before the start of the performance. Prices are more modest than the scale prevailing in both Geneva and Zürich: starting at a low of FS 17 to a high of FS 60.

Tourist information is available in the station, but it is a bit difficult to find and not clearly marked. After you come up out of the tunnel leading from the train platforms turn left (or turn right if you are coming into the station from outside) and go past the ticket windows and towards the area designated "France/SNCF." Just before the area where the restaurants are located turn sharply left. The Information Office is open Mondays through Fridays from 0830 to 1900; on Saturdays from 0830 to 1800; and on Sundays from 1400 to 1700. If you are coming to Basel from France, the Information Office will be on your right just after you pass the line of eating places and shops bordering the corridor that leads into the main part of the station.

There are a number of good and very modestly-priced hotels off to your right when you come out of the station. The higher-priced hotels will be off to your left facing the long, narrow square in front of the station. In the neighborhood of the Stadttheater I've seen only banks and no hotels.

A Tramkarte good for 24 hours or one day (until the last tram or bus runs) costs FS 5. These may be bought at ticket windows inside the station if you are wary of testing the machines in use at the larger trolley stops.

Money may be changed inside the station seven days a week between 0630 and 2215. As you face the ticket windows the bank will be off to your left. American Express and Cook's each have an office in Bâle.

GENEVA (in French: Genève; German: Genf) enjoys a site of incomparable beauty: the magnificent lake, the panorama of the snow-capped French Alps on the opposite shore, and the crystal-clear water of the Rhone at its starting-point, dividing the city into its two parts. Geneva is an international city economically (the banks) and politically (the United Nations and the many world-wide organizations that maintain their headquarters there), but it is also a city in which a strong French cultural influence is felt. In the size of its population, oddly, Geneva ranks after Zürich and Basel, though physically and in the way it is laid out, it appears to be much larger. It is not a city with any especially interesting monuments. The birthplace of its most famous citizen, Jean-Jacques Rousseau, was levelled in the last century, as if too many reminders of the revolutionary Rousseau might disturb the tranquillity of the city's bankers. For more warmth and charm than Geneva can offer, but in much the same setting (the lake and the distant Alps) I prefer Lausanne, Vevey, and Montreux, all within a few minutes by frequent train-service from Geneva.

Operas are performed in the **Grand Théâtre de Genève,** a handsome, late nineteenth-century building that lives up to its somewhat bloated name. It faces a busy intersection at one end of the Promenade des Bastions, a large park which contains the impressive monument to the leaders of the Reformation. Unfortunately the theater lies at some distance from the Cornavin railroad station, on the other side of the Rhone, more than a mile away (roughly 1 ½ kilometers); if you take the #23 bus, you will still have to walk some distance from the front of the station to the bus terminal where that line starts. The bus terminal, as you come out of the train station, is off to your right, on the other side of the church at the far end of the square, the Place de Cornavin. Or the #4 bus from right in front of the train station will put you within three long blocks of the opera if you get off at the third stop: Place du Cirque. (As you make your way to the Grand Théâtre on foot from the bus you will probably pass Victoria-Hall where the Orchestre de la Suisse Romande regularly performs.) If you choose to walk from the station, what with heavy traffic, it should take you at least 45 to 50 minutes to reach the theater.

The Grand Théâtre is somewhat like the Paris Opéra: the outer public rooms for promenading are quite spacious but the seating area inside is comparatively small, holding only a few more than 1400 patrons. Though the theater was extensively redesigned after a bad fire in 1951, there are still many seats to the sides, on all three levels or tiers, with only a partial view of the stage. The acoustics however are now quite good, and as the basic design of the hall is rather shallow (the *Parterre* or orchestra section is only 17 rows deep), this means that in the third and top-most tier, the very large and deep *Amphithéâtre*, the seats at the back are still not too far from the stage. Avoid if possible the Boxes grouped in a circle behind the open rows of seating on the first and second tiers (the *Balcon* and *Galerie*); too many people (five or six) are stuffed into these small and confining cubicles where both the sound and sight-lines are quite poor.

Geneva is not a repertory company, but between September and June it offers a different event each month, for a total of ten for the season. In recent years each season has been made up of seven operas, at least two evenings of ballet, and one musical comedy or operetta. Within the same month there are at least four repeats of the same opera in the subscription series and one or perhaps two performances offered to non-subscribers. (Additional performances, with no tickets sold to the general public, are reserved for special groups.) Between performances there will be a gap of two or three days when the theater remains closed. From season to season, even with this limited number of works, Geneva shows no single "national" prejudice and gives its audiences a balanced sampling of operas drawn from throughout the repertory.

With most of the operas the big rôles are sung by "big names" brought in from the outside, while the smaller parts are taken by singers chosen from all over the world; Italy, England, and the USA provide most of the voices for these secondary rôles. Strangely, Geneva seems to show no inclination towards developing a steady repertory company by using these same singers in more than one opera. With but very few exceptions each new work brings in a totally new group. Geneva is meticulous however in demanding adequate rehearsal time for its productions, and this is evident in the quality of the performances. It should be noted that the Orchestre de la Suisse Romande is the "house" orchestra, with both the operas and the ballets.

The times when the Box Office is open are made extremely complicated by the fact that the first performance of each opera may begin on a different date within each month. The first day for buying a ticket begins seven days before the first performance (if this performance should fall on a Sunday, the Box Office opens the Monday before). And on the first day for selling tickets the Box Office opens earlier, at 0800; on the second day and thereafter, until the final performance of the work, the opening hour is at 1000; during this period the Box Office closes at 1900, but on Saturdays the closing hour is 1700. There is someone in the Box Office one hour before curtain-time for each performance. There are two price scales in effect with a significant margin between them: the lowest-priced tickets start at either FS 16 or FS 29, and the highest vary between either FS 79 or FS 98. The telephone number for ticket service is: (022) 21-23-11.

Tourist information is readily available in the train station, at street level, opposite the main, central entrance. Their hours are as follows: Monday through Friday: 0830 to 2000; Saturday: 0900 to 1800; and on Sunday:

1600 to 2000. They are very helpful in locating hotels for visitors. Their telephone number is: (022) 45-52-00.

There is no shortage of hotels in Geneva, and many in all categories, from the modest to five-star luxury, can be found just across the street from the station and in many of the adjacent streets. Lockers for storing your baggage are available near the exit to the station; in order to use the lockers you will need the correct change in coins.

Money can be changed inside the station, again at street level, with many signs clearly pointing in that direction. Their hours, seven days a week, are as follows: 0600 to 2000. Both American Express and Cook's have more than one branch in Geneva, and in one instance they are close neighbors on the Rue du Mont Blanc.

ZÜRICH

is a rich and handsome city, its population of around 350,-000 making it the largest in Switzerland, but most of its citizens seem to have a friendly, "laid-back" attitude, hardly the outlook one would expect from the natives of one of the world's most important banking centers. Or maybe knowing that much of the world's gold supply is stored in their vaults gives its citizens a relaxed self-confidence that others lack. With the lake at its edge and three streams flowing through its center, Zürich offers the sightseer who chooses to walk many interesting things to visit. And as the oldest part of the city is so compact, most of it can be seen in one day, leaving time to tour some of the many other interesting towns and villages lying just outside the city. In season a boat trip on the lake is something that should not be missed.

The **Zürich Opera House** is approximately one mile from the Hauptbahnhof, a very pleasant walk of about twenty-five to thirty minutes if you elect to follow the route along Limmat Quai and then along Uto Quai bordering the lake. Or take the #4 tram, leaving from the southeast side of the station, and get off at either Belle-Vue or Opernplatz, a 6–10 minute ride depending on traffic. The fare for one trip will be FS 1,50, as this is a "short" trip *(Kurze Strecke)* as opposed to a "long" trip. A day-card or *Tageskarte,* good for an unlimited number of bus or trolley rides, costs only FS 5. (The tram and bus stops are found off at the far, left end of the station when you go out any of the doors facing the main part of the city.)

The opera house itself is an elegant and conservative beaux-arts structure, facing a small park with the lake at its side. It is a small gem inside, its 1891-version of French eighteenth-century roccoco now glistening since a recent refurbishing. During the 1984 renovations the bold step was taken to remove on all levels all of the partitions separating the old loges; this has had the effect of making the theater appear much more spacious and more important, greatly improving the acoustics which now, throughout the house, are excellent. (One wishes that Paris would follow the Zürich example and do the same with its old, uncomfortable, and creaky Palais Garnier!) There are three levels of rings with a fair number of seats concentrated at the center rear of each balcony, but even with the removal of the walls between the old loges there are still problems with sight-lines in many seats on the sides; near the stage only those sitting on the front rows will have an unobstructed view. The theater seats approximately 1200 people.

I cannot understand why Zürich is not cited more often when the "big" houses on the Continent are discussed. Certainly it does not rank alongside Vienna, Munich, and La Scala for the grandness of its productions and the large number of renowned singers steadily attracted to its stage, but Zürich strives for quality and deserves much more attention from those who pride themselves on keeping up with what is new in the world of opera. The excellent singers who make up this ensemble are for the most part young and come from all over the world. Some are just beginning to appear on the stages of other, more prestigious houses, and in the past few years Zürich has with pride watched some of those who began their careers with the company gain international acclaim. One reason perhaps why in critical circles the company is slighted is that for a few times in the course of a season long runs of musicals are presented, but the musicals, except in June, usually are sandwiched in between a varied schedule of operas. Zürich does have its share of well-known singers of star-quality, and it has long had a reputation for its productions of the operas of Richard Strauss. The composer himself often used to visit and frequently conducted his own works. The repertory includes about thirty different productions throughout the year, and each month one can usually expect a scattering of some three to five evenings turned over to dance. Generally there is no opera scheduled for Monday night, but this policy is not rigorously followed because there are exceptions. Beginning in June, when a musical occupies the stage of the opera house, the company puts on a "giant" and colorful opera spectacle in the **Hallenstadion,** a large sports arena in the suburbs. In 1988 the choice was *Turandot,* and for 1989 *Nabucco* was scheduled. The season opens in September and closes late in June.

There is a Box Office at the opera house, but far more convenient is the ticket office in the center of the city, just a few minutes, five at most, from the Hauptbahnhof. This small, glass-walled pavilion (Billet-Zentrale) serves as the main booking and information agency for all of the cultural events taking place in Zürich. (To find this pavilion, when you leave the station by the main entrance, take an escalator outside and down one level to avoid the congested streets in front of the station and then find the "up" escalator leading to Bahnhof-Strasse, the wide, main artery heading directly into the city. Stay on the left-hand side of the street. Go past two streets on your left and then at the third block turn left. Just a short distance in front of you is a small, quiet park in the center of a small square. In the middle of the square, Werdmühleplatz, is the ticket office, a very quick walk from the Hauptbahnhof.) Someone is there on Mondays through Fridays from 1000 until 1830; on Saturdays from 1000 until 1400; closed on Sundays and holidays. The telephone number is (01) 221-22-83.

The Box Office at the opera house (off to the right of the theater in a modern annex) maintains a slightly different schedule and is open longer on Saturdays and briefly on Sundays: Mondays through Saturdays from 1000 until 1830; on Sundays from 1000 to 1200. The telephone numbers are: (01) 251-69-22 or 251-69-23. They are good about answering their telephones but will sometimes say that a performance is sold out when in fact a few tickets may still be available. An Abendkasse in the same annex to the theater opens one hour before curtain-time. Prices follow several different scales but on the average start at a low of FS 13 and at the top vary between FS 91 and FS 111.

Tourist information is to be found in the Hauptbahnhof, but the entrance is only from the outside, off to the left when you come out the main doors nearest the train platforms. Construction barricades probably for some time to come will make it difficult to spot the tourist office, but if you stay to the left, hugging the outside wall of the station, you cannot miss it. From March through October they are open as follows: Monday through Friday, 0800 to 2200; Saturday and Sunday, 0800 to 2030. From November through February: Monday through Thursday, 0800 to 2000; Fridays: 0800 to 2200; Saturdays and Sundays: 0900 to 1800. The telephone number is (01) 211-40-00.

There is no shortage of good hotels in Zürich, but only the more expensive ones are clearly visible in the area immediately surrounding the Hauptbahnhof. You might want to choose a hotel in the vicinity of the opera house. There are a number of small ones, very reasonably priced (by Swiss standards), both facing the lake and on some of the side-streets near the theater. But it is advisable to have confirmation of your space at the tourist office before you go that distance. There are also some modestly-priced and good hotels not too far from the station, but once again it is best to reserve a room before maybe getting lost in some of the smaller, out-of-the-way streets.

Money can be changed in the Hauptbahnhof seven days a week from 0700 to 2200. At this writing (May 1990) the station is still torn up by some major structural changes, and access to the bank may have been altered yet once again. In any case directions to the bank are marked. The bank is presently located on the right side of the last corridor that leads straight away from the train platforms closest to the exit to the station. Both American Express and Cook's have offices in Zürich.

SUMMER FESTIVALS

For the summer tourist, when most of Europe's opera companies have closed their doors for the season, there are still many opportunities for hearing and seeing opera outside of the major cities and often in ravishingly beautiful settings, either natural or historic. Just as in the USA, European cities can become very hot in June and July, and with those few companies that do extend their seasons into these months, attending a performance in an unairconditioned theater can sometimes be excruciating torture. For my taste the most desirable of the summer festivals are those that are held out-of-doors or at least in country or small-town surroundings. There are a few festivals, such as Bayreuth, Glyndebourne, and Salzburg, where in spite of the rural or small-town setting an atmosphere of somewhat stiff formality still prevails, but these are exceptions. At most of the others, where the audiences are more diverse and usually less affluent, informality is more the rule, offering a pleasant contrast to winter opera-going indoors. I would rate the most interesting of these open-air festivals to be those at Aix-en-Provence, Bregenz, and Verona. Then finally there are the "hybrid" festivals which are little more than many diverse attractions added on to the end of the regular season of an opera company; in this category one could place Florence's Maggio Musicale, Munich's July homage to Richard Strauss, the Holland Festival, and Vienna's Festwochen. In compiling this list I have included only those festivals that offer at least a minimum of two operas. In both France and Germany the term "festival" has come to be much abused, with many towns, seeking to draw vacationers, pretentiously designating as a "festival" a brief cluster of summer recitals or chamber music concerts.

There are however some good small ones that on occasion do present an interesting opera. For information about these smaller festivals not furnished here, you can use the sources I give below to inquire about repertory and dates. Usually the complete schedules are available in a brochure or flyer, and you can ask for these when you write or call one of the branches of the European government tourist agencies found in Appendix II: Useful Addresses.

From the vantage-point of the USA, it is usually much easier to obtain detailed information about a festival in Europe than to find the schedule, during its regular season, of an opera house. For some years *Opera News* in a spring issue (either April or May) has been listing by country the major festivals, giving the names of the operas, precise performance dates, and the casts. For some entries addresses are included; for others not. Most of the hotels and restaurants that are mentioned, unless specifically cited as moderate in price, will not be of much use for the budget-minded traveler because many of them fall into the four- and five-star categories. Write or call: *Opera News,* Metropolitan Opera Guild, 1865 Broadway, New York, New York 10023; telephone (212) 582-7500. Single issues are priced at $2.50. (A separate spring issue of *Opera News* gives information about festivals in the USA and Canada.) Quite useful in a different way is the new annual supplement to *Musical America / Opus* appearing in mid-April. Entitled *Festivals '00* (the date corresponds to the year), this special issue could be purchased separately in 1988 but in 1989 was given as a "bonus" to subscribers and the magazine's advertisers. As indicated by its name the supplement contains an exhaustive listing of festivals throughout the world during the entire year, not just the summer. No distinction is made between opera festivals and those devoted to many other types of music (jazz, folk, popular, etc.), but the main usefulness of the supplement is in the completeness of the addresses (a weakness of the *Opera News* calendar). For almost all of the foreign listings both the name of the festival and single-word descriptions ("opera," "dance," "choral," etc.) are the only hints as to what sort of music is on the schedule; no names of operas to be presented, no casts, and such are provided, simply the word "opera." For inquiries about copies write: *Musical America,* 825 Seventh Avenue, New York, New York 10019; telephone (212) 265-8360. (In 1988 copies of *Festivals '88* cost $9.95.) All of the European opera publications publish quite comprehensive information about festivals, whenever, beginning in the fall and winter, the schedules are released to the press, but one would have to follow each magazine month by month throughout the year in order to have the same information that is available in one copy of *Opera News.* In short, none of them pulls all of the information together into one issue; complete schedules are of course given for each of the summer months when the magazines appear, which by then, for ordering tickets, could be too late.

Dailey-Thorp, the large New York-based agency that organizes opera tours to Europe, also serves as the agent in the USA and Canada for the Association of European Festivals, an organization comprised of some 52 festivals, not all of them however offering opera. Daily-Thorp publishes a schedule in the spring and can supply tickets for individuals not participating in their group tours, but unfortunately there are a number of exceptions: tickets for many of the most popular opera festivals (Aix-en-Provence, Bayreuth, Glyndebourne, Munich, Salzburg, and Verona) are not available through their New York representative. These festivals require that requests for tickets be placed directly to them (or through booking agencies in Europe). When and where Dailey-Thorp can supply tickets, I have so noted the fact in the list below. For information write or call Dailey-Thorp Travel, Inc., 315 West 57th Street, New York, New York 10019; telephone: (212) 307-1555.

Finally, a cautionary note: with most of the more popular festivals, orders for tickets should be made as early as possible, and with your travel agent you should book hotel space very early as well. Brochures describing some of the next summer's festivals are often available in the late fall. You can get in touch with the proper European government travel agency or write directly to the festival headquarters to be put on their mailing list.

AUSTRIA

BREGENZ (from mid- or late July to mid- or late August, usually one month in length). Distinguished by the open-air stage floating on Lake Constanz, also with another opera usually scheduled on the city's indoor stage. Bregenz Festival, Postfach 119, Festspiel-u. Kongresshaus, A-6900 Bregenz, Austria. Telephone: 22-811/ Fax: 22 811-242 / Cable: FEST-SPIELE. Tickets also available through Dailey-Thorp.

CARINTHIAN SUMMER (late June through late August). A few performances of opera (not a major component of the festival) interspersed with concerts, recitals, and other events, situated in one of the loveliest parts of rural Austria. Learn what operas are to be performed (and the limited dates) before you decide to go. Sekretariat, Carinthischer Sommer, A-9570 Ossiach; telephone: 502-510/ Telex: 45666.

SALZBURG FESTIVAL (late July to late August). One of Europe's oldest, most prestigious, and most expensive festivals. Originally intended as a homage to native-son Mozart (who quarreled bitterly with the town's Archbishop), the festival changed its focus under Karajan, somewhat away from Mozart and on to Karajan himself. It will be interesting to see how the festival changes with Gerard Mortier of La Monnaie and the Vlaamse Opera now in charge. Tickets and hotel space are quite tight and very expensive. Opera tickets are usually sold by booking agencies as a "package" with at least one other non-operatic event (less in demand). For tickets bought from agents, see under "Vienna" in the main part of this guide. Salzburg Festival, Box 140, A-5010 Salzburg; telephone: 84-25-41/ Telex: 633880/ Fax: 842541-401.

WIENER FESTWOCHEN (The Vienna Festival Weeks, early May to mid-June). One of the "hybrid" festivals mentioned above, with special events scheduled while the Staatsoper is ending its season. Vienna plays host to opera companies from outside Austria, and they perform in various theaters in the city. At present the "festival" is a greatly scaled-down version of the more ambitious and illustrious Vienna Festival inaugurated in 1950 and at least for the opera-goer offers little that is not already available during the regular season. Wiener Festwochen, 11 Lehárgasse, A-1060 Vienna; telephone: 586-16-76/ Telex: 111 383/ Fax: 586-16-76-49.

CZECHOSLOVAKIA

PRAGUE SPRING FESTIVAL (mid-May through early June). While the Tyl Theater still remains closed for extensive repairs, Prague's two other houses, the National and Smetana Theaters, continue their seasons through May. Visiting companies from Eastern-bloc countries perform some of their specialties during a crowded schedule of recitals and other musical events. Information, tickets, visas, and travel arrangements (with hotels) should be made through Cedok, the Czech National Tourist Agency, 10 East 40th Street, New York, New York 10036; telephone: (212) 698-9720. Tickets are also available through Dailey-Thorp.

FINLAND

SAVONLINNA FESTIVAL (July). The main courtyard of Olavin-linna Castle in Savonlinna serves as the site for presentations of at least one Finnish opera and two or three other works drawn from the general reper-tory. Some are done in Finnish translation, others as written. In some years for a limited number of performances the festival is host to a visiting company from another country. Information available in the USA: Finnish Tourist Board, 655 Third Avenue, New York, New York 10017; telephone (212) 949-2333. Or directly from Finland: Savonlinna Opera Festival, 35 Olavin-katu, SF-33100 Savonlinna; telephone: 514-700/ Telex: 81057007 OPERA SF/ Fax: 21866. Tickets available through Dailey-Thorp.

FRANCE

AIX-EN-PROVENCE FESTIVAL (the more ponderous title is *Le Festival International d'Art Lyrique et de Musique*) (early July through early August). A long history of excellent performances of Mozart operas, given in the open-air courtyard of the former Archbishop's Palace; other works occasionally done indoors in the Théâtre Municipal. Each opera is repeated between three and six times. The cathedral of Saint-Sauveur serves for con-certs. Aix with its elegant Cours Mirabeau is one of the handsomest small cities in all of Europe. Breathtakingly beautiful is the sight in early evening of the city's old buildings gradually turning a rich golden color against the deep blue of the Midi sky. To explore the varied beauty of Provence one really needs to have a car. Connections out of Aix and Marseille by train are not very good for adequately seeing the region. Arles, Avignon, les Baux, Nîmes, and Orange, only the most famous of the many not-to-be-missed sites in the area, all lie to the west of Aix, and by train it is necessary to double-back to Marseille and then out again in another direction. Festival d'Aix-en-Provence, Palais de l'Ancien Archevêché,13100 Aix-en-Provence; telephone: 42-23-37-81/ Telex: 410065 F.

(CARPENTRAS) FESTIVAL INTERNATIONAL: OF-FENBACH ET SON TEMPS (late July to early August). Offenbach operettas, usually two or three of them, performed out-of-doors in a square in the center of this mid-sized town in Provence. Carpentras is pleasant but appreciated more for its importance as a fresh fruit and vegetable center than for its historical or artistic monuments. Yet because the town is never overrun with tourists the visitor who lingers for a few days should soon be captivated by the easy-going life-style of the Provençaux. To reach Carpentras you will need a car, as the nearest rail service is either at Orange or Avignon, both towns (on the main line from Paris) only 15 miles (24 k.) distant; Vaison-la-Romaine, the site of another festival, is due north and slightly further, but by a most scenic route. Three addresses, depending on when you write or call, should be used in seeking information or booking tickets. During the winter and spring, before 30 June, an address in Paris may be used: Festival International Offenbach et Son Temps, 79 rue Jouffroy, 75017 Paris: telephone: 42-27-59-13; before 30 June in Carpentras: "La Charité," 77 rue Cottier, B. P. 113, 84204 Carpentras; telephone: 90-63-46-35; and after 1 July in Carpentras: Bureau du Festival, Théâtre de Plein Air, rue d'Inguimbert, 84204; telephone: 90-63-05-72.

(ORANGE) LES CHORÉGIES D'ORANGE (early July to early August).

The ancient Roman theater, still in a remarkable state of preservation, serves as the setting for all of the operas presented in Orange. Orange has always mustered first-class casts for its productions (in 1988 they did a complete *Ring* that was very highly praised), but unfortunately most of their offerings are now limited to a single performance each. There is no general pattern to the repertory from year to year, but tickets can be hard to find. Orange, a town of less than 30,000, lies approximately 60 miles (100 k.) northeast of Aix near the northern edge of Provence; a wider range of hotel accommodations can be found in Avignon, which is about 15 miles (25 k.) to the south. Chorégies d'Orange, Maison du Théâtre, Place des Frères-Mounet, 84100 Orange; telephone: 90-34-24-04.

FESTIVAL DE PARIS (mid-May through the end of June).

This festival, begun in 1988 under the patronage of the Mayor of Paris, is a rather strange grab-bag of events scattered around the city in churches, theaters, and concert halls. Bitter-tongued critics have complained that the festival lacked any over-all purpose and that it was merely an effort on the part of Paris' Mayor, a bitter opponent of the Mitterand government, to show that he too was a supporter of culture on a grand scale. In any case a few operas are presented in the course of the festival, some of them productions brought in from other countries or from the French provinces. Most are heard only one or two times (in 1989 an exception was made for a zarzuela, brought in from Spain and repeated on three nights). There are several addresses for information and for tickets: Festival de Paris, 38 rue des Blancs-Manteaux,

75004 Paris; telephone: 40-27-99-07; or: 2 rue Edouard-Colonne, 75001 Paris; telephone: 42-33-44-44/Telex: 215362 F. Six weeks before the Festival opens tickets for all of the events included in the series may be bought at the Box Office of the Théâtre des Champs-Elysées, 15 Avenue Montaigne, 75008 Paris. The Box Office is open daily from 1100 to 1900.

FESTIVAL DE MUSIQUE DE STRASBOURG (early June through early July).

Generally two or three works, repeated two or three times, are presented in a festival that moves from the opera house to the much larger Palais des Congrès at some distance from the "downtown" area. For details about this handsome city see the entry for Strasbourg under "France." Two addresses exist for information and tickets: Festival de Strasbourg, 24 rue de la Mésange, 67000 Strasbourg (in the heart of the city); telephone: 88-32-43-10; and 18 Quai Zorn, 67000 Strasbourg.

FESTIVAL DE VAISON-LA-ROMAINE (early July to early August).

(For lack of funds the Festival scheduled for the summer of 1990 was cancelled. It is hoped that money can be found to revive the Festival by the summer of 1991.) This festival, begun in the early 1950's, like that of Orange makes use of the ruins of the town's impressive Roman amphitheater. Two operas are presented and repeated only twice, but if these are not to your liking there is a modest offering of other entertainment: ballets, recitals, chamber music, and plays. An excursion to Vaison can be justified by a visit of the Roman ruins, in particular the well-preserved ruins of the houses, and then a walk through the streets of the old town where many medieval houses have been preserved and restored. As Vaison has only around 6000 inhabitants, hotel space is quite limited. Avignon is 30 miles away (50 k.) and Orange 17 miles (27 k.); there is bus service (with many stops) but no train service to Vaison. Highly recommended in conjunction with the Aix Festival (see above). Information about the Vaison festival may be obtained through a Paris address or from the town itself: (Paris) Festival de Vaison-la-Romaine, 12 rue Chabanais, 75002 Paris; telephone: 42-61-81-03; or: (Vaison) Hôtel de Ville, 84110 Vaison-la-Romaine; telephone: 90-36-24-79.

GERMANY

BAYREUTH (late July to the end of August). The "holy of holies" and the oldest of all the current music festivals. Wagner's *Ring* is usually repeated three times (within a six-day period); before and after each complete cycle three other of the master's works are then offered (not necessarily the same ones each year). It is often possible to see seven operas in ten or eleven days. There is little argument that Bayreuth no longer sets the style that others follow, and perhaps better productions can now be found elsewhere, but at least once in one's life a Wagner fan should make the pilgrimage to the shrine. Tickets are difficult to come by (witness the lively classified ads in the winter issues of *Opernwelt*) and are sold out usually two years in advance, but one knowledgeable critic advises that you write Bayreuth and have your name put on their mailing list. Your application will be honored in two or three years. Except for *Das Rheingold* and *Der fliegende Holländer*, which begin at 1900, all the other operas begin at 1600 and include a long break later for dinner. Getting to and from Bayreuth by train is convenient and takes only about an hour and fifteen minutes from Nürnberg. Accommodations in and around Bayreuth can be reserved through the office of the Festival; these range from the luxurious to the very reasonable and modest. Bayreuther Festspiele, P. O. Box 100262, 8580 Bayreuth 2; telephone: 20221.

(DRESDEN) DRESDNER MUSIKFESTSPIELE (from mid-May to early June). Added on to Dresden's regular season at the Semper Opera are visits from various companies in other Eastern-block countries, from Leipzig, and on occasion from the West. During the time of the festival a full schedule of operas, ballets, orchestral concerts, and recitals is offered in venues throughout the city. Arrangements for travel in what used to be East Germany are in a state of flux as the government-owned and -operated hotels are gradually turned over to private investors. Residents of European countries (other than Czechs and Poles) are now no longer restricted in travel to Dresden, but a visa, costing DM 15, is still required of all others (as of August 1990). General information about travel and tours in what was formerly the DDR may be obtained from Impact Travel Marketing, P. O. Box 802315, Chicago, Illinois 60680-2315; telephone: (312) 527-2966. The main office of what used to be the East German government travel agency in East Berlin has been "privatized" and its name changed to the Europäisches Reisebüro; it is still located at 5 Alexanderplatz, 1026 Berlin (DDR) (East Germany); telephone: (37) (2) 2150/Fax: 212 6528.

LUDWIGSBURG CASTLE FESTIVAL (LUDWIGS-BURGER SCHLOSSFESTSPIELE) (early May through the end of September). Ludwigsburg, a small city about 8.5 miles (14 k.) outside of Stuttgart and linked to the latter by frequent suburban service, is the site of an immense baroque château and gardens built in the early 1700's as a German evocation of Versailles. Some of the diverse events scheduled during the festival are given in the château itself; others in several theaters in the surrounding town. An interesting array of some four to five operas is offered, ranging from the 18th century to the very contemporary, performed by various visiting ensembles. The number of performances of each work varies greatly, so you are advised to consult the schedule. Ludwigsburger Schlossfestspiele, Postfach 1022, 7140 Ludwigsburg; telephone: 25035/ Telex: 7264451 LUSF D/ Fax: 90 10 11. Tickets available through Dailey-Thorp.

MUNICH OPERA FESTIVAL (July). A non-subscription appendage to Munich's regular season, in some years the festival is made up of only Strauss operas; in other years the repertory is a mix from Mozart to the contemporary, but always with some scattering of Strauss. Usually there is at least one work scheduled for performance in the delightful baroque Cuvilliés theater. Festival tickets are as difficult to obtain as tickets during Munich's regular season, but put your name in early. (For other details about Munich see the entry in the main part of this guide.) Munich Opera Festival, Brieffach 745, 8000 Munich; telephone: 2-18-51/ Telefax: 2185-304.

SCHWETZINGEN FESTIVAL (late April to early June). Several companies are invited to present operas in the 18th-century court theater in the elaborate gardens adjoining the summer residence of the Palatine Electors. In recent years Schwetzingen has been presenting a Rossini cycle along with one other opera. Each of the two or three operas is repeated three or four times. The dates of the festival also happen to coincide with the height of the asparagus season, a specialty of the region that attracts to this small town both music- and asparagus-lovers. Mannheim lies some 8.5 miles (14 k.) to the north and is connected to Schwetzingen by frequent suburban train service; Heidelberg is about the same distance to the east but is linked only by slower bus service. Schwetzinger Festspiele, Schlossplatz, 6830 Schwetzingen; telephone: 4933. Tickets available through Dailey-Thorp.

GREAT BRITAIN

ALDEBURGH FESTIVAL OF MUSIC AND THE ARTS (from early to late June). Founded by Benjamin Britten shortly after the war, the festival is held in a seaside town some 110 miles northeast of London. Vocal and operatic works by Britten (and occasionally by other composers, usually in student performances), interspersed with a generous assortment of recitals and chamber music concerts by first-rate artists. Aldeburgh Foundation, High Street, Aldeburgh, Suffolk IP15 5AX; telephone: 2935/ Fax: 2715.

BATH INTERNATIONAL FESTIVAL OF MUSIC AND THE ARTS (late May to mid-June). Includes a few single-night performances of opera in magnificent settings in and around Bath. The main attractions of the festival are however the concerts by visiting orchestras. From Paddington (London) about an hour and a quarter by fast, direct train. Bath Festival, Linley House, 1 Pierrepont Pl., Bath, Avon BA1 1JY; telephone: 62231 or 60030/ Telex: 449212 LANTEL G/ Fax: 445551.

BUXTON FESTIVAL (late July to mid-August). Slim opera offerings (just enough to qualify for this list!) in a scenically-interesting part of England north of the Midlands. Not to be missed is nearby Chatsworth House with its magnificent gardens. Buxton is approximately 21 miles (35 k.) southeast of Manchester, some two-and-one-half hours north of London by train. Buxton Festival, 1 Crescent View, Buxton, Derbyshire SK17 6EN; telephone: 70395.

CHELTENHAM INTERNATIONAL FESTIVAL OF MUSIC (the first two weeks of July). A small city, known for its spa, in the heart of the Cotswolds and a little more than two hours from London by connecting train (direct trains are not numerous). Programs of opera vary in type and in frequency from year to year; most works are repeated at least once. Numerous other musical and dance events scheduled in the Everyman Theatre, the Town Hall, and the Regency-built Pittville Pump Room. Cheltenham International Festival of Music, Town Hall, Imperial Square, Cheltenham, Gloucestershire GL50 1QA; telephone: 521-621/ Cable: TOWN-HALL/ Fax: 221 569.

EDINBURGH INTERNATIONAL FESTIVAL (mid-August to early Sept.). Though relatively short in length (three weeks) Edinburgh has probably the most crowded and ambitious schedule of any festival now going. It justifies as well the "international" in its name by attracting cultural events from all over the world. While orchestral and chamber music concerts, plays, recitals, ballet, jazz, lectures, and art exhibitions vie for the visitor's time, opera remains an extremely important component of the festival. Visiting companies from abroad and from other parts of Great Britain (as well as local Scottish groups) offer an impressively varied choice of works. Each opera (or music-theater piece), of which there were six during the 1989 festival, is repeated at least two or three times, some of them more. Fortunately, with so many events scheduled in so many different places in and around the city, the organizers of the festival provide the visitor with a good map. Edinburgh, so often by-passed by the average tourist, is one of the great cities of Europe; allow yourself several days just to explore its many treasures. Tickets for the festival may be ordered by credit card in the USA and Canada through overseas branches of the London booking firm of Edwards and Edwards: for reservations from the USA, telephone in New York City: (212) 944-0290; from Canada: (Montreal) (514) 393-9971; these orders include a service charge and VAT. Beginning the last of May tickets may be ordered directly from the festival Box Office, again with credit cards: Edinburgh Festival Society, 21 Market Street, Edinburgh EH1 1BW; telephone: 225 5756.

GLYNDEBOURNE (mid-May to late August). The most exclusive—and elusive—of all the summer opera festivals because the demand for tickets is so great. Since it began in the early 1930's with performances of Mozart on the Christie's country estate in Sussex, much has changed about the festival. There is now a much larger repertory (running from Monteverdi to world premières of new works), a considerably longer and fuller season (made up now of six different operas), more frequent performances (an average of four or five each week and then in August almost every night), and finally the increased use of international stars among the singers. But other things have remained the same: long rehearsal times, which means superb ensemble work, at least one Mozart opera in the annual repertory, an atmosphere of intimacy (the audience is limited to 800 people, larger than pre-war audiences but still quite small by any measure), and the famous extended intermissions when the patrons find a nice spot in the garden, open up their picnic hampers, and sit down to enjoy a supper of champagne, smoked salmon, and fresh strawberries. (Cold suppers can now be ordered for those who don't arrive in their chauffeur-driven Bentleys with a well-stocked trunk.) Formal dress is still expected but not required.

Glyndebourne is essentially an exclusive club, with each member paying an annual £50 fee which in turn allows that member to have two tickets to each of two of the six operas. The waiting list is now so long that it may take between 10 and 14 years before anyone new is admitted to membership. "Outsiders" may obtain tickets in any of three ways: by telephoning the Box Office when a few tickets are turned in (usually for mid-week performances), from watching closely the "for sale" ads in the more serious English newspapers, and finally from friends who are members. Tickets are not available through any of London's ticket agents. Getting to and from Glyndebourne, some 50 miles south of London, is too complicated to risk going with the hope of finding a ticket at the last minute (unless you have a car and are endowed with a remarkable talent for persuasion). Trains (on the Brighton/Hastings line) leave Victoria Station in London around 1400 for the hour-long ride to Lewes, where special busses are arranged for the short trip to Glyndebourne. Performances usually begin in the late afternoon and end around 2200 (with a long intermission somewhere in-between, in the Bayreuth tradition, for that leisurely supper). The current practice is to have six operas in the repertory, with two performed in tandem. As one is phased out, a new one begins, making it possible a few times in the summer to see three in succession. Generally each opera is repeated twelve times, the Mozart more and one or two others less. Most of the audience is seated on orchestra-level (in "stalls").

There is vague talk about increasing the size of the theater built onto the Christie manor house, expanding it so as to accommodate 1400 people. Many are unhappy because this could destroy the intimate ambiance of the festival. Do not expect this to happen, if it ever does, any time soon.

Bookings for the summer's season open April 1, but usually by that time all the tickets have been given out to members and business supporters. You might however be lucky and come up with a ticket. Write or call: Glyndebourne Festival Opera, Glyndebourne, Lewes, Sussex BN8 5UU; telephone: 812321/ Telex: 877862 GLYOP G/ Fax: 812783.

LONDON INTERNATIONAL OPERA FESTIVAL (mid-May to the end of June). An interesting mix of works, new and old, standard full-length operas and brief one-acters, performed in various theaters scattered throughout the city. Lectures, exhibitions, film-showings, and recitals are also important elements of the schedule. This festival was "born" in 1985 with the aim of promoting enthusiasm for opera among young people—or at least those under 30—who benefit from a number of special discounts on tickets to Covent Garden, the Coliseum, and to other events. Of more interest than the performances scheduled in the "big" houses (which can be seen at other times because most are repeated) are the many one-time-only performances of rarely-heard works and the considerable number of world premières of new works by young British composers. In some cases the artists are brought in from the Continent and from the USA. Application for the under-30 discount membership closes as of April 1. Credit cards (Visa, Access-MasterCard, American Express) may be used. London International Opera Festival, 78 Neal Street, WC2H 9PA London; telephone: 836-0008.

GREECE

ATHENS FESTIVAL (early June through mid-September). The splendid setting here is the almost perfectly preserved outdoor theater on the side of the Acropolis, the Odeon of Herodes Atticus. Among the many international events on the schedule is the visit of at least one foreign opera company. The National Opera of Greece also performs. The dates for the operas vary from year to year, and between each cluster of performances there can be long gaps, filled with concerts, ballets, and plays. Consult the schedule if you want to see opera. Information and tickets may be obtained in New York from the Greek National Tourist Organization, 645 Fifth Avenue, New York, New York 10022; telephone (212) 421-5777. The address in Athens is as follows: Athens Festival, 1 Voukourestiou St., 10564 Athens; telephone: 322-1459/ Telex: 215832 GRTA GR. Tickets are also available from Dailey-Thorp.

HOLLAND

HOLLAND FESTIVAL (June). Opera is usually highlighted by tours of visiting companies, from both the Old and the New World. Many of the same events are shifted from Amsterdam to the Hague (45 minutes away by train) and to Rotterdam (just over an hour away). Visiting dance companies and orchestras also figure prominently in the schedule of the festival. With its handsome new opera house and the newly renovated Concertgebouw, Amsterdam is best able to offer the most concentrated choice of interesting events. The Hague, which also has a new theater, should be included in the visitor's itinerary because it is such a lovely city of quiet yet elegant charm. For information and tickets: Holland Festival, 21 Kleine Gartmanplantsoen, 1071 RP Amsterdam; telephone: 276-566/ Telex: 11218 HFAUB/Telefax: 253140. Tickets also available through Dailey-Thorp.

ITALY

(BARGA) OPERA BARGA (late July to early August). The tiny town of Barga has won some notoriety in recent years by inaugurating a short festival of rarely produced operas. The works, repeated at least twice, are generally chosen according to some kind of theme. You will need a fairly large-scale map of Italy just to locate Barga and a car to get there. Barga lies about 25 miles (40 k.) due north of Lucca (Lucca is twelve miles northeast of Pisa on the *autostrada* that connects Florence, 60 miles to the west, with the coast). Tickets and information from Opera Barga, Casa Baldi, 11 Via della Fornaceta, 55051 Barga.

(FLORENCE) MAGGIO MUSICALE FIOREN-TINO (May through June). See the entry for Florence in the main part of this guide.

(MACERATA) ESTATE MACERATESE (the dates vary from year to year: usually in July and sometimes into August). Why a music festival in Macerata, a town some 60 miles (100 k.) southeast of Rimini, neither high up in the Apennines nor right on the Adriatic coast? The neighboring town of Recanati, some twelve miles (21 k.) closer to the sea, has the distinction of being the birthplace of Beniamino Gigli (complete with a Gigli museum) and commands as well a spectacular view of both the mountains and the Adriatic, but Macerata? The town owns a large *sferisterio,* an outdoor stadium seating 6000 designed for the now seldom-played ball game of *pallone,* and beginning in 1967 the local authorities decided to put the structure to good use with summer opera. The festival has been a surprising success. Three popular works are performed with first-rate casts and scheduled on an alternate basis throughout the month-long season. There is good train service from the main cities in the north to Ancona, but you will need a car for the 30 miles (49 k.) inland and up into the hills to Macerata. Arena Sferisterio, Servizio Prenotazione, Casella Postale 92, 62100 Macerata; telephone: (733) 40-735.

(MARTINA FRANCA) VALLE D'ITRIA FESTIVAL (late July to early August). A little-known festival in Martina Franca, a small inland town near the bottom tip of Italy, close to where the "heel" joins the main part of the "boot," and a quite unlikely place for a tourist to go unless lured by an interesting festival. Usually three or four works from the Italian repertory are presented, and according to the pattern of recent years, at least two of them, repeated twice, are rarities from the 18th or early 19th centuries. The operas are presented in the courtyard of the Palazzo Ducale. There is good and frequent train service from the north and from Naples to towns nearby: Bari, Brindisi, or Taranto, but you will need a car to reach Martina Franca. Write: Centro Artistico Musicale "Paolo Grassi," Palazzo Ducale, 74015 Martina Franca; telephone: (80) 707-191. Tickets also available through Dailey-Thorp.

PESARO ROSSINI OPERA FESTIVAL (mid-August to early September).

Three operas by Rossini are performed by the growing number of singers who specialize in the style of singing thought to be authentic for this composer. Performances also are often the first to conform to the latest critical editions. Each opera is repeated four times, and two of the three can be heard in tandem; the third and last is usually presented by itself in September. The number of available opera tickets is limited because the Teatro Comunale holds only 900, and other concerts, recitals, lectures, and exhibitions are held there. Pesaro, Rossini's birthplace, is on the Adriatic coast, some 50 miles (80 k.) south of Ravenna and on the direct rail line linking the cities of the north with Bari and Brindisi far to the south. As with every inch of ground in Italy, there are interesting things to see in Pesaro itself and in many nearby towns, most of which can be reached easily by train. Rossini Opera Festival, 37 T Via Rossini, 61100 Pesaro; telephone: 30-161 or 61-927/ Telex: 560215 PP PS I/Fax: 30-979. Tickets also available through Dailey-Thorp.

RAVENNA (early July to early August).

Three operas, usually from the Italian repertory, are presented in the courtyard of the massive ruins of the old Venetian fortress Rocca de Brancaleone; on occasion the Teatro Alighieri (indoors) is used instead. Each work repeated three or four times with casts of international caliber. Fanciers of organ music will also want to take in some of the concerts sponsored by the Festival de Musica d'Organo which runs simultaneously throughout July and early August in San Vitale, the site as well of some the city's most famous mosaics. Ravenna possesses a dazzling array of monuments evoking the early evolution of Christianity in the fifth and sixth centuries: first as the capital of a Christianized Roman Empire, then under the rule of Gothic kings who had converted, and finally as the western outpost of Byzantium. Festival di Ravenna, Biglietteria del Teatro Alighieri, 2 Via Mariani, 48100 Ravenna. Tickets may also be purchased through Dailey-Thorp.

(ROME) CARACALLA (July to mid-August). Bread and circuses, modern Italian-style, in the ruins of the Roman Baths of Caracalla. Usually two operas and a ballet, unfortunately not given every night, are scattered throughout July and the first two weeks of August (some seven to nine performances of each), often with outstanding casts. *Aïda* is usually on the schedule, complete with many of the inmates of the Rome zoo. Tickets in advance from the Box Office at the Rome opera house or at the entrance to Caracalla on the day of the performance, at 2000, one hour before the starting-time. Regular tram and bus service to the Baths, with special night service after the performances. With some 6000 other opera lovers, a most enjoyable way, out-of-doors, to find relief from Rome's oppressive summer heat. Teatro dell'Opera, 1 Piazza Beniamino Gigli, Rome; telephone: (6) 46-17-55 or 46-36-41, daily except Monday, from 0930 to 1800.

(SPOLETO) FESTIVAL OF TWO WORLDS (late June to middle July). Unusual repertory and/or innovative staging distinguish this early-summer festival initiated and still managed by composer Gian Carlo Menotti. Two or three operas figure on average in the schedule, each usually repeated four to six times. Casts are often made up of young singers poised for promising careers. Many other events: concerts, recitals, dance, and drama fill up the days between opera performances. Spoleto, which lies 84 miles (141 k.) northeast of Rome, though small, is of considerable interest tourist-wise but can become over-crowded while the festival is in progress. By train it is less than an hour and a half from Rome. Other nearby towns, Assisi and Perugia, are also worth a visit and can be reached easily by connecting train; for Todi, an important Etruscan center, you will have to rent a car. Four addresses may be used for information and tickets: Spoleto USA, P. O. Box 157, Charleston, S. C. 29402; telephone: (803) 722-2764; Festival dei Due Mondi, Palazzo Ancaiani, 06049 Spoleto/Cable: FESPOLETO or (Rome): 17 Via Margutta, 00187 Rome. Tickets also available through Dailey-Thorp.

TORRE DEL LAGO PUCCINI (last part of July through mid-August). An annual tribute to Puccini, born in nearby Lucca, who lived in Torre del Lago and is buried there. Generally two Puccini operas are on the summer schedule and are repeated four or five times. In some years a short work by another composer is billed on the same evening with a Puccini one-acter. The theater is out-of-doors by the lake. Torre del Lago is a few miles inland from the Ligurian coast, between the seaside resort town of Viareggio and Pisa. There is good, fast train service connecting northern cities to both of those towns, and fairly frequent local service between them and Torre del Lago; Florence, some 60 miles (100 k.) to the east has good service to Pisa. Torre del Lago Puccini, Biglietteria del Teatro, 4 Belvedere Puccini, 55048 Torre del Lago Puccini; telephone: (584) 343-322.

(VERONA) ARENA DI VERONA (July and August). A spectacular outdoor setting in the nearly intact Roman arena that seats up to 25,000. Usually three or four works are on the schedule, with each repeated an average of ten times (sometimes more). First-class casts. The superb acoustics of the arena mean as well that audience noises are also loud, but relax and share the enthusiasm (or displeasure) of the crowd. There is much to explore in Verona and in all of the art- and architecture-rich towns that surround it (Vicenza, Mantua, Padua). Venice, too, is only an hour and a half away by train. Everything in Verona is within easy walking-distance, the Arena is in the heart of town, but the station is about a mile from Piazza Brà and the festival activities. Unless you stay somewhere well outside Verona, lodging within the city should be arranged well in advance of the opera season. Spettacoli Lirici Arena di Verona, 28 Piazza Brà, 37121 Verona; telephone: (45) 590-966/telex: 480869 OPERVR I.

SWEDEN

DROTTNINGHOLM COURT THEATER (late May or early June through early September). A short distance outside of Stockholm, the small theater of the royal palace, complete with its original stage machinery, remains much as it was when constructed in the 18th century. Three operas are customarily on the summer schedule, performed by mostly Swedish singers; sometimes a recent or new Swedish work is featured. Mozart has become a "specialty of the house." Usually only one opera at a time is on the calendar; hence there will be a gap of one or two days between each performance. Eurailpasses are valid for transportation to Stockholm, but opera-goers go by bus or steamer to Drottningholm. Drottningholms Slottsteater, Box 27050, 10251 Stockholm. Tickets also available through Dailey-Thorp.

USEFUL ADDRESSES

Listed below are a number of addresses that could prove useful in planning a trip to Europe in search of opera.

Under (A) are addresses of foreign government tourist offices in the USA and Canada, along with the offices of their respective national railway systems (where such exist).

Under (B) is the address of the USA agent for copies of Thomas Cook's *European Timetable.*

Under (C) is where to write to obtain the free booklets giving the addresses of the offices of American Express and of Thomas Cook/Wagons-Lits found in many of the cities mentioned in this guide.

(A) EUROPEAN GOVERNMENT TRAVEL OFFICES

AUSTRIA (main office in New York City): Austrian National Tourist Office, 500 Fifth Avenue, New York, New York 10110; tel: (212) 944-6880.

(Chicago): 500 North Michigan Avenue, Suite 544, Chicago, Illinois 60611; tel: (312) 644-5556.

(Houston): 4800 San Felipe Street, Suite 500, Houston, Texas 77056; tel: (713) 850-9999.

(Los Angeles): 11601 Wilshire Boulevard, Suite 2480, Los Angeles, California 90025; tel: (213) 477-3332; for California only: (800) 252-0468; for the West Coast: (800) 421-8281.

In Canada: (in Montreal): Office National Autrichien du Tourisme, 1010 Ouest Rue Sherbrooke, Suite 1410, Montreal, Québec H3A 2R7; tel: (514) 849-3709.

(Toronto): Austrian National Tourist Office, 2 Bloor St. East, Suite 3330, Toronto M4W 1A8; tel: (416) 967-3381.

(Vancouver): 736 Granville St., Suite 1220-1223, Vancouver, B. C. V6Z 1J2; tel: (604) 683-5808.

BELGIUM: Belgian National Tourist Office, 745 Fifth Ave., New York, New York 10151; tel: (212) 758-8130.

In Canada (Montreal): 187 Place d'Yonville, Montreal, Québec H2Y 2B2; tel: (514) 845-7500.

CZECHOSLOVAKIA: Cedok, Czechoslovakian National Tourist Agency, 10 East 40th St., New York, New York 10036; tel: (212) 698-9720.

FINLAND (Main office in New York City): Scandinavian Tourist Boards (Finland), 655 Third Ave., New York, New York 10017; tel: (212) 949-2333.

FRANCE: The French Government Tourist Office since 1987 has been renamed Maison de la France. There are seven offices in the USA and Canada.

(New York City, the main office): Maison de la France, 610 Fifth Ave., New York, New York 10020-2452; tel: (212) 757-1125.

(Chicago): 645 North Michigan Ave., Suite 630, Chicago, Illinois 60611; tel: (312) 337-6301.

(Dallas): World Trade Center, No. 103, 2050 Stemmons Freeway, P. O. Box 58610, Dallas, Texas 75258; tel: (214) 741-7011/7012.

(Los Angeles): 9401 Wilshire Blvd., Beverly Hills, Los Angeles, California 90212-2967; tel: (213) 272-2661.

(San Francisco): Suite 250, 1 Hallidie Plaza, San Francisco, California 94102; tel: (415) 986-4174.

In Canada (Montreal, the main office): 1981 McGill College T Esso, Suite 490, Montreal, Québec H3A 2W9; tel: (514) 288-4264.

(Toronto): 1 Dundas Street West-Suite 2405, Box 8, Toronto, Ontario M5G 1Z3: tel: (416) 593-4723.

The French National Railroads (S. N. C. F.) have seven offices in the USA and Canada. The VISA card (in France called the CARTE BLEUE) is accepted in most train stations for train and sleeper service.

(New York City, the main office): French National Railroads, 610 Fifth Ave., New York, New York 10020; tel. (in New York state): (212) 582-4813; tel. (East Coast): (800) 223-5252.

(Chicago): 11 East Adams St., Chicago, Illinois 60603; tel. (in Illinois): (312) 427-8691; tel. (Middle West): (800) 621-4460.

(Los Angeles): 9465 Wilshire Blvd., Beverly Hills, Los Angeles, California 90212; tel. (California): (213) 274-6934; (outside California): (800) 421-4583.

(Miami): 2121 Ponce de Leon Blvd., Coral Gables, Miami, Florida 33134; tel. (in Florida): (305) 445-8648; (outside Florida): (800) 327-9656.

(San Francisco): 360 Post Street on Union Square, San Francisco, California 94102; tel. (California): (415) 982-1993; (outside California): (800) 227-4813.

In Canada (Montreal): 1500 Stanley St., Suite 436, Montreal, Québec H3A IR3; tel. (in Ontario): (514) 288-8255; and: (800) 381-8052.

(Vancouver): 409 Granville St., Suite 452, Vancouver, B. C. V6C 1T2; tel. (in British Columbia): (604) 688-6707.

GERMANY (EAST): Although the two Germanies should be politically reunited by the end of 1990, certain restrictions regarding travel will for some time probably remain in effect for non-Europeans. As of August of 1990 Europeans (except for Czechs and Poles) are free to travel in what used to be East Germany; those who live in other parts of the world are still required to have a visa. The visa costs DM 15 and is necessary for an overnight-stay in any part of what used to be the Eastern Zone, including East Berlin. (The visa is stamped on your passport by the hotel, a different procedure from the earlier rule requiring a voucher for your hotel reservation *before* you were allowed to cross the border into the Eastern Zone. But with hotel space in such short supply, it would be very unwise to make travel plans without first having a confirmed reservation, which in the end differs little from the old requirements.) While the few available hotels in East Germany are now being shifted from government ownership to private investors, that part of the country is still poorly equipped to receive many tourists. I have retained this seemingly out-of-date entry for East Germany because of two addresses which could still prove to be useful. For information about tours and other travel conditions write or call the agency that before reunification served officially as the USA-representative for DDR tourism: Impact Travel

Marketing, Inc., P. O. Box 802315, Chicago, Illinois 60680-2315; or use the street address: 540 North Lakeshore Drive, Suite 305, Chicago, Illinois 60611; tel: (312) 527-2966. What in East Berlin used to be the official (and only) government travel office for all of the DDR has changed its name and is now privately operated. They now call themselves the Europäisches Reisebüro, but they occupy the same office at 5 Alexanderplatz, PSF 77, 1026 Berlin, (DDR) (East Germany); telephone in East Berlin: (37) (2) 2150; telex: 114648/114651/114652. Eventually, but no one yet knows for sure the date, the German National Tourist Office (now limited to West Germany) will provide tourist information about the East.

GERMANY (WEST) (main office in New York City): German National Tourist Office, 747 Third Ave., New York, New York 10017; tel. (212) 308-3300.

(Los Angeles): 444 South Flower St., Suite 2230, Los Angeles, California 90071; tel: (213) 688-7332.

In Canada (Toronto): 175 Bloor Street East, North Tower, 6th floor, Toronto, Ontario M4W 3R8; tel: (416) 968-1570.

The German National Railways have offices in the USA and Canada. The main office in New York is at the same address as the Tourist Office, but the telephone number is different: (212) 308-3106.

(New York): German Rail, 747 Third Ave., New York, New York 10017; tel: (212) 308-3106.

(San Francisco): 323 Geary Street, Suite 501, San Francisco, California 94102; tel: (415) 362-6206.

GREAT BRITAIN (main office in New York City): British Tourist Authority, 40 West 57th Street, New York, New York 10019-4001; tel: (212) 581-4700.

(Atlanta): 2580 Cumberland Parkway, Suite 470, Atlanta, Georgia 30339-3909; tel: (404) 432-9635.

(Chicago): 625 N. Michigan Ave., Suite 1510, Chicago, Illinois 60611; tel: (312) 787-0490.

(Dallas): Cedar Maple Plaza, 2305 Cedar Springs, Dallas, Texas 75201-1814; tel: (214) 720-4040.

(Los Angeles): World Trade Center, 350 South Figueroa Street, Suite 450, Los Angeles, California 90071-1203; tel: (213) 628-3525.

British Rail has offices in the USA and Canada for arranging train travel throughout the British Isles. The main office is in New York City: BritRail Travel International, 630 Third Ave., New York, New York 10017; tel: (212) 599-5400.

(Dallas): Suite 210, Cedar Maple Plaza, 2305 Cedar Springs, Dallas, Texas 75201; tel: (214) 748-0860.

(Los Angeles): Suite 603, 800 South Hope St., Los Angeles, California 90017-4697; tel: (213) 624-8787.

In Canada (Toronto): 94 Cumberland St., Toronto, Ontario M5R 1A3; tel: (416) 929-3333.

(Vancouver): 409 Granville St., Vancouver, B. C. V6C 1T2; tel: (604) 683-6896.

GREECE: Greek National Tourist Organization, 645 Fifth Ave., New York, New York 10022; tel: (212) 421-5777.

HOLLAND (the main office in New York City): The Netherlands Board of Tourism, 355 Lexington Ave., (21st floor), New York, New York 10017; tel: (212) 370-7367.

(Chicago): 225 North Michigan Ave., Suite 326, Chicago, Illinois 60601; tel: (312) 819-0300.

(San Francisco): 90 New Montgomery St., Suite 305, San Francisco, California 94105; tel: (415) 543-6772.

In Canada (Toronto): 25 Adelaide Street East, Suite 710, Toronto, Ontario M5C 1Y2; tel: (416) 363-1577.

HUNGARY: IBUSZ, Hungarian State Travel Office, Rockefeller Center, Suite 2455, 630 Fifth Ave., New York, New York 10111; tel: (212) 562-7412.

ITALY (main office in New York City): Italian Government Travel Office (E. N. I. T.), 630 Fifth Avenue, Suite 1565, New York, New York 10111; telephone: (212) 245-4961/4962/4963/4964. A helpful little book, "An Italian Year," is distributed annually giving addresses and dates for many upcoming important cultural and commercial events throughout Italy. A few opera companies submit their schedules, but the list is very far from complete.

(Chicago): 500 North Michigan Avenue, Suite 1046, Chicago, Illinois 60611; tel: (312) 644-0990/0991.

(San Francisco): 360 Post Street, Suite 801, San Francisco, California 94108; tel: (415) 392-6206.

In Canada (Montreal): Place Ville Marie no. 1, Suite 2414, Montreal, Québec HEB 3M9, Canada; tel: (514) 866-7667.

C. I. T. is the travel and information division of the Italian State Railway system, with offices all over Italy and in many foreign countries. C. I. T., 666 Fifth Avenue, New York, New York 10103; tel: (212) 397-2667.

(Chicago): 500 North Michigan Ave., Chicago, Illinois 60611; tel: (312) 644-6651.

(Encino, California): 15760 Ventura Blvd., Suite 819, Encino, California 91436; tel: (818) 783-7245.

(Los Angeles): 6033 West Century Blvd., Suite 1090, Los Angeles, California 90045; tel: (213) 338-8620.

In Canada (Montreal): 2055 Peel St., Montreal, Québec H3A IV4; tel: (514) 845-9101.

(Toronto): 13 Balmuto St., Toronto, Ontario H3B 2E3; tel: (416) 927-7712.

SCANDINAVIA (for all four Scandinavian countries): Scandinavian Tourist Boards, 655 Third Ave., New York, New York 10017; tel: (212) 949-2333. There is a referral service, with an 800 number, in Norwood, Minnesota for requesting general information about travel in the four Scandinavian countries: Scandinavian Tourist Boards, P. O. Box 5527, Norwood, Minnesota 55383-5527; tel: (800) "SCANFUN" or (800) 722-6386.

SPAIN (main office in New York City): National Tourist Office of Spain, 665 Fifth Ave. (at 53rd St.), New York, New York 10022; tel: (212) 759-8822.

(Chicago): Water Tower Place, Suite 915 East, 845 North Michigan Ave., Chicago, Illinois 60611; tel: (312) 642-1992.

(Los Angeles): San Vicente Plaza Bldg., 8383 Wilshire Blvd., Suite 960, Beverly Hills, Los Angeles, California 90211; tel: (213) 658-7188.

(Miami): 1221 Brickell Avenue, Suite 1850, Miami, Florida 33131; tel: (305) 358-1992.

In Canada (Toronto): 60 Bloor St. West, Suite 201, Toronto, Ontario M4W 3B8; tel: (416) 961-3131.

SWEDEN (the main office is in New York City): Scandinavian Tourist Boards (Sweden), 655 Third Ave., New York, New York 10017; tel: (212) 949-2333.

SWITZERLAND (the main office is in New York City): Swiss National Tourist Office, 608 Fifth Ave., New York, New York 10020; tel: (212) 757-5944.

(Chicago): 150 North Michigan Ave., Chicago, Illinois 60601; tel: (312) 630-5840.

(San Francisco): 260 Stockton St., San Francisco, California 94108; tel: (415) 362-2260.

In Canada (Toronto): P. O. Box 215,, Commerce Court West, Toronto, Ontario M5L 1E8; tel: (416) 868-0584.

(B) FOR PURCHASING COOK'S *EUROPEAN TIMETABLE*

The Forsyth Travel Library, Inc., is the sole distributor in North America of Thomas Cook's *European Timetable,* the monthly guide, printed in England, that gives the schedules of all railroad lines for the British Isles, Ireland, and the Continent. Each issue, containing more than 500 pages, contains full details about international service as well as current schedules for trains within each country; there are also timetables for ferry and steamer service, which in many cases is "free" for holders of either Eurailpasses or the passes for individual countries. Forsyth charges $19.95, plus $3.00 for postage, for each copy of the Cook's guide. In addition to the various formats for the Eurailpass, Forsyth also specializes in the many rail passes for single countries. They also have, free on request, an extensive catalog of books, guides, and maps related to travel worldwide. Write or call: Forsyth Travel Library, Inc., 9154 West 57th St., P. O. Box 2975, Shawnee Mission, Kansas 66201-1375; tel: (800) "FORSYTH" (Kansas residents call: (913) 384-3440); 24-hour Fax: (913) 384-3553. Visa, MasterCard, and American Express are accepted on all purchases (with some restrictions on the use of American Express in charging rail passes).

(C) OFFICES OF AMERICAN EXPRESS AND THOMAS COOK IN EUROPE

American Express publishes a small booklet, called the *American Express Traveler's Companion,* listing their branches throughout the world. Free copies may be obtained from any American Express office or by writing to the following address: *American Express Traveler's Companion,* P. O. Box 678, Canal Street Station, New York, New York 10013. This booklet gives the address and telephone number of each branch office. If the office you intend to use in Europe is not nearby, it is often advisable to call ahead to be sure of their hours; in some countries, following local custom, the offices close for a lengthy lunch period. The booklet also indicates which branches offer the convenient (and free) mail-handling service.

Thomas Cook also publishes a similar booklet with all the addresses, telephone numbers, and telex digits for their offices and those of their affiliate, Wagons-Lits Tourisme. With those countries in which a long lunch-hour closing is customary, a particularly useful and time-saving feature of this list is the fact that it gives in detail the specific hours when these offices are open. As the booklet is updated every two months, seasonal variations in the hours (and days) are indicated as well. Free copies of this booklet *(Office Addresses Worldwide)* may be obtained from any Thomas Cook office or by writing or telephoning: Thomas Cook Travel Inc., 2 Penn Plaza, 18th floor, New York, New York 10121; telephone: (212) 967-4390; telex: 910 250 0 4982. In Canada write or call: Thomas Cook Travel (Canada) Inc., 111 Avenue Road, Suite 303, Toronto, Ontario M5R 3J8; telephone: (416) 968-9424; telex: 495 9061.

CURRENCY TABLE

The figures given below correspond roughly to the value of the dollar when converted into the various European currencies as listed in a newspaper of October 1990. The values are given only as a guide and do not take into account the taxes and conversion fees that are usually deducted from the "official" exchange rate. Between parentheses with each country I have listed the smaller unit of currency, when such exists, into which the larger unit is divided—e. g.: franc (centimes). For a more up-to-date listing of the exchange rates consult the financial pages of your newspaper.

Country	Large Unit by Which the Dollar Is Valued:	One () Is Worth in US Currency:	One US Dollar Will Buy:
Austria	Schilling (100 Groschen)	.0935	10.69
Belgium	Franc	.0319	31.31
France	Franc (100 Centimes)	.1964	5.0490
Germany	Mark (100 Pfennig)	.6592	1.5170
Great Britain	Pound (100 Pence)	1.9435	.5145
Holland	Guilder (100 Cents)	.5834	1.7140
Hungary	Forint	Ask your travel agent or consult the Hungarian Travel Office in New York City	
Italy	Lira	.000880	1137.00
Spain	Peseta	.010471	95.50
Switzerland	Franc (Rappen or Centimes)	.7873	1.2702

ABOUT THE AUTHOR

Born and raised in Chapel Hill, John Philip Couch graduated from the University of North Carolina in 1949 with a major in French and spent the following year in France on a Fulbright Scholarship. (That summer, in Vienna, he brushed up on his German and almost nightly attended operas and concerts.) In 1954 he was awarded a Ph.D. in French from Yale University. Then, after two years of military service, Mr. Couch started his full-time teaching career at Wake Forest University. He was a member of the Romance Languages faculty of the University of North Carolina at Greensboro from 1958 to 1988, when he retired from teaching.

The author of various academic publications, Mr. Couch translated the libretto of *Manon* for the Beverly Sills recording that first appeared on ABC-Treasury Records. He also did a translation of an Offenbach libretto for the now-dormant "Offenbach Project," as well as an English version of Pirandello's *Enrico Quattro* that has been used by the North Carolina School of the Arts and the Tyrone Guthrie Theater in Minneapolis.

Mr. Couch's addiction to opera began when he was a child listening to Metropolitan Opera radio broadcasts and to opera records, which he had started to collect by the time he was twelve. While he was at prep school and later at Yale, frequent visits to New York found him regularly attending performances at the old Met and at the City Center.

After his stint in the military, made tolerable by his proximity to the San Francisco Opera, Mr. Couch began an almost yearly habit of spending his summers in Europe, visiting music and opera festivals in England and throughout the Continent. Taking time off from teaching, he spent many a spring or fall semester sampling the airs of all the major European opera houses. Jet travel since the late 1960's has made it possible for Mr. Couch to return to Europe usually on the average of twice a year and, most important for the writing of this guide, for extended periods when opera houses are open during their regular seasons.